Concepts in Health Care Entrepreneurship

First Edition

JENSON HAGEN, CPA, MSFA

Remedy Books

Portland, Oregon

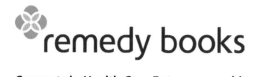

Concepts in Health Care Entrepreneurship

First Edition

Copyright @ 2012 Remedy Books

PO Box 1182
Portland, OR 97207

Library of Congress Control Number: 2012914530
ISBN: 978-0-9839510-0-1

For permission to use material from this textbook, please submit a request using our online submission form at RemedyBooks.com.

Warning: Not all chapters have been technically reviewed for accuracy.

Cover photo © Nejron Photo – Fotolia.com

ABOUT THE AUTHOR

Author: Jenson Hagen, CPA, MSFA

Jenson Hagen has worked for some of the top investment and accounting firms in the nation. He has passed six professional examinations in various areas of business, including the Certified Public Accountant exam and Level II of the Chartered Financial Analyst exam. He holds a master's of science degree in Financial Analysis, a program of study that provides detailed training on how to conduct business valuations.

Contributing Author: John M. Hagen, DC

John M. Hagen runs a highly successful practice in the Vancouver, Washington area. He has over 30 years of experience as a doctor of chiropractic medicine. He developed many of the concepts in this book related to the patient experience and patient care.

RemedyBooks.com Website

Please access the resources at http://www.remedybooks.com under the *Students* and *Teachers* tabs. You will find many free downloadable resources for use in operating your business and as learning tools.

Under the *Students* tab:

Territory Worksheet

Retention Checklist

Financial Ratios Spreadsheet

Business Valuation Assignment

Self-Study Guide

Student Links

Under the *Teachers* tab:

Sales Luncheon Business Project

Cash v. Accrual Accounting Methods

Business Valuation Results

Guide to Selecting Guest Lecturers

Answer Guides

Reviewers

The following health care students and professionals conducted a peer review of one or more chapters to ensure that the author conveyed a clear understanding of the material.

Amanda Buffington

Lisa Fortes-Schramm

Krista Weikel-Delaplane

Kelly Raylinsky

Julie Rose

Nusaybah Bey

Heidi Clark

Aimee Perkins

Anorah Schostag

Robert Strait

Andrew Litchy

Alison Schulz

Thalia Farshchian

The following technical experts conducted a technical review of one or more chapters to ensure that the author correctly presented the material.

John Hagen, DC

Stephen Liston, DC

Marne Garcia, PHR

Jacob Redding, IT Professional

Don Warnecke, CPA

BRIEF CONTENTS

CONTENTS

SECTION IV Management

Marketing Principles

AUTHOR'S NOTE

Pay special attention to the discussion on *holistic philosophy* because that is the mindset that an entrepreneur needs the most. A holistic approach toward thinking can take time and experience to develop because it merges the larger picture of what you're trying to accomplish with all the little details of running a business. Understand the concept of gross domestic product (GDP), which will serve as a foundation for financial research later. The main goal of a business is to earn a sufficient level of *net profit* that properly compensates the owner for the effort involved with starting and operating the venture. The last half of the chapter tries to engender the notion that people are all different and you must plan for those differences. It is necessary to understand what people want and then tailor services appropriately.

The best marketing is FREE: Foster Relationships Energetically Everywhere.

A business in its most rudimentary form provides products or services to consumers. A mixture of time, effort, and knowledge empowers an entrepreneur to form a strong relationship between consumers and the business organization. As the relationship unfolds in terms of controllable and uncontrollable forces in the marketplace, an entrepreneur must continually adapt to changes that take place. This provision for adaptability requires theoretical knowledge, work experience, and a bit of creativity. An entrepreneur must see the marketplace holistically and introduce changes to the business organization in response to events. Figuring out the best way to respond often requires intimate knowledge of the marketplace that a third-party expert is not able to possess. An entrepreneur can lack knowledge of accounting, finance, and even management with the intention of relying upon skilled experts, but marketing activities cannot easily be outsourced.

The first section of this book starts by teaching you how to market as a health care provider. Whether the intention is to start a business or work as an employee, marketing has extensive value over the lifetime of a health care provider's career. The ability to recruit new patients, improve the patient experience, and encourage the spread of positive word of mouth are essential for reaching high levels of success. It's important to understand how patient care can suffer if marketing efforts are underdeveloped or absent.

This chapter reviews general principles that are important for understanding the field of business in general. It will take time to build a portfolio of skills, attitudes, and habits necessary to run a successful health care practice; it can easily take several years to develop a network of relationships extensive enough to support a practice financially. Learn business concepts, gain from experiences, and foster relationships—as early as possible. The achievement of success will not occur spontaneously or rapidly. Why is it truly important to start marketing efforts early? Understand one core principle of consumption: *People will buy a product or service only when they need or want it.* Knowing a lot of people over time increases the chance that someone will eventually encounter a health care need. You must then connect that person's health care need with the services you provide. Forming that connection may take a few short minutes or it might take several years.

1.1   Holistic Philosophy

What comes to mind when the term "marketing" is used? You may instantly think about a TV advertisement or glossy brochure—these are *marketing tools*. A traditional definition of marketing touches upon forming and developing relationships with consumers. An entrepreneur needs to understand that marketing involves any issue that can impact the relationship a consumer has with an organization's products or services. For example, an employee who dresses inappropriately is a human resource concern as well as a marketing concern. Addressing the topic legally and tactfully with the employee requires knowledge of human resource concepts, but an entrepreneur cannot ignore how employee attire will impact the patient experience. How will patients judge your organization upon seeing an employee who is dressed unprofessionally?

In the context of health care, every detail of the experience carries significant weight for several reasons including the following:

1. A patient remains in an office for some time.
2. A patient's general expectation of quality is high.
3. Positive word of mouth is needed to generate more business.

Negative experiences may lead a patient to speak about your health care organization in a negative light or terminate care prematurely. On the other hand, a positive experience may cause a patient to spread positive word of mouth and continue with care unabated.

CASE STUDY

Holistic Philosophy

A holistic philosophy requires thinking about all aspects of the business in tandem. Imagine an office that has poor accessibility because of traffic congestion in the surrounding area. Patients may grow tired of the time and money (gas) burden imposed by sitting in an automobile. This may lead them to complain about the experience, seek care elsewhere, or stop care altogether. Negative feelings regarding this one aspect of the experience can easily seep into conversations with others. Patients might feel comfortable telling others about your services and mention them in a positive light but, unbeknownst to you, they might also insert a negative point about poor accessibility. You are receiving positive and negative word of mouth concurrently in this situation. If patients continue care as planned, then a secondary problem arises down the road when patients confront the idea of restarting care to address a *future* need. That negative feeling felt in the past will weigh upon their decision to return in the future, thus impacting repeat business.

One solution to poor clinic accessibility might involve understanding the general flow of traffic in the area to determine what times are best for commuting. The clinic may need to change the general hours of operation after surveying the patient base and understanding optimal commute times.

Approaching the full organization with a holistic philosophy allows you to unearth problems and provide an appropriate solution. Keeping a tight watch over patients and the organization provides more opportunity to solve problems through feedback and analysis. By asking general questions of patients and paying attention to their overall experience, you should be able to ascertain if a problem exists in one area of the business. Holistically, you know that a problem can spill into other areas of the business and impact the relationship maintained between patients and your health care products and services.

A holistic perspective takes time to develop because the human brain requires knowledge and experience to see more easily how pieces of an organization fit together. Employees, the building, the location, service options, and so forth combine to form the patient experience. The better the experience, the more likely a patient will continue care, return in the future, and issue positive word of mouth. As you continue reading, bear in mind how everything connects and how the patient experience might draw from different elements of an organization. Think about possible solutions in a holistic manner, taking into account more than the actual problem at hand. As you make changes, think about who or what might be impacted. The problem and solution can easily involve other parts of the organization indirectly.

The best method of approaching change involves a proactive instead of reactive response. For instance, even if an upcoming change never impacts a particular staff

Success requires close attention to details in all areas of business.

member, communicate with that staff member in advance to ensure problems will not arise. The business organization is a system much like the human body where all parts work together dynamically. The whole organization can suffer even if only one part of the organization is weak.

Summary

Marketing attempts to build and maximize the relationship that exists between patients and the services and products offered by an organization. This relationship underscores the reason why every health care provider goes into practice. Other parts of the organization work to support this core relationship and consequently branch into the field of marketing. A problem in one area of an organization can spill into other areas and impact the patient experience. Negative experiences can lead patients to discontinue care and speak negatively about your clinic. By adopting a holistic philosophy when approaching marketing, management, finance, and accounting issues, a health care organization will function more smoothly and provide patients with a better experience overall. In turn, the organization can allocate more resources to patient care as opposed to marketing efforts.

1.2   Concept Evolution

Remember that the brain loves carbohydrates and blood flow in order to stay alert and active. Snack and take breaks as needed!

Entrepreneurship best refers to a desire to provide services or products within a marketplace. An entrepreneur can launch into activities ill-prepared and hope to stay afloat financially through luck. Or, an entrepreneur can seek the highest rungs of success possible by planning appropriately. The first stage of planning involves developing a conceptual picture of what a future business might encompass. A concept can evolve in a multitude of ways and it allows memory centers to form in the brain. In turn, as you read business books and gain work experience, new information will flow into these memory centers more easily.

The core reason a person would consume time, energy, and money (resources) to visit your clinic is to access *needed* health care services. Your experiences in school or practice allow you to craft a general preference for how you want to treat patients. Make a list of how you would ideally deliver health care services and consider if patients would want to access your services in this way. The full organization should then be built around this core concept. How will the name read in front of your building? Can you envision staff members circling around each other as patients walk through the door? What will the waiting room, treatment rooms, and front office look like? Table 1.1 provides ideas on what to consider when forming and expanding upon a business concept.

TABLE 1.1	Concept Evolution
Consider items in the following table when generating ideas.	
Category	**Example Items**
Appearance	Clothes, posture, and presentation
Treatment style	Primary and secondary services
Staff members	Number, type, and appearance
Office interior	Waiting area and treatment rooms
Office exterior	Building, landscape, and parking lot
General vicinity	City, neighborhood, and stores

Within this dream of starting a business or working as a health care provider, think holistically about the details of your ideal practice. Include every dimension in this mental picture to consider all the pieces that might play a role in the actual business later. Dreaming about the future helps when setting goals. Creating a clear vision about the future increases motivation and provides a general sense of purpose.

Dreaming is the backbone of entrepreneurship even after establishing a solid organization. An entrepreneur will constantly need to modify processes or confront a new dilemma. The ability to think abstractly about a situation that has not yet occurred or take into account the big picture once it does occur is vital to running a successful health care practice—and it represents one of the most enjoyable aspects of being an entrepreneur. Take the time to outline ideas, expand upon them, and meet periodically with others to generate feedback.

1. Conjure up a mental picture of your ideal practice.
2. Write down the various elements in a journal.
3. Organize a meeting with other professionals to discuss ideas.

Summary

An entrepreneur should formulate concepts about future activity to properly consider all relevant matters. As a health care provider studies other businesses and puts together an actual practice, having a clear vision and detailed list of ideas helps create direction and purpose. The process of developing concepts should consider health care services first and expand outward to showcase how the whole organization will function holistically.

1.3   Market Research

After developing the full conceptual picture, an entrepreneur should research a concept's viability in the marketplace before initiating future activity. A practice management firm can be hired to conduct market research and provide additional insights into a concept's viability, but an entrepreneur will always want to personally understand how the marketplace will react to a concept.

> The health care industry centers on people and their opinions.

The first stages of research might involve Internet searches, library resources, or information presented by professional associations, journals, or conferences. Grassroots research carries the most weight within the field of health care. Talking to people in the surrounding area gives a first-hand sense of what *market participants* consider relevant. Understanding the likes and dislikes of a cross section of market participants will help when evaluating **normative views** felt about service lines, prices, a desired location, and so forth. Local business owners can have a strong sense of what will work within a given marketplace and can form an integral part of a health care provider's network.

> **Normative Views:** Standard perceptions of an idea, event, or situation.

Macroeconomic Analysis

Macroeconomics is the study of forces that influence the general economy, such as the rate of inflation and unemployment. This field of economics gives insight into the health of the general marketplace. The number of products and services produced within a distinct country, referred to as **gross domestic product (GDP)**, provides a good indication of overall economic strength. When GDP levels fall for consecutive periods of time, economists refer to this event as a recession. As a recession settles and the economy improves, a trough is reached and the economy then enters an expansionary phase where wages, employment, and product inventories normally begin to rise. GDP levels rise during an economy's expansionary phase and continue to grow until the economy reaches the peak of the business cycle. An economy normally experiences a full business cycle that includes a recession, trough, expansion, and peak before cycling through to another recession. The **central bank** and government policies attempt to maintain the health of the banking system as a way

> **Macroeconomics:** Field of economics focused on the study of nationwide economic activity.
>
> **Gross Domestic Product (GDP):** Amount of products and services produced in a country.
>
> **Central Bank:** The entity in charge of an economy's banking system. A central bank normally controls the amount of loans that lending institutions can extend.

to stimulate economic activity and keep recessions short. The central bank of the United Stated is called the *Federal Reserve*.

Understanding the business cycle helps a health care provider figure out the best time to initiate future activity within the marketplace. If a loan is required, interest rates tend to be *high* during the peak of a business cycle and *low* at the trough as presented in Table 1.2. Entering the marketplace at an economic peak or during the initial moments of a recession may amplify risks and result in above-average interest costs. *Despite the appearance of strong economic activity, the peak of the business cycle represents the worst time to initiate new business activity.* An experienced entrepreneur will spot the trough of the business cycle when economic conditions seem dire and favor initiating business activity then. While reading financial news and conducting research online, *try to ascertain the current phase of the business cycle.*

1. Does this business cycle differ from historical trends?
2. What is the forecasted interest rate going forward?
3. What level of general economic activity is necessary for the organization to survive as planned?

TABLE 1.2   Business Cycle Trends

The following list represents normal economic conditions present during each phase of the business cycle. In contrast to what is shown, *stagflation* occurs when high interest rates are present during a recession.

	Interest Rates	Employment	GDP	Leading Indicators
Recession	Decreasing	Decreasing	Negative	Decreasing
Trough	Lowest	Lowest	Slightly positive	Starting to increase
Expansion	Increasing	Increasing	Increasing	Increasing
Peak	Highest	Highest	Decreasing	Starting to decrease

Economic Indicators Various economic indicators provide insights into the health of an economy. *Lagging indicators* look backward at what has occurred over the past several months. *Coincident indicators* explain the current economic environment. Economists mainly use *leading economic indicators* as a way of predicting future activity. The Conference Board Leading Economic Index™ as presented in Table 1.3 contains some of the most important leading indicators weighted according to their respective importance in predicting future economic activity.

TABLE 1.3   Conference Board Leading Economic Index™

1. Money supply (most important)
2. S&P 500 stock index
3. Consumer expectations
4. Long- versus short-term interest rates
5. New building permits
6. New orders of nondefense capital goods
7. New orders of consumer goods
8. Average manufacturing employee workweek
9. Initial claims for unemployment
10. Index of supplier deliveries

Source: www.conference-board.org

ECONOMIC ANALYSIS		
Bureau of Economic Analysis	bea.gov	U.S. GDP and balance of trade
Bureau of Labor Statistics	bls.gov	U.S. wages, employment, and inflation
Economic Indicators	economicindicators.gov	U.S. leading economic indicators
Daily FX	dailyfx.com/calendar	Global economic calendar
Bloomberg News	bloomberg.com	Financial news
Reuters	reuters.com	Business and financial news
Federal Reserve Bank of NY	ny.frb.org	U.S. central bank

Microeconomic Analysis

Microeconomics explores the relationship between supply and demand factors in relation to price levels. As seen in Table 1.4, if consumers *demand* 200 barrels of oil per day and *supply* is reduced to 190 barrels, then microeconomic forces, in theory, will cause prices to rise until consumer demand drops to 190 barrels. Within the health care industry, similar price corrections may not occur in such a straightforward manner. Food, shelter, and health care enjoy a much greater degree of **price inelasticity** wherein prices do not rapidly adjust per demand and supply factors. Consumers place greater importance on health care services and will generally pay more to address a health care need. As a result, increasing the price of health care services may not significantly impact demand levels.

Microeconomics: Field of economics focused on the connection between demand and supply forces.

Price Inelasticity: Resistance to price changes as supply levels vary given a constant demand level or vice versa. Opposite of price elasticity where price changes strongly correspond to changes in supply levels given a constant level of demand or vice versa.

TABLE 1.4	Supply and Demand

As the supply of oil falls over time, prices adjust upward, squeezing off demand until equilibrium is reached at $55 per barrel.

	Time 1	Time 2	Time 3
Demand	200	195	190
Supply	200	190	190
Difference	–	(5)	–
Price	$40/barrel	$50/barrel	$55/barrel

CASE STUDY

Causes of a Recession

Economic activity normally burns out after some time because of resource limitations or when too many **unproductive assets** have been placed into service. Imagine a scenario where homebuilders construct 2,000 units in a particular year. If consumers purchase those units, homebuilders will normally react by building another 2,000 (or more) units during the following year. The economy would benefit from stable employment and money would cycle through the economy as housing companies and their employees expend profits and paychecks. However, at some point the economy will peak, most likely due to a resource limitation. In this example, consumers may be limited by the amount of housing debt they can assume. If lending institutions cannot extend loans so that consumers can buy all 2,000 homes, then a shortfall of housing purchases will occur. Assume that only 1,800 units are purchased out of an available 2,000 homes as presented in Table 1.5. The 200 (2,000−1,800) homes that went unsold would impact how many future homes are built.

Unproductive Assets: Business ventures that do not generate a positive return on investment because of management inefficiencies or weak demand levels.

TABLE 1.5	Supply Overproduction		

Housing overproduction in Year 2 results in a sharp fall in Year 3 production. This sharp change in building can lead to an economy-wide recession.

	Built	Demand	Difference
Year 1	2,000	2,000	–
Year 2	2,000	1,800	200
Year 3	1,400	1,600	(200)

Suppose the homebuilders become scared and revise overall demand expectations downward to 1,600 units. In trying to meet this estimated 1,600-unit demand level, only 1,400 units (1,600 − 200) would actually be built—down 600 units from the prior year. The economy would peak at the point of maximum activity and then slow going forward. Homebuilders would respond to overproduction by decreasing prices and cutting employment. As a result, the lack of building activity would slow the cycle of money and cause the industry to contract. This downshift in housing could spill into other areas of the economy and lead to a recession overall. The central bank and government would try to minimize the recession, but the passage of time is necessary to increase bank lending, remove unproductive assets, and move the economy into another expansionary phase.

Competitor Research

The term *profit* can also be referred to as *income* or *earnings*. These three words mean the same thing and are used interchangeably throughout this book.

Despite the existence of competitors in an area, the decision to initiate new business activity should be based solely on an entrepreneur's ability to capture a sufficient level of **net profit** that properly compensates for the risks and effort involved with starting and operating the new business. When conducting competitor research, it becomes important to define a general area (on a map) where marketing resources will be expended and figure out if health care providers earn a satisfactory amount of net profit.

Net profit: Amount remaining after deducting all necessary business expenses from revenue.

An area might have 40 health care providers per 10,000 people and enjoy an average net profit of $80,000. A second area with a similar standard of living might contain 50 health care providers per 10,000 residents yet provide an average of $90,000 in net profit. Different legal environments, insurance offerings, or demographic variables might cause the second area to offer more net profit on average despite the greater density of health care providers. In theory, new entrants would gravitate toward the second area in hopes of accessing a higher level of net profit. The inclusion of more health care providers in that area would then drive average net profit levels down until reaching equilibrium with the first area. The **revenue** levels of each competitor could also be considered, but net profit reflects what an entrepreneur keeps for personal use.

Since net profit is computed after deducting business expenses from revenue, organizations that are improperly managed can cause the marketplace to reach a point of saturation quicker than expected.

Revenue: The total inflow of cash or value derived by exchanging services or products with consumers.

An area will not reach a point of saturation until the available net profit potential falls below desired levels across the board. Entrepreneurs should properly research the marketplace by analyzing competitors and discover if net profit potential is acceptable. Even where profit levels are low within a marketplace, an entrepreneur may attempt to push out competitors through superior service quality or focus on a specific group of patients where profit potential is greater than average. Consider the following questions:

How will the marketplace evolve? The marketplace might provide a high degree of profit potential now, but will that profit potential remain high over the course of your career?

1. What is the average net profit level that health care providers earn in the area where you would like to practice?

2. Do the net profit levels disperse over a wide statistical range or do they fall close to the average?
3. Based on the expected number of competitors and the amount patients are expected to spend on health care, will the marketplace continue to provide enough net profit in the future?
4. At what point would net profit potential become so constrained that competitors would start to feel dissatisfied with what they are earning overall?

Talk to your competitors and ask if their incomes meet expectations.

Target Market

Figuring out what type of patient group provides the greatest amount of profit potential, positive word of mouth, and practitioner enjoyment is an essential part of market research. Taking all market participants and segmenting them into smaller categories permits a strategic allocation of resources. Competitive forces may cause a health care provider to focus more on a specific group or there may be a personal reason for wanting to offer unique services. Often, the **target market** evolves organically by way of a characteristic group that more readily frequents a health care organization. For instance, word of mouth may spread haphazardly among coworkers at a specific local business resulting in a higher rate of new patients from that particular source. Knowing the sources of patients is important and should shape how marketing resources are allocated during future efforts. In order to target a certain group better, a health care provider can acquire specialized skills or tailor marketing efforts in a specific manner.

Target Market: A defined group of market participants that receive a unique allocation of marketing resources.

As listed in Table 1.6, items to consider when defining a target market include *demographic variables*, occupations, locations, community organizations, and health conditions. Demographic variables are a way of segmenting market participants according to unique personal characteristics including gender, age, height, weight, educational level, and so forth.

Take caution when focusing almost exclusively on a specialized skill set or when seeing a unique type of patient. You may struggle to recruit or properly care for patients outside of that specialization.

TABLE 1.6	Target Market Categories
The table contains six categories specifying how a target market could be defined.	

Demographic Variables	Specific Health Conditions
• Gender • Age • Height • Weight • Educational level • Other key characteristics	• Most common health problems experienced in the marketplace • Most common health problems seen by the organization • Unique health conditions where being an "expert" is desired
Community Organizations • Attended by entrepreneur • Attended by network participants	**Geographical Locations** • General area within the marketplace • Near a specific location
Occupations • Specific companies in the marketplace • General category of occupation	**Interests and Hobbies** • Enjoyed by entrepreneur • Enjoyed by network participants

CASE STUDY

Target Market

A health care provider who enjoys running may want to target various types of runners. As Figure 1.1 shows, runners within this sample marketplace could be categorized into three *subtarget* markets. Defining a subtarget market can further increase the efficiency of how marketing resources are spent.

FIGURE 1.1 Target and Subtarget Markets

Local runners
(Target market)

Running stores   Running clubs   Friends that run
(Subtarget markets)

The following list represents ways to expend marketing resources per each subtarget market:

1. List local running stores, connect with the respective owners and employees, and set up sales luncheons to form relationships.
2. Participate on runs organized by local running clubs, get to know the members, and expand relationships where rapport is strong.
3. Discover friends who like to run, invite these friends to local runs or running club events, and train these friends on how to market on your behalf to other runners.

Summary

Understanding the full marketplace involves an extensive amount of work. Practice management firms can provide certain information, but a health care provider should have an intimate personal understanding of the marketplace. The Internet, libraries, and professional resources are great first-line sources for market information. Talking to residents in a neighborhood, networking with local business owners, and simply walking around the area can provide the best insights. Knowing the current phase of the business cycle is important when initiating a new venture. In terms of entering into a new marketplace, a health care provider should focus almost exclusively on the average net-profit levels available. Once a marketplace is defined, targeted patient groups that promote the greatest amount of net profit, word of mouth, and enjoyment should receive the greatest allocation of marketing resources.

1.4   Consumer Behavior

A successful business offers products or services that consumers want or need. Structuring the health care experience in a way that is personally relevant might not directly satisfy consumer demand. A balancing act exists between finding optimal enjoyment in what you do and providing services that are wanted or needed. Pinpointing that spot in between these two objectives requires getting a sense of your likes and dislikes as well as the consumer's. Table 1.7 outlines the various types of behavior that influence consumer demand categorized as *group*, *individual*, and *purchase*.

Group Behavior

One set of behavior is based on factors in the general environment. These include cultural phenomena, soft impressions, evaluations, and direct recommendations. *Cultural phenomena* act as a giant wave over a distinct population. The general topics heard and seen on a daily basis from media sources, advertisements, or group conversations have an influence over behavior and thinking. For example, people tend to have a strong sensitivity to gas prices. As prices rise, conversations among people and on TV begin to change and this cultural focus then enters the consumer's psyche when making decisions on such things as what car to buy or how far to travel.

Individuals a consumer comes in contact with every day can greatly influence the decision-making process. These individuals can deposit *soft impressions* based on the likes and dislikes they express about a subject. A consumer makes adjustments because of subtle thoughts and feelings that subsequently develop. To illustrate this point, a friend might express dissatisfaction after seeing a new movie, thus causing others to feel doubtful about it as well. Consumers can also manifest beliefs about what they think the likes and dislikes of others are and alter the decision-making process based on the perceived *evaluation* that could ensue. The fear of a negative evaluation or hope for a positive evaluation can easily influence a purchase decision. For instance, a consumer may decide to buy an expensive pair of jeans thinking it will grab the attention of others.

Finally, a *direct recommendation* to avoid or try something has perhaps the most profound impact on a consumer, especially in the context of health care. Direct recommendations are of tremendous importance for health care providers who must rely heavily on word of mouth. Health care providers should try to encourage patients who had a positive experience to pass along direct recommendations.

> A *referral* is a type of direct recommendation within the context of health care.

Individual Behavior

Another set of behavior is based on personal experiences. These include customary behavior, hard impressions, cognitive dissonance, and genetic attributes. Perceptions that individuals accumulate as children tend to carry forward through life as *customary behavior*. Political

---

TABLE 1.7	**Consumer Behavior**
Group Behavior	
Cultural phenomena	Being influenced by current trends or public opinion
Soft impressions	Taking into account the likes and dislikes of others
Evaluations	Taking into account the perceived likes and dislikes of others
Direct recommendations	Receipt of a direct suggestion or set of instructions
Individual Behavior	
Customary behavior	Traditional way that a person acts or thinks
Hard impressions	Intense moments that influence how a person acts or thinks
Cognitive dissonance	Ignoring new information that conflicts with old information
Genetic attributes	Predispositions based on a person's physical or emotional state
Purchase Behavior	
Willing customer	Has the desire and resources to spend willingly
Bargain hunter	Wants to preserve resources and find a good fit
Onlooker	May cling to resources or have no interest in services offered

affiliation, hygiene, study habits, language, and so forth become well established in the brain. This behavior persists even when the environment later changes because the brain cannot be instantly rewired to account for new understandings.

Hard impressions tend to form as a result of intense personal experiences that may be highly unique. Imagine a person who is rear-ended by a semitruck and must endure a year of rehabilitation. That patient may establish a strong bias toward semitrucks and refrain from liking them even after several years. When making a purchase decision, the consumer will most likely consider the safety features of a new vehicle.

The synaptic network of the brain has tremendous psychological influence over consumer behavior. If something goes against the general belief system of a consumer, it might be dismissed so that the consumer remains comfortable with current beliefs. People often resist changing what they perceive as customary because of *cognitive dissonance*. Dissonance factors refer to the conflict that occurs between new unfamiliar information and old familiar information. As the science of health care evolves, new forms of treatment can arise. A patient might expect to receive old forms of treatment and feel uncertain about anything new being recommended. To modify patient behavior, a health care provider must properly communicate in a way that helps transition a patient's thinking.

Finally, there are *genetic attributes* that influence consumer behavior unrelated to personal experiences. Individuals display behavior based on how their bodies function naturally. For example, people will generally avoid hot foods and drinks during hot weather and gravitate more toward colder items.

Purchase Behavior

A consumer will approach the decision-making process in one of three ways. As a *willing customer*, the consumer has a strong desire to consummate a sale. A child in a candy store with $5 would likely be a willing customer. Often, a willing customer has a strong emotional attachment to a certain product or company that results in alternative products being ignored.

A *bargain hunter* wants to browse various products or services, weigh different options, and find a good fit at the right price. A bargain hunter will consummate a sale if the circumstances are right. The emotional ties to a certain product or company tend to be minimal for a bargain hunter.

Finally, an *onlooker* might be open to hearing ideas but has an aversion to making a purchase decision either to save money or because of disinterest. Preconceived notions may also block the decision-making process before thoughtful deliberation is allowed to take place. An onlooker can morph into a bargain hunter or willing customer through proper communication, but this category of consumer will have the least propensity to purchase something.

Industry Trends

Bad experiences within the health care industry may emerge in the media or through other sources of public communication causing the formation of negative cultural phenomena. Regulatory and legal changes can also impact an industry. These events might lead to decreased revenue for the industry as a whole. Professional associations should set in place infrastructure to receive warnings from members and to prepare an appropriate response at the public level to defend against negative press. Individual health care providers should have a strategy to address concerns proactively with their patients. Responses can be placed in printed materials, such as a newsletter, or discussed directly with patients when they come in for a visit. Professionals should remain vigilant in supporting their industry and address negative cultural phenomena proactively.

Some contemporary trends can increase cash flows into an industry. Positive media coverage can give rise to supportive cultural phenomena. The addition of new health care providers may draw more net profit into the marketplace as a result of increased marketing efforts and a broader patient base. A professional association can enact marketing initiatives that help expand the industry. As available net profit increases, more health care providers can enter the marketplace and remain satisfied with what they earn.

Reviewing industry trends is part of conducting ongoing microeconomic analysis.

Industry growth patterns may increase, decrease, or fall in line with the average growth rate of the general economy. An industry that experiences rates of growth higher than the general economy will ultimately reach a peak and either flatten out, fall back to the level of the general economy, or slip below it. This is viewed as the *industry cycle*. Unlike the general business cycle, the peak of an industry may not lead to a recessionary period for that industry. A health care provider who intends on entering the marketplace or expanding operations has to consider how future industry and business-cycle trends will unfold. Organizations that suddenly invest heavily in new equipment, such as a building, around the peak of an industry or business cycle might be caught in a financial bind as the industry or general economy shift into different growth patterns. Where above-average growth patterns currently exist, a health care provider should prepare strategic alternatives for an eventual change in those growth rates.

> Since the industry cycle and business cycle will always revert back to sustainable rates of growth, an entrepreneur should remain mindful that current economic conditions may not hold going forward.

Summary

The relationship between what a patient wants and the services an organization provides will greatly impact an organization's success. Building this relationship requires an understanding of consumer behavior. Group behavior that impacts a consumer includes cultural phenomena, soft impressions, evaluations, and direct recommendations. Individual experiences throughout life can lead to the formation of customary behavior and hard impressions. Challenging the understanding brought about by these experiences may result in cognitive dissonance. A person might possess certain genetic attributes that influence behavior as well. Depending upon the circumstances surrounding a purchase decision, a consumer might act as a willing customer, bargain hunter, or onlooker.

A health care provider should focus on potential regulatory or legal changes and shocks to consumer behavior from contemporary trends. Research should include a review of industry and business-cycle growth patterns. A health care provider must anticipate that current growth patterns *will* eventually change and prepare a strategic response.

1.5   Strategic Planning

Entrepreneurs mistakenly refrain from starting a new organization that resembles an existing one. Why would anyone start a business where one already exists? When conducting market research, the main question becomes, "Can I derive a sufficient level of net profit from this venture?" Competitive pressures should be evaluated, but profitability carries the most significance overall. Can the existence of another business allow all competitors to remain profitable at a sufficient level? Market research should indicate if a marketplace has enough capacity to support additional competitors.

Strategic planning helps an organization solidify market share in the face of existing or changing competitive pressures. Strategic planning is an important part of generating optimal levels of net profit before and after starting a practice. Even in an environment with high profit potential (because competitive pressures are low), a starting practice needs to grow until adequate profitability is reached. In an area with low profit potential, strategic planning has even more importance as competitors struggle to remain sufficiently profitable.

In general business theory, competitive strategies are categorized as either **cost leadership** or **differentiation**. Health care providers can also compete using a strategy of **integration**. An organization that adheres to a strategy of cost leadership attempts to offer products similar to its competitors but at a lower cost. In the health care field, a strategy of cost leadership is pursued infrequently since reducing prices too low tends to carry a negative connotation about the quality of care being offered. The general public already expects to pay a fair amount for health care services and will become skeptical about a "good" deal. Health care providers tend to operate most often using a strategy of differentiation as a result.

With a differentiation strategy, the organization offers unique features that cannot be easily duplicated and does not attempt to reduce prices below competitors. Health care providers can differentiate their services based on the overall level of quality. Patients tend to

Strategic Planning: The main approach an organization takes when attempting to form and maintain a relationship with consumers.

Cost Leadership: Offering products or services similar to competitors but at lower prices.

Differentiation: Offering products or services with unique, high-quality features at similar or higher prices than competitors.

Integration: Forming an organization with other types of health care providers giving patients access to a broader range of services.

accept standard or above-average prices when the patient experience warrants them. Along those same lines, health care professionals often form integrated health care clinics to provide a greater range of health care services or deliver a better overall experience. An office might contain a medical doctor, naturopath, acupuncturist, chiropractor, massage therapist, dietician, and so forth. The individual health care providers might offer a standard array of services, but access to the various health care providers can heighten the overall patient experience. An integrated clinic must be properly managed to ensure patients are directed to other health care providers when necessary and the patient experience remains positive.

SWOT Analysis

SWOT Analysis: Strengths, weaknesses, opportunities, and threats of an organization in relation to competitive pressures.

A **SWOT analysis** divides competitor research according to an organization's strengths, weaknesses, opportunities, and threats. A SWOT analysis reviews the organization's market position in relation to its competitors and is usually included in the marketing section of a business plan. If a desired marketplace cannot provide enough net profit for all competitors, then all organizations will have to fervently compete for market share. This may result in a competitor leaving the marketplace or new entrants looking elsewhere to initiate operations. Some organizations that become unprofitable may try to survive financially in the short term and hope that conditions will improve. If sufficient profitability cannot be maintained over the long term, an entrepreneur will not be properly compensated for the risk and effort involved with operating an organization. This scenario may lead the entrepreneur to move to a different marketplace or go into bankruptcy if severe.

Refer to the marketing plan at the end of Chapter 5 for more information on what a SWOT analysis entails.

Summary

An entrepreneur should ask if enough net profit is available to all competitors before initiating new activity in a marketplace. A new entrant may not encounter strong competitive pressures if a marketplace offers high profit potential. Where average net profit is inadequate or a new organization needs to capture market share rapidly, strategic planning becomes increasingly important. In the health care profession, competitive strategies include cost leadership, differentiation, and integration.

CHAPTER ASSIGNMENT

Working in a group of three to four students or fellow professionals, complete the following items.

1. Work through evolving a concept using Table 1.1. Write down a complete list of items and then review how each particular element might impact the other elements holistically.

2. Conduct research online and figure out what business cycle the economy is in currently. Also, give reasons for why you believe the economy will be in a particular part of the business cycle two years from now.

3. Ensure that each group member understands why profitability is more important than the total number of competitors in a marketplace. Have each group member outline an initiative involving a target market that could be launched to obtain more market share.

4. Reflect on what an individual might think about when considering a health care provider and write down examples of how each of the 11 types of consumer behavior might relate.

5. Have each group member give at least one example of a contemporary trend affecting the health care profession. Has the professional association made attempts to address the matter?

6. If competition is high, how might a health care provider use a strategy of differentiation?

Territory Management

AUTHOR'S NOTE

Taking human nature into account, opening up an office and expecting patients to flood in seems unreasonable. Health care is a personal matter and prospective patients must feel comfortable with the thought of accessing a new health care provider. Patients must be willing to expend resources and be motivated to initiate the health care process. Building a patient base takes time and examining your marketplace is a crucial part of making the most efficient use of your time. Discover where to find the most effective sources of referrals, patients, and networking opportunities by leaving no stone unturned as you sift through every square inch of your marketplace. Keep track of everything as explained in this chapter, either using a territory worksheet or a software program. Make this investment now and your marketing efforts will become more effective down the road.

The best marketing is FREE: Foster Relationships Energetically Everywhere.

Marketing efforts should be initiated at the earliest possible moment since it can easily take several years to develop a **network** of relationships extensive enough to support a practice financially. This time factor exists because people may not possess an immediate need for health care services or they may not currently have the right frame of mind toward health. Expecting immediate results from last-minute marketing efforts is unreasonable. Marketing efforts spread out over several years have more potential to be converted into something of value than a conversation that took place sometime in the prior day.

You cannot foresee all future events or predict how people will interact inside a marketplace. Do not be quick to dismiss anyone who currently seems apprehensive about using your services. A person might use your services at a later point in time or simply pass along a *direct recommendation*. Running a successful practice means setting wheels in motion and making a long-term investment toward building a broad and meaningful community. Every relationship has the potential to contribute to success—some more than others—and answering *how* is impossible. Even before becoming licensed, a health care student should never hesitate to foster relationships energetically everywhere (FREE). How will relationships evolve after becoming licensed? The only way to find out is by forming a network, expanding it, and cultivating referrals from it.

The personal nature of health care services creates a mental barrier to accessing an unknown health care provider. Individuals tend to shy away from modifying a daily routine to include health care appointments as well. What will make individuals comfortable with the decision to start something new and place you in charge of it? Years of **branding** efforts can allow individuals to grow comfortable with your organization. It is necessary to cultivate relationships over the long term in an effective manner tailored to each situation. As relationships are built, general word of mouth will permeate through the marketplace and lead to greater exposure.

Since networking and marketing efforts consume resources, research help determine their most efficient allocation. The best allocation of **marketing resources** will minimize the amount of time spent on marketing and maximize the time spent with patients. Since *current* marketing efforts produce value in the *future*, a health care organization must think about its needs in advance. A software database program is essential for keeping track of marketing efforts and members of a community over time. This chapter closes with a review of Daylite by Marketcircle, a contact relationship management (CRM) software program.

Network: Collection of people with awareness of you or some aspect of your organization.

Branding: Inspiring a particular feel or reputation through a common name, icon, message, or marketing campaign.

Marketing Resources: Time, energy, and money spent in relation to marketing efforts.

2.1   Territory Mapping

An entrepreneur must take note of every aspect of a marketplace. Marketing ideas demonstrating the best way to expend resources will emerge only after examining people, places, events, and objects in depth. Take, for instance, a health care provider who participates in a book club. How could knowing the area surrounding where the book club meets prove beneficial? The health care provider could connect book club members with local business owners or make recommendations on where to eat after the meeting adjourns. Making these connections supports the growth of a referral system where local business owners refer to you and vice versa. Becoming familiar with various books can support conversations held with individuals outside of the book club.

> A health care provider needs to maintain a general list of discussion topics to ensure conversations evolve and do not fade prematurely.

An intimate understanding of a marketplace can provide countless benefits. Discovering more about a marketplace is a matter of venturing around it, making detailed observations, and talking with everyone possible. You would be amazed when and where opportunity will present itself. Consider the following responses to a common question about directions.

DIALOGUE

Passerby: Excuse me. Do you know where Main Street is?

Person A: I don't know exactly. It should be over in that direction.

Versus

Passerby: Excuse me. Do you know where Main Street is?

Person B: Go down this street four blocks, turn left, and continue for about a mile. What are you looking for exactly?

Passerby: There's a new restaurant that just opened up called Romana's.

Person B: Right! That's a great place. I know the manager, Greg. Tell him I said hello if you see him. My name is Jeff Smith. I have a health care practice a mile in that direction on Lincoln Street. I hope you enjoy your meal.

Discussion Person A does not have a good understanding of the marketplace and the conversation abruptly ends. Continuing further, the passerby meets Person B who has an intimate understanding of the marketplace and can provide useful directions. Moreover, Person B has found an opportunity to strike up a short conversation and insert meaningful references. To what extent could those references culminate in something of value?

Use an actual map to outline your marketing **territory** and keep track of major people, places, events, and objects in it. Buy a map and place it on a wall somewhere visible in order to keep the territory within plain sight. Use pins or markers to label areas and keep track of important items as shown in Figure 2.1.

> **Territory:** A defined area where the expenditure of marketing resources is planned.

A territory houses many unique hotspots that draw people together. Get to know the geographic layout and identify major venues. Parks, schools, shopping malls, office buildings, hospitals, and so forth contain many marketing opportunities. What public events will take place at a nearby park? What people can you encounter while walking a dog or shopping for groceries? Find out what is happening at various locations using websites, newspapers, flyers, or other listings that contain upcoming events. How many events can you reasonably attend and what would provide the best allocation of marketing resources? Taking a cooking class for $60 that allows a high level of interaction among a few people might prove more valuable than an outdoor concert that costs $20 and provides limited opportunity for conversation despite the large number of people in attendance.

> Q. How should I define my marketing territory?
>
> A. It's any area on a map where you want to expend marketing resources.

FIGURE 2.1 Territory Map

Source: © Laralova, Fotolia.com

Leave no stone unturned as you scour the marketplace. Even the most trivial objects can generate a range of useful ideas. Imagine a bus stop that stands 20 yards from a desired office location. How can this object be used for marketing purposes? Bus riders might feel more willing to frequent a business along the route, for example. Are there ways to put flyers near the bus stop? Could changing the location of a sign increase its visibility to people while they wait at the bus stop? The bus itself is another object to take into account. Is there a way to advertise on the inside or outside of the bus? Ride the bus one day and talk to the driver. Build rapport and ask if the driver knows of coworkers, riders, or other individuals who could use your services.

Community organizations represent a powerful marketing resource for health care providers. Organizations tend to center on religion, politics, philanthropic causes, sports, or hobbies. Toastmasters International clubs can be found throughout the world and are a great way to improve public-speaking skills. Effective relationships are often best formed through face-to-face contact where public-speaking skills will come in handy. It becomes important to arrange meetings, join community organizations, and strike up conversations at random with market participants.

To create an environment centered on health care, stage community events or presentations yourself and offer free health screenings. Health care providers often set up tradeshow booths at conventions or community events where health care will be of interest to participants. Another option involves asking to be a guest speaker at such events.

COMMUNITY ORGANIZATIONS		
Toastmasters International	toastmasters.org	Public speaking
Rotary International	rotary.org	Serving the community
Lions Clubs International	lionsclubs.org	Serving the community
National Association of Investors Corp	betterinvesting.org	Investment club
Optimist International	optimist.org	Focused on children
Kiwanis International	kiwanis.org	Focused on children
Soroptimist International	soroptimist.org	Women's club
U.S. Chamber of Commerce	uschamber.com	Business federation

Territory Worksheet

A physical map cannot display all the information needed to manage all the people, places, events, and objects in a territory. A **territory worksheet** uses categories called *classifications* to keep track of marketing details. In its most basic form, the worksheet should contain three columns. The first column specifies the general classification—the group that best represents the overall marketing opportunity. For example, a target market, community organization, family member, or major referral source could have its own classification. The second column defines attributes, such as facts, figures, or specific names. Once an attribute gains in importance, it can be placed into its own classification. The final column should include highlights of past marketing efforts and ideas on how to expend marketing resources going forward.

Make sure to continuously update the worksheet. Set reminders on a calendar in order to keep motivated to make updates. Table 2.1 illustrates how a territory worksheet could be arranged for a hypothetical health care provider. Take note of how main categories of people, places, events, and objects have been placed into classifications. Attributes define each classification in more detail and marketing notes describe the nature of proposed marketing efforts.

Territory Worksheet: A listing of important people, places, events, and objects in a marketplace along with details on related marketing efforts.

Go online to remedybooks.com and download a free territory worksheet under the Students tab.

Simply drive or walk around your marketplace. Stop into businesses and see what marketing ideas come to mind. Take note of everything on a territory worksheet.

TABLE 2.1	Sample Territory Worksheet

This territory worksheet shows elements of a marketplace divided into relevant classifications along with attributes and marketing notes detailing each classification.

Classification	Attributes	Marketing Notes
Relatives	Parents Siblings Uncle Frank Aunt Betty	• Annual event: replenish business cards and remind about referring • Have Aunt Betty decorate clinic
Cycling club	38 members Low turnover 14 race events	• Get to know a family member of each cyclist • Get a race calendar and show up for events with business cards • Throw a **BBQ** next month and invite members
Nearby shopping mall	4 restaurants 1 dry cleaner 1 grocery store 1 flower shop 1 gas station	• Leave business cards after eating at each restaurant • Meet owner of dry cleaner • Advertise in flower shop's newsletter • Mention office location while getting gas or groceries
Mr. Smith, Attorney at Law	Business attorney with 800 current clients	• Take him to lunch and try to join his professional networking group • Send him a holiday card and learn his family members' names

Summary

An intimate knowledge of the marketplace helps when attempting to connect with market participants. Everything matters including people, places, events, and objects. Understanding all aspects of a marketplace will unearth new opportunities and provide conversation topics. Keeping a physical map somewhere visible along with a more detailed territory worksheet keeps marketing efforts focused and organized. Unique marketing ideas should be noted in relation to classifications on a territory worksheet.

2.2 Network Development

Since marketing efforts usually take time before producing results, an entrepreneur should work on building relationships with market participants as soon as possible. Building strong relationships takes time, energy, and money. A thorough examination of a marketplace using territory-mapping concepts enables an entrepreneur to find the most ideal market participants. A territory worksheet could be more than 20 pages and is used to pinpoint relevant sources of **prospects**, such as trade shows, companies, seminars, community organizations, and so forth. Marketing notes need to contain details about how to effectively market each territory classification.

The next step in marketing involves organizing market participants into a structured network. A network forms the backbone of a health care provider's success. Whether in practice as a business owner or working as an employee, a strong network of people operates as a bridge to opportunity. It can serve as a source for new jobs, employees, or equipment. In fact, most *network participants* will not become patients. A network contributes to success by spreading word of mouth, furnishing resources, and providing access to new patients. Marketing efforts should center on building strong relationships with people who already possess a large and valuable network, such as attorneys, small-business owners, or employees of large companies.

In developing an extensive network, it is not necessary to make everyone your best friend. Relationships can exist on a purely professional level. A successful network will normally involve several thousand people where forming strong friendships with each will prove impossible. A network should contain a central core that consists of *direct* relationships. As seen in Figure 2.2, a network then radiates outward indirectly through word of mouth spread among the communities maintained by your core network participants. Learning names is an important part of building relationships, but an extensive *indirect* network will not easily form if your name is hard to remember. You may need to modify your name or associate it with a memorable concept in order to ensure it gets passed along.

Prospects: People who have the potential to become network participants, referral sources, or patients.

FIGURE 2.2 Network Participation
Direct network participants can present you to networks they have formed, expanding awareness of you indirectly.

How much exposure do you have within a particular marketplace? Network participants must talk about you in a constructive manner in order for you to build an extensive community. Awareness will more easily spread into successive divisions of people far beyond your immediate network core when communication efforts are structured. An **applied network** exists whenever network participants are trained to speak on your behalf. A network must become more than a collection of people who talk about you in a haphazard fashion. It becomes critical to maintain control over your market *brand* and ensure the most productive use of your network. The following dialogue illustrates how a health care provider can build a network and create *applications* for network participants.

Applied Network: Network participants with a trained ability to market on your behalf.

DIALOGUE

Provider: Would you mind taking a moment to think about all of the individuals at your workplace? Is there anyone that might need my services?

Relative: No one really comes to mind. I'm not sure I can be of much help.

Provider: That's okay. Whenever you have a conversation about health related matters, could you mention me? Bring my name up in conversation and the location of my office. Tell others that I offer a free *no-obligation consultation* for new patients. I could use everyone's help in growing my practice. I will give you a stack of business cards to keep at work in case anyone shows interest.

Relative: Sure. I'd be happy to help anyway I can.

Discussion In this example, a relative becomes an applied network participant. The health care provider tries to seek out specific referrals at first and then follows with a specific set of instructions to help build general awareness. Getting network participants to think or act in a specific way has tremendous value. Imagine the benefit if someone suddenly has a health care need and a network participant has been trained on how to communicate on your behalf. Important information will become relayed whereas it might have otherwise been forgotten or overlooked.

When meeting a new person, how often will they ask or wonder what you do for a living? The human brain likes to have a point of identification in order to reduce ambiguity and start filing away memories. Occupations tend to serve as a focal point most of the time. Discussing a particular hobby or achievement can also make people more comfortable with you. Taking an initial encounter and turning it into an effective relationship that endures over time often requires a (1) common interest, (2) **interconnection**, or (3) personal touch. Sharing a *common interest* decreases ambiguity about who you are and allows for a reliable point of conversation. You're more likely to be invited into new communities when common interests are shared. A territory worksheet should allude to where an entrepreneur can find people who share a common interest.

Along those same lines, an *interconnection* offers a point of identification by virtue of having common knowledge of people, places, events, or objects. A strong relationship forms vicariously as people understand you through the context of someone or something else. Interconnections can form in relation to mutually known people, businesses, community organizations, neighborhoods, parks, and so forth. The chance of having an interconnection with prospects greatly increases by simply knowing more about a marketplace.

Finally, a health care provider should impart certain *personal touches* that reaffirm quality when interacting with others. The general expectation is that health care providers are well educated and they genuinely care about people. Remembering names, looking someone in the eye, smiling, offering a firm handshake, and dressing appropriately at all times can affirm someone's perception of you as a quality health care provider.

> Interconnection: The act of knowing people, places, events, or objects in common with another person.

> People who have never used your services need some way of judging your service potential. Your personal presentation needs to parallel your abilities.

DIALOGUE

Provider: That's interesting. You play chess every Thursday downtown? I love a good chess match. How's your game?

Acquaintance: I don't win as much as I'd like but I really enjoy playing. You should join us some time. We play at the Northwest Community Center.

Provider: I would really like to play a few games but I'm starting a practice and it keeps me fairly busy. If I can't make it, could you tell others about my new practice?

Acquaintance: Sure. I'll keep you in mind.

> Discussion　In this example, the health care provider explores a *common interest* with this other person— chess playing. The common interest provides a reliable conversation topic and presents the health care provider with an opportunity to meet more people. If time is limited, the health care provider can create an application for this acquaintance in an attempt to spread word of mouth indirectly within the chess-playing community.

Summary

Success does not hinge upon close friendships, but rather effective professional relationships that can radiate outward through successive communities. Network applications aid the movement of word of mouth in a coordinated manner. It becomes important to specifically tell people what to say on your behalf. Sharing common interests or interconnections with people and using personal touches can promote the formation of effective relationships faster.

2.3　Referral System

The purpose of developing a network is to form and solidify effective relationships as part of creating opportunity. As relationships strengthen, attention should be turned toward building a **referral system** among select network participants. A valuable referral source will have an extensive network and will follow *applications* when communicating on your behalf. Understand how reputations are on the line when asking others to serve as a source of referrals. You must express a high degree of confidence that the referral source has nothing to worry about. Imagine meeting with an attorney and agreeing to cross-refer clients and patients to one another. Three months later the attorney calls because a client was complaining about your services. The attorney will probably hesitate before referring additional clients and may become angered over being put in an awkward position.

Start with straightforward prospects who may not react strongly to a negative event. As you gain both marketing and health care experience, slowly approach more sophisticated network participants. For example, work with an attorney new to practice who can relate to your situation and has the time to carry on an in-depth conversation. Later, market to a well-established attorney who has only 15 minutes to converse and may hold you to higher standards.

> **Referral System:** Collection of network participants trained to provide others with direct recommendations regarding seeking care from you.

> By not giving referral sources specific instructions on how to deliver the referral, you will lose control over what is communicated.

> Consider sending out an annual referral letter to specific network participants encouraging them to keep you in mind in case anyone they know has a health care need.

DIALOGUE

Initial contact

Provider: Hello. Is an owner of the firm available?

Provider: Hello. I run a health care practice nearby and would like to set up a meeting with you. I would like to bring lunch and give you the opportunity to meet me. I would also like to know your firm better in case my patients are in need of legal services. Would a day next week work?

During the meeting

Provider: I want to thank you for letting me stop by and introduce myself. I run a health care practice nearby and would like to connect with other business owners in the area. I have strong roots in this community and will remain here for the duration of my career. I would like to discuss some unique aspects of my background and style of care in case you have clients with matching needs. Later, I would like to learn what you specifically focus on as attorneys. That way I can direct my patients to you if the need arises.

Discussion This type of luncheon event is very common. A health care provider can call around and set referral meetings with other local business owners using food as an incentive. Mentioning reciprocity of referrals encourages listeners to sit through this type of meeting as well. Note how the health care provider has a structured dialogue that is being followed during the initial phone call and at the meeting.

Instead of establishing a disorganized referral system, dialogue applications provide verbiage that a referral source can use when providing a *direct recommendation*. First, ensure that a network participant thinks highly of you as a professional or a patient thinks highly of the overall health care experience. You want to make certain that the referral source will deliver only positive statements. Then, ask the referral source to consider individuals who may need your services. Finally, give examples of specific verbiage to use when communicating a referral. A prospect will more likely take action when given set instructions by the referral source. A referral made without an application can easily lack the kind of substance needed to make the referral effective.

DIALOGUE

Provider: How has your experience with my office been? I want to make sure I am offering the best level of service available.

Patient: I really like coming in. I think you take great care of me.

Provider: Is there anyone else in your family—or perhaps friends or coworkers—who could benefit from my care?

Patient: A few of my coworkers come to mind.

Provider: For those who come to mind, could you suggest that they call my office and set up an appointment? I can give you business cards to provide my complete contact information.

Discussion The health care provider ascertains that the patient has had a positive experience with all aspects of the organization. Since the patient appears to be a good source of referrals, the health care provider lists people to consider and then offers a specific set of instructions when approaching people on the organization's behalf. These applications increase the chance that the person receiving the referral will act upon it.

DIALOGUE

Provider: Do you know anyone who could benefit from my health care services, perhaps a family member, friend, or coworker?

Patient: Yes, my brother probably could. We were talking about his health the other night.

Provider: You should direct him to my website and encourage him to contact me about setting an appointment. It would be nice to meet more of your family members.

Patient: I'll see him next week and can talk to him then.

Discussion The health care provider asks a direct question about the patient's community and offers examples of whom to consider. The health care provider follows with an application on how to approach the brother specifically. The patient might not know how to properly communicate on the provider's behalf without these clear instructions.

Once a referral culminates in a new patient, try to gather feedback. Instead of waiting for negative feedback to filter back to the referral source, ask a patient directly how the experience went. If a problem exists, talk to the referral source directly before the patient has time to complain. Talking to the referral source proactively can also unearth problems that have not been automatically communicated to you by a referred patient. Do not expect a referral source to always call when problems exist. Gathering feedback and contacting people directly is critical to improving the patient experience and strengthening referral relationships. Thank a referral source for both successful and unsuccessful attempts at referring.

Have a stack of thank-you cards that can be quickly filled out and placed in the mail.

DIALOGUE

Provider: I'm calling to thank you for referring patients to me. I had three new ones because of your help.

Firefighter: No problem. I'm just trying to help my fellow firefighters.

Provider: The next time you see them, ask how their care was and let me know if there were any problems. The last thing I want is for them to have a bad experience.

Firefighter: I bump into them here and there. I'll see what they thought.

Discussion Never expect people to carry out a task automatically. Effective communication involves giving people very specific instructions (applications). The health care provider ultimately wants the referral source to gather feedback from the people being referred. By calling the referral source, the health care provider has a chance to give thanks and uproot any hidden problems.

Referral sources should be categorized using a territory worksheet in an effort to maximize marketing efforts. Those who proactively refer a large number of new patients or have valuable networks should be classified together. A provider can plan an annual event or offer unique perks for top referrers. Network participants who occasionally refer new patients can then be categorized separately. Other referral classifications can be established for unique purposes, such as a target market. A territory worksheet is an ideal form for keeping track of this type of marketing information.

Summary

A health care provider should ask a network participant to serve as a referral source when the relationship appears strong. Ask a referral source to consider specific people and then give specific instructions (applications) on how to communicate the referral properly. Feedback helps evaluate the quality of care being offered and can prevent a referral source from being blindsided with complaints. Always thank a referral source by some form of communication, such as a letter or phone call. Use a territory worksheet to organize your marketplace, network community, and referral system.

2.4   Marketing Campaigns

The best marketing is FREE: Foster Relationships Energetically Everywhere.

A structured marketing campaign attempts to communicate to a designated audience in a strategic manner using marketing tools and direct contact. A marketing campaign could attempt to convey general information or relay details about a significant event, such as a location change, sale of a practice, or new service line. Marketing tools provide a platform to display information and solidify relationships. Such tools include collateral pieces, websites, advertisements, and media spots. Successful marketing campaigns will include follow-up contact to further solidify relationships, bearing in mind the negative or diminished value from excessive contact.

To optimize effectiveness, all interaction through marketing tools or direct contact should be reviewed in terms of **frequency** and **intensity**. Repeated exposure to the same stimulus increases the brain's potential to write a long-term memory, but frequent and intense forms of interaction can become counterproductive. Imagine a network participant receiving an email every day from your organization versus once a quarter. How might different levels of frequency and intensity be perceived? Excessive frequency or intensity can result in the subsequent decline of marketing effectiveness leading to wasted resources.

Use a territory worksheet or software program to keep track of marketing campaign efforts. Start with a small, general audience until enough experience has been gained. Work with close relationships or other professionals starting a business at first and then slowly expand marketing efforts to involve a larger, sophisticated audience later.

Collateral

Collateral pieces represent the most common marketing tool used by health care organizations and include such materials as letters, business cards, brochures, newsletters, pamphlets, and electronic mail. Being handed a collateral piece directly will carry more intensity in a person's mind than receiving one in the mail or electronically. A graphic designer can create a marketing kit, including a logo, or a design template to ensure that materials look professional and consistent. The cost of designing, printing, and sending collateral pieces tends to be reasonable. For example, a newsletter can take a few hours to write and cost a few hundred dollars to completely distribute. A health care organization has more control over who receives collateral pieces as well. A newsletter or brochure can be sent to a target audience in a fairly controlled manner.

Health care providers often maintain several brochures that (1) explain specific health care services, (2) provide an overview on specific health concerns, and (3) display general information about the organization. Passing along business cards and giving allotments to network participants and referral sources help disseminate contact information and maintain awareness. Even before starting a long-term practice, a student or beginning health care provider can pass along personal cards. *Promotional items*, such as stickers, mugs, pens, magnets, shirts, or bookmarks can serve a useful purpose and display general information about the organization as well. Printing shops normally have catalogues full of different promotional items.

Websites

An online presence can help form and solidify relationships by providing information to patients and unknown market participants. In some instances, people will randomly search for health care providers using a search engine. Using the right *keywords* in between your website's title tags can move your website higher on search engine results. Linking to other websites and placing a web address on collateral increases awareness of a health care organization's own website. The web in general has become a valuable tool to connect with new people and stay in contact from a distance. If you wish to someday practice in a faraway marketplace, attempt to form an online presence beforehand. For instance, use a blog to write articles and give readers an opportunity to interact. Offer a way for people to submit topic ideas for the blog.

The first step in forming a website involves registering a domain name. This process can be difficult because many names have already been taken or an available domain name would appear too similar to another company. An organization has three options when attempting to build a website: (1) Hire a web designer, (2) use an all-in-one website service that offers templates and building tools, or (3) download a template and modify it with software, such as Adobe Dreamweaver. A website must be uploaded to a hosting

Frequency: The amount of exposure over a given time period to an organization's marketing efforts.

Intensity: Impact on the consumer from one or more instances of exposure to an organization's marketing efforts.

Collateral: Print or electronic documents that display information about an organization.

Would sending collateral to 50 people ten times result in a better response rate than reaching an audience of 500 people once?

Gather collateral pieces from other businesses to generate ideas for putting together your own collateral.

Instruct patients through a disclaimer on your website not to send health information via email or a submission form.

server with a company that has permission to house websites. Websites that offer blog or all-in-one website services normally include hosting.

Online scheduling services are available through various companies allowing patients to schedule appointments directly through your website. The company will provide website code that embeds into your website.

WEBSITE CREATION		
GoDaddy	godaddy.com	Domain names and hosting
Template Monster	templatemonster.com	Website templates
Weebly, Inc.	weebly.com	All-in-one service (free)
Adobe Systems	adobe.com	Web-building software
Blogger	blogger.com	Blogspace
Genbook	genbook.com	Appointment scheduling
Schedulicity	schedulicity.com	Appointment scheduling

Advertisements

Advertisement: Information about an organization displayed by a third-party vendor.

An **advertisement** (or ad) is an informational piece placed with a third-party vendor. It can vary in size from a small section in a phone book to a large billboard next to a roadway. A typical ad provides readers with general information and can cost a great deal to create and display. Most health care providers report a low volume of new patients from phone book ads yet phone book companies charge a high amount for even small placements. Inserting an ad with a coupon book or other *direct mailer* tends to target *bargain hunters* and can cost much less. Examine your marketplace to find appropriate third-party vendors that could display an ad. Look inside businesses or on objects, such as a city bus, to generate ideas. Where are ads currently shown in your marketplace and what businesses have potential untapped ad space?

Media Spots

Media Spots: Audio or video clips placed on a website or transmitted by TV or radio stations.

Media spots require a great deal of work to create, cost a fair amount, and may not easily communicate the perception of quality health care. A TV or radio station has the equipment to create the actual recording. A health care organization must closely match the organization's image with the associated TV show or radio program. Producing a movie or audio clip and placing it on websites represents another option. Media spots and ads do not always form a strong connection with audience members. Their high cost and low efficacy for health care organizations tend to limit their extensive use. However, creating general awareness through media spots or ads can assist with other marketing efforts.

Place a video on youtube.com.

Branding

An integrated clinic can combine marketing efforts to reduce costs, but it would need to coordinate how the clinic is branded.

What should come to mind when people think about your organization? *Branding* refers to inspiring a particular feel or reputation about an organization. Consider your reaction upon hearing the name of a well-known corporation. An understanding of what the company represents comes about by simply reflecting upon its name. It can take years to establish a strong brand in the marketplace as well as form meaningful relationships that will help support a successful practice.

Over time, the human brain will start to absorb the same stimulation without consciously taking it into account. A health care organization needs to slightly modify marketing efforts over time to stimulate a conscious observation while retaining a consistent branding theme that will accumulate layers of familiarity. An effective marketing campaign should attempt to develop a unique feel with an intended audience and evolve over time through feedback and development. Suppose a collateral piece sent to 4,000 market participants within a particular demographic generates 14 new patients. Two years later a similar marketing campaign targets that same audience. What will be the result? A health care organization could generate patient activity from one of the following.

1. One of the 14 original patients renewing care.
2. Market participants reacting to the latest marketing campaign only.
3. Market participants reacting to the accumulated effect of both marketing campaigns.

A marketing campaign needs to have many strategic layers to produce its intended branding effect. For instance, reaching out to market participants informally through media spots can create a first round of general awareness. Individuals may attempt to call an organization or access a website thereafter. An analysis of respondents may allow for the establishment of a target market. Then, collateral pieces could be tailored to this new-found target market in order to brand the organization in a specific manner. Table 2.2 lists common goals that branding efforts involve.

TABLE 2.2	Branding Efforts
1. Build awareness	
2. Modify perceptions	
3. Create attraction	
4. Showcase value	

> Viral or buzz marketing techniques involve eccentric activities that combine creativity and intensity to rapidly connect with market participants.

Summary

A health care organization needs to control its image within the marketplace. Branding refers to the coordinated effort of creating a particular feel or reputation for an organization. Marketing tools can assist with marketing efforts and include collateral, media spots, advertisements, and websites. The marketing tools most common to the health care profession are collateral pieces, such as business cards, newsletters, and brochures. Collateral pieces usually cost a reasonable amount and can support human interaction, marketing campaigns, or branding efforts. Media spots occur less frequently because of high production costs and poor connection strength. Health care providers commonly use ads in phone books despite these same drawbacks. A coupon book might provide better results than a phone book advertisement and appeal to bargain hunters. Websites can support marketing efforts by showcasing information that market participants seek. Human interaction still remains the best method for building a network, referral system, and patient base.

2.5 Resource Allocation

A natural relationship exists between the outflow of *current* marketing resources and the *future* level of patient volume. This **marketing pendulum** swings back and forth in relation to how historical marketing efforts influence future business activity as illustrated in Figure 2.3. As a practice builds, resources allocated to organizing and marketing should diminish and become replaced with patients. A health care organization should keep in mind that marketing efforts *lead* to the generation of new business. As the patient base builds, the need to market may seemingly diminish. *A practice can suffer later if an organization has not currently invested enough resources into marketing for future estimated needs.* The marketing pendulum will start to swing backward away from desired patient levels

> **Marketing Pendulum:** A symbolic representation of the relationship between seeing patients and engaging in marketing efforts.

FIGURE 2.3 Marketing Pendulum

The current level of marketing efforts helps define the future level of patient activity. If patient activity is low, then more resources must be centered on marketing efforts.

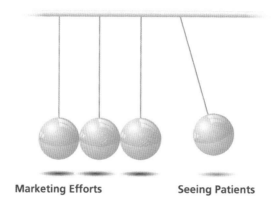

Marketing Efforts   Seeing Patients

because of insufficient historical marketing efforts. In order to prevent this backward slide, a continual investment in marketing must be made according to estimated future needs. Beginning health care providers who purchase a practice easily fall victim to the timing difference inherent in this marketing pendulum.

1. A health care provider takes over a well-sized practice and sees no apparent need to market.
2. As turnover occurs among patients and network relationships fade, the patient volume begins to diminish.
3. The health care provider reacts by initiating marketing efforts but undergoes a period of suboptimal performance because future needs were not properly anticipated and marketing efforts require time to take hold.

Experience running a practice helps when determining the amount of current marketing resources to be used to support a desired level of future activity. Excessive marketing can aggravate market participants or cause growth to occur faster than can be managed. An insufficient investment in marketing resources can cause relationships to fade and patient levels to decline. A successful practice will maintain a stable marketing pendulum and put as few resources as possible toward marketing. Still, there will never come a time when marketing efforts can completely cease.

Since networks can radiate outward unpredictably, a resource assessment should focus on the value involved with maintaining specific long-term relationships. A new patient questionnaire as shown in Figure 2.4 is vital to figuring out the source of new patients and what exposure patients had to different marketing efforts. Categorize patients based on responses and then look into accounting records to determine the amount of resources spent attracting the various types of patients. Subtract related expenses from patient revenue to find the net profit figure for each patient category. An evaluation of net profit should steer the course for new marketing efforts.

Accounting concepts learned later will help with conducting this evaluation.

Summary

Since marketing efforts may not immediately produce anything of value, a health care organization should expend marketing resources currently to meet estimated future needs. Because of resource limitations, a health care organization should allocate time, energy, and money in the most efficient way possible. Figuring out the source of new patients and comparing this to the amount of net profit patients generate help determine the best allocation of marketing resources.

FIGURE 2.4 New Patient Questionnaire

New Patient Questionnaire
Please take a moment and answer these questions so we may better service our customers. Thank you.

1. How did you first hear about our office?
    _____
    _____
    _____

2. Have you heard about our office on other occasions? If so, please explain.
    _____
    _____
    _____

3. Why did you decide to come in to us for services?
    _____
    _____
    _____

2.6 Marketing Software

This section is an independent learning module and is not affiliated with, nor has it been authorized, sponsored, or otherwise approved by Marketcircle™, Inc. Daylite™ product screenshots reprinted with permission from Marketcircle™, Inc. Information presented in the screenshots has been added by the author.

A territory can become cumbersome to manage without the help of a customer relationship management (CRM) software program. Many practice management software programs include a CRM application. A CRM application or individual program should enable the user to categorize people, events, and organizations while keeping notes and tracking marketing campaigns. Companies selling CRM software typically provide online demonstrations or free trial versions. In order to show examples of how a CRM program can support marketing efforts, this chapter closes with an overview of Daylite, a Marketcircle product available only for Apple computer systems. This CRM program works in tandem with Apple Mail and is available as an iPhone, iPad, or iPod application.

The following overview by no means captures all the capabilities of Daylite. This overview should not be construed as a recommendation to use or buy Daylite. The following screenshots are only meant to illustrate how a CRM program can help with managing a network, referral system, patient base, and marketing campaigns. The reader of this software overview should properly assess the appropriateness of a particular CRM program. Some CRM programs store information online and assess ongoing service fees. A health care organization must ensure that access to a CRM program is kept password protected and file transfers over the Internet are performed only through encrypted lines.

After properly installing the Daylite software, click on *New Contact* in the ribbon and begin adding contact information for network participants. Assume that a health care provider enjoys running and would like to target the running community. Figure 2.5 shows the main user interface and is currently highlighting contact information for the store manager of a fictitious running store.

FIGURE 2.5 Contact Screen

Clicking on *New Organization* will bring up the screen shown in Figure 2.6. This feature allows the user to categorize network contacts as part of effective territory management. Attributes (network contacts) can be linked to a classification (organization). Individuals can be classified according to a company, community organization, or event. In this example, three individuals along with an active marketing campaign have been linked to OPQ Sports as presented in the upper-right side of the screen.

FIGURE 2.6 New Organization

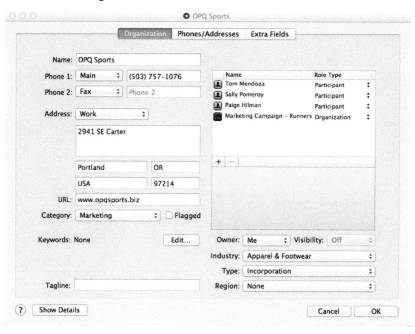

By clicking on *New Opportunity* in the main ribbon, the user can track a marketing campaign as demonstrated in Figure 2.7. Notice how four organizations have been linked to this example marketing campaign. The probability of success has been estimated at 80%. Clicking on the *Estimate* button allows the user to keep track of expenses related to the marketing campaign.

FIGURE 2.7 New Opportunity

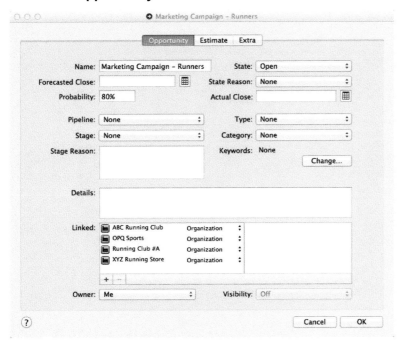

Assume that the health care provider in this example contacted OPQ Sports to organize a lunch meeting in hopes of forming relationships with store employees. Figure 2.8 displays a note made after the lunch meeting detailing what took place. A note can be started by clicking on *New Note* in the main ribbon. The word *Timestamp* and the date have been added to assist the user with keeping track of marketing efforts.

FIGURE 2.8 New Note

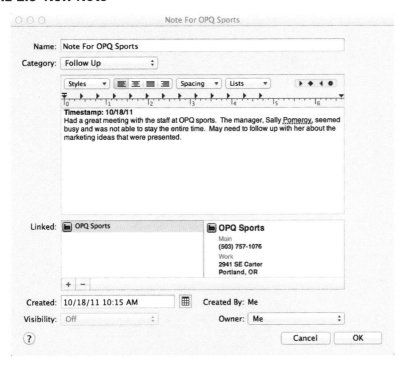

The health care provider in this example would like to send a thank-you card to the employees of OPQ Sports as part of building strong professional relationships. A task reminder has been created as shown in Figure 2.9 to ensure a card is sent. The task screen will appear after clicking on *New Task* in the main ribbon.

FIGURE 2.9 New Task

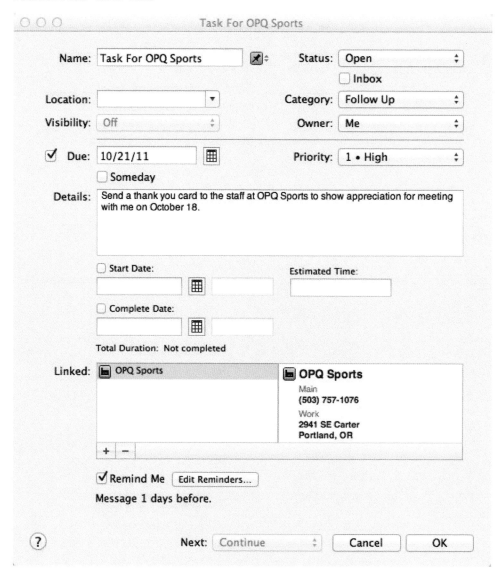

Figure 2.10 provides a list of organizations and highlights activity related to the OPQ Sports store specifically. Notice how the note made previously appears in the lower-right side of the screen. Information related to the marketing campaign involving the OPQ Sports store is listed in the upper-right side. Apart from the features shown previously, the user could keep track of marketing appointments and maintain a calendar of events using Daylite. Emails sent using Apple Mail are automatically recorded by the Daylite program if they relate to a network contact. An email can be initiated through the Daylite interface as well.

FIGURE 2.10 Organization Screen

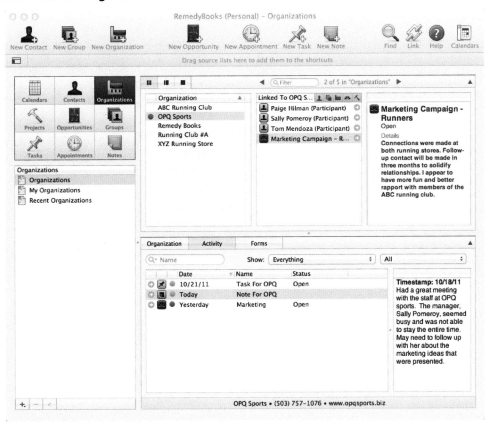

CRM PROGRAMS		
Outlook 2010 with Business Contact Manager	microsoft.com	CRM application
Sage Act!, Contact and Customer Manager	act.com	CRM program
Daylite by Marketcircle (Apple users only)	marketcircle.com	CRM program
Google Contacts	gmail.com	Integrates with Gmail
Prophet 5	avidian.com	Integrates with Outlook

CHAPTER ASSIGNMENT

Working in a group of three to four students or fellow professionals, complete the following items.

1. Get a map of the area around your school or a desired practice location (you can print one from maps.google.com). Travel around the immediate area or conduct research online and compile a territory worksheet. Dedicate at least two classifications to each of the four categories: people, places, events, and objects. Define attributes for each classification and compile marketing notes. Finally, highlight items on the map using pins and markers.

2. Fill out a territory worksheet involving ten separate network participants. The worksheet should include at least four classifications. An individual can function as a

classification or exist as an attribute of another classification. Consider friends, family, significant others, or random persons. Do any target markets come to mind?

3. Fill out a territory worksheet involving ten separate referral sources. The worksheet should include at least four classifications. An individual can function as a classification or exist as an attribute of another classification. Consider friends, family, significant others, or random persons. You may need to create fictitious referral sources if none currently exist.

4. Outline a marketing campaign involving three to four local small businesses. Consider restaurants, attorneys, grocery stores, and so forth. Include the frequency and form of intensity that seems appropriate. List how each of the four types of marketing tools will be employed.

5. Formulate a questionnaire with three to four questions meant to determine the number of new patients who came from the preceding marketing campaign.

6. Imagine a questionnaire showed that 8 new patients came from a specific advertising campaign directly; 4 new patients had heard about the organization before, but the marketing campaign served as a useful reminder to initiate care; an additional 2 new patients had heard about the organization before but had already planned to set an appointment. How should revenues from these 14 new patients be allocated against marketing expenses in figuring net profit?

Professional Sales

AUTHOR'S NOTE

Professional sales is not about selling anything. This chapter is about learning how to form relationships in an effective manner. Some of those relationships will go nowhere; others will contribute positive word of mouth, referrals, or business resources; and another group will become patients. A health care provider must reach out to as many people as possible because very few people who have a current health care need will want to address it with you right away.

The most successful practices are built by fostering long-lasting and mutually beneficial relationships with as many community members as possible. The concepts expressed in this chapter center on the belief that forming long-term relationships should be assisted with planning and structure. People who have never been in your office or received care from you have no idea what to expect. *You must learn how to present a quality image so that people can assume your office and service potential are of equal quality.* The main goal overall should be to foster relationships in a positive and meaningful way—and that may require you to approach people in a coordinated manner.

The best marketing is FREE: Foster Relationships Energetically Everywhere.

Qualification: Affirming that a long-term and mutually beneficial relationship between a health care organization and prospect can form.

Territory management involves forming an understanding of your marketplace and building a presence within a community of people. A professional sales approach represents a systematic way of developing the actual relationships. The general selling process contains four parts that need to be followed in sequence: introduction, rapport building, **qualification**, and sales approach. Health care providers will often overlook the need to develop a professional sales approach, accepting instead to casually interact with people. Conversations take place organically and relationships evolve without much management. A health care provider may have great success forming long-term relationships in this manner based on a natural talent to build rapport and connect with people. Often, the sensitive nature of health care and the expectation of high quality preclude a health care provider from approaching people informally, especially when considering the need to establish a large and diverse network. Professional sales techniques offer a framework for creating a formal presentation meant to indirectly *brand* your services as high quality.

Why is placing structure around your interaction with others important? Review the following question: *Do you know anyone who could benefit from coming in and receiving care at my office?* This question has a defined constituency and clear intent. It instructs the listener to consider anyone who could experience a benefit from receiving health care services. Nonetheless, the question attempts to prompt a thought process that might not have otherwise occurred. Consider the mental and physical energy along with the time and money needed to wade through a health care appointment or act as a referral source. Even the simple act of someone bringing up your name in conversations requires a degree of vigilance in remembering to keep you in mind.

When conducting sales in a *professional* manner, a health care provider can advance the profession and demonstrate how people can benefit from health care services. Learning how to listen and communicating in a structured manner promote a stronger connection and help a relationship evolve over time in a more managed fashion. In terms of the *marketing pendulum*, using professional sales techniques can decrease the need to allocate significant time to marketing efforts. This means a better allocation of resources to what matters most—treating patients.

Sales techniques attempt to change thought processes and provoke action. Hard sales tactics work because they lock people into taking action using potent emotions, but the average person can easily become frustrated after being made to feel those emotions. Health care providers can harm the profession by using aggressive tactics that lead to unsuitable or excessive health care treatments or that simply place the listener in an uncomfortable position. Aggressive sales tactics can spoil relationships, increase negative word of mouth, or even trigger disciplinary action by a licensing board. Health care providers who struggle to form relationships often resort to aggressive tactics unaware that a better approach exists.

The term *professional* should be stressed within the context of health care sales. Any aggressive action that could hinder the formation of a long-term relationship would not be considered a professional sales technique. A professional sales approach uses the power of time and planning to offer people the opportunity to realize how your services can be of benefit. Combining professional selling efforts with a marketing campaign creates a long-term, dynamic approach to cultivating effective relationships. It becomes essential to keep track of information using a territory worksheet or relevant software program; otherwise, time will erode memories and relationships.

You might come across other professional selling processes that make similar recommendations, such as **consultative selling, trust-based selling**, or **SPIN selling**. Mastering this chapter will prove highly beneficial in understanding the basic function and objective of different professional sales approaches. Practice using different selling techniques and find what works best for you. Discover what makes you, as well as the person you are engaging in conversation, comfortable.

Consultative Selling: The express use of questioning tactics to build rapport and configure how a customer's needs best match with an organization's services.

Trust-Based Selling: Showing clear effort to build a supportive relationship with a customer, overlooking any short-term advantage.

SPIN Selling: A selling process that incorporates four categories of questions: situation, problem, implication, and need-payoff (SPIN).

3.1   Introduction

The selling process starts long before actually meeting with people. Examine your marketplace to find community events, organizations, businesses, or groups that might serve as optimal sources of human interaction. Ensure that you have planned each day appropriately before leaving your residence. An **introduction** can take place randomly as a community builds in size. Proper attire should always be worn in public and behavior should be professional. Avoid looking disheveled even when running a quick errand. Remember to take business cards, carry around a positive attitude, and be ready to show excitement when running across a familiar face.

Use proper phone etiquette when making an introduction over the phone. Call at the right times and explain how you obtained the person's number. When going to an event, do as much research as possible. Gather names, job titles, or any available information on individuals who might be in attendance. Suppose a friend calls to invite you to a barbeque. Ask who will be there, write down the names, and tell your friend to please remember to introduce you to everyone there. Becoming familiar with names in advance helps when being presented with names during introductions at an event. Dress according to the occasion and behave in a fitting manner. Ask an acquaintance to accompany you who either

Introduction: The process related to coming into contact with a person whether for the first time or after some delay.

knows people already or is willing to help with meeting new people. When attending an event alone, make the effort to connect with an unfamiliar person and then ask that person to help with making further introductions. This way, you will not feel fatigued after meeting a sizable number of new people.

An introduction refers more specifically to what should occur after making contact with a person whether for the first time or after some delay. An introduction can occur over the phone or in person and should lead to conversation. When initiating contact, assess what would be an appropriate way to greet the person, considering cultural norms, personality types, and mental health conditions. Approach the person slowly and without overbearing gestures that might invade personal space. Greet the person warmly and extend a nice smile. A common introduction involves making eye contact, offering a firm handshake, and exchanging names—but this is not always the case.

GREETING PEOPLE APPROPRIATELY

Try to assess how to greet a person bearing in mind religious and cultural norms, different personality types, and health conditions that could influence how a person likes to be approached. Conduct research when possible to learn how to approach someone in the most appropriate way. Determine what topics the person might find controversial or negative before attempting to build rapport. In a clinical setting, a health care organization may want to ask about such information on an intake form:

Is there a particular way that you like to be greeted?

Mental health conditions may impact how a person interacts socially, whereas a person with physical limitations may not be able to shake hands easily and move about freely. Using another person to facilitate introductions can help when deciding the best way to approach new contacts. The other person may already know how a specific person likes to be greeted. Make an assessment and, when in doubt, approach others in the gentlest way possible.

How can you make your name more memorable?

Alert! Make sure information is password-protected in case a device is lost or stolen. People will not like hearing that sensitive information about them has been compromised.

If a person does not state your name, make mention of it proactively to prevent feelings of awkwardness and to ensure your name is easily remembered. Always ensure that the person you have just met can remember your name. Passing along a direct recommendation or making a referral on your behalf is more difficult if your name and information cannot be recalled. You must provide a clear memory of your name and that may mean modifying it or associating it with something memorable.

Professional selling techniques work because they make people feel important. Remembering information shows courtesy and respect toward others. Do you feel more upbeat when people remember your name, birthday, occupation, and so forth, especially after significant time has passed? Nothing will engender a greater connection than remembering information about people. Take along a personal digital assistant (PDA) or cell phone to ensure you can access information or record new information when presented with it. Make sure to transfer information to a territory worksheet or CRM program later. Successful marketing efforts require research and good notes.

Confidence Builder

What promotes the desire to seek new prospects time and again? Researching your marketplace will provide a better sense of where ideal prospects can be found. Discovering people who share *common interests* or possess a willing attitude toward health will undoubtedly provide more satisfaction than dealing with *onlookers* or people with dissimilar personalities. Other professionals or business owners can refine ideas or provide emotional support when interacting with people continuously. Before going out in public, have fun with the process of getting ready. Browse through marketing notes as if looking through an old photo album. Remember the positive aspects of prior encounters while getting up to speed with recorded information. Think about how good it will feel to come prepared. Within a group setting, ask a familiar person to help with making new introductions. This can reduce the exhaustion felt from constantly greeting new people.

Potential Barriers

Mental barriers, such as nervousness, might create discomfort when making introductions. These mental barriers could reduce the willingness over time to seek new forms of human interaction. Toastmasters International clubs offer an ideal environment to practice public speaking and work through anxiety. Experiment by making introductions with fellow students or professionals and discover ways to reduce mental barriers.

Feelings of discomfort might be felt when using selling techniques. Keep in mind that a successful practice will help a tremendous number of people and that should be the main focus of a health care provider. Professional sales techniques are meant to foster relationships in a comfortable and appropriate manner. Such techniques would not be considered *professional* if used in an aggressive way. Approach people with the intention of helping them feel better and enjoy life more. Hold a positive focus about what you are truly doing instead of dwelling on your use of sales techniques.

> Don't make it about you! Focus your attention on how this other person may need your help.

Finding new sources of introduction can consume time and energy. Set aside time to review your marketplace. Network with other professionals who need to grow a business as well. Ask network participants to contribute marketing ideas and put forth the effort to keep you informed of events. Subscribe to email lists or newsletters that will automatically update you on networking opportunities. Getting into the habit of updating a territory worksheet might prove tiresome at first, but it will lead to greater marketing efficiency later.

Feedback

The introduction can provide immediate feedback about a prospect. Does this relationship have the ability to progress? Does the other person appear engaged or distracted? Figure out what could have made a bad introduction better. Ask fellow students or professionals to assess your *personal touches* and appearance.

DIALOGUE

Provider: Hello. I read about this event online and I wanted to check it out. I see by your name tag that you are Jeff. I'm Doug Barnes. Do you have these events often?

Member: Yes, every month.

Provider: How long have you been a member?

Member: About four years. I used to be the treasurer.

Provider: Oh, that's great. I respect anyone who volunteers for such positions. Have you always been in this building? It's very nice.

Member: As long as I've been a member we've been in here.

Provider: This seems like an enjoyable group of people. Since I'm new, would you mind introducing me to others here? Again, my name is Doug.

Member: Sure, there are a lot of new faces, but I can introduce you to some of my friends.

Discussion The health care provider has shown up at a community event and started a conversation with someone who looks like an established member. After feeling comfortable with this person, the health care provider solicits help in making more introductions. The contact person's name, prior position as treasurer, and length of membership (four years) could be recorded. The health care provider could conduct further research on the building or surrounding area to have a broader understanding of the territory.

Summary

Researching the marketplace can unearth ideas about where to find the best sources of human contact. Take the initiative to make introductions at events and ask contacts to help make further introductions. Shake hands firmly, give good eye contact, and use names if the situation permits. Make sure to dress and behave appropriately while out in public. Take into account personal space and offer a warm smile. Carry a PDA or cell phone to record and recall information.

3.2   Rapport Building

After making an introduction, either for the first time or after some delay, the goal is to build rapport and solidify the relationship. Rapport building follows three stages:

1. Set a point of identification
2. Form a connection with the prospect
3. Highlight the organization

Point of Identification

Memories form best around one memorable reference point. The human brain usually sets that reference point around what it commonly reflects upon. Your physical appearance, handshake, occupation, and so forth tend to stand out in another person's mind. Consider using names as the key point of identification. The human brain reacts sharply to names, especially a person's own name. Take a moment to clearly exchange names at the beginning of a conversation. The brain's ability to store and recall information, such as a name, is enhanced through multiple associations with common everyday sights, sounds, shapes, tastes, smells, emotions, and objects.

DIALOGUE

Provider: Hello! My name is Deborah Shaw. My initials D and S also refer to what I do for a living. I provide Doctor Services. This is a way to remember my name.

Forming a Connection

> Common interests, interconnections, and personal touches increase the chance that a strong connection will form with a prospect.

Spending time on names ensures that they will be remembered and that new memories have somewhere to attach. Thereafter, it becomes important to begin a general conversation and allow the other person to gain familiarity with you. A prospect might start talking about health right away if you immediately note your occupation. Realize that talking about health is different from wanting to go see a health care provider. A person may be comfortable talking to you about a health issue, but setting an appointment with your organization might be a completely different matter. Attempt to build rapport before progressing to the subject of health.

Try to engage in light conversation about general interest topics as listed in Table 3.1. Read newspapers and community publications to gather current conversation topics.

TABLE 3.1	Conversation Topics
Weather	Community events
Food	Restaurants
Sports	Vacation ideas
Movies	Hobbies
Jokes	Music and concerts
Theater	Outdoor activities

Interacting with people on a regular basis and researching a marketplace can reveal mainstream topics currently being discussed. Take an opportunity to mention a restaurant or other local business in your referral system. Being slightly versed on a range of topics permits a conversation to move forward without fading. Topics to avoid include controversial or negative matters—items that can raise eyebrows or blood pressure.

Rapport building can occur over a short or long period of time depending on the situation. As a conversation evolves, rapport-building efforts can gradually intensify to touch upon more personal topics. You could ask about prior areas of residency, schools attended, family members, friends, interests, and so forth. For instance, you might ask about a prospect's occupation in order to get a sense of this person's average day. Since people often enjoy talking about themselves, rapport building can be one-sided. *A health care provider can simply ask questions and keep the conversation focused on what the other person has to say.* In fact, try not to dominate a conversation or come across as an expert on all topics. Ask specific questions related to what you know this other person will find relevant.

Getting to know a prospect allows a health care provider to figure out how the relationship can best develop. Should this person become a network participant, referral source, patient, or none of the above?

> The full selling process may take ten minutes or it may take ten months. Each situation is different.

> Asking questions is recommended by most professional selling processes.

Highlight the Organization

As a relationship evolves even further, determine if a prospect would want to hear about your health care organization. Hearing a description of your business may not be received with interest if a sufficient level of rapport does not exist. Consider the possibility of continuing a conversation at a later time to continue building rapport, especially if attending a reoccurring event. If rapport appears sufficient, mentioning your health care organization at this juncture enables you to define it in your own terms. A prospect will view your organization in relation to what is known about you instead of a *preconceived notion*. Maintaining control over your organization's brand enables you to frame the health care experience in a positive manner. By knowing a person well, you can determine the best way to communicate how your organization operates. Important elements to highlight may include services, years of experience, health care philosophy, staff members, or location. Are there any free services, such as a *no-obligation consultation*, that could motivate a prospect? Lead a conversation with strong features that *differentiate* your particular organization and make the health care experience appear beneficial.

There will be times when you will not need to review your health care organization. A prospect may be a *willing customer* or describing your organization does not fit within a conversation's flow. Even though a prospect might want to consummate a sale at this point, attempt to work through the remaining parts of the selling process to properly solidify a long-lasting and mutually beneficial relationship.

Confidence Builder

Practice rapport-building efforts with fellow students or professionals by finding topics to discuss and engaging one another in conversation. Ask close members of your community to help guide this process if self-reflection proves difficult. Keep a list of conversation topics in a wallet or purse related to current events, funny stories, or leisure pursuits. The list should include topics with which you have sufficient knowledge and familiarity. Before going to a known event, read up on topics related to the area, individuals who will be present, or the theme of the event.

Potential Barriers

Conversations can fade if topics do not hold enough interest or one party lacks knowledge on a subject. A balance exists between what will engage a person and what you can talk about at length. Reading general news, talking regularly with others, and experimenting with different interests can provide more conversation ideas. Memorizing a list of topics can ensure the flow of a conversation continues. Many conversation topics will surface on the "spur of the moment" as interests, hobbies, and unique situations are revealed. Knowing a little bit about a lot of different topics allows you to stay engaged in conversations. Researching your marketplace provides more opportunity to connect with community members. Meeting with others where you share at least one common interest or interconnection can help expedite rapport building. Have a close community member with good communication skills join you at events. Three or more people can stand around and converse more easily than two. In creating a connection, remember that it becomes more important to communicate effectively than at length.

You may feel devious about carrying on a conversation for the sole purpose of selling. This seems to defy what it means to care for others. Unfortunately, telling people to call if they *perhaps* feel the need for health care services will result in a low response rate. Most people will not automatically rise to the occasion and say, "Yes, I need your services so I will take charge and set an appointment right away." That sort of reaction simply does not happen in the real world because wading through health care appointments or acting as a referral source takes time, energy, and money. Bear in mind that your true motive is to encourage people to obtain health care services and it's not really to engage in selling. You have ultimate control over the content and execution of the selling process. Enjoy conversations, allow others to benefit from your positive attitude, and stay focused on how you are trying to help your community.

Feedback

During this phase of the selling process, you again have an opportunity to figure out where the relationship will potentially head. Would this person make a good network participant, referral source, patient, or none of the above? You may want to end a conversation if **disengagement** appears noticeable. Do not expend finite marketing resources on unproductive efforts. If a conversation has soured, state your name again and present a nice transition. **Resistance** to the selling process will most likely occur when rapport is insufficient, a prospect wants to digest matters further, or a prospect is simply not interested. Reassess why a conversation did not go well and consider if more planning would help. Ask members of your close community what they think about conversation topics. Practice rapport building with other students or professionals regularly.

Disengagement: A noticeable desire to discontinue with a certain line of conversation.

Resistance: Objections or barriers to fostering an effective long-term relationship.

DIALOGUE

Provider: We should have nice weather next week. What plans do you have?

Member: None that I know of.

Provider: You should consider going to Rock Pointe. The area is beautiful. They have all sorts of outdoor activities.

Member: I don't have much time right now. I just work and hang out with the family.

Provider: What family members do you have?

Member: I have two kids.

Provider: How old are they?

Member: My son's 14 and my daughter will turn 12 soon.

Provider: Is work always busy?

Member: Pretty much.

Provider: I run a health care office and there is so much involved. I can understand how work can dominate a person's life.

Discussion The member of this community organization seems a bit disengaged from the start of the conversation. The responses are short and lack substance. The health care provider tries to guide the conversation by asking questions and ties together how both individuals are busy in order to mention the health care organization. Discussing the health care organization at this point seems premature for this conversation. The health care provider may want to build more rapport or transition out of the selling process. A future encounter with this person may result in a better conversation.

Be careful when asking specific questions about a person's family to avoid a sensitive matter, such as death or divorce.

Summary

A conversation during the rapport-building phase should be general and light. A conversation can reach greater depth as rapport is built, allowing a health care provider to discover more about a prospect's daily life. Knowing what matters on a personal level allows a health care provider to assess how a relationship can best develop. Finally, a discussion about the health care organization will permit a conversation to transition over to health. Key features that differentiate your organization should be highlighted. A person might already be ready to act as a new patient, referral source, or network participant once rapport has been sufficiently built. Later stages of the selling process should still be accessed to ensure the relationship is properly formed.

3.3 Qualification

The *qualification* phase of the selling process works to define motives. If you have any concern over the integrity of selling techniques, then the qualification phase works to buffer against inappropriate actions. Here, a health care provider must consider another person's complete situation and pay adequate attention to the value proposition being offered. *The qualification verifies that a health care organization can benefit a prospect in a specific manner.* As such, a qualification ensures that a long-lasting and mutually beneficial relationship can be formed.

Should a person serve as a network participant, referral source, patient, or none of the above? Information gathered during the rapport-building phase of the selling process helps when figuring out a prospect's ability to fit into one of these roles. The scope of a conversation, the type of rapport, and what a person needs will determine how a relationship should best unfold. If rapport is insufficient and a qualification cannot be clearly made, pushing forward with the selling process could lead to negative word of mouth, resource inefficiencies, or uncomfortable feelings.

Imagine that a health care provider decides a prospect would serve well as a network participant who could support the organization by expanding awareness. Do not overlook how a prospect could benefit your organization over the long term. Maintaining a relationship might result in a network participant serving as a referral source later, becoming a patient, or providing resources.

If a network participant invites you to events or aids in the expansion of positive word of mouth, show appreciation and consider ways to return the favor. A network participant might benefit mutually by simply being made to feel important. The structure placed around the introduction and rapport-building phases is meant to ensure that you make others feel important. When it pertains to a prospective referral source, show appreciation directly and consider referring patients reciprocally. Keep the business cards of referral sources handy and learn how to communicate a referral *on each referral source's behalf.*

A prospective patient must have a **qualified health care need**. The selling process should not proceed forward otherwise. Although qualifying a health care need is required in a clinical setting, be mindful of probing health care needs to gain a sales advantage. A health care provider should refrain from discussing health matters in profound depth when out in public from both legal and professional standpoints. Bear in mind privacy issues and what types of conversations could be considered inappropriate. In-depth conversations should wait until a person appears in the clinic. In terms of the selling process, focus more on why a person should expend resources, set an appointment, and have a health care issue addressed. Of note, a health care provider should determine if a person's quality of life has been impacted by a health problem. Imagine learning that a prospect can no longer play sports because of a physical limitation. To what extent could this person's life change as a result of accessing services you offer?

The goal is to ascertain a prospective patient's health care needs and then match those needs with services that your organization offers. Formulating this match would be difficult, if not impossible, without effective rapport. Taking this phase seriously means that you are actively trying to avoid unnecessary care. Where a qualification is weak, a health care provider should refrain from encouraging services. Advocating for unqualified care requires more aggressive sales tactics, which do not fit within the context of *professional* sales.

On occasion, forming relationships with certain individuals can prove draining or counterproductive. Nothing is wrong with blocking the formation of a relationship. If it has been concluded that a mutually beneficial relationship exists, the selling process should continue to its final stage after making a qualification. The final *sales approach* is used to draw a picture about how best to continue a relationship, either as a patient, referral source, or network participant.

Confidence Builder

Addressing a qualified health care need falls under the scope of what a health care provider does every day in a clinical setting. A thoughtful qualification ensures that no one will receive unnecessary or improper care, or form an unwanted relationship. This process filters out any negative or selfish aspects normally seen in a sales environment. Building solid rapport with another person ensures that a qualification will be appropriate. Listen and learn about your community members. Take an interest in what matters to them. These actions are what a health care provider should always be doing.

Potential Barriers

How can a prospect benefit by forming a relationship with you? If rapport-building efforts do not sufficiently evolve, you will not find the correct answer. Maintaining a good line of conversation during the rapport-building phase of the selling process will support qualification efforts. It is essential to form a proper relationship before discussing health matters or trying to link into a person's network or referral system. When a conversation is rushed and poor attempts to qualify needs are made, disengagement and resistance during the final sales approach are likely.

Simply ask, "Is there anything I can do in return?"

Qualified Health Care Need: Identifying how a prospective patient will benefit by receiving specific health care services.

Ignoring the need to work through the full selling process may result in someone forming an unwanted relationship with you.

Feedback

When a proper qualification is made, a person will connect with it. Work with fellow students or professionals to practice making effective qualifications. Review to see if the proper amount and type of information have been gathered and brainstorm ideas on how best to form a mutually beneficial relationship in a given situation.

SELF-DIALOGUE

Provider: What does this prospect consider important? This prospect likes to fish, hunt, and camp with friends. This prospect works as an engineer for a large manufacturing company.

Provider: How can I make improvements to this person's quality of life? This prospect has health limitations that make everyday tasks somewhat hard at times. By coming in for care, this prospect could enjoy recreational activities more and perform better at work.

Discussion This internal dialogue should occur as a natural part of being a health care provider. Discovering how a relationship can be mutually beneficial will require information that can only be gathered by building effective rapport. In this self-dialogue, the health care provider is evaluating if a prospect's quality of life will improve by receiving health care services.

Summary

While working through the introduction and rapport-building phases, consider what would be the best relationship to form with another person. Should the person become a network participant, referral source, patient, or none of the above? A proper qualification ensures that a person is not asked to serve in one of these roles improperly. A qualification attempts to identify what type of benefit a prospect will experience by forming a relationship with you. As such, a qualification must be reached before continuing to the final stage of the selling process.

3.4 Sales Approach

The final phase of the selling process is used to communicate a qualification to a prospect. All prior phases of the selling process should be completed in sequence before attempting this phase. Decide to wait until a more appropriate time to discuss a qualification if a situation does not appear ideal. Remember that the most successful practices are built via thousands of long-term and mutually beneficial relationships. The goal is to build relationships over time instead of launching toward opportunity at full speed in an aggressive manner. Allow a relationship to evolve until it becomes certain that you share a connection with a prospect. The sales approach is then used to communicate the benefit of forming a relationship and how the relationship should progress.

SALES TRANSITION

A sales approach sometimes begins with a brief and generic transition either in question or statement form, such as, "Would you like to regain your health?" A prospect should be in agreement and wait for additional discussion.

A professional sales approach works by creating structure around forming relationships. The sales-approach phase of the selling process can be used to communicate qualified reasons why a prospect should want to become a network participant, referral source, or patient. The sales-approach phase follows four stages:

1. Explain the qualification
2. Motivate the prospect to take action
3. Address sales resistance
4. Propose continuing the relationship

The following discussion looks at each of these four stages in relation to prospective patients, but aspects of this discussion also relate to forming relationships with network participants and referral sources.

Explain the Qualification

Most people fail to consider all the personal benefits of being in great health. You can discover qualified reasons why a person should receive your services after forming a sufficient level of rapport. Explaining how mental or physical changes will take place in the body is one matter. How will those items affect all other aspects of a person's life? Explain how a person will enjoy activities more, become more productive at work, or regain abandoned interests. What is a person truly passing up by not addressing a health care problem? Place context around how a person's life will improve after receiving care from your organization.

Motivate the Prospect

You should understand a prospect well enough to know how much motivation is needed to arrive at a point where setting a health care appointment will become a possibility. Use an effective sales approach to lower the energy required to initiate a new daily routine. Imagine speaking with a prospective patient who has a chronic health problem. Simply saying, "I can help with this problem so come see me" is usually not sufficient to motivate a person to modify a daily routine and expend resources. The prospect needs a clear reason why initiating change would be well worth the effort. Explain how effortless setting an appointment will be and consider offering some form of price or service incentive if necessary.

Address Resistance

A prospect might see the complete picture of how your health care services could prove beneficial, but what are the possible sources of resistance? You should not look negatively on sales resistance, but rather anticipate, welcome, and address it proactively. Table 3.2 lists the main forms of sales resistance. Time, energy, and money are the ones most commonly experienced. A person's preconceived notions about an organization or profession might create a hindrance if occupations are discussed during the initial part of the rapport-building phase.

TABLE 3.2	Forms of Sales Resistance
1. Time	
2. Energy	
3. Money	
4. Preconceived notions of the organization	
5. Preconceived notions of the profession	
6. Already uses a health care provider	
7. Bad prior experience (in general)	
8. Unspoken resistance	

Resistance may occur because a person already has a health care provider or had a bad experience in the past. Be prepared to discuss points of resistance that have been directly or indirectly mentioned during the rapport-building phase and show empathy for the point of resistance. In many cases, *unspoken* resistance exists and it blocks a relationship from evolving. Address issues proactively and be mindful of any resistance that might be kept hidden.

Continuance

A health care provider will want to end the selling process by reaching a point of **continuance**. As long as a prospect has not disengaged from the selling process by this point, a health care provider needs to figure out how best to proceed with a relationship. Since you are interested in forming long-lasting and mutually beneficial relationships, look for the best possible method of continuance instead of worrying about locking a prospect into a purchase decision. In a traditional sales environment, this action is called *closing* when a prospect is pressured into making a purchase. Professional sales techniques lead to the formation of long-lasting and mutually beneficial relationships that never *close*. A mindset that focuses on developing long-term relationships will produce the greatest success over time.

> **Continuance:** Moving forward with a long-term relationship through mutually agreeable actions.

Would it be appropriate at this point to suggest setting an appointment? Each situation differs and approaching a prospect about becoming a patient may be warranted. A health care provider may end the selling process by simply asking a prospect to think about a qualification more. The point of continuance might involve sending a prospect an email, brochure, or packet of information. For a referral source, a health care provider could ask for a commitment to meet again in three months to evaluate the relationship's effectiveness. A health care provider might also ask a network participant to pass along business cards or attend events.

In order to maintain professionalism, the form of continuance should be appropriately tailored to each specific prospect. An action plan for continuance may require a prospect to put forth effort next or the health care provider might need to complete tasks first. Ask the prospect to consider what the best form of continuance would be. If a person resists part or all of a plan for continuance, reframe the original one, offer a secondary option, or transition out of the selling process altogether. Note what went wrong and review the situation with fellow students or professionals.

Narratives

Take note of how proper forms of communication can be complex. Although communicating a qualification can take place organically, memorizing brief **narratives** will support the sales approach by allowing you to (1) sound professional, (2) convey essential points, and (3) prevent disengagement. Narratives protect against making incorrect or inappropriate statements and they ensure that key matters are expressed as desired. A narrative is a preplanned dialogue structured to effectively communicate important matters, generally in terms of the health care experience. A narrative is usually one paragraph (three to five sentences), covers a specific subject, and is committed to memory. Although a person's qualification or a given situation may be unique, establishing narratives in advance provides a general framework to guide each ensuing conversation.

> **Narratives:** Memorized dialogues structured to effectively communicate important matters.

> Sales professionals may memorize up to ten pages of narratives in total.

Over the course of time, practicing with narratives will ensure effective conveyance without the need to repeat dialogue verbatim and sound robotic. Because each sales situation differs, a health care provider should commit to memory as many narratives as possible and have sufficient fluency to modify them on the fly. Table 3.3 lists common objectives to consider when establishing narratives. Keep a log of narratives that work well and develop them over time as new ideas surface.

> The sales luncheon assignment found online at remedy-books.com under the Teachers tab represents the main business project for this book.

Communicate at least one narrative during a sales approach but insert more into the conversation if the need arises. Making a sales call or leading a sales luncheon may involve an extensive use of longer narratives—as many as five pages of dialogue. A longer narrative should include sales *applications* meant to instruct prospects on how to communicate a referral and offer a *direct recommendation* on an organization's behalf.

TABLE 3.3	Use of Narratives
1. Describe yourself
2. Describe your profession
3. Highlight your organization
4. Address sales resistance
5. Provide a quality guarantee
6. Describe services or products
7. Educate a prospect on health matters
8. Change the subject if a prospect appears disengaged

Sample Narratives

The following narratives illustrate dialogue that could be formed in advance to address hypothetical situations a health care provider might encounter.

Purpose To encourage preventative care at a sales luncheon.

Preventative care is just as important as treating a current health problem, if not more so. I want to make sure that patients live well and avoid uncomfortable, painful, and even life-threatening problems. It's hard to predict the future but a large percentage of the population contracts at least one chronic disease. Once a health problem sets in, such as type 2 diabetes, reversing it becomes difficult, if not impossible. I have procedures in place to ensure that I cover a range of topics, such as nutrition, exercise, and workplace ergonomics, with every patient as a way of preventing disease. I offer a range of supplements and vitamins at wholesale cost as well.

Purpose To encourage a prospective patient to use multiple health care providers.

You should definitely consider the benefit of working with multiple health care providers as part of your care plan. I normally advise patients to seek the advice of at least one other health care provider who can offer a second opinion and protect you from an incorrect or deficient diagnosis. Health care providers trained in a different field can also supplement a treatment plan with insights from their particular scope of practice.

Purpose To address the high costs of health care with a prospective patient.

Without insurance or other coverage, receiving care from a health care provider can be expensive. I have cash discounts and several payment options. In the end, you have to decide the value of the care you receive. Will treatment give you the ability to [insert qualification]? Will it allow you to move forward and do things you've never been able to do? I feel that, based on your circumstances, spending the time and money will be worth it.

Purpose To address disengagement or an emphatic *no.*

Sorry if I get excited about encouraging people to come see me. I personally have benefited from receiving health care services. I only hope others can have that same experience. If you ever have questions, I am always available to answer them.

DIALOGUE

Aggressive: You should consider setting an appointment with my office. I have openings next week. Let's get you in and get started. Let me grab your number and we can go from there.

Professional: I would greatly enjoy being your health care provider. True, it will take time out of your day, but in talking to you, it seems worth your effort. I'm not sure if you'd like to set an appointment now. What do you think would be the best way to proceed?

Aggressive: You know, there's some material I can send that might answer a lot of your questions. How about I send you some? Should everything go to your home or work address?

Professional: There is ample opportunity to stay connected with me. If you are interested in getting more information, I can pass along my website or printed materials. I also have free classes you are welcome to attend and I maintain a blog. I hope that you think about your needs and access my services when you feel ready.

What makes the preceding dialogues *aggressive*? In the first sentence of each aggressive sales approach, the speaker sounds unconcerned about what the other person really needs. That assumes the speaker does not have sufficient rapport to properly qualify needs and cannot properly initiate a *professional* sales approach. Thereafter, the speaker uses aggressive sales tactics to lock the prospect into setting an appointment or receiving care. *Patients should decide to make you their health care provider because they enjoy the relationship and they understand how you can improve their health.* Using aggressive tactics that make a person feel uncomfortable might work in the short term but such tactics can lead to rapid patient turnover, negative word of mouth, or decreased referrals.

What makes the preceding dialogues *professional*? The speaker starts each professional sales approach with a strong sentence that reaffirms the relationship and shows that the other person matters. In the first example, the speaker decides to address potential sales resistance. The idea of making an appointment is suggested but not forced. How best to continue the relationship is left to the listener to decide. Instead of locking the prospect into unwanted services, the speaker simply asks for appropriate ideas. With the second example, the speaker provides a host of ideas on how to stay connected. The health care provider recognizes that change occurs slowly and frames a message that implies waiting to take action is understandable.

Confidence Builder

A health care provider must feel certain that the selling process takes into account a prospect's best interests. A valid qualification ensures that a prospect will react positively to the sales approach. Rapport helps determine what type of relationship to form and how it could best continue. It becomes important to design and memorize effective narratives in order to sound professional. When rejection or disengagement occurs, understand that a person may not have a qualifying need. Also, some people are tenacious *onlookers* and feverishly resist changing habits or thought processes. Nothing is wrong with letting go of static relationships and focusing energy on other market participants.

A health care provider cannot feel hesitant when entering or executing this phase of the selling process out of fear of making someone else uncomfortable or getting rejected personally. As long as a prospect has a qualified need, your services will be of benefit. The selling process works to ensure that community members are properly matched with health care services they need. *Failing to direct market participants to services they need means that people in your community will continue experiencing poor health needlessly.*

Potential Barriers

The sales approach can become awkward or uncomfortable if a prospect disengages from a conversation or rejects a plan for continuance. The selling process should follow one course: to form a long-lasting and mutually beneficial relationship. If a prospect does not understand the importance of the relationship or becomes uninterested, a health care provider should transition away from the conversation in a professional manner. Experience will help filter out unqualified prospects and enable you to communicate more effectively in instances where a qualification exists. Luckily, a health care student or current practitioner has ample opportunity to practice marketing techniques with fellow students or professionals as long as an effort is made to meet together.

Lack of confidence forms the greatest barrier to this phase of the selling process. Many health care providers might have preconceived notions or internal conflicts when making the sales approach. Health care providers have limited familiarity with health care sales and base their understanding on the behavior of other aggressive approaches more commonly employed. Disinterest toward the performance of this phase of the selling process would not be unusual. Rehearsing the sales approach with fellow students or professionals can provide clarification on whether a particular approach has come across as professional or has created feelings of discomfort. Planning will ensure that the line of communication occurs as intended and does not cross over into aggressive territory.

Feedback

Did a prospect really have a genuine health care need that you could service? A negative or neutral response to the selling process means that a qualification, narrative, or plan of continuance might have been deficient. A prospect might be a tenacious onlooker, unwilling to form a relationship with you no matter what you say. Review what occurred during the selling process and brainstorm about what could have worked better. Narratives should be well structured beforehand and practiced repeatedly in order to avoid sounding robotic. An action plan for continuance might result in a negative or neutral response at first. Progressing forward to a positive response might take additional forms of communication. A health care provider will receive feedback based on the ultimate decision of a prospect. A *no* means that the selling process did not work or a qualification did not truly exist. A *yes* means that it has worked but could still be improved.

DIALOGUE

Provider: Would you like to eliminate the pain you feel and get back to your old routine without any limitations?

Prospect: Yeah, but I've got so many other things going on.

Provider: I know how busy people's lives can become. I'm sensitive to that, which is why I never schedule more than ten people on Thursdays. That ensures I never fall behind on that day. If your appointment is at 10:30, you will be in the treatment room with me at 10:30. I can also come in on the weekend by appointment, or I would be happy to recommend someone closer to you.

Provider: I became a health care professional to improve the lives of others. There are many ways that I can help you. If you would like to eliminate the pain you feel, then we should discuss your different health care options.

Provider: I maintain a lot of information on exercises that you can do at home. If money is a concern, let's explore other other options.

Provider: I would like to give you my business card. You can contact me any hour of the day. Unless you are ready to set an appointment now, give what I have said some thought.

Discussion Throughout this entire sales approach, the prospect says very little. The prospect agrees with the initial question but tries to avert an affirmation. Resistance is expressed because of time constraints, but there might still be other unidentified and unspoken forms of resistance. The health care provider uses several narrative to (1) address sales resistance, (2) expand the conversation, and (3) showcase how the prospect has options. The narratives allow the prospect to view matters in a different light. The health care provider is even willing to sacrifice a sale altogether by recommending the prospect see someone closer. Finally, the health care provider brings up the idea of setting an appointment but suggests taking a moment to digest the current conversation.

Summary

The sales approach invokes the use of narratives to precisely communicate a qualification that has already been established. A health care provider should commit a wide range of narratives to memory to use in cases of sales resistance or other various situations. A narrative ensures that a discussion sounds professional, essential points are conveyed, and the prospect remains engaged. The selling process should end with an action plan that outlines how best to continue the relationship.

3.5   Maintaining Relationships

Professional sales are about creating long-lasting and mutually beneficial relationships. Never start this process with short-term goals in mind such as locking a prospect into an appointment. Attempting to lock a prospect into an appointment after a brief conversation may easily be met with resistance. The accumulation and strengthening of effective relationships over time will net a greater benefit than securing an instant sale. Be patient with the selling process and allow relationships to grow and evolve. A health care provider might recommend meeting again, exploring a website, or speaking with others to keep a relationship progressing. An action plan for continuance might not result in anything of value instantly. You might find that a prospect is more open to forming a long-term relationship during a future encounter.

It is not uncommon for six months to lapse before a person finally decides to take action. Take note of how the human brain has complex connectivity that will not rewire itself overnight. Each person will take a varied amount of time before the motivation to alter a daily routine or initiate a new activity surfaces. Look around where you live. Have you ever let a chore slide for a month or more? You will get around to performing the chore at some point because some form of reminder exists. Instead of expecting a prospect to take immediate action, take a professional approach that involves developing a relationship in practical stages bearing in mind the *frequency* and *intensity* of contact.

Set reminders about when to reconnect with a prospect. Avoid using selling dialogue during every conversation. Understand when to back away and give a person space to digest the relationship. Use other forms of communication or marketing tools, such as emails or newsletters, to remain in contact in a subtle manner. Holiday cards provide a great way to remain in contact and affirm that you view a person as important. Staff members can assist with calling, emailing, or writing as well. A person could be part of a marketing campaign meant to maintain relationships or individualized contact might be more appropriate. Each situation differs and having sufficient rapport helps you realize what type of marketing effort would work best. Do not forget qualifications made in the past or important details provided during prior conversations. Keep good notes in a territory worksheet or CRM program. Review your notes before reconnecting with someone and remain prepared for any chance encounter with a patient, network participant, or referral source while in public. Be available to field phone calls or emails late at night, on the weekend, or during a vacation.

When initiating contact again, take the time to rebuild rapport and reassess the relationship before attempting any new sales approach. A prospect might have new reasons to resist setting an appointment or taking other forms of action. Even if a prospect agrees to set an appointment, a fair amount of time might lapse before the appointment finally takes place.

Patience will generate patients.

Think of every phone call as a $1,000 opportunity that should not be missed or sent to voice mail.

Events could transpire in the interim that might make a prospect want to cancel the appointment. A prospect should receive a reminder phone call or email a few days before an initial visit to prevent a missed appointment. Ask existing patients directly if they believe your services are well matched with their needs in order to prevent any unnecessary care or disinterest.

DIALOGUE

Provider: It was nice talking with you the other night. I am calling to follow up with our conversation as you suggested. I mentioned having you come in for a free consultation. I was wondering if you still had any concerns or if you want to set an appointment.

Prospect: I might think about this more and then contact you when I decide.

Provider: Let me know if meeting outside of regular office hours would be better. I can easily adjust my schedule. You have my business card as well. Please pass my contact information along to anyone you think could benefit from receiving health care services from me. Thank you again for the great conversation.

Prospect: I will keep everything in mind. Good night.

Discussion The health care provider followed up with an agreed-upon action plan for continuance, but the prospect sounded disengaged and perhaps had already thought about how to avoid committing to an appointment. Instead of pursuing the issue further, the health care provider felt the existence of unspoken resistance and wanted to give the prospect breathing room. A general narrative was used to encourage word of mouth and transition the conversation. The health care provider may want to review the plan for continuance and consider whether it was too aggressive for this situation.

Summary

The selling process encompasses four phases: introduction, rapport building, qualification, and sales approach. Following the proper order helps a relationship build successfully. Interaction meant to maintain a relationship should adhere to this same format. Meeting with someone on a future occasion, sending collateral pieces, or adding a person to a broader marketing campaign exemplify ways to stay connected. A health care provider should bear in mind the frequency and intensity of efforts related to maintaining a relationship. Good notes serve as a reminder of what took place previously.

3.6 Microsales

Elevator Pitch: A brief sales narrative that could be expressed within the time it would theoretically take to ride an elevator.

Microsale: A condensed sales approach that lacks either a sufficient introduction, buildup of rapport, or qualification.

Often called an **elevator pitch**, a **microsale** excludes one or more parts of the selling process. Review the following conversation taking place with the wait staff at a restaurant.

DIALOGUE

Provider: Hi. I included a business card with the bill. I run a health care practice nearby. Please look over my website when you have a moment. If you or anyone you know needs my services, including anyone who works here, do not hesitate to call.

Executing the full selling process in this situation may not be possible since the wait staff is busy. A health care provider may be able to run through the full selling process over the course of time or by organizing a meeting at the restaurant. Forming long-term relationships will occur more easily when using the full selling process. Heavy reliance on microsales can be counterproductive because they do not generally motivate a person to initiate a new activity and it might deter prospects from interacting with the organization in the future. Will trying to rope in a few patients in the current moment hurt any chance of forming long-term relationships with community members over time? A microsale does not allow a health care provider time to qualify needs, creating the potential for the sales approach to come across as aggressive.

A microsale can be conducted in an effort to build general awareness and support future selling efforts. There are many situations where a microsale may be the best option. Create narratives based on the more common situations in order to have a portfolio of dialogue. Offer a business card during an encounter and encourage the person to mention your clinic to others. As always, keep track of notes in a territory worksheet or CRM program.

Summary

A microsale can work but usually with diminished efficacy as compared to the full selling process. A microsale is often used to build general awareness within a marketplace. Make use of narratives and maintain good notes even when conducting a microsale.

3.7   Professional Perseverance

A health care provider needs to walk a fine line between faint confidence and aggressive maneuvering when approaching people. A health care provider must pay strict attention to the level of **professional perseverance** when conversing with a prospect or encouraging existing patients to continue care. In traditional sales, if a prospect says *no* to something, the next course of action involves rephrasing the question, asking for something else, or revisiting earlier phases of the selling process. This idea of *don't take no for an answer* should never apply to professional health care sales. Health care providers should act professionally when making an introduction, building rapport, qualifying services, and communicating how those services could fulfill a health care need. The goal involves forming a long-term relationship and not locking a prospect into a purchase decision.

> **Professional Perseverance:** The frequency and intensity of contact with a person viewed in terms of professional appropriateness.

On the other hand, maintaining confidence during the selling process is crucial. A health care provider who is new to sales or resists the selling process tends to invoke *easy outs* to avoid discomfort or failure. This approach usually results in the expression of generic dialogue that has limited sales value. The following two statements illustrate differences in confidence.

DIALOGUE

Statement 1: If you'd like, you can call to set up an appointment. I am open from 9 A.M. until 6 P.M. every day.

Statement 2: Give proper thought to setting an appointment. If you are feeling hesitant, let me know the reasons why. I am always available to take your phone call.

In the first statement, the health care provider places the decision squarely in the other person's hands. Maybe this statement is appropriate given the circumstances but, more commonly, this type of approach originates from feelings of aversion. Prospects will usually ignore this type of statement because it offers no clear directive. The energy required to initiate a new activity can easily outweigh a prospect's willingness to seek care. The second statement involves a more confident approach in which the health care provider ends up more exposed to rejection. The statement contains bold instructions meant to help motivate and guide the listener.

For someone who has never accessed your services before and does not understand what to expect at your clinic, other factors will play a role in that assessment. If you don't work through the selling process in a confident manner, prospects can easily dismiss your value as a health care provider. Would you want to set an appointment with a health care provider who sounds timid or incoherent? Your presentation in terms of communication skills and appearance must match or exceed your service potential. Do not expect prospects to feel confident in your professional abilities if your recommendation for care is conveyed in a disorganized manner.

Professionalism encompasses good judgment, and every situation will have unique variables that work to define appropriateness. Would you be comfortable with someone communicating in a similar manner? The greatest feelings of discomfort for a prospect or existing patient might occur during the continuance stage of the sales approach. As a general rule, do not try to execute more than two attempts at affirming a plan of continuance. Make sure you have enough rapport to know what type of action plan would work best. Pay strict attention to how a plan is phrased and maintain a list of ideas so that various options can be suggested. Once a person appears disengaged or emphatically says *no*, transition out of the selling process in a professional manner. Never take rejection personally or revert to more aggressive tactics. Acting unprofessionally can lead to negative word of mouth, injure your reputation, result in disciplinary action, or hurt the profession as a whole. Developing long-standing and mutually beneficial relationships will engender positive word of mouth, support practice growth, reduce time spent marketing, and boost your profession's image. It becomes important to adopt a holistic philosophy in all aspects of the selling process.

Be a long-term, holistic salesperson.

Summary

Professional perseverance straddles a fine line between not enough confidence and overaggressive sales tactics. Perceptions about your abilities could diminish when prospects are approached in a weak or disorganized manner. Pushing forward with the selling process when prospects appear uncomfortable or disengaged could similarly hurt perceptions of quality. As a professional, you must judge the appropriateness of each situation and act accordingly. Adequate preparation can ensure that executing the selling process occurs in an effective manner.

CHAPTER ASSIGNMENT

Working in a group of three to four students or fellow professionals, complete the following items.

1. As a group, greet each member in a professional manner and provide a way for everyone to remember your name.

2. Write eight narratives related to each category of sales resistance: time, energy, money, preconceived notions of the organization, preconceived notions of the profession, already uses a health care provider, bad prior experience, and unspoken resistance.

3. Read the case studies in Appendix I and consider ways to improve the introduction, rapport-building effort, qualification, and sales approach for each.

4. As a group, seek out an area business willing to host a sales luncheon. Explain that the project relates to a school assignment and that you will bring food (either purchased or made). Ask if they have any food preferences. Later, call the day before to confirm that the meeting will still take place. At the luncheon event, make proper introductions and ensure that names are remembered. Build general rapport and then transition into a health presentation relevant to the designated audience members. At the conclusion of the meeting, refer to each person by name, pass out business cards, and deliver an action plan for continuance. For example, ask audience members how they might see the relationship unfolding going forward. After returning from the luncheon, discuss qualifications that came to mind and record notes on the entire day. Brainstorm ways that the selling process, including the presentation, could be improved. Finally, maintain the relationship by sending a written thank-you letter.

Note: This chapter assignment represents the main business project of this book. Group members should work on the project while continuing to study the remaining material in the book. More information about this project can be found online at remedybooks.com under the *Teachers* tab.

Appendix I Case Studies on Professional Sales

Case Study A

This case study reviews an extended narrative that a health care provider put together to better form referral arrangements with attorneys. Presentation of this narrative would work best during a sales luncheon at a law firm.

Introduction Thank you for spending your lunch hour with me. My name is Dr. Jack Wisehart. Let me write that down so people have the correct spelling. I will also pass out business cards at the end. I operate a clinic near the downtown movie theatre on NW Main and Cleveland Street. Is everyone familiar with the location?

Rapport Building

1. Keep updated on current events and community news as a way of building general rapport.
2. Review current legislation and matters important to the profession.
3. Conduct Internet research on organization members expected to attend the luncheon.

Main Narrative I'm enjoying this opportunity to get to know all of you better. I arranged this luncheon to introduce myself and also to learn what you do. It is common for patients to need legal services and I want to make sure I send patients to the right attorneys. Let's work around the table and each of you can mention your individual areas of expertise. We'll start with you.

I would like to tell you more about my practice now. I specialize in auto accidents almost exclusively. My office is equipped with the latest technology enabling a detailed examination to take place. I purchased this equipment to diagnose patients more accurately and to uncover any hard-to-see problems. All new patients undergo a thorough examination process guided by strict internal controls as a way to guarantee that health problems are never overlooked.

This process makes your job easier. I have the capacity to thoroughly assess the extent of physical damage caused by an auto accident. If a case ever goes to court, I have a concise way of explaining how my equipment works and what the results show. I feel comfortable that I can clearly articulate related health problems in court or during a deposition. I will also not charge for my time since I am grateful for having you refer the patient in the first place.

I appreciate any referral that you make and I will ensure your clients are treated properly. You will find that my office is well managed and that patients report a high degree of satisfaction with their experience. I have taken every possible step to ensure that your clients will receive great service and will not come back and complain to you. I would like to provide a small brochure that highlights some of the key features that differentiate my practice from others. Inside you will also find my business card. I would like to stop now and see if any of you have questions. Please let me know if I did not address any issues that you view as important.

Continuance Now that I have gotten to know all of you and the services you provide, I would like to refer a couple of patients when the next opportunity arises. If my patients have a good experience using this firm, then I would like to steadily refer patients here. I encourage all of you to work with me in a similar manner. Feel free to refer one or two clients and then gather feedback. If the clients appear satisfied—which I will work hard to assure—then I would appreciate your continued support.

Case Study B

In the following case study, a health care provider has drafted a letter to send to former and existing patients to determine if they would serve as referral sources.

[Insert logo]

March 31, 2013

Dear [Insert name],

After three successful years of providing acupuncture services, I continue to grow and expand my practice thanks to the support of great patients like you. Your word of mouth has allowed so many individuals to receive the health care services they need.

I decided to become a health care provider to help our community members tackle the tough health issues they must endure. I have made significant new investments in my practice resulting in a broader range of services being offered. Some of the key features include the following:

1. Free 10 minutes of massage therapy before each session.
2. Renovation of my waiting room, including new recliner chairs.
3. Health courses viewable online and on CD-Rom.

My intent has always been to improve the health of my patients and give them the best health care experience possible. I would like to continue developing a greater range of services that all community members can enjoy. Your assistance is a critical piece of this mission.

Please take a moment to consider how friends, family members, coworkers, or other individuals you know could benefit from health care services involving acupuncture and massage therapy. Let the members of your community know about my services and how they can contact me. Together, we can make a difference in the lives of so many.

Kind Regards,
Dr. Jack Wisehart

[Insert address]

[Insert contact info]

Case Study C

This next case study looks at *aggressive* tactics that *should be avoided* when trying to conduct a *professional* sale. This conversation takes place between a health care provider and a new patient.

Sales Approach

Provider: Do you want to see improvements to your health that will allow you to regain an active lifestyle?

Patient: That is exactly what I would like to accomplish.

Provider: By not taking care of your body on a regular basis, you could end up with an irreversible health condition. I not only want to treat your current health care problem, but I would also like to set you up with a treatment plan with the goal of preventing the onset of new diseases.

Provider: I have a brochure here with examples of preventable diseases that people have contracted simply because they have ignored the need for ongoing maintenance care. I would hate to see you end up in the same position. You should take care of your body as you would a house or car. Maintenance care for your body is essential.

Provider: I would like to see you for 12 more visits over the remainder of the year. With this treatment plan, you will receive a 10% discount. Your health care needs will be met with this treatment plan, plus you will benefit from the discount. Let's go ahead and set these appointments up at the front desk.

Patient: Well, how much will this cost me exactly?

Provider: If you are concerned about the cost, we can set up a payment plan where you pay a portion each month. For what will amount to a low monthly price, you will be doing something of tremendous value for your health.

Patient: Well, I understand that I should take care of my body. I'm a little hesitant setting 12 appointments right now. I would like to review my finances and explore less expensive options if at all possible.

Provider: It's your body and I can't force you into anything. I would hate to see your health deteriorate. How about we go ahead and set the appointments? You can always call and cancel them if you change your mind.

Patient: Thank you, but I feel that I should wait before setting the appointments and spending any money.

Provider: I will follow up with a phone call in two to three days to see how you responded to today's treatment. We can discuss the treatment plan again at that time.

Case Study D

In contrast to the last case study, the following dialogue highlights how to conduct the selling process in a professional manner. This conversation takes place between a health care provider and a former patient who accidentally run into each other.

Rapport Building

Provider: Hello Judy! How have you been? It's Dr. Jack Wisehart. It's been about two years since I've seen you last.

Judy: Yes, things are great. I started a new job about six months ago and I'm pretty happy with this new company.

Provider: You were working at an engineering firm if I remember correctly. Are you doing something different now?

Judy: Still at an engineering firm. It's actually one of the competitors. They stole me away.

Provider: And you seem to be in high spirits at the moment. Is your health holding up as desired?

Judy: Oh yes! My back gets a little sore sitting all day, but I still do some of the same exercises you prescribed.

Qualification

This former patient appears to be in good health. There is only a slight health care need, which may not be great enough to provoke a renewal of care. I might introduce a narrative featuring key updates at the clinic and also one about referring community members.

Sales Approach

Provider: Let me know if you would like any new exercises. I would hate for you to grow disinterested with the old ones.

Provider: I have new classes at night and several new pieces of equipment as well. Let me give you a business card with my web address. When you have a spare moment, look at the services page and you'll see a few upgrades. Give some thought to revisiting the clinic. I would love to see you again as a patient.

Provider: Also, please keep me in mind in case anyone you know is looking for a health care provider. Maybe someone at your new office has a health care need.

Judy: I can do that. Well, I need to get going. I have a few errands to run. Thanks for the card. I'll check out your website.

Provider: It was really nice running into you. Good luck at the new job and I hope to see you again.

Case Study E

This final case study has two parts. A sales dialogue is used at first to speak with management about the benefits of arranging a health care presentation for employees. The second part outlines the actual presentation that will be given.

Initial Discussion

Provider: Thank you again for meeting with me. I know your time is limited so I will make this brief. Every time an employee gets injured or sick, your company experiences a loss in productivity. In order to counteract such potential losses, I would like to present your employees with free information on workplace safety as well as disease prevention. The presentation will last about 20 minutes and will include a segment on ergonomics and another on nutrition. If your employees would like to come in as patients, that will be their decision. I prefer to use this opportunity to provide your company with an invaluable service in hopes of building a positive reputation within the community. I can send you a copy of my presentation as well as a list of optimal dates. Do you have any questions of me at this time?

Manager: It was nice meeting you. I'm glad we had a chance to get together in person. You appear professional and I feel comfortable having you present information to my employees. Please go ahead and email me your presentation and we can set a date thereafter.

Presentation Outline

Introduction: Remember to highlight my name and take note of employee names.

Rapport Building: Research the company's website beforehand and browse the Internet for current news articles that involve the company. Read through general current events and community news right before the presentation in order to support rapport building efforts.

Presentation: Ergonomics Segment

1. Ask how employees feel after a day at work.
2. Show examples of healthy body positions at various workstations.
3. Discuss the need to engage in light exercise during breaks and at lunch.
4. Briefly recommend exercises and stretches to do at work or at home.

Presentation: Nutrition Segment

5. Ask how employees feel after eating meals.
6. Review the importance of eating the right foods to increase energy.
7. List out meal options considered nutritious and enjoyable.
8. Mention ways that employees can initiate nutrition-related programs at work.

Question and Answer: Allow the employees to ask questions or insert comments.

Continuance: Pass out business cards and mention upcoming events. Thank everyone for attending and encourage them to speak with management about conducting another presentation in six months.

Patient Experience

AUTHOR'S NOTE

This chapter is the backbone of this book and underscores the importance of adopting a holistic philosophy. Every part of what a patient experiences, whether inside or outside of the clinic, weighs upon the patient's decision to continue care, spread word of mouth, or refer others. Everything spills into the patient experience, making it essential to pay attention to all aspects of your organization. Why learn accounting? You must ensure that patient accounts are correct and the business provides you with a sufficient level of net profit. Why learn professional sales techniques? You must possess an ability to form long-lasting and mutually beneficial relationships. Creating an amazing patient experience requires a health care provider to learn about all areas of business and put business concepts to use properly.

The best marketing is FREE: Foster Relationships Energetically Everywhere.

The whole experience with your organization, starting with exposure to marketing efforts, will weigh on a person's decision to initiate services, continue receiving care, or end the relationship. Previous chapters demonstrate how to manage your territory and build long-lasting and mutually beneficial relationships. This chapter continues the discussion by looking at what happens after marketing efforts take hold and a prospect decides to become a patient. A prospect must first enjoy the experience of making an appointment. The area around the building and the waiting room interior form the first impression of a clinic. Meeting with a health care provider occurs next and represents the most important aspect of patient retention. The main reason for expending time, energy, and money is for a patient to obtain health care services. A patient will normally deal with billing, scheduling, and other administrative matters at the end of an appointment. Finally, a patient will leave the clinic and commute elsewhere.

A negative experience at any point along this journey tends to leave a firm mental imprint and is often expressed to others. Even subtle negative elements of the patient experience can leave an impression over time and become communicated to others through word of mouth. An overall positive experience may be overshadowed by any element of the experience that proves negative. Any comment containing negative feelings toward a health care organization can rifle through the marketplace and greatly disturb your *brand*. Imagine that a patient is asked for a referral from a coworker and consequently says, "I like my health care provider—but it's hard to find parking in the area." Understand how this one issue clouds the entire conversation and puts the listener on alert. This one negative aspect has the power to reduce patient retention, referrals, and network participation.

Theory of Mind: A personal observation that considers how another person could be observing situations.

In order to ensure that a patient's experience remains completely positive, a health care organization needs to examine every detail of what a patient encounters. In psychology, **theory of mind** refers to making an assumed observation about what another person could be experiencing. It becomes important to consider life through the perspective of others. Thoughtful analysis of the patient experience in advance can prevent negative experiences from occurring. Of equal importance, proactive communication with patients can reveal any feelings of displeasure that would otherwise go unspoken. Be respectful of patient sacrifices and take to heart patient complaints. Understand the cause of any problems and make sufficient effort to derive an appropriate solution.

What is the true value of ensuring that patients have a positive experience? By perfecting the patient experience, a health care provider can benefit indirectly from positive word of mouth, strong referrals, and decreased patient turnover. An organization that does not provide a strong experience will need to devote more resources toward marketing new business.

4.1   First Impressions

A patient's experience with an organization first begins when encountering some form of marketing effort. An individual will become familiar with an organization and eventually make a decision to initiate services. From this point forward, a health care organization must maintain the relationship and ensure premature turnover does not take place because of a negative experience. A health care organization must realize that negative experiences can arise from both internal and external factors. Every aspect of what a person might encounter as a result of trying to obtain health care services should be considered relevant.

A patient will form an impression about the overall organization according to what is experienced when making an appointment, commuting to a clinic, and viewing the external and internal areas. The impressions that form can easily influence how the remaining aspects of the patient experience are perceived.

Making an Appointment

A patient will often call to make an initial appointment or one for a subsequent visit. Every phone call must be answered within two to three rings during regular working hours. Outside of regular hours, an organization member must respond within 24 hours if a phone call is allowed to go to voice mail. A health care provider could have phone calls forwarded to a personal cell phone or home phone in order to prevent missed opportunities. A messaging service could be hired by the organization so that patients reach a live person after hours, although the person answering the phone will not be part of the organization and may not have the ability to provide much information. An organization may allow patients to make appointments via email or through a website submission form. Email is a great way of staying connected with patients in general. An organization member must respond to an email within 24 hours as well.

Can you have calls forwarded to a family member or friend?

After setting an initial appointment, give a brief overview of what will take place during the visit and clarify that a staff member may be in contact to remind the patient of the appointment. Take note of the best form of communication with a patient, either via telephone or email.

A patient should receive a reminder card when setting a subsequent visit in person. A reminder card should have the appointment time, contact information of the organization, and business logo on one side. Tell each patient to place the reminder card somewhere visible at work or home. Offer free magnets so that the reminder card (and the magnet) will remain on the refrigerator door for the entire household to see.

Magnets are a promotional item that can be produced by a printing company or online website.

Require that patients call 24 hours in advance to cancel an appointment. Refer to a policy that states patients will be charged for missed appointments not canceled in time. The policy is meant to deter missed appointments, but patients should rarely be charged for not canceling an appointment within 24 hours, especially if the time slot is subsequently filled. If a patient cancels an appointment, try to reschedule the patient and consider calling other patients or posting the opening on your organization's website in an attempt to fill the time slot. Charging patients for missed visits will greatly impact the experience and could result in a discontinuance of care altogether. Review the long-term payout of maintaining a positive experience versus the need to prevent a series of missed appointments.

Commuting

A patient must commute to your clinic to receive services and then commute to a destination once an appointment has ended. The commute itself may result in a negative experience if the distance or traffic proves excessive. A health care organization should try to schedule office hours in a way that provides the best commuting environment. An organization may want to refer a patient with a long commute to a more proximate health care provider. Doing so might cause the loss of a patient but may promote positive word of mouth or eliminate complaining. Train staff members to uncover any problems with a patient's commute and appointment time by asking relevant questions.

DIALOGUE

Staff Member: Did you have any problems getting here? Was this a suitable time to schedule your appointment?

Asking about the commute can bring forth more information about a patient's life. Knowing where a patient commuted from can unearth details about where the patient spends time during the day. In turn, this knowledge can lead to a conversation useful in building rapport as well as discovering factors that might be causing health issues. Talking about a commute may bring to light sacrifices that a patient must endure to keep an appointment. Does a patient have to put children in daycare, take time off from work, or not eat during a lunch hour? Being mindful of these sacrifices and showing empathy for what a patient must endure can prevent subtle negative elements from ruining the patient experience.

If a patient arrives late for an appointment, how will the organization react? Perceived penalties can motivate against tardiness, but imposing actual penalties may greatly frustrate a patient. Strike a balance between maintaining a positive experience and managing the patient flow. Consider whether trying to squeeze in a patient who arrived late or a walk-in visit will impact later patients. Form a policy that takes into account the experience of all patients and reschedule late arrivals or walk-ins if the organization simply cannot accommodate them.

Exterior Surroundings

The external area surrounding a clinic also shapes the experience. A health care organization should examine roadway and parking-lot accessibility, the building exterior, landscaping, and neighboring amenities. Roadways should contain good signage and form a clear maneuverable path to an office. Close forms of public transportation will benefit patients who do not have access to a vehicle. A parking lot or street parking should be available for those who drive, offer ample space, and provide for easy maneuvering. Examine walkways for hazards such as buckled sidewalks or icy patches (in the winter). Ensure that disabled patients, including those blind or using a wheelchair, can move around the area without complication. Ensure that property codes are met and the building exterior and landscaping appear clean and professional. Signs alluding to the organization need to be visible from afar and should be positioned toward high-traffic areas.

A commercial lease of **real property** may contain provisions that limit an organization's ability to modify landscaping or a building's exterior (and sometimes aspects of the interior). A standard commercial property lease, called a **triple net lease**, specifies that the lessor (property owner) has responsibility for the outside area and the lessee (person leasing) has control over the inside area. Upgrades to an outdated building facade that appears unattractive may not be allowed without special permission. Make sure to read lease agreements thoroughly and negotiate for the ability to modify a building's exterior. Take heed that amounts spent by a lessee to upgrade leased property may never be easily recovered. If significant modifications are needed to make a building's exterior or interior appear professional, stipulate in the lease contract that the landlord must fund the money or you should explore other locations.

A patient's day can be enhanced if a neighboring area contains additional amenities. Does the area have a bank, supermarket, gym, or other stores in case patients want to run errands or enjoy leisure activities? Parks, restaurants, and coffee shops offer patients a place to pass the time. Neighboring stores or establishments can play a key role in network

Real Property: Land or larger structures placed on land with a definite long-term use.

Triple Net Lease: A form of lease agreement where the lessor (property owner) has main responsibility for the outside area and the lessee (person leasing) has main control over the inside area.

Caution! You will lose money invested in leased property if you move locations or the landlord exercises the right to have you vacate the property.

and referral system development. Do not overlook the cleanliness of neighboring locations. Garbage floating around the streets or a neighboring business with uncut grass will make the entire area look unprofessional. You might have to make the effort to pick up garbage, mow surrounding lawns, or discuss matters with neighboring establishments.

Waiting Room

Upon entering the office, a patient will spend time at the front desk and in the waiting room. Staff members should dress appropriately and receive proper training on how to greet patients. A greeting begins with a warm smile and positive attitude and follows with recalling names, initiating a conversation, and quickly checking in a patient. Whenever appointments have been set in advance, staff members should have a list of information on patients to read in the morning. By using a CRM or practice management software program, notes from prior conversations can be reviewed. Suppose a family member of a patient comes to an appointment and staff members know about this person from prior conversations with a patient. If the family member is made to feel important, this person could spread positive word of mouth, refer others, or become a patient. This is a great example of how the best marketing is free. Never miss an opportunity to foster relationships energetically everywhere.

A waiting room should include comfortable chairs and enjoyable reading materials. Furniture and decorations on the wall should appear professional and provide nourishing energy. Do the furniture, decorations, or paint need to be modernized? Maintain a collection of general-interest magazines, books, and health care journals. Leave newsletters, business cards, or brochures on a counter. Consider organizing a row of binders related to different health subjects where patients can read or contribute articles. Put a corkboard in the waiting room that contains the latest positive research and news articles about the profession. Remember to throw away outdated reading materials regularly. Toys, games, or specific reading materials should be available for children. Businesses increasingly have televisions to improve the waiting experience. However, a television can distract working staff members or patients wanting to relax. Take into account noises emanating from any TV, radio, or external source. In terms of smells, does the waiting room contain any strange odors or strong potpourri scents? Especially in the bathroom, make sure smells are well regulated and that surfaces remain clean and tidy. Perform general cleaning often, including dusting and vacuuming. Less frequently, have the carpets and upholstery cleaned.

A normal waiting experience includes access to water or warm beverages such as tea and coffee. Think about offering healthy food options instead of candy. Despite the fact that people enjoy junk food, healthy foods fit better within the context of health care. Staff members can offer food and beverage options directly to patients, especially to buffer against long wait times. The waiting experience should remain short and allow patients to engage in supportive activities. *Patients should spend this time filling out a small form indicating what they want to review with the health care provider.* Noting this information gives patients a stronger voice and it ultimately saves everyone time. Waiting times can also be used to gather general information about the patient experience with a survey or questionnaire. *Preliminary* forms of care allow the health care process to begin even before the patient meets with a health care provider. A massage chair or warm pack can fill time and mentally prepare a patient for treatment. Preliminary forms of care can serve as a conversation topic for patients outside of the office, thus encouraging positive word of mouth.

When a patient's wait time becomes long or excessive, a health care provider should speak with the patient directly. An organization member needs to apologize and affirm that this does not happen often and that more will be done next time to prevent another occurrence. Communicating with a patient proactively and offering unique activities can soften the impact of an excessively long wait. Consider such ideas as plugging in a health-related video or presenting a patient with special amenities. In the worst-case scenario, a patient might have to be rescheduled. Suppose a health care provider's car breaks down while returning from lunch or a patient has other obligations. A patient may decide that

A building inspector can confirm if a property meets city code or requires improvements.

Give an estimate for how long the wait might be.

One of the most significant indicators of a poorly managed clinic is the presence of outdated magazines. It shows a clear lack of managing every detail of the patient experience.

coming back another time would be more convenient than enduring a long wait. Under these circumstances, the organization may decide to offer a rebate on services, provide a coupon for a local business, or insist that the next visit will be free. Following up with a phone call after such an incident would support patient retention and prevent the formation of negative word of mouth. If long wait times become chronic, reassess how patients are scheduled, review the amount of time being spent with each patient, or reduce the number of new patients seen.

Treatment Room

A patient will be placed into a treatment room to eventually meet with a health care provider. Ensure that each treatment room meets the same standard of quality as the waiting room. Reading materials and other forms of entertainment should remain available. What sounds emanate into the room and can anything dampen the noise? Smells are another important concern, especially where solvents have been used to clean tables and surfaces. Masking bad odors with potpourri can work as long as the scent is not overbearing. A treatment room should contain nice furniture, decorations, and paint as well as offer space for guests, such as a child or spouse. Time spent in a treatment room before a health care provider appears should be kept to a minimum. When wait times become long or excessive, steps should be taken to occupy time and soften the impact. A staff member could offer food and beverages directly to a patient or offer preliminary forms of service similar to those that would take place in a waiting room.

Summary

The patient experience needs to be holistically managed. Ensure that every phone call is answered within two to three rings or that phone and electronic messages receive a response within 24 hours. Eliminate barriers or hazards involved with reaching the office and ensure the entire area looks professional. Upon entering the interior of an office building, a patient will need to check in and wait. A waiting room should be clean, nicely decorated, and contain forms of entertainment. Other areas of an office, including the bathroom, should be maintained in a similar manner. In order to bolster the waiting experience, an organization can provide preliminary services that mentally prepare the patient for treatment. As a patient migrates into a treatment room, the experience should parallel that of the waiting room. Take into account cleanliness, smells, noises, decorations, furniture, and forms of entertainment. When long wait times become systematic, a health care organization needs to address how patients are scheduled. If a long wait time occurs in isolation, apologize to the patient and provide some form of remedy.

4.2   Patient Care

A thorough examination of patient care is discussed in Chapter 17. This section highlights key aspects of what a patient will specifically experience when first meeting with a health care provider as part of the health care process.

Introduction

Review the introduction and rapport-building phases of the selling process in Chapter 3.

A morning meeting among organization members serves as a great opportunity to review patient files and marketing notes so that a strong introduction can be made with each patient. A health care provider should greet a patient appropriately and acknowledge anyone else in the room. Bear in mind cultural norms, personalities, and potential health problems that may alter how a person should be approached. The same standards applicable to the introduction phase of the professional selling process apply to this situation. Maintain a professional appearance and present a positive attitude. Get haircuts frequently, keep fingernails tidy, and wear nice clothing. Prevent any potential bad breath by using mouthwash in the morning and keeping some at the clinic. As you gain in affluence, consider making upgrades to clothing and jewelry, but not to the point where it strains finances or appears flashy. Health care providers often have difficulty transitioning from the loose standards of school to a professional environment where more is expected. Especially toward the end of your educational process, begin to maintain a more professional image.

> Does your image convey a sense of quality health care?

Rapport Building

Remember that you are a memorable event for a patient. Even though everything appears routine on your end, this experience does not represent an everyday, nonstop occurrence for a patient. By taking good notes on prior instances of contact, you can weave a current conversation together with ones held in the past and give the impression that a patient matters. Unlike professional sales, rapport building in a clinic setting does not have to reach the same level of depth. Patients are often eager to address health care issues and may already feel comfortable with you. Build rapport briefly using light conversation before commencing the health care process. Listen for ways in which a patient has made sacrifices to undertake the appointment. Thank each patient for making sacrifices without dwelling on issues too long and reinforcing negative perceptions. Merely get a sense of the sacrifices in order to empathize a bit.

DIALOGUE

Provider: I really appreciate the fact you're using time off from work to take care of your health. This may not seem like the best way to spend your day, but maintaining your health is very important. It's hard to enjoy life without good health.

Keep a positive attitude at all times and avoid subjects that could engender unpleasant feelings, such as inserting opinions about politics or talking negatively about matters. If a patient begins discussing a touchy subject, work to alter the conversation to something positive and appropriate.

Health Care Process

When rapport appears sufficient, begin the health care process by qualifying a patient's health care needs. A health care provider should understand if qualifications made in the past still apply by asking, "Has anything changed since we last met?" Conduct an inquiry into current health care qualifications by reviewing any forms filled out during the preliminary wait or by asking, "What would you like to work on today?" The health care process involves learning about a patient's health concerns through an intake and determining if your health care organization can properly address such concerns.

> The health care process is explored in much greater detail in Chapter 17.

If a patient has particular expectations of care that appear unnecessary, communicate the reasons for pursuing another course of action. Always *ask the patient* for feedback about what is being proposed in order to confirm that recommendations fall in line with what a patient really wants. Although a patient may go along with a recommendation at the moment, feelings of discontent can arise later. If a patient fails to follow a recommendation for care, determine if barriers exist and *ask the patient* what a better course of action might be. Ask questions to ensure that a recommendation is considered reasonable given a patient's lifestyle. *Nothing will damage the experience more than advocating for unnecessary or unwanted services.*

> A *qualified* health care need is one that could be properly addressed by your organization.

Communicate what the health care process involves and how it relates to a patient's quality of life. This conversation parallels what takes place during the sales approach phase of a professional sale. Patients will usually accept more care overall if they enjoy the health care process and understand the reasons for it. If a qualified health care need still persists after the first visit, thoroughly explain what will take place during any subsequent visits to avoid surprises. At first, a patient might have trouble digesting a mountain of new information. Keep the dialogue simple and consistent by using *bullet points*. Take into account the patient's ability to understand complex health issues. As a patient returns for more visits, expand the discussion on health to include more complex topics and explore matters in greater depth. A patient may not ask for information, but consider how the human brain actively seeks to understand context and looks to eliminate ambiguity.

Support the communication effort with a packet of written materials. Make the effort to write down specific exercises, stretches, or items to purchase. Do not expect a patient to keep notes on what you say during a visit. Mention if an associate health care provider might assist with a patient's ongoing care. Describe classes or events at your clinic or within the community that a patient might find useful.

CASE STUDY

Scenario 1: Imagine a patient returns home and a spouse asks what took place after an initial visit. The patient had not been given materials to bring home and nothing was communicated about how the health care process addressed a qualified need, causing the patient's spouse to suggest that the visit was a waste of money. The patient does not return for another visit and the spouse complains to coworkers about having to spend a lot of money on some silly health care provider.

Scenario 2: Another health care provider effectively communicates during an initial visit about how the patient's quality of life will improve and then hands out written materials for the patient to take home. The spouse is able to read a treatment plan and understand what the health care provider is trying to achieve. As a result of the health care provider understanding that the family lives on a tight budget, the patient is instructed to discuss the cost of care with the spouse. The patient had very nice things to say about the entire experience and feels adamant about continuing care. The spouse has no complaints about what has taken place and later decides to become a patient and refer coworkers.

Ask the patient! Never dump a recommendation on a patient without gathering feedback. Never get frustrated if a recommendation is not followed.

Synthesize the ongoing treatment of a qualified need into short-term and long-term plans (after a few visits) and effectively communicate provisions that each plan contains. Focus on achieving specific goals at various stages that fit within a patient's ability to adapt to change. Print a copy for the patient and mention any contingent events that may occur that could disrupt the set timeline. When a qualified health care need is being resolved, a health care provider should thoughtfully assess how much additional care a patient needs.

DIALOGUE

Provider: You seem to be doing much better. Your body seems to be reacting well to treatment and doesn't appear symptomatic. We may only need to see each other one or two more times. After that, we can discuss routine preventative care to keep you in good working order. Does this course of action appear reasonable to you or do you have other ideas?

Do not overtreat under any circumstances based on the financial needs of your organization. Health care providers will often extend treatment over multiple visits as part of a sales plan. For instance, the first visit might be to assess a patient's needs and then the next appointment is meant to provide care. Excess care can provide a great source of revenue in the short term, but a sales ploy could result in low patient retention and negative word of mouth over the long term. The long-term prospects are best served by developing a strong network, referral system, and patient base. To this extent, a health care provider should build long-lasting and mutually beneficial relationships by providing patients with the best care possible.

Care Management

Create a system of checks and balances to confirm that services being provided are complete and proper. A health care provider needs a framework that will guarantee steps are not overlooked. The patient experience will quickly sour if a patient's care becomes mismanaged. Following a written set of procedures will ensure that the health care process takes place as desired. Written procedures work well for common health conditions. Consider having a staff member assist with note taking or researching information when busy or faced with uncertain situations. More than anything, the experience with a health care provider will carry the most weight in terms of patient retention, positive word of mouth, and referrals. Uphold the values of intellectual curiosity and strive to maintain excellence in providing care. *Take continuing education classes, study new bodies of knowledge, keep on top of the professional literature, and take time to research issues specific to a patient.* These actions will ensure that you are providing quality health care services, which are an integral part of the patient experience.

An organization should consider offering *secondary* services to enhance the patient experience. These additional services should support the health care experience without placing demands on a health care provider's time. Secondary services are normally free or low-cost and provide enjoyment. Giving a patient a warm pack or blanket could relax muscles, but it mainly serves to mentally heighten the overall health care experience. Other ideas include (1) setting up a separate room with massage equipment or exercise machines, (2) keeping a room completely dark and silent, or (3) placing yoga mats on the floor for stretching and relaxation. Classes, seminars, or workshops offer a means to educate patients about health and establish a place for patients to connect with one another. Offering products, such as supplements, cookbooks, shoe insoles, or therapy equipment, can benefit patients as well. However, patients will already be spending money on primary services and may quickly become frustrated if an organization makes *active* attempts to sell secondary products or services.

Secondary services often encourage the spread of positive word of mouth even when not accessed. A patient could easily be heard saying, "I go to this great health care clinic that has several massage chairs and a beautiful waiting room with a water fountain." If secondary services become extravagant or require significant time to manage, a financial assessment should be made. Be mindful of secondary services that consume a high degree of time, energy, and money without a compensatory increase in revenues or word of mouth.

DIALOGUE

Provider: Good afternoon, Todd. I see you brought your son in with you. How are you both doing?

Patient: He's been sick the last few days and so he's out of school.

Provider: That's not good to hear. He probably likes hanging out with his dad, though.

Patient: Yeah, I get to take him everywhere with me.

Provider: Do you have a lot to do today?

Patient: I need to make a few stops after this and then it's back home.

Provider: I will try to make this quick seeing how your son doesn't feel well and you have errands to run. Has everything been improving?

Patient: I was feeling better, but the last week was pretty rough.

Provider: Did something change last week? Could you identify anything that might have made last week different from others?

Patient: Nothing that I know of. Probably just stress.

Provider runs through the health care process

Provider: How did everything go for you today? Is there anything specific you want done differently?

Patient: Everything went well. There's nothing that I wanted done differently.

Provider: Why don't you stay in here with your son and relax for a minute. Let's plan on meeting at least one more time before doing a reevaluation. We can decide then if more visits would be beneficial. I'm also going to give you this packet full of new stretches and nutrition tips. Please schedule your next appointment at the front desk, but I am going to a conference the first part of June. If you would like to schedule an appointment in June, Dr. Smith will be filling in for me. You can find her bio on my website.

Provider: Thank you both for coming in. I look forward to seeing you next time. Contact me if you have questions or concerns.

Discussion The health care provider enters the treatment room, makes an introduction, and then briefly builds rapport. An effort is made to understand and empathize with what the patient faces personally. The patient has an opportunity to bring forth any unmet wants or expectations at the end of the health care process. A reevaluation point is set allowing the patient to feel comfortable about the overall quantity of care being recommended. Information is provided during the last part of the visit to prevent any surprises.

Summary

When entering a treatment room to begin the health care process, make an introduction and quickly build a sufficient level of rapport. Review past qualifications and establish what the current qualification involves. Effective communication about a qualified need will reduce ambiguity about the reasons for receiving care. Over time, a patient should become increasingly aware of how services rendered address a qualified health care need. Do not overtreat patients or sell them on unnecessary care plans. Such tactics might work well in the short term, but long-term success is better achieved by forming a satisfied network, referral system, and patient base. Discuss what will take place during any subsequent visits to avoid unexpected surprises.

4.3 Posttreatment

A patient will normally return to the front desk area at the end of an appointment. Make an attempt to schedule a patient's next appointment first (if applicable). Then, obtain payment for the current visit. A patient should already have a sense of what the charges will be. Finally, confirm with a patient that all concerns have been properly addressed.

Scheduling

A health care provider may suggest setting subsequent appointments if a qualified health care need still exists. Work through setting an appointment first before discussing other topics. If a patient hesitates about setting an appointment, that reaction could signify that an unspoken problem exists. Use this opportunity to gather feedback about the patient experience and check for problems. Light conversation can reveal if the hesitation relates to an unspoken problem or if a patient simply wants to wait before making an appointment. If a problem exists, the matter should be discussed with an organization member in a position of authority, such as an office manager or a health care provider, in order to find an effective solution.

DIALOGUE

Scheduler: Let me take a look at your card. We want to see you three more times it looks like. Are there any particular dates and times that would work best?

Patient: Well, I'm not sure what is best with my schedule. Let me give you a call later this week.

Scheduler: Please call us anytime to set up an appointment. Did everything go well today and did we answer all your questions?

Patient: Yes, thank you.

Scheduler: It looks as if you're all set then. I look forward to hearing from you. Have a great day!

Discussion   The scheduler tried to set an appointment, but the patient cited a reason for waiting. The patient was then asked a question to make certain hidden problems did not exist. Since no concerns were expressed, the scheduler brought the conversation to an end.

When setting an initial or subsequent appointment, the availability of appointment times becomes a key factor in the patient experience. By not seeing a patient at a time perceived as convenient, a conflict could arise with a patient's daily routine. For example, a patient might become stuck in traffic if the visit ends at the beginning of rush hour. Evaluate the need to modify hours of operation and consider structuring a distinct schedule. To prevent patients from complaining to others or failing to address a health care concern altogether, gather feedback about a patient's scheduling experience and make a referral to another health care provider when necessary. As long as working late at night or on the weekend occurs infrequently, being flexible with a patient on one visit may lead to several more visits being set during normal office hours. Imagine the cost from declining one *irregular* appointment request to lose out on ten future visits because a patient goes elsewhere.

> Ask the patient! "Was this time convenient for you?"

> Always consider the long-term payout when making decisions.

Provide enough variation in the weekly schedule in order to capture different brackets of time. For instance, the office could stay open until 7:00 P.M. each Wednesday in order to cater to patients with irregular work hours. The office could open every other Saturday to benefit patients who have time constraints during the regular workweek. After setting the hours of operation, review the number of patients who can be seen in a given time period to prevent long waits and allow enough spread between time slots to absorb drop-in visits, late arrivals, or urgent cases.

The scheduler can ask how everything went for a patient after setting an appointment. If a patient expresses a concern, it should be communicated to the organization member in charge of such matters. If no concerns exist, ask if the patient is ready to make payment.

Billing

Avoid surprises! Let patients know in advance what the charges will be.

Superbill forms need to be filled out by a health care provider running a cash practice and handed to the patient for submission to an insurance company.

CareCredit Healthcare Financing, carecredit.com

Point-of-Sale (POS) System: Electronic devices used to manage data and process payments related to the sale of products or services.

A POS system can also be extermely helpful when managing large amounts of inventory.

Bad Debt: The amount of a valid billable charge that is never collected.

Clearly indicate before a patient arrives at an appointment what the approximate charges will be. It is best to research the sources of payment before the visit occurs and clearly mark any instructions on a patient's file. For instance, does insurance cover part of a visit and to what extent? Ensure that the parties responsible for payment are charged their proper share. Patients will become agitated if they are quoted or billed the wrong amounts. Consider billing insurance companies on behalf of patients instead of running a cash practice in order to lessen the burden on patients. By learning how to bill insurance companies or government agencies early in one's career, a health care provider will not feel as overwhelmed with the billing process upon managing a busy practice. If a health care provider decides to run a cash practice, give each patient clear instructions on how to submit paperwork to an insurance company. Consider handing a patient a stamped envelope with the relevant insurance company's address preprinted to make the billing process as easy as possible.

Some health care organizations handle billing matters at the start of an appointment. This arrangement can fill wait times and it allows a patient to quickly leave once a visit has ended. If a patient confronts a billing issue, which can easily occur, any feelings of anger or frustration can prove very disruptive to the health care process. Most organizations work through the billing process at the end of a visit as a result. A patient may want to include more services or buy additional products as well. An organization can also use a mix of either billing approach depending on the circumstances.

The organization member in charge of billing may want to revisit the policy about missed visits or late arrivals if a concern arises. A patient needs to be called after a missed visit in order to assess the reason and to set a new appointment. Even though an organization may threaten to charge patients for a missed visit, imposing such penalties could lead to negative word of mouth or the loss of a patient. Giving a patient a free pass and explaining organization policy should alleviate a future recurrence. The chance of several missed appointments or late arrivals increases if a patient comes in frequently for care; thus more than one free pass may be given to a long-term patient.

Along with poor patient care and lack of rapport, monetary concerns will cause a high degree of patient turnover. A patient will react differently to being charged small amounts several times versus one large amount all at once. Maintain payment-plan options that act as artificial extensions of credit or use a third-party vendor that can extend credit to patients. Review the interest rate to ensure patients will not become overextended financially. A **point-of-sale (POS) system** that accepts debit or credit cards can facilitate the actual billing transaction. Autodraw can be set up on charge cards enabling amounts to be withdrawn automatically over multiple time periods. Be careful using payment plans that charge a flat fee for unlimited care or that provide a sharp discount for multiple visits because insurance companies will raise objections whenever a cash payor is allowed to pay considerably less than a covered patient for the same level of care. Also, an organization should only provide services that address a qualified health care need in contrast to a general package of care.

When patients dispute charges, an organization member needs to research the matter thoroughly and determine if the charges are valid. Patients who have not yet paid a valid charge establish an unpaid balance. Hold firm and make attempts to collect the full amount. Send general letters at first that outline payment options and then start to introduce repercussions for not paying. An organization could express how the patient might be barred from future services, incur fees and penalties, or face a negative credit rating from a collection effort. After an unpaid balance reaches a certain age, such as 180 days, call the patient to structure an individualized payment plan or find a fair compromise on the amount to pay. Amounts that are not collected turn into a **bad debt**. Consider receiving a reduced amount from active patients who still want to come in but cannot afford the full fee. Instead of pursuing the full unpaid balance and receiving nothing, be flexible and negotiate with the patient for a lower amount conditional upon timely payment. If no agreement can be reached, then the account could be turned over to a collection agency whereby the relationship will most likely sour. A collection agency will take a portion of amounts that are recovered. Assess the importance of the person as a network participant or referral source beforehand. Make every attempt to resolve the matter professionally and do not allow tensions to mount.

As a result of health care organizations becoming frustrated over poor collection rates, many have switched to requiring full payment at the time of service. This approach does not provide patients with the flexibility of long-term payment options. The impact on patient retention may or may not outweigh the cost of bad debts or collection efforts. Review the needs of both patients and the organization when setting billing policies.

Final Orientation

Light conversation during the final moments of a visit is an important part of building rapport. Asking where a patient is headed afterward provides feedback about a patient's daily routine and turns the focus away from administrative matters. This final contact allows an organization member to mention upcoming events or inform patients of a substantial change that will take place in the future. This final orientation is meant to confirm that all matters have been resolved and a patient will not feel unsettled after leaving.

When future appointments have been decided against, ask if a patient would like to remain in contact with the organization. Mention free events, newsletters, or an online blog that the organization maintains. Once a patient leaves, make sure notes are updated in order to ensure the beginning of the next appointment, no matter when that might occur, resumes in a seamless manner—*right where the patient will remember it finished!*

> Try not to put personal information unrelated to the health care process in a patient's medical chart. Store unrelated personal information in a CRM program or territory worksheet.

Summary

A patient should stop at the front desk before leaving and schedule a next appointment (if applicable). Having adequate availability helps when setting appointments and it can keep the patient experience from turning negative. Offer each patient a reminder card with information on one side and clarify that someone will make contact before the next visit as a courtesy reminder. Contact patients who miss an appointment and review the office policy with them. An organization member should clearly indicate to patients what their payment responsibility will be before the appointment gets underway. Patients should receive a bill or make a payment after any scheduling occurs at the end of a visit. When closing the visit, mention upcoming events, provide informational materials, and steer the conversation away from administrative matters. This final orientation allows a patient to feel comfortable that all matters have been settled.

4.4   Maintaining Relationships

The connection made previously with a patient will begin to fade as time progresses. Organization members have an opportunity to rebuild rapport and further strengthen the relationship during each visit. Various marketing tools work to maintain contact between visits. Examples include holiday cards, weekly workshops, and tip-of-the-month emails. Patients can submit articles for a newsletter or online blog, thereby giving them a sense of involvement and reducing the time required to put the information together. Instruct patients to keep an appointment reminder card visible, such as with a magnet on a refrigerator, to build awareness of your organization and prevent a missed appointment. Any effort that supports the formation of a positive reminder about your organization helps with spreading word of mouth, expanding a referral system, and maintaining a patient base. A health care organization should consider the frequency and intensity of marketing efforts to avoid overloading patients.

As a patient's next visit approaches, have an organization member contact the patient as a reminder. Until a patient gets into the regular habit of coming in for care, a missed appointment has a greater chance of occurring. When calling or emailing about an upcoming appointment, use this opportunity to encourage the patient to bring any concerns that might have surfaced *to the appointment*.

DIALOGUE

Scheduler: Hello. I'm calling to remind you about your appointment tomorrow at 3:00 P.M. Bring with you any questions you might have. We are looking forward to seeing you again. Have a great day!

Discussion   The scheduler has instructed the patient to think about questions in general that may be negative, neutral, or positive. In an effort to gather feedback that could improve patient retention or avoid the formation of negative word of mouth, the patient has been given the green light to discuss matters. Instead of discussing these issues on the phone, the scheduler suggests that the best time would be during the next visit.

A patient can easily have unspoken resistance toward continuing care. An organization would not receive feedback crucial to improving the patient experience if it's left unspoken. Patient retention is placed in jeopardy and negative experiences can become intertwined with word of mouth if problems fester. Organization members need to proactively communicate with patients and ask questions in order to uncover hidden problems.

If a patient stops care for some time, an organization may want to subtly reconnect at a later point in an effort to renew care. Be careful not to overcontact former patients and disrupt the long-term relationship. Former patients may already be receiving a newsletter or some other marketing tool and additional contact might appear redundant or bothersome. A former patient may simply have no current qualified need yet has thoroughly enjoyed the experience thus far and could be spreading positive word of mouth and offering referrals. A health care organization should consider organizing an event specifically for former patients who have a track record of making referrals. When contacting former patients, professional sales techniques can assist with the entire conversation and ensure a qualified need actually exists in case renewing care is a possibility.

Summary

Have ways to remain in contact with patients between visits. General marketing materials, such as holiday cards, newsletters, and email, help. Make sure that all telephone calls are answered during regular office hours and that any phone message or email receives a response within 24 hours. Contact with a patient may occur at random while in public. Carry a PDA or cell phone to ensure you can remember and recall the many names and details of patients, referral sources, and network participants. Remembering information supports the formation of long-term relationships by making people feel important. An organization member may also contact former patients in an effort to renew care. The communication effort should be properly managed, taking into account frequency and intensity.

4.5   Experience Management

On a holistic level, the entire experience for a patient should leave only a positive impression. A slight annoyance over time can build up and lead to negative word of mouth or the loss of a patient. When turnover occurs prematurely, an organization is forced to allocate additional resources to marketing. An organization might observe friction when trying to expand a network or referral system because of invasive word of mouth that has been allowed to form. Ensuring that each patient has a positive experience denotes professionalism and ensures that relationships hold their optimum value.

Think about every aspect of what a patient might encounter as part of working through an appointment. A health care organization should act out simulated patient visits to train staff members and discover what patients might experience. A **mystery shopper** hired by a health care organization could assess the entire experience in secret, especially the conduct of staff members. Use a close community member or hire someone from an agency that keeps the mystery shopper's identity secret even from you. Schedule time at least once a year to conduct an exhaustive review of the entire patient experience, including marketing efforts and sales narratives. Consider forming a group with other professionals or business owners to discuss problems and brainstorm solutions. This collegial approach to problem solving represents a free and significantly valuable way to manage an organization.

If a problem does surface, take action to address its cause and provide remedies for individuals who have been impacted. For example, suppose road construction begins in the area, negatively impacting patient commutes. Figure out when it will end, communicate relevant information to patients, and offset the impact through indirect measures. An organization could offer discounts or free services, or modify office hours until the construction ends. Talking with patients and staff members is the best way to unearth problems and form a solution.

> **Mystery Shopper:** A "fake" patient hired by a health care organization to work through an appointment as a way of secretly assessing the patient experience.

> Telling staff members that you use a mystery shopper can make them feel anxious or paranoid.

Quality Control

Quality-control measures establish barriers that support the delivery of high-quality services. These measures might contain an alert that becomes triggered if an unwanted activity takes place. A system of quality-control measures can ensure that nothing will be overlooked in the health care process. Quality-control measures might involve reviewing another person's work or needing to complete one task before being able to move on to a new task.

As part of maintaining controls over patient care, ask patients direct questions and take a moment to make personal observations. Meet with staff members regularly and theorize about what patients might be experiencing. Contact referral sources to gather feedback and maintain the referral relationship. Send out anonymous questionnaires or encourage patients to fill ones out while waiting. The questionnaires should contain general questions but also reference specific items that organization members believe are a concern. Training staff members sufficiently and carefully managing their work will help protect against poor work performance that could undermine the patient experience as well.

> **Quality-Control Measures:** Structured processes that ensure steps are not overlooked or improper actions are not taken without some form of alert or barrier.

Summary

Subtle issues over time can lead a patient to convey negative word of mouth or cease treatment altogether. Opening lines of communication with patients and staff members is the best way to uncover problems. Carrying on discussions with referral sources and sending out questionnaires represent other key forms of feedback. In terms of assessing a problem and devising a solution, adopt a holistic philosophy that encompasses the whole organization. Quality-control measures work to prevent problems from occurring in the first place. Such measures might involve having organization members review each other's work or creating steps that must be completed before moving on to later stages of a task.

CHAPTER ASSIGNMENT

Working in a group of three to four students or fellow professionals, complete the following item.

1. Find a local health care clinic willing to allow your group to review the full patient experience. A patient retention checklist can be downloaded online at remedybooks. com under the *Students* tab. Describe the nature of each item listed on the checklist in relation to this clinic, mention if problems exist, and provide ideas for improvement. Feel free to review additional items not contained on the checklist.

Market Planning

AUTHOR'S NOTE

It's important to review the marketing plan presented in this chapter, create an outline of all the headings, and begin to compile your own marketing plan. If you have already put together a marketing plan, make sure it is updated periodically. When reading through the sections on pricing and service mix, pay attention to how accessibility is just as important as profitability. Take note of how an organization could incur various indirect expenses when trying to augment its service mix; that is, increased management time or cannibalization.

The best marketing is FREE: Foster Relationships Energetically Everywhere.

Marketing efforts are meant to uncover opportunity in the marketplace necessary for building a network and referral system along with recruiting and retaining patients. The ultimate goal of marketing involves linking patient needs with services and products offered by a health care organization. Marketing principles also play a key role in optimizing the patient experience. As patients come into contact with an organization, all aspects of the experience need to remain positive in an effort to support a long-term relationship.

This final marketing chapter examines administrative matters, many of which impact the patient experience. Most notably, what is the exact nature of services a health care organization will provide and at what price? The service offerings are usually based on a health care provider's clinical expertise. Most health care organizations extend a primary set of services to either a general audience or a target market. Another secondary level of services might be offered in addition to the primary ones.

Revenue
− Expenses
= Net Profit

It is important to pinpoint how much to charge patients for primary and secondary service offerings. A health care provider might want to establish low prices in order to extend services at an affordable rate. From a profitability standpoint, high prices do not always generate the greatest financial benefit because expenses need to be factored into the equation. *Net profit* matters the most when evaluating the value of activity. Keeping to one low-priced service that requires few support costs may generate more profit and accessibility than a dynamic organization with high prices and multiple service lines that require an extensive amount of resources to maintain. Figuring out profitability levels can require extensive feedback and analysis on prices and service lines. A marketing information system creates the right framework for generating information useful in making this assessment.

The marketing section of a business plan establishes what marketing efforts should entail. A health care provider with a stable practice could benefit from writing a marketing plan in an effort to pull more resources away from marketing activities and direct them toward patient care. A health care student or beginning provider will have significant problems attaining success without a marketing plan. Putting together a marketing plan will assist with preparing for the future, whether the potential goal is to develop a patient base from scratch or secure money to purchase one. Writing a *full* business plan becomes feasible after understanding the remaining fields of business: accounting, finance, and management. In writing a business plan, a person is forced to think about the organization as a whole and prepare a foundation of knowledge to handle potential events. As circumstances change, a business plan should be modified accordingly.

5.1   Pricing Strategy

In the health care industry, prices are often influenced by a **third-party payor**, such as an insurance company or government agency. Based on the particular type of service, a third-party payor might offer a fixed amount or a percentage of the total billable charge. A health care provider must remain active in learning about insurance pricing and billing code guidelines, which can change frequently. An organization member will most likely need to attend periodic seminars to stay up-to-date but should then train other organization members on the subjects covered.

Prices need to remain balanced among the various payor types. Insurance companies (especially) will protest **price discrimination** if cash patients receive steep discounts while patients with health care coverage are charged higher rates for the same services. An organization that offers long-term care packages to cash patients must be careful not to offer steep price discounts indirectly. Cash prices for a particular service need to closely approximate what an organization would bill an insurance company, including any deductible or copayment, even if an insurance company reduces the amount it will ultimately reimburse. Although an insurance company might not cover a particular service, a health care organization is still expected to provide the same overall level of care to covered patients. Failure to treat or bill covered patients the same as cash patients could cause an insurance company to not renew any contract it has with a health care provider. Improperly billing an insurance company could also result in a legal dispute.

A **cash practice** can circumvent price discrimination by charging full prices upfront and then handing each patient a *superbill* listing treatment codes that the patient uses to seek reimbursement from a respective insurance provider. Each patient would only be reimbursed for an amount that coverage allows. The patient experience can suffer when running a cash practice as a result of higher costs to the patient and the increased paperwork burden. A health care organization should provide patients with a stamped envelope containing the insurance company's address and easy-to-read instructions on how to submit forms as a way of reducing hassles. As a way of minimizing surprises to the patient, a health care organization should always call an insurance provider to verify coverage and then explain that coverage to the patient.

Initial Price Setting

Most health care organizations have a fair degree of flexibility in managing price levels despite some limits to setting prices freely. When trying to figure out what to charge overall, begin by looking at competitors to establish a rough estimate of market rates. Call around and note what similar organizations charge and gather feedback from health care providers and patients about such price levels. Take into account the exact nature of service lines you intend to provide and find organizations that work amid similar conditions. Knowing the range of prices from comparable health care organizations helps assess reasonability. This research on prices might uncover general ideas about the types of services that patients like as well. Figure out if **substitutes** exist in the marketplace and also take into account their price levels. Would a patient pursue a completely different health care option if your prices increased too much?

Strategic Initiatives

Since low prices tend to denote low quality, be mindful of the psychological implications of a *cost leadership* strategy. Decreasing prices below those of competitors as a way to adjust for low patient retention is not an appropriate solution since perceptions of quality can diminish. The best way to fix low patient retention is to heighten the overall patient experience, which may require an increase in prices. Structuring a strong patient experience will engender loyalty, lead to positive word of mouth, and promote trusted referrals. High patient retention means that patients see value in receiving care and might be willing to pay more for services as a result. Effective *branding* efforts play a role in getting patients to bear in mind the value your organization provides. As a patient base grows, filling the schedule to maximum capacity signals that price levels can further increase (if desired).

Third-Party Payor: A corporate or government institution that makes health care payments on behalf of a covered recipient.

Price Discrimination: Charging distinct groups of customers different rates based on source or type of payment.

Laws regarding price discrimination can vary per state.

Cash Practice: A health care organization that does not accept third-party coverage directly but provides treatment codes (*superbill*) to patients so they can seek reimbursement personally.

Do not expect patients to understand the complex nature of insurance billing.

Substitutes: Completely different products or services, usually of lower quality and price, but able to still satisfy a customer's same demand.

Occasionally remind patients how your services contribute value to their lives.

How might prospective patients view prices in relation to an organization's quality? Pursuing a strategy of *differentiation* means that the nature or quality of services provided is somehow perceived as better than those of competitors or substitutes. The ability to set high prices will be difficult if patients do not truly take notice of this value proposition. Sales narratives and a coordinated marketing campaign can assist with branding efforts. Clearly articulating the reasons for care (*qualification*) to patients can elicit a high degree of motivation on their part. If a patient fails to appreciate the reasons for specific price levels or has general concerns about money, then resistance can exist toward accepting care.

Price Incentives

Price Incentive: A product or service provided at a steep discount or free of charge as a way to entice customers into patronizing an organization and further buying products and services.

Although setting an initial appointment can require a great deal of effort, the act of undergoing appointments tends to become easier after a patient has settled into a health care routine. In order to move beyond that initial energy barrier, a health care organization could offer a **price incentive** to provide motivation. People often want to receive *free stuff* or at least feel like they are *getting a deal*. In isolation, charging a uniquely low price one time for initial or renewed services—to motivate a patient to jumpstart care—will probably not cause an insurance company or government agency to voice concerns about price discrimination. An initial low price on services may not diminish perceptions of quality either.

Consider how a fast-food restaurant could offer a 50-cent product at a loss hoping that this price incentive would encourage customers to stop in and buy other profitable food items.

When a qualified need is indeterminate, a *no-obligation consultation* gives a health care provider the opportunity to showcase the value of care to a patient who is worried about money. The patient only faces expenditures related to the commute. Consider expenditures for gas, food, and time when talking to patients about a no-obligation consultation.

DIALOGUE

Provider: I'd like you to address your health care concerns with me. I know this will take time out of your day, but I'm not going to charge you anything. I want you to see the value that comes from your health improving. This should be well worth your time.

Pricing Economics

The business cycle can influence price levels that consumers will accept. Willingness to spend money increases during the growth stage of the economy. As the economy peaks and turns recessionary, consumers begin to budget more and favor less-expensive substitutes. Focusing on a specific target market can help isolate market participants able and willing to pay regular prices during harder economic times.

Elasticity of Demand: The degree to which price changes inversely impact demand levels for a product or service.

Microeconomic forces play a more significant role in terms of health care pricing. The health care industry in particular faces an overall steady demand for services because of the importance people place on their health. **Elasticity of demand** is an economic concept that relates the total change in demand to a given change in price. Elasticity means that consumers have a high sensitivity to prices and will greatly decrease consumption patterns if prices increase. If prices were to increase 5% and demand subsequently falls by 100%, then that relationship is said to display *perfect elasticity*. Having substitute services in the marketplace or strong competitive pressures can lead to greater price elasticity.

Price Inelasticity: Reflects the extent to which demand levels for a product or service are not significantly influenced by price changes.

If prices increase 5% and demand falls less than 5% (or even increases), then the relationship would display **price inelasticity**. Although inelasticity runs higher for the health care industry compared to other industries, the inelasticity is not a perfect 100%. Increasing prices too high will stifle demand or be met with opposition from third-party payors. Overall, the health care industry enjoys a fair degree of price inelasticity, which varies according to the actual service provided. Consumers perceive health care as an important need, similar to food and shelter, and will often forego other items before giving up seeing a health care provider or stopping medications. Health care coverage helps to augment price inelasticity, especially when patients are charged only a low standard copayment. A health care provider can differentiate services, boost the patient experience, and target specific market groups in an effort to further stabilize demand levels.

The concept of price inelasticity is also covered in Chapter 1.

Profit Maximization

The optimum price level is one that generates sufficient accessibility and profitability. Health care covers an important need and patients must have access to affordable services. Luckily, high-priced services do not always generate the most profit. Setting prices at zero would encourage demand but would automatically result in no revenue. At the opposite end, incredibly high prices will stifle demand, resulting in no revenue either. Figure 5.1 shows three separate lines that illustrate the point of maximum profitability. The blue line corresponds to revenue, which is derived by multiplying the price and demand for a service together. The red line represents the costs needed to support revenue at a given level of demand. Finally, an amount for *net profit*, which represents revenue less expenses, is shown as the green line. The point of greatest distance between the revenue line and the cost line represents where profits are maximized.

FIGURE 5.1 Maximum Profitability

Net profit is at its maximum when the revenue line is farthest from the expense line.

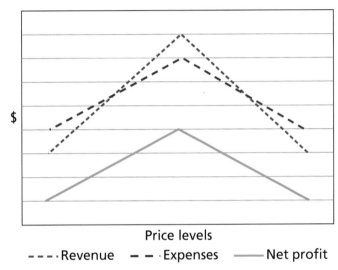

Price levels

- - - · Revenue   - - · Expenses   ——— Net profit

Summary

When evaluating what prices to charge, the assessment should take into account competitors, substitutes, and third-party payors. Excessive price discounts for covered patients may cause third-party payors to voice concerns, but one-time discounts or no-obligation consultations may provide the incentive needed to motivate patients to start care without causing any negative backlash from such entities. Economic forces also play a role in setting prices. A health care organization must look at the macroeconomic and microeconomic factors that influence demand levels. The health care industry normally enjoys a fairly inelastic demand for its services wherein patients still demand care when prices are high.

5.2   Service Mix

The mere presence of various service options can increase revenue if they cause patients to think more highly of an organization or spread positive word of mouth. The main reason behind establishing an integrated clinic involves increasing service diversity. A **complementary service** that has a mutual connection can raise the odds of a patient wanting to combine services. For instance, a patient who buys an exercise ball might also want any corresponding workout video. An organization might find that it can charge higher prices for uniquely differentiated services when focusing on a target market. However,

Complementary Service: A type of service that fits within the scope of other services leading customers to demand items together.

an organization may face pressure to keep prices down if other patients accessing those services do not notice a similar type of value.

Arriving at a price point for different services is often a deliberative process that examines a number of variables. True, having additional services might lead to higher revenue, but an organization also needs to review how expenses play a role. How much do service lines cost in terms of time, energy, and money? As the service mix increases in scope, providing services at an appropriate level of quality can become more challenging. Profit levels can fall across the board if an organization becomes harder to manage after adding more service lines. This often occurs when an organization hires an additional health care provider in an attempt to offer patients more service diversity. The costs related to increased management efforts as well as the additional employee wages may outweigh any increase in revenue.

Profit maximization involves a tug-of-war between price and demand factors along with resource expenditures. Simply bringing in high revenue through a specific service line does not necessarily equate to high profit levels. Services that result in less revenue could actually lead to higher profitability if expenses diminish and improvements to the patient experience enhance consumption patterns. Even then, a less profitable service line might (1) appear more attractive to prospective patients, (2) complement demand for another service line, or (3) enhance the patient experience to a greater extent, leading patients to demand more services overall.

Additions to the service mix start to become counterproductive when they consume too many resources or reduce demand for highly profitable service lines. **Cannibalization** of highly profitable service lines could decrease profit levels overall unless demand for a less profitable service line is substantial enough. An organization that experiences a decrease in profit levels might react by boosting prices, thus decreasing accessibility for patients. In addition, an increase in prices could soften demand and lower profit levels even further. In order to maximize accessibility and profitability, an organization must operate efficiently, review price versus demand factors for each service, and take note of the various expenses required to support each service line.

Cannibalization: The loss of demand for one type of service because of the addition of a more desirable one within an organization's service mix.

Price Setting

Feedback from patients and staff members along with a *cost-benefit analysis* assists in setting prices at their optimal level. Structuring the accounting system properly will provide information for use in a cost-benefit analysis. Revenues and expenses should be separated according to each particular service line in order to calculate individual net profit figures. An organization can calculate how much time organization members spend performing work related to a particular service line by using a system of job codes. Other nonlabor expenses can be allocated to service lines based on employee time or by another reasonable factor. Use of job codes also ensures that organization members are not wasting time.

Concepts related to conducting a cost-benefit analysis are reviewed in greater depth during later chapters in this book.

An understanding of what drives expenses can influence what to charge for services. For example, a particular patient group may place significant demands on a health care provider's time, require special equipment, or take up extra space in an office. An organization may want to charge per procedure, per visit, or apply an addendum charge to better reflect the costs associated with a type of service or patient concern. For example, patients with chronic health problems may require longer initial visits than patients with acute issues. A health care organization could structure different time lengths for initial visits at varying prices.

Changing prices later may not be easy since patients will grow accustomed to price levels. A series of announcements should be communicated for several weeks before major price changes take effect to avoid surprises. Newsletter postings, flyers placed in the waiting room, and direct communication should take place. Insurance restrictions and accessibility concerns might preclude large adjustments to current prices (or even the achievement of optimal prices).

Summary

A health care organization should take heed before offering a large range of services. Does a particular service line complement or cannibalize demand for another service line? The relative level of expenses must also be taken into account through a cost-benefit analysis to determine the profitability of each service line. The health care provider's time and energy should be factored into this analysis. The optimal service mix will generate a high level of profit in association with an appropriate amount of management. Accessibility and profitability after consideration of business expenses ultimately guide the optimum price level for services. When changing prices, an organization should make announcements several weeks in advance to properly inform patients.

5.3   Marketing Information System

An **information system** may involve computer software or manual activities as part of its process. A *marketing information system* refers specifically to the collection, transmission, and dissemination of information related to marketing efforts.

Information System: A framework that enhances the collection, transmission, and dissemination of information.

Collection

A marketing information system's first goal is to collect information from external and internal sources. Information can be gathered through feedback forms, human contact, or personal observations.

Feedback Forms With today's technology, feedback forms can be placed on a website or sent out electronically for greater access. Types of feedback forms include surveys, questionnaires, and suggestion boxes. Because patients often feel uncomfortable opening up about concerns, especially ones that are ancillary to the care they receive, mail-in surveys are a great method to obtain candid feedback about the patient experience. A mail-in survey should have a self-addressed, stamped envelope attached. Surveys can be handed to patients as they leave the clinic or sent to the homes of former patients. Since surveys are best kept anonymous, a sign at the front desk should remind patients to please respond. A message on the survey itself can stress the importance of responding. Because motivated or frustrated patients may reply in higher numbers, consider if the response group provides a good statistical representation of the entire population under observation.

Survey items may focus on a specific problem or attempt to gather general information. Open-ended questions should be included to provide responders with an opportunity to add ideas or talk about matters not directly covered by a survey. Developing a rating system as illustrated by the two sample survey forms in Figures 5.2 and 5.3 creates a value framework to view the extent of concerns and allows responses to be tracked over time.

Human Contact Directly communicating with people is another means to gather information. A health care provider can ask questions of fellow health care providers, business owners, or professionals in other fields to brainstorm ideas. An organization may consider hiring a professional consultant to get expert advice on more complex issues, such as accounting or human resource matters. As for patient care, a health care provider must maintain an open dialogue with patients and keep good notes.

Personal Observations Conduct a thorough review of the internal and external issues (at least annually) that could impact the patient experience. Information should be collected by conducting research, contacting competitors, reading publications, or driving around the marketplace. Incorporate an examination of price and service diversity. Adopt a holistic philosophy and think through all the permutations of what could impact service quality, paying strict attention to how everything plays out in real life.

FIGURE 5.2 **First Sample Survey**

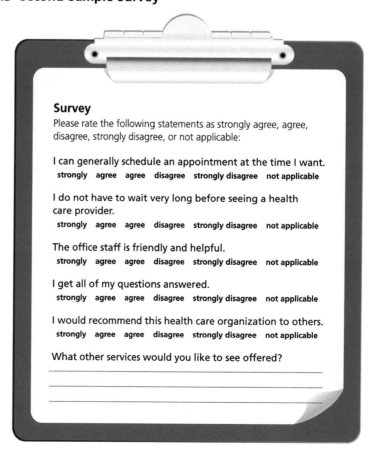

FIGURE 5.3 **Second Sample Survey**

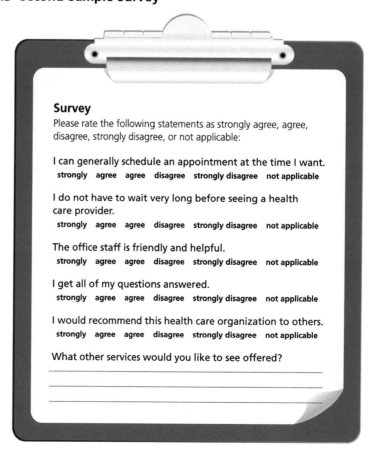

Transmission

The worst form of feedback occurs when someone complains directly to an organization member or through community-based word of mouth. A complaint means that a problem has reached a level where it places long-term relationships in jeopardy. In an effort to stop problems from happening, information about problems must reach the right organization member in a position of authority. An organization should establish processes and enact *quality-control measures* to ensure information is properly communicated. Ask staff members, patients, referral sources, and network participants to bring forth issues or make suggestions at any time. Regular staff meetings, written job duties, and proper training help with placing information in the hands of the right decision makers. A computer system centralizes the storage of information and can provide an easy method for transmission as well.

Dissemination

Sending information externally into the marketplace helps an organization connect with new market participants or remain connected with current network participants, referral sources, and patients. When attempting to resolve a problem, the form of communication should be direct, such as through a phone call or meeting.

A marketing campaign is an organized effort to promote an organization and may include the use of marketing tools, such as ads, media spots, websites, or collateral. The most influential forms of marketing tend to cost very little. For example, a small *promotional item* could help maintain relationships by displaying an organization's contact information. Word of mouth represents one of the most powerful forms of marketing and often costs nothing. An organization should confirm that a person has had a positive experience and then offer an *application* exemplifying what to communicate on the organization's behalf. Never assume anyone will automatically spread word of mouth in a constructive manner. Word of mouth in general falls into one of three categories: positive, neutral, and negative.

Applications are discussed in Chapter 2.

Positive An organization should aspire to reach 100% positive word of mouth. When positive word of mouth flows through the marketplace, more resources can be allocated to patient care instead of marketing. Positive word of mouth can support branding efforts and enhance the formation of a strong network. It is necessary to ensure each patient has a 100% positive experience and to instruct patients on how to communicate on an organization's behalf using applications.

Certain individuals feed on drama and can view events in a negative light despite the existence of a 100% positive experience.

Neutral Neutral word of mouth does not convey meaningful information or appear as a recommendation for or against using an organization's services. Although it does not inflict damage upon an organization, an opportunity has been lost to convey positive sentiments. Neutral word of mouth may help build awareness, but an organization should make attempts to guide network participants, referral sources, and patients on how to speak positively on an organization's behalf.

Negative The most powerful form of word of mouth is usually driven by negative experiences. One negative aspect of the patient experience could override everything that appears good. The issue could be a long wait time, billing error, treatment concern, or an unpleasant staff member. The rate of dissemination and overall impact from negative word of mouth can be significant. Overcoming invasive negativity may require an extensive reallocation of resources away from patient care toward marketing efforts. Negative word of mouth can result in lost revenue from multiple sources. Imagine the loss of a patient, referral source, and network participant all at once. Taking the time to ensure every patient has a positive experience may not always result in positive word of mouth, but it will help to prevent anything negative from being said within your marketplace.

Summary

An effective marketing information system allows information to be collected, transmitted, and disseminated. Feedback forms, human contact, and personal observations collect information for an organization. Circulating information to the right organization member requires regular staff meetings, clearly defined job duties, and well-established processes. A computer system can simplify the transmission of information and may include built-in quality-control measures. Sending information externally into a marketplace helps an organization create and maintain connections. Word of mouth represents the most effective way to disseminate information externally. An organization should take steps to encourage the spread of positive word of mouth using dialogue applications. By striving to create a 100% positive experience and designing effective solutions to problems, negative word of mouth can be kept to a minimum.

5.4   Sample Marketing Plan

The marketing section of a business plan should illustrate how an organization intends to form a connection between patients and services being offered. Other aspects of a business plan involve (1) hypothetical estimates of profitability (financial plan) and (2) objectives to reach when operating a business (management plan). The accounting elements of a business plan are interwoven into the financial section. The following *hypothetical* marketing plan involves a student who intends to work as an employee for one year before transitioning patients over to a personal practice. All details in this plan are fictitious and the content of your actual marketing plan may differ substantially.

Marketplace Defined

The intended area of operation is in the city of Rosewood, which encompasses the southern area of the region. The population according to the U.S. Census of 2010 was 146,500 citizens. The city planning office reported over the phone that the growth rate has averaged 3% since this time, resulting in a current population of 150,900.

The attached map [not shown] outlines three major zones in which to direct marketing efforts. The zones give a general sense of the concentration of potential network participants. Zone 1 has a high concentration of prospective patients because consumer demographics favor services my organization will provide. Zones 2 and 3 represent areas where marketing efforts will also be concentrated, but with a smaller allocation of resources. It has been observed that many new health care offices are forming to the west in an area of high development. I intend to find commercial property space in the southern portion of Rosewood to practice away from this high-growth area. The southern portion offers better transportation accessibility and contains a dense population. Area residents here are older and would prefer access to a local health care office. Although the cost for office space is moderate to high, analysis shows that competitors charge above-average prices in the southern region of town and experience strong net profit levels. Table A shows a breakdown of price levels among competitors that have a comparable service mix.

TABLE A	Competitive Analysis	
	Number of Providers	**Average Prices**
Western competitors	16	105
Eastern competitors	14	118
Northern competitors	24	74
Southern competitors	38	124

Market Analysis

The local marketplace has a strong economy that has been supported by the increase in new technology companies. If the economy weakens, the technology companies could come under financial stress and impact the overall marketplace economy. In previous recessions, the economy has performed well according to Tom Smith of the Small Business Administration (SBA). Mr. Smith informed me that the local economy has become increasingly diverse and exports to developing nations should boost local economic activity.

Macroeconomic Outlook

According to the financial press, the national economy is midway through an economic correction. The economy slowed in the first quarter because of a European banking crisis that started last year. According to Mr. Smith at the SBA, the national economy has not been greatly impacted by this crisis. The Bureau of Labor Statistics reports an unemployment rate of 9.3% in Rosewood and this number has slowly improved over the last several quarters. The Federal Reserve has also held interest rates steady. Both of these indicators support the notion that the business cycle should move into an expansionary phase at some point soon. Financial research shows that an expansionary phase typically lasts 10 to 12 years before peaking and recessions last 1 to 2 years on average. The organization should start in a positive economic environment with an estimated decade of strong economic activity ahead. The financial plan [not shown] outlines several ways that the organization will prepare for the next recession.

Industry Trends

The demand for health care providers in the area has grown steadily for the last decade while this rate of growth has sharply increased over the last three years. According to several health care organizations and the U.S. Department of Health and Human Services, this trend should continue for the foreseeable future as the baby-boomer generation ages and increases its demand for health care. Currently, the area has 1,800 health care providers among the different professions, of which 92 work in the same field as I do. The legal and political environment favors the profession's inclusion on insurance panels. A lobbyist with the professional association said over the phone that the health care subcommittee greatly supports the profession. A large portion of the population carries health insurance coverage and only needs to make a copayment at time of service. During a recession, this should make demand for my health care services more inelastic, thus supporting steady price levels.

Marketplace Trends

This section outlines significant items occurring in the marketplace. The local transportation website lists several upcoming projects, none of which should impact my organization. Most patients are expected to come from roads with no current transportation improvement plans. Commercial office space around the area remains moderately priced, but prices may change as the economy expands. Barbara Jones, a reputable commercial lease agent with 20 years of experience, has been helping me search for office space and will work to ensure lease agreement terms are appropriate.

The western area has experienced the most population growth and economic development by providing cheap space for new inhabitants and companies. Efforts should be made to watch as new opportunities take shape in this part of the region.

Competitive Analysis

In talking with 15 established health care providers, most agreed that competitive forces are low. Only two with proximate offices in the southern part of the region mentioned high competitive pressures. When asked on a scale from 1 to 10 if they thought that their profit levels met expectations, the average score equaled 8.7. None of the health care providers expressed any complaints when asked about financial concerns.

Competitor List

Zone 1 contains 6 health care providers who work in my same health care field. Zones 2 and 3 contain 13 and 16 related health care providers, respectively. A description of the main competitors in Zone 1 follows.

Competitor 1 has practiced for 8 years and charges $100 for a standard visit. No other service lines are offered. Office hours occur during regular business hours and on Saturday every other weekend.

Competitor 2 has practiced for 16 years and offers a service line comparable to what this plan contains. Prices range from $90 to $120 per visit depending on the type of service obtained. There are no office hours on Thursday or the weekend.

Competitor 3 has practiced for 4 years and has several other licenses for unrelated service lines. Prices range from $60 to $150 per visit, but charges equal $100 for service lines that are similar to my own. The office is open during regular business hours and the health care provider accepts special appointments.

Competitor 4 has practiced for 23 years and is not taking new patients currently. Service lines compare to what this plan contains. Prices are between $105 and $130 per visit. The office is open during regular business hours, and the health care provider does not accept special appointments.

Competitor 5 has 3 years of experience and works underneath Competitor 4. Service lines are similar to the ones contained in this plan. Prices charged range between $85 and $95 per visit. The office is open during regular business hours and the health care provider accepts special appointments.

Competitor 6 has 14 years of experience and offers a broad range of services. Prices range from $80 to $140 per visit. The office is open during regular business hours and the health care provider accepts special appointments. I took Competitor 6 to lunch and was encouraged to start a practice in the area.

SWOT Analysis

The following is a well-recognized planning tool called a SWOT analysis to examine the organization's strengths, weaknesses, opportunities, and threats in relation to competitive pressures.

Strengths

The health care profession has evolved fairly significantly over the last ten years. As a graduating student, my patients will benefit by having access to the most up-to-date knowledge base. The intended location within the marketplace has strategic value and appears optimal based on conversations with current health care providers. An allocation of two hours per week dedicated to planning the organization has helped me gather information, analyze it, and plan accordingly.

Weaknesses

My experience level with marketing needs to increase. The services I make available will not be largely differentiated from competitors. I will need some time before perfecting the patient experience as well. My current network appears comparatively small despite efforts to build awareness in the community. Other well-established health care providers have large networks from which they generate referrals.

Opportunities

New development to the west should allow the marketplace to continually expand. Baby boomers in the 65 and older demographic should steadily represent a larger percentage of market participants accessing the health care industry. I could provide a greater range of services than competitors by obtaining additional certifications and licenses. I have a strong desire to learn new skills as a way of differentiating my services.

Threats

Unforeseen new entrants could make gaining marketshare harder. If current health care providers increase their service lines or decrease prices, those changes could make it harder to gain market share. Growth in the economy could falter, leading to a recession.

Substitutes

Market participants could access other nonprofessionals, especially if prices rise too high or a recession hits. Currently, the market for substitutes has remained small mainly because substitute services are of a lesser quality and remain relatively expensive. Based on phone calls to respective businesses, patients should expect to pay $50 to $60 to receive unlicensed services that meet lower standards of quality.

Service Offerings

Because the educational curriculum within health care schools has undergone dramatic transformation to reflect changes within the profession, I might have the opportunity to differentiate the treatment experience by offering services in an up-to-date manner.

Primary Services

Several primary service lines will be offered regardless of the circumstances. These appear comparable to existing competitors. The technique used should differ somewhat from competitors who received their education years ago. I have not considered modifying the service lines around a target market or demographic.

Secondary Services

To provide a better patient experience, I could acquire two certifications that very few competitors possess. These will allow me to offer a greater service mix if necessary. I do not intend to rely heavily on revenue from secondary services because I need to focus on gaining management skills first. I may at some point focus more heavily on secondary service lines to boost profitability as long as they do not cannibalize profit from my primary service lines.

Pricing

Initial prices should fall within the range of $80 to $90 per visit based on what competitors charge. After one year, I have made plans to adjust prices based on qualitative feedback and a quantitative cost-benefit analysis. One year should provide enough time to gauge the strength of demand factors and the ability of patients to access my services.

Future Services

If market conditions change significantly, I could acquire two other certifications. If a recession occurs or the political environment changes, I can conduct a cost-benefit analysis to verify if any additional forms of service would help the organization remain profitable.

Marketing Strategy

The following marketing strategy was created with a friend who has a background in marketing. A budget of $2,000 will be allocated to marketing efforts during the first year of operation and will grow at 10% per year for five years. In each of the next three years, a varied percentage of time spent on marketing will be allocated to each of the three predefined marketplace zones as listed in Table B.

TABLE B	Allocation of Marketing Time			
Total hours spent marketing are allocated to each marketplace zone according to the percentage rates shown.				
Year	Total Hours	Zone 1	Zone 2	Zone 3
One	200	80%	15%	5%
Two	150	75%	20%	5%
Three	100	70%	20%	10%

Network Participants

I currently belong to a community organization with about 200 active members. Many of these members have known me for several years and have shown great interest in my transition from student to health care provider. I have frequented two philanthropic organizations over the last year and I volunteer at the Food Bank. I have no family members residing inside the marketplace, but an uncle who used to live in the vicinity has put me in touch with friends. I have made friends of my own inside the marketplace and have created a list of 40 strong friendships and 135 acquaintances. I have put together a 22-page territory worksheet that lists people, places, events, and objects with additional notes on how each one holds value for marketing purposes.

Referral Sources

I will speak to close community members about referring new patients. My friend with a marketing background suggested giving out a $5 gift certificate to anyone who refers a patient. I plan to organize a one-time softball game to bring people together. In addition, my territory worksheet contains a listing of 300 businesses that might accept a request to meet for lunch (sales luncheon) in order to discuss referring customers. In an effort to more effectively communicate with network participants and referral sources, I have worked consistently with a fellow student one hour each week for the last year to practice sales techniques. The local community college regularly offers adult noncredit classes on sales techniques as well.

Marketing Tools

A graphic designer has designed my logo and business card. I currently hand out personal business cards with my general contact information on a regular basis. I learned how to put together a newsletter using online resources and expect to disseminate one on a quarterly basis. I put together a nice website using a free, all-in-one hosting service. The local radio station has a popular health show and related media spots are only $25 per airing. A minimum of 20 spots must be purchased in order to get a discount on production assistance. Mr. Bergman, director of marketing at the station, stated that a 15-second commercial should cost $400 to produce. The full cost of $900 ($25 × 20 spots + $400) to run the marketing campaign should generate awareness among listeners in all marketplace zones and greatly enhance other marketing efforts. A local print shop can produce 1,200 brochures for roughly $350 as well.

Patient Retention Strategy

As a student, I always strived for excellence. Graduating with honors and involvement in several extracurricular activities illustrate this commitment. My philosophy in practice will be to provide an excellent experience for each patient who walks through the door. Good planning beforehand will ensure that I am ready to grow a successful practice from the first day.

Exterior

With help from a commercial leasing agent, I am looking for office space in a specific area of town that does not experience much traffic congestion. The road system functions on a grid, so alternate routes generally exist if needed. The area has a good system of public transportation. The surrounding neighborhoods are densely populated and stores are placed uniformly throughout. Most commercial office buildings have well-kept exteriors and landscaping.

Interior

For the interior, $8,000 has been budgeted for office improvements and equipment. Most of the equipment can be purchased from classified postings listed on the professional association's website. An interior designer I met through another friend has agreed to help decorate the office at a low price. I have gathered subscription cards from magazines that together only cost $48 per year. A second TV that I own could provide entertainment for patients as they wait.

Staff Members

I will try to hire a regular staff member after two to four months in business, depending on profit levels. A temporary employee from a staffing agency will be used in the beginning to help at the front desk. I have received human resources documents and training manuals from another health care provider who recently retired.

Patient Care

Procedures under development will ensure that patients receive high-quality health care. Quality-control measures put in place will ensure that procedures are properly followed. In order to create a strong impression when meeting with patients, I started asking family members to send nice clothes as gifts. The licensing board requires 20 hours of continuing education classes each year. In order to maintain a reputation for quality, I will attend 40 hours in total.

Scheduling and Billing

A temporary employee will first help with scheduling until a full-time staff member comes onboard. Personnel will receive adequate training on how to greet patients, schedule appointments, and manage billing forms. A graphic designer has already created a reminder card with the organization's logo on the front. The office will remain open from 9 A.M. until 7 P.M. during the regular workweek at first, including half-days on Saturday. These longer hours of operation will continue until the practice grows.

CHAPTER ASSIGNMENT

Working in a group of three to four students or fellow professionals, complete the following items.

1. How might an insurance company respond to price discrimination? What are the advantages and disadvantages to running a cash practice?

2. Define price inelasticity and explain why the health care industry might not experience a sizable decrease in demand levels if prices increase. How might higher prices impact accessibility and profitability, especially when considering expenses?

3. Once an organization establishes its primary lines of service, what might cause the organization to hesitate about introducing additional lines of service? Under what circumstances would the introduction of secondary service lines lower overall profitability?

4. Call approximately ten health care providers and ask what general services they offer as well as their fees. Mention that the question relates to a homework assignment if necessary and assure the respondent that answers will be kept confidential. Create a list of responses using only general labels, that is, competitor 1 through competitor 10.

5. Each group member should formulate a marketing plan outline comparable to the hypothetical one presented in this chapter. Provide assistance to group members who know where they intend to practice and work together to list ideas under each heading.

General Accounting

AUTHOR'S NOTE

Health care providers often have an aversion to dealing
with money issues. Unfortunately, the world revolves
around money and the subject cannot be avoided. Ignoring
the need to understand the flow of money can easily translate into waste that ultimately costs patients. Instead of
requiring high levels of revenue to offset needless expenses,
an organization that runs efficiently can set prices lower for
patients and still achieve desired levels of net profit. This
chapter should provide enough knowledge to maneuver
through an accounting system without getting too lost. The
next chapter provides much more detail on how to treat
specific transactions. It's very important to understand the
general framework of an accounting system. The balance
sheet shows a complete history of all transactions whereas
the income statement takes a closer look at business activity
within the current period. The statement of retained earnings provides a vital link between these two reports. The
statement of cash flows represents another common financial statement, but this book does not provide coverage
because of its complex structure and limited value for a
small business.

Accounting concepts are vital for the internal administration of an organization and can take a fair amount of time to master. Fortunately, a health care provider can get by without extensive knowledge of accounting concepts by using the help of tax, legal, or bookkeeping experts. A basic understanding of accounting concepts will enable you to have a better discussion with these outside experts. Many individuals make a good living helping small business owners tackle the maze of rules and regulations—and usually have extensive networks with which to connect. Although it might cost $1,500 to have a tax return prepared, effective relationship-building techniques (professional sales) can be used to develop a very valuable referral source. Some of these technical functions can occur in-house at a much lower cost by gaining knowledge of accounting concepts and properly staffing your organization. It would be unrealistic to assume that a health care provider can acquire a sufficient understanding of technical matters to avoid using outside experts altogether. In fact, payroll should rarely occur in-house because of the related complexity and penalty repercussions for not filing correctly or on time.

Many small business owners understand accounting only to the extent necessary to gather information and send it to outside experts. However, accounting information can offer tremendous detail about both quantitative and qualitative events taking place within an organization. An organization can better understand elements of the patient experience and uncover problems by structuring the accounting system properly and knowing how to read the numbers. Imagine that revenue declined soon after hiring a new staff member. The numbers simply alert you to the fact that a problem exists. A new staff member might be impacting the patient experience directly, or perhaps insufficient marketing efforts were made during the previous month due to time being allocated to interviewing and training the new staff member. An examination should take place to determine what the numbers mean.

Accounting information plays a role among the financial and management concepts seen in later chapters. Becoming familiar with how accounting information flows will take time and experience. Each chapter builds a cumulative layer of understanding of accounting treatment, reporting, and analysis. After completing this section on accounting, consider the value of taking additional classes or watching online tutorials. Find bookkeeping software, such as Quickbooks, and use the program as a training mechanism. Staff members are invited to read through this book as well. In total, having knowledge of accounting will make bookkeeping duties easier, reduce the cost of using very expensive tax professionals, and equip you with the ability to produce and analyze information useful in running a successful organization.

Find online tutorials at youtube.com.

6.1   Introductory Concepts

The field of accounting has a collection of standard principles that guide the recording and reporting of financial information. Although an organization is welcome to record transactions in an individualized manner, following standard rules is important whenever third parties will rely on an organization's accounting information. A typical health care organization will need to report activity to tax authorities, lending institutions, and sometimes even investors—all of which may want the organization to follow strict reporting standards.

Double Entry

At the heart of accounting sit the almighty debit and credit. These two marvels oppose each other at every conceivable moment to help protect the integrity of data. Do not think of debits and credits in terms of positive and negative amounts. They are simply two sides of an equation of which the summation of one side must always equal the other. Accounting uses the **double-entry accounting system** as a *quality-control measure*. If total debits do not equal total credits, then the person inputting information knows automatically that an error exists. When faced with thousands of transactions over the course of a year, the double-entry system offers some protection against generating erroneous accounting information. Errors can still go undetected if the same double-sided entry is made twice or amounts are recorded to an improper account.

> **Double-Entry Accounting System:** A recording system for accounting information that uses debits and opposing credits as a quality-control measure.

Does making a double-sided entry result in the doubling up of amounts? Think of one side as an adjustment to cash and the other side as a *description* of what has transpired with cash. The vast majority of transactions will involve an increase or decrease in cash with only a small percentage involving noncash items. Various noncash items will be discussed later. As the debit or credit reflects the change to cash held in, say, a checking account, an opposing credit or debit describes what a transaction involves. The **description account** used in an entry is what provides the main detail for reporting purposes whereas the other side of the dual entry only modifies the cash account. Figure 6.1 illustrates the standard format used to record a double-sided entry.

> **Description Account:** An account that serves no other purpose than to describe what has occurred with cash or sometimes noncash items.

Materiality

Accurate information supports the decision-making process internally. An organization should strive to record information accurately 100% of the time since billing or collection errors can easily disrupt the patient experience. Externally, lending institutions and tax authorities usually only pay attention to *material* items. External parties will generally not care about items deemed immaterial. In order to verify the accuracy of accounting information, auditors representing an external party may come in to review a random sample of transactions. An audit will most likely ignore immaterial items unless they form part of a larger group of transactions or involve illegal activity. How is **materiality** defined exactly? Accounting professionals tend to have a better understanding of what

> **Materiality:** A quantitative benchmark constituting a significant amount set in reference to the particular circumstances of an organization or transaction.

FIGURE 6.1 Sample Double-Sided Entry

Account	Debit	Credit	
Cash	500		A debit always reflects an increase to cash.
Patient Revenue		500	A revenue account describes what occurred with cash and opposes the debit.
Payroll Expense	2,000		An expense account describes what occurred with cash and opposes the credit.
Cash		2,000	A credit always reflects a decrease to cash.

constitutes a material amount based on their experience looking at a range of businesses and transactions. A $9,000 error may seem material for a small health care organization, but that amount should not matter for a large-scale corporation. Every organization possesses a unique yardstick in terms of what constitutes a material amount and that yardstick may change depending on the circumstances. A health care organization should seek help from outside experts if faced with a situation that requires a judgment about materiality.

Accounting Methods

An accounting method sets forth a general framework to follow when recording and reporting information. The cash and accrual methods represent the two main accounting methods whereas the tax method incorporates tax rules into either of these other two main methods.

Cash Method   The **cash method** of accounting is the most basic type. Under the cash method, rules state that transactions are reportable events only when cash is exchanged. The use of checks and charge cards is considered *equivalent* to cash. Many external parties who need to review accurate accounting information do not favor the cash method since it allows more room for manipulation. After performing services, an organization can simply wait to bill customers and push recording revenue into the next time period. An organization with financial problems tends to wait longer before paying vendors, boosting net profit levels artificially.

Accrual Method   The **accrual method** differs from the cash method by requiring that transactions be recorded when a *business exchange* occurs. Manipulation becomes much more difficult because cash is not the specimen that defines when to record a transaction. For example, an organization will need to record having rendered services even if a patient has not yet paid. The double-sided entry used to record this event would not initially impact cash. Two description accounts would be used initially, and then once a patient pays for services, another double-sided entry would show the increase to cash and wipe away one of the original description accounts. Figure 6.2 compares the cash method with the accrual method.

For internal purposes, an organization might choose to follow the accrual method of accounting in order to support the decision-making process. The accrual method tends to provide the most accurate information for the purpose of business analysis and projecting future cash flows as explained in later chapters. An organization with substantial loans may face having to follow Generally Accepted Accounting Principles (GAAP), which are set forth by a special professional accounting board. Lending institutions

FIGURE 6.2 Comparison of Accounting Methods

Cash Method	Debit	Credit	
Cash	150		A debit records an increase to cash when received.
Patient Revenue		150	A revenue account describes the business exchange and opposes the debit.
Accrual Method	**Debit**	**Credit**	
Account Receivable	150		A debit account describes the status of cash.
Patient Revenue		150	A revenue account describes the business exchange and opposes the debit.
Cash	150		A debit records an increase to cash when received.
Account Receivable		150	The original account describing the status of cash is reversed.

may require compliance with GAAP per a loan agreement because such rules attempt to minimize accounting manipulation and provide a strict framework for presenting information. GAAP combines the accrual method of accounting along with additional reporting rules.

Tax Method   A hybrid basis of accounting called the **tax method** integrates tax rules with the cash method of accounting. Most small businesses use the cash method and incorporate elements of the tax code to the extent possible as a way of preparing information useful for compiling tax returns. Recording every transaction in full accordance with the tax code is not realistic because the tax code is highly complex and it changes frequently. A licensed tax professional should assist with the preparation of tax documents and make adjustments where necessary.

Historical Cost

Values recorded in the accounting system normally reflect the original purchase price of an item. If an item that was purchased subsequently increases in **market value**, the accounting system will not be adjusted to reflect that enhancement in value. An organization could make an adjustment for internal reporting purposes, but the tax code and GAAP do not permit an organization to present an increase to an item's market value. When looking at accounting reports of other organizations, bear in mind that the value being presented will represent historical cost and not current market value.

The tax code and GAAP may require adjustments for large *decreases* in market value. Inventory is often reported at either the current market value or historical cost—whichever is lower. Any subsequent increase in market value will not be captured later. In other words, if an item is modified for a decrease in value, it will remain reported at its reduced value until sold.

Summary

A double-sided accounting system that involves a debit on one side and a credit on the other serves as a quality-control measure ensuring amounts are recorded in full. In the majority of instances, one side of an entry impacts cash while the other side *describes* what has occurred with cash. An accounting system could still contain errors if a transaction is mistakenly recorded twice or the wrong description account is used. An organization should employ other quality-control measures to ensure all transactions are recorded accurately. Under most circumstances, a health care organization will follow the cash method of accounting to record transactions—and possibly make attempts to incorporate elements of the tax code. A transaction is not recorded until cash is exchanged according to the cash method. The accrual method of accounting requires that a transaction be recorded once a business exchange occurs and again when cash is finally exchanged. Values presented in accounting reports most likely reflect historical cost unless an adjustment has been made for a specific decline in market value.

6.2   Chart of Accounts

The **chart of accounts** exists as a list of all the accounts that an organization maintains and should be viewed as a highly fluid document that can be modified at any time. A typical chart of accounts is divided into seven different categories that correspond to time-honored reports that are common in the accounting profession: the balance sheet and income statement. The first three categories listed in Figure 6.3, **assets**, **liabilities**, and **equity**, contain accounts that flow directly into the *balance sheet*. The remaining four categories,

---

A lending institution will usually require compliance with GAAP when the loan is several million dollars or more.

Tax Method: System of accounting that incorporates tax code rules.

A licensed tax professional should be consulted when attempting to determine what type of accounting method an organization will need to follow for external reporting purposes.

Market Value: The price at which two willing parties agree to exchange goods or services.

Inventory is not reported under the cash method.

Chart of Accounts: A complete listing of active and inactive accounts used by an organization.

FIGURE 6.3 Chart of Accounts

The accounts listed are meant to serve as an example only and may not be used by your organization. All income statement accounts will eventually flow over to the balance sheet.

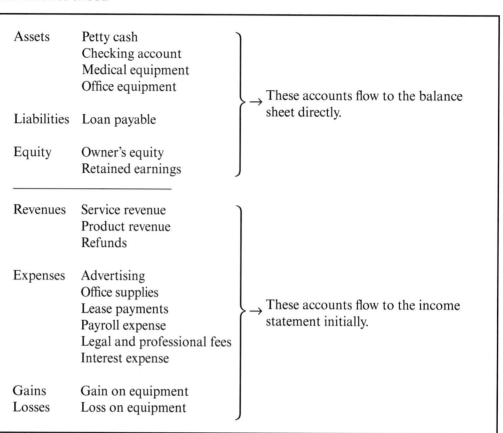

Assets: Items that have value extending into future time periods.

Liabilities: Obligations to pay that extend into future time periods.

Equity: The residual amount of value held by a business owner after subtracting liabilities from assets.

Certain equity accounts flow to the statement of retained earnings first before being transported onto the balance sheet.

Revenues: Inflow of value or cash as part of an ordinary business transaction.

Expenses: Outflow of value or cash necessary to support the production of revenue.

Gains: Inflow of value or cash as part of a nonstandard transaction (usually related to fixed assets).

Losses: Outflow of value or cash as part of a nonstandard transaction (usually related to fixed assets).

Journal Entry: A listing of debits and credits related to a transaction along with an explanation of the transaction.

Adjusting Journal Entry (AJE): A secondary journal entry used to modify amounts already recorded in the accounting system according to an original journal entry.

revenues, **expenses**, **gains**, and **losses**, contain accounts that flow to the *income statement*. The balance sheet presents a snapshot of items that hold value going into future time periods. Amounts relating to inflows and outflows from business activity in the current time period are captured in the income statement initially before being transported onto the balance sheet. Both of these reports are explained in more detail later.

Journal Entries

The accounting profession uses a standard format called a **journal entry** as a way of listing the debits and credits involved with a transaction. A journal entry begins by listing all debit items first, followed by all credit items (indented) second. A brief explanation is included to provide a better understanding of what a transaction involves. After making an original journal entry, it may become necessary to adjust amounts in the accounting system. Instead of erasing a journal entry and losing the record of activity, an **adjusting journal entry (AJE)** is used to modify a previously recorded transaction. In rare instances, a reversing journal entry (RJE) is used to correct timing differences. When using an RJE, the journal entry will appear in one time period and then an opposing RJE will clear amounts from a subsequent time period.

A journal entry can involve two or more accounts depending on the nature of a transaction. Figure 6.4 presents a hypothetical set of journal entries that could be used when setting up an organization. The first journal entry records three items related to money coming into the organization originally from a personal contribution and bank loan. The loan payable and owner's equity accounts are description accounts that let the reader

FIGURE 6.4 Recording Initial Business Activity

Account	Debit	Credit	
Cash	32,000		⟶ Balance Sheet
Loan Payable		22,000	⟶ Balance Sheet
Owner's Equity		10,000	⟶ Balance Sheet
To record a bank loan and owner's contribution deposited into the business checking account.			
Equipment	13,000		⟶ Balance Sheet
Cash		13,000	⟶ Balance Sheet
To record the purchase of a treatment table, six chairs, and a computer. See receipt for cost detail.			
Loss on Equipment	1,000		⟶ Income Statement
Equipment		1,000	⟶ Balance Sheet
To record loss on computer that suffered damages and was not under warranty.			

know more about the source of cash. The second journal entry shows that amounts were spent to purchase equipment. Again, the equipment account serves to describe what occurred with the cash. The third journal entry describes a noncash event wherein a piece of computer equipment was damaged and no longer holds any value for the organization. Since cash is not exchanged in this last event, both sides of the journal entry serve only as descriptions.

> Some adjusting journal entries are referred to as reclassifying journal entries if amounts are simply being moved between accounts within the same chart of accounts category.

General Ledger

The **general ledger** showcases a more detailed listing of the journalized transactions that have been posted to each account. Double-sided entries ensure that each transaction will show up in the general ledger under at least two separate accounts, one of which is usually cash. Accounting software programs typically allow a user to bring up the chart of accounts and then click through to a particular account to examine its detail. Figure 6.5 presents the general ledger for a hypothetical medical equipment account. Note how this general ledger presentation starts with a beginning balance and then includes a list of all transactions before showing the ending balance for the period. This new ending balance reflects what would be presented on the balance sheet under the asset category.

> **General Ledger:** Summary of all journalized transactions posted to each individual account.

Subsidiary Ledger

The use of a **subsidiary ledger** helps to summarize accounting information found within the general ledger in a more structured manner. Figure 6.6 shows the chart of accounts, general ledger, and subsidiary ledger related to accounts payable. The general ledger

> **Subsidiary Ledger:** Detailed listing of information within a particular general ledger account categorized by relevant criteria.

FIGURE 6.5 General Ledger

A general ledger presents all the detail of each transaction contained within a particular account.

Chart of Accounts		General Ledger	
Assets	Petty Cash	**Medical Equipment**	
	Checking Account	Beginning Balance	–
	Medical Equipment	Purchased new treatment table	7,200
	Office Equipment	Sold old treatment table	(1,200)
		Purchased used x-ray machine	12,000
		Ending Balance	18,000

FIGURE 6.6 Subsidiary Ledger

A subsidiary ledger categorizes transactions shown in a general ledger. Accounts payable usually only apply to the accrual method of accounting and not to the cash method. However, the accounting system should still house a record of amounts owed to vendors.

Chart of Accounts		Subsidiary Ledger		
Accounts Payable	1,250	**Accounts Payable**		
		Bagel Palace	25	
		Total Bagel Palace		25
General Ledger				
Accounts Payable		HR Design Services	150	
Beginning Balance	—	HR Design Services	175	
HR Design Services	150	Total HR Design Services		325
Payroll Service Center	75			
J&L Legal Firm	680	J&L Legal Firm	680	
HR Design Services	175	Total J&L Legal Firm		680
Payroll Service Center	145			
Bagel Palace	25	Payroll Service Center	75	
Ending Balance	1,250	Payroll Service Center	145	
		Total Payroll Service Center		220
		Total Accounts Payable		1,250

may show detail on the individual accounts payable, but the subsidiary ledger further categorizes amounts according to each particular vendor. Subsidiary ledgers are typically used to better categorize accounts receivable, accounts payable, and inventory based on relevant criteria.

Summary

Setting up an accounting system begins by arranging a chart of accounts, which represents a complete listing of accounts an organization intends to use. The chart of accounts should be divided into seven categories. Asset, liability, and equity accounts flow to the balance sheet while revenue, expense, gain, and loss accounts flow to the income statement. A journal entry represents the standard format used to list the debits and credits involved with a transaction along with a brief explanation. Once a transaction is posted using a journal entry, an adjusting journal entry can be used to modify amounts if necessary, but the original journal entry is always left untouched. The journal entries posted to each account are displayed in a general ledger. A subsidiary ledger can be used to better categorize transactions reported on the general ledger according to relevant criteria.

6.3 Financial Statements

A massive collection of accounting information would be hard to understand if only presented in a ledger format. The accounting profession makes use of a standard set of reports called the financial statements to present information in a more coherent manner. This chapter provides an overview of the balance sheet, income statement, and statement of retained earnings whereas the next chapter goes into more detail on how to record specific transactions and present information on each financial statement. The statement of cash flows can be created to describe the sources and uses of cash according to operating, investing, and financing activities. Because the statement of cash flows can be difficult to produce and may not provide the best information compared to other reports, this chapter excludes a discussion on this statement.

Balance Sheet

Items that relate to more than one time period are posted to a balance sheet account. Think of this in terms of what would happen if an organization closed its doors and did not see one more patient. The assets of an organization carry a positive value and could be converted (in theory) into cash to pay liabilities. The liabilities represent obligations that must be satisfied before a business owner can pocket any value as equity. The equity balance is what remains after subtracting liabilities from assets. As such, the balance sheet must always *balance*.

Liabilities
+ Equity
= Assets

The balance sheet does not offer a perfect assessment of the true market value of equity because accounting information is normally presented at *historical cost*. The market value of assets will change according to demand and supply factors, but the balance sheet will *not* change accordingly. The extent to which assets can truly cover liabilities represents the market value of equity possessed by a business owner. This true market value of equity will almost always differ from what the balance sheet presents—this difference could range from something minor to a substantial amount in either an upward or downward direction.

In rare situations, when an asset has lost considerable value, an **impairment** might need to be recorded, causing the balance sheet to present a value lower than historical cost. An asset subject to impairment normally remains at its reduced value until sold. Proper balance sheet presentation normally does not allow for upward adjustments upon any subsequent increase in an asset's market value. Most liabilities are not readily bought or sold in the marketplace and rarely change in market value. In other words, no one really wants to buy your obligation to pay something.

Impairment: Adjusting an asset's historical cost downward to reflect a material reduction in the asset's market value.

Figure 6.7 reflects a sample balance sheet with only a few accounts. The presentation of balance sheet accounts follows a general set of rules. Assets are reported first and normally show as debit balances, although certain credit balances are listed under the asset category. The liability and equity accounts are reported next in a combined listing and normally involve credit balances. The asset side must equal the combined total of liabilities and equity. It's important not to view credit balances as positive or negative figures because liabilities reveal obligations of an organization and equity accounts report value held by owners (at historical cost). A debit balance reported under the equity section usually results from an organization experiencing net losses.

The general order of accounts listed on the balance sheet relates to how long the underlying amounts will be a concern. Cash is listed first while other asset accounts are listed in order of their general **liquidity**, which is the ability to convert an asset into cash. On the liability side, the account order is the general due date of the underlying obligations. The order of both asset and liability accounts usually follows a standard sequence. Pay attention to the order of accounts in sample balance sheets found in this book as they allude to this standard order.

Liquidity: Reflects the rate at which an asset can be converted into cash.

Income Statement

Accounts used to report standard and nonstandard business activity flow to the income statement. Revenue accounts show inflows of value or cash from standard activity while expenses reflect outflows of value or cash meant to support the production of revenue. Not all expenses are immediately placed on the income statement, however. Accounting methods try to match expenses against the revenue they help generate and a particular expense may support the generation of revenue across multiple time periods. A larger expense that

FIGURE 6.7 Sample Balance Sheet

Note the account order in this sample balance sheet along with how assets equal the total of liabilities and equity. A balance sheet prepared according to the accrual method of accounting would most likely present different amounts.

Balance Sheet - Cash Method		
For the month ending January 31		
Assets		
Petty cash	200	
Checking account	1,950	
Medical equipment	18,000	
Office equipment	6,500	
Total assets		26,650
Liabilities		
Loan payable	22,000	
Total liabilities		22,000
Equity		
Owner's equity	10,000	
Retained earnings	(5,350)	
Total equity		4,650
Total liabilities and equity		26,650

Capitalization: The act of taking a material expense applicable to multiple time periods and holding it on the balance sheet.

Depreciation Expense: The amount of a capitalized expense that is applied to a specific time period.

Careful! An organization's capitalization policy should consider requirements set by external parties, such as tax authorities. Consult a licensed tax professional to verify what items can be expensed and what must be capitalized.

applies to more than one time period would be subject to **capitalization** on the balance sheet, and then part of the amount capitalized would flow to the income statement as **depreciation expense** in each of the relevant time periods. For example, the cost of a treatment table might be capitalized on the balance sheet at first and then the cost of that table would be apportioned to the income statement over the next several years. Expenses deemed immaterial or which do not support the production of revenue over multiple time periods would be fully expensed on the income statement in the current period. For instance, a $22 clock may continue running for several years, but the full amount is immaterial and should be expensed when purchased.

An organization must review the *materiality* of an item before deciding upon its proper treatment. This level of materiality for a small to midsized health care organization normally ranges between $500 and $1,000, meaning that anything below this level would be fully expensed on the income statement in the current time period even in situations where an expense supports the production of revenue over multiple time periods. Of course, large expenses above this threshold would also be fully expensed if they only support the production of revenue within the current time period. An organization will need to establish a *capitalization policy* that clearly outlines how items should be treated.

Once an expense becomes capitalized on the balance sheet, it will remain presented in full as a *fixed asset* until sold. The portion that represents depreciation expense is shown as an offset to the fixed asset account and does not impact the value of fixed assets directly. Suppose a treatment table has a useful life of seven years. In each of those seven years, a percentage of the treatment table's cost would flow to the income statement as depreciation expense. The accumulated amounts for depreciation would be reported on the balance sheet separately. The historical cost of the treatment table would not be modified until sold. The overall net value of fixed assets shown on the balance sheet would be indirectly reduced by the *accumulated depreciation* being reported. Although an organization may calculate depreciation expense, a licensed tax professional will usually make an adjusting journal entry once a year to correct for any miscalculations.

Methods of calculating depreciation are examined in greater depth in Chapter 7.

When fixed assets on the balance sheet are eventually sold, the *net* value of the item must be considered. An asset's net value reflects the historical cost still presented on the balance sheet less any accumulated depreciation as presented. Land is the only long-term asset not subject to depreciation—although improvements made to land are often capitalized and subject to depreciation. A gain occurs when the sales price (market value) of an asset is greater than its net value reported on the balance sheet. A loss reflects how an asset was sold for less than its net balance sheet value. Gains and losses involve *nonstandard* business activity, such as the sale of capitalized assets, and are usually reported separately at the bottom of the income statement. The main section of the income statement is reserved for transactions involving *standard* business activity.

Selling fixed assets is not an everyday part of your business. As such, the sale of fixed assets is presented separately on the income statement.

CASE STUDY

Financial Statement Preparation

Suppose after building relationships with network participants and referral sources, a health care organization is able to generate some new patients. This health care organization plans on following the cash method of accounting and will record transactions only when cash actually exchanges hands. The journal entries presented in Figure 6.8 are used to record activity from operations occurring in the first month.

FIGURE 6.8 Recording Operating Activity

Account	Debit	Credit	
Cash	225		→ Balance Sheet
Service Revenue		225	→ Income Statement
To record copayments received from patients during the first week of operations.			
Cash	475		→ Balance Sheet
Service Revenue		375	→ Income Statement
Product Revenue		100	→ Income Statement
To record copayments received from patients and the sale of supplements.			
Payroll Expense	1,450		→ Income Statement
Cash		1,450	→ Balance Sheet
To record amounts paid for biweekly wages.			
Lease Payments	1,500		→ Income Statement
Cash		1,500	→ Balance Sheet
To record the monthly lease payment due before month's end.			
Legal and Professional Fees	3,100		→ Income Statement
Cash		3,100	→ Balance Sheet
To record legal fees related to filing incorporation documents.			
Depreciation Expense	3,500		→ Income Statement
Accumulated Depreciation		3,500	→ Balance Sheet
To record depreciation on equipment.			

Since this organization uses the cash method, copayments are journalized immediately as cash is exchanged, but the full amount due from having rendered services will not be recorded until the remaining amounts are received from third-party payors. In terms of fixed assets, a bit of value has been sliced from the balance sheet and passed over to the income statement as depreciation expense. Figure 6.9 reflects how the income statement would appear after posting these journal entries.

FIGURE 6.9 Sample Income Statement

Income Statement - Cash Method For the month ending January 31		
Revenues		
Product revenue	100	
Service revenue	600	
Total revenues		700
Expenses		
Depreciation expense	3,500	
Lease payments	1,500	
Legal and professional fees	3,100	
Payroll expense	1,450	
Total expenses		9,550
Net profit (or loss) from operations		(8,850)

The accounts are also listed in alphabetical order on the income statement with revenues being separated from expenses. The income statement currently shows a net loss because revenue will not be received from third-party payors right away. Note how revenues and expenses are shown as positive amounts on the income statement even though expenses will be deducted to arrive at net profit (or loss). Only the net loss figure is shown as a negative amount.

Balance Sheet Result

As a result of the journal entry related to depreciation, the balance sheet shown in Figure 6.7 would change according to what is illustrated in Figure 6.10. Total assets in this sample balance sheet dropped by $3,500, reflecting *accumulated depreciation* on equipment. The historical cost of the individual fixed assets reported on the balance sheet is not impacted by this entry. Since the income statement becomes rolled into retained earnings, the $3,500 of depreciation expense placed on the income statement eventually reduces the equity section of the balance sheet. Because both the asset side and the equity side of the balance sheet drop by $3,500, the balance sheet remains in balance. The journal entry used to record this transaction would involve a debit to depreciation expense followed by a credit to accumulated depreciation. Note how both accounts are noncash items involving descriptions only. The actual cash traded hands previously when the individual fixed assets were purchased.

FIGURE 6.10 Sample Balance Sheet (updated)

Balance Sheet - Cash Method
For the month ending January 31

Assets

Petty cash	200	
Checking account	1,950	
Medical equipment	18,000	
Office equipment	6,500	
Accumulated depreciation	(3,500)	
Total assets		23,150

Liabilities

Loan payable	22,000	
Total liabilities		22,000

Equity

Owner's equity	10,000	
Retained earnings	(8,850)	
Total equity		1,150
Total liabilities and equity		23,150

Statement of Retained Earnings

The double-entry system of accounting requires that all credits and debits be presented on the balance sheet. How exactly do all these amounts reported on all the various financial statements find their way onto the balance sheet? Revenue, expense, gain, and loss accounts flow to the income statement first. They are then netted together and placed on the statement of retained earnings. The asset, liability, and equity accounts flow directly to the balance sheet except for distributions made to owners. The statement of retained earnings could be considered a mixing bowl where the net earnings (or loss) coming from the income statement is further netted against owner distributions. Upon deducting owner distributions from net earnings, the remaining balance reflects the earnings that have been *retained* by an organization. Figure 6.11 illustrates how accounts flow among the various financial statements. *The income statement accounts and owner distribution account are what make up the retained earnings account presented in the equity section of the balance sheet.* The retained earnings account on the balance sheet represents a collection of all the profits (and losses) that have been accumulated by an organization over time along with any distributions of profit to owners.

The statement of retained earnings can present details on other equity accounts as well out of convenience to the reader. When a health care provider starts an organization from scratch, the retained earnings account will equal zero since there is no profit (or loss) from a prior period. As operations continue across multiple time periods, net earnings as reported on the income statement can be retained by an organization or distributed

FIGURE 6.11 Flow of Accounts

Net earnings that are *not* distributed are *retained* and presented on the equity section of the balance sheet as *retained earnings* (RE).

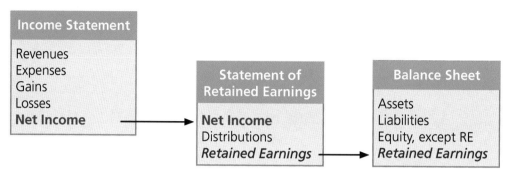

to owners. Earnings are generally not retained indefinitely but distributed to owners at strategic points in time bearing in mind the need to reinvest profit to fund new projects or ventures. The owner of an organization will want to weigh the benefit of keeping money inside an organization for growth against the desire to make a distribution for personal use.

In the sample shown in Figure 6.12, no distributions have been made because the retained earnings account shows a loss. The following statement of retained earnings presents additional information on equity accounts, such as owner contributions and owner's equity.

FIGURE 6.12 Sample Statement of Retained Earnings

Statement of Retained Earnings - Cash Method	
For the month ending January 31	
Beginning retained earnings	—
Net profit or loss	(8,850)
Distributions	—
Ending retained earnings	(8,850)
Contributions	10,000
Total owner's equity	1,150

Summary

The accounting profession uses four standard reports called the financial statements to present accounting information. The balance sheet contains all the amounts ever posted to the accounting system via journal entries. The income statement presents the revenue, expense, gain, and loss accounts related to the current time period only. The net amount of these various income statement accounts flows to the statement of retained earnings before continuing forward to the balance sheet. Owner distributions are also reported on the statement of retained earnings and reduce the amount of earnings *retained* by an organization. The statement of cash flows has not been included in this book because of its complexity and limited use for a small business.

6.4   Bookkeeping

Bookkeeping refers to the tasks involved in maintaining accurate accounting records. When using a software program to perform bookkeeping functions, journal entries post digitally and balances are automatically modified in the accounting records. An organization may still need to maintain paper documentation to ensure that proper support exists for amounts reported in the accounting system unless the paper documents are scanned into a digital file.

Bookkeeping Documents

Tax authorities require that an expense have a legitimate business purpose; otherwise, it cannot be used to reduce taxable income. Tax authorities recommend keeping all receipts and writing notes about their specific business purpose on the reverse side. Since almost every transaction involves cash, bank statements serve as an additional means of support for accounting records. Many banks allow businesses to download records directly into a software program via a transaction file, greatly reducing the time spent inputting data. Proper explanations need to be written on transactions uploaded into the accounting system. Memories fade, hence detailed explanations assist with finding and understanding accounting records.

> Feel free to stuff all your receipts in a brown paper bag with the year written on the front side in case your organization is ever audited by an external party.

An organization will also make use of several different types of bookkeeping documents when communicating with external parties about requesting or making payment.

Requesting Payment   In an attempt to request payment from a patient or third-party payor, an organization will send an **invoice** outlining the amount due, length of time the amount has been outstanding, and method for submission. If payment is not received after a fair amount of time has passed (90 to 180 days), an organization should begin to communicate differently in order to hasten payment. Figure 6.13 provides a sample of what an invoice should communicate.

> **Invoice:** A document used to request payment from an external party that includes relevant payment terms.

Making Payment   Large organizations typically require that an authorized **purchase order** be filled out before buying products or services from an external vendor. The purchase order would go to the vendor and act as a request form. A copy of the purchase order would be retained by the organization making the request and would be matched against the actual products once they were delivered along with an *invoice* that the vendor provides. All documents would be forwarded to the accounting department to be reviewed and recorded. If the documents appear legitimate and proper, a **payment voucher** would be drafted. The payment voucher, invoice, and purchase order would finally be sent to the accounts payable department in order to have a check issued.

> **Purchase Order:** A form used to make a request for services or products.

This documentation process might not contain as many steps in a smaller health care organization. Most small businesses do not use purchase orders or payment vouchers. Still, an organization should have systems in place to ensure the accuracy and legitimacy of amounts paid to external parties. An organization member should at least review vendor invoices, figure out if products were actually received, and then confirm later that proper payment was made. A different organization member should be responsible for issuing checks based on the receipt of valid invoices from vendors. In order to assist the vendor, each check stub should include the vendor's original invoice number or some other explanation of the check's purpose. A vendor might receive thousands of checks daily and could easily make a recording error without proper notation from your organization. In addition to an invoice, a vendor might send a *debit memo* to report any payment deficiency or issue a *credit memo* to reflect an overpayment or purchase return.

> **Payment Voucher:** An internal petition used to request payment be made to an external party.

FIGURE 6.13
Sample Invoice
Statement

INVOICE

Office Phone Number	**Invoice Date** 7/31/13
503-757-1076	
	Invoice Number 36275634
Mailing Address	
PO Box 1182	**Current Balance** 91.00
Portland, OR 97207	

Service Date	Description	Total Charges	Insurance Coverage	Patient Balance
5/5/13	Initial Visit	200.00	(120.00)	80.00
6/15/13	Venipuncture	15.00	(4.00)	11.00

Under 30 Days	Over 30 Days	Over 60 Days	Over 90 Days	Overdue Charges
0.00	11.00	80.00	0.00	0.00

Please make checks payable to **XYZ Clinic**.

The patient balance is due within 30 days of the invoice date.
Overdue charges sent to a collections agency will incur additional fees.

Internal Controls

> Internal control measures are similar to quality-control measures except the former refers more specifically to the integrity of administrative processes instead of the quality of products and services.

An organization that hires employees or independent contractors to perform administrative tasks needs to maintain proper *internal controls* over accounting functions in an effort to prevent errors and fraud. A business owner will likely have a staff member attempt to commit theft at some point. Ensure that job functions are properly *segregated*, meaning that one staff member should not have sole and complete control over an administrative process. Either an organization member's work needs to be reviewed or the organization member should only be allowed to perform part of a full job process. For example, an organization member who has the ability to modify the accounting system should not be allowed to handle any item sensitive to theft, such as cash.

Revenue Controls   When one organization member can receive money from patients and also modify data in the accounting system, that arrangement leaves tremendous room for the theft of cash without any recorded trace. Internal controls should be instituted to prevent errors related to the billing process as well. If amounts are incorrectly billed to patients or third-party payors, an organization may not receive the full amount due or overbilling might cause the patient experience to sour. Consider the following process for handling payments.

1. An organization member picks up mail each morning at the post office.
2. Checks are separated and listed individually on a bank deposit slip. The slip is handed to the business owner for verification purposes.

3. A different organization member takes the checks and updates accounting records and patient files. A daily report is then generated, showing the journal entry made to record the checks. The checks, bank deposit slip, and accounting report are handed back to the business owner for verification purposes.

4. The business owner reviews the journal entry to confirm that the checks were posted to the right patient accounts and in the correct amounts. The report is also compared to the bank deposit slip received earlier in the day to confirm that none of the checks has gone missing.

5. After work, the business owner delivers the checks along with the deposit slip to the bank.

Because this business owner has taken the time to review accounting information and job duties have been properly segregated, the possibility for errors or fraud has been minimized. An organization could further segregate duties by using an external bookkeeper to compile accounting records instead of an internal staff member. An external bookkeeper would not have access to checks being received through the mail; thus, would not have an opportunity to simultaneously steal checks and modify accounting records.

Expense Controls   To illustrate with another example, imagine that a staff member has ties to another business. That other business could submit an illegitimate invoice, allowing the staff member to make payment fraudulently. The staff member would post information to the accounting system correctly but has been allowed to pay an illegitimate invoice sent in by an accomplice. The staff member should not be allowed to write a check to an *unknown* vendor. In order to place a new vendor in the system, another organization member should review the vendor beforehand for internal control purposes and then review the check register on occasion to verify the legitimacy of checks written to *known* vendors. Software programs often come equipped with internal control measures that govern what users can and cannot do.

> A health care provider working alone would not need to segregate job duties to prevent fraud. Internal-control measures should still be in place to prevent errors.

Summary

Bookkeeping functions involve administrative tasks related to accounting records. An organization will normally collect money by sending an invoice that includes where to submit payment, the amount due, and how long amounts have been outstanding. The opposite occurs when purchasing items wherein a vendor will be the one sending an invoice. Internal control measures protect the organization against error or fraud in receiving money or paying vendor invoices.

CHAPTER ASSIGNMENT

Working in a group of three to four students or fellow professionals, complete the following items.

1. What is the purpose of the double-entry accounting system? What do the debits and credits represent?

2. What does it mean to use a description account and how would such an account oppose cash?

3. Please provide a definition for each of the seven categories of accounts: asset, liability, equity, revenue, expense, gain, and loss. To what accounting report(s) do these accounts originally flow?

4. Describe the difference between a journal entry and an adjusting journal entry.

5. Suppose an organization just received $244 to cover payment for services administered to a patient the previous month. Write two sets of journal entries according to the cash method and accrual method of accounting.

6. Explain the difference between a general ledger and a subsidiary ledger. How might a subsidiary ledger be structured in relation to the accounts receivable, accounts payable, or inventory account?

7. What is the total amount of liabilities presented on the balance sheet if net assets equal $50,000 and an organization has negative $5,000 in equity?

8. Under what circumstances would you increase the value of an asset to reflect its current market value? When might you record an impairment?

9. How does the statement of retained earnings link the income statement to the balance sheet? What account(s) are normally listed on the statement of retained earnings?

10. Write a journal entry to report the purchase of the following long-term equipment: an $800 computer, a $1,500 treatment table, and a $2,300 telephone system. Assume that the organization has a capitalization policy of $1,000 that complies with what tax authorities prescribe.

11. What might happen if a tax authority audits an organization and expenses cannot be supported with documentation? What type of documentation could an organization provide?

12. Why is it important to prevent one person from both handling cash and being allowed access to modify the accounting system?

Accounting Treatment

AUTHOR'S NOTE

Make sure you thoroughly understand the difference between the cash method and the accrual method of accounting before tackling this chapter. You may need to revisit the explanation of accounting methods in Chapter 6. Pay close attention to whether the cash method or the accrual method is being explained, or when the explanation of accounting treatment applies to both methods. Do not become overwhelmed by all the rules presented in this chapter. You will probably always need to work with accounting professionals throughout your entire career because of the sheer complexity—and not all of the complexity you will be faced with is presented here. Becoming familiar with these concepts will minimize the need to rely on expensive outside professionals and it will empower you to manage your organization better.

The financial statements serve as a great starting point for discussing how to account for transactions properly. Revenues, expenses, gains, and losses flow to the income statement originally. The net balance of earnings from the income statement is rolled into the statement of retained earnings, causing the income statement accounts to be reset to zero each period. The net earnings figure presented on the statement of retained earnings is reduced by any owner distributions. Any remainder of earnings that have not been distributed represent value that will be *retained* for future time periods. As such, retained earnings are transferred to the balance sheet and presented along with all other amounts that will carry forward into future time periods, including assets, liabilities, and other equity accounts. Since all debits and credits eventually flow to the balance sheet, either directly or indirectly, most of the rules governing the proper presentation of accounting information involve the balance sheet.

There is a fairly extensive list of rules that govern the appropriate presentation of financial statements. Tax authorities add to these rules in an attempt to clearly isolate taxable income. If an organization takes out substantial loans, a lending institution can further add to this list by requiring that accounting information be presented in accordance with Generally Accepted Accounting Principles (GAAP). By following GAAP, an organization is less able to manipulate information and a common framework is used to present accounting information to external parties. A loan agreement will specify if GAAP statements are required and also what will happen if an organization's financial position deteriorates too much. Instead of allowing an organization to consume all loan proceeds in times of distress, a lending institution will look at the financial statements and force bankruptcy in order to recuperate as much loan balance as possible. It is uncommon for banks to require small or midsized companies to compile financial data according to GAAP. *Most small and mid-sized organizations follow a modified cash method of accounting that incorporates tax rules to the extent possible.* At year's end, a licensed tax professional will take accounting information and make adjusting journal entries that correct any bookkeeping mistakes and isolate taxable income.

An organization that follows the cash method for external purposes may want to follow the accrual method internally in order to conduct business analysis as explained in later chapters. Many accounting software programs allow users to switch back and forth between these two accounting methods by a mere click of the mouse. Although many elements of the accrual method are explained here, this chapter does not attempt to include all the rules regarding complete presentation according to GAAP or the tax method. This chapter extends the discussion of financial statements, excluding the statement of cash flows.

7.1 Balance Sheet

At a given point in time, the balance sheet gives the reader an overview of what amounts will carry forward into future time periods. Assets are ordinarily reported at cost (or lower if transferred in) and do not generally reflect market value. If a business suddenly closes, the assets would need to be converted into cash to cover liabilities. Any amount that remained after satisfying liabilities would flow to equity holders. The exact amounts that would be involved with such an event cannot be determined by looking at the current balance sheet since it reports amounts at their historical cost.

If transactions will be completed within one year, amounts within an account are listed within the *current* section of the balance sheet. Accounts that involve amounts extending beyond one year are reported as noncurrent or long term. An account may have amounts in both the current and noncurrent sections of the balance sheet based on timing differences.

Assets

An organization should strive to possess assets that will produce the greatest amount of value in the future. Holding onto cash for strategic purposes, as during a recession, might be in an organization's best interest. An organization will want to continually look for new *productive assets* to purchase and seek ways to increase the productivity of current assets. In cases where new assets will not add value and cash serves no strategic purpose, a business owner should consider making a distribution.

> A new asset becomes productive when it leads to increases in net profit levels.

Asset accounts are typically listed according to their general *liquidity*, meaning how quickly they can be converted into cash. This has led to a commonly accepted order in which to present asset accounts. Figure 7.1 reflects the asset section of a sample balance sheet under the accrual method of accounting. This asset section is referenced throughout the next part of this chapter to exemplify concepts. A cash method balance sheet would not contain all the accounts shown.

> Pay attention to the order in which accounts are listed in this chapter.

A. Cash and Cash Equivalents It is customary for businesses to hold cash in multiple places, including a checking account or a clinic's petty-cash lockbox. In either case, the actual cash or **cash equivalent** used to carry out a transaction may include hard currency, a check, cashier's check, money order, or debit card. When making payments using these instruments, the *outflow* of cash would be recorded when amounts are made available to the other party. As soon as a check is placed in the mail or a debit card is swiped, cash, in theory, has been encumbered and no longer remains the organization's property. However, when sending a *postdated* check, a liability account will need to be established until passage of the date printed on the check or earlier if a bank processes the check prematurely.

> Cash Equivalent: Any financial instrument that can function like cash, such as a check or charge card.

An organization can wait until a credit card statement arrives to report amounts using the dates listed by the credit card company in relation to each particular transaction. The actual transaction may have occurred a few days before its posting date, but using the later credit card date is an accepted practice. Not paying a credit card balance in full gives rise to a liability (account payable) on the unpaid portion even under the cash method since a credit card transaction equates to borrowing money. Overpaying a credit card has the opposite effect whereby an account receivable would be established since an organization did not consummate a valid transaction and no expense exists.

> These rules apply to both the cash and accrual methods.

An *inflow* of cash occurs when currency or a check arrives in the mail, is handed to an organization member, or a charge card is swiped. Combining bank accounts on the balance sheet would make it difficult to manage bank account balances properly. Each bank account should be separately presented on the balance sheet in case an *overdraft* occurs. If an overdraft is not fixed and a negative balance remains, this amount should be classified as a current liability. Although the entire cash balance may be positive, an overdraft occurring in one bank account should be moved to the liability section of the balance sheet.

FIGURE 7.1 Sample Balance Sheet (asset side)

The alphabetic values A through H correspond to the explanation of asset accounts.

	Balance Sheet - Accrual Method *For the year ending December 31*		
			2012
	Assets		
	Current assets		
A	Petty cash	350	
A	Checking account — general	4,295	
A	Checking account — payroll	2,850	
B	Investments	1,588	
C	Accounts receivable, net	8,964	
D	Inventory	377	
E	Prepaid expenses	200	
F	Current portion of note receivable	3,000	
	Total current assets		21,624
F	**Note receivable**		9,000
	Fixed assets		
G	Office equipment	6,200	
G	Medical equipment	20,000	
G	Building	185,000	
G	Land	40,000	
G	Accumulated depreciation	(18,450)	
	Fixed assets, net		232,750
	Intangible assets		
H	Organizational costs	2,500	
H	Accumulated amortization	(333)	
	Intangible assets, net		2,167
	TOTAL ASSETS		265,541

Bank Reconciliation: The process of matching the cash balance reported on a bank statement against the corresponding cash balance reported on the balance sheet.

Bank Reconciliation

Since nearly all transactions involve cash, a bank statement functions as an effective internal control measure over the accounting system. Amounts reported in an organization's accounting system might differ from what a bank reports, either due to an error or transaction delay. A **bank reconciliation** takes the cash balance reported by a bank and accounts for any unprocessed transactions. A transaction delay can involve a deposit that a bank has not processed yet. A bank statement would underreport the cash balance as compared to the accounting system in this case. An organization might also have made a purchase and recorded the event as an outflow of cash, but a bank may not have processed the transaction yet. Most delays involve checks or debit card transactions because they can be routed through various channels before being processed by a bank. Until a bank processes an outflow of cash, the bank statement will overstate the cash balance as compared to the accounting system. If amounts still do not reconcile after making adjustments, an organization knows a recording error has been made, setting off an oftentimes difficult hunt to find the mistake.

BANK RECORD

Consider using a charge card or check to make every transaction so that the bank will house a record of transactions. If documentation is lost or damaged, your organization will have a secondary record maintained by the bank. Recording errors are also minimized since two entities—your organization and the bank—are compiling accounting information separately.

In conducting a bank reconciliation, an organization should list each bank account separately as illustrated in Figure 7.2 and have the corresponding bank statements. An organization should note the date range on a bank statement or download an online bank statement according to a specific date range and compare what is listed in the accounting system using that same date range. Starting with a bank statement balance, add any deposits the bank has not processed yet. Then, subtract any checks or purchase transactions reported in the accounting system that have not yet cleared the bank. By adding unreported cash inflows and subtracting unreported cash outflows, a bank statement should reconcile to the corresponding cash account reported on the balance sheet.

FIGURE 7.2 Cash Accounts

Each cash account is listed separately on the balance sheet to assist the reader.

Balance Sheet	
For the year ending December 31	
Assets	
Current assets	
Petty cash	350
Checking account — general	4,295
Checking account — payroll	2,850

The reconciliation of the general checking account as listed in Figure 7.3 shows a difference of $54, meaning that (1) an amount has been left off the reconciliation by mistake, (2) the organization has made an accounting error, or (3) the bank has made an accounting error. Tracking down an error does not have to involve multiple time periods if bank accounts are reconciled often. The bank reconciliation of the payroll checking account balances in this example, but it indicates that an overdraft could occur if the checks clear before the deposit is processed. An organization should watch to make sure a cash balance does not turn negative in order to protect against overdraft fees and bounced checks.

FIGURE 7.3 Bank Reconciliation

Add cash deposits and subtract purchase transactions that have not been processed by the bank yet in order to reconcile the cash balance for each bank account listed on the balance sheet.

Checking Account — General			Checking Account — Payroll		
Balance per bank statement		5,423	Balance per bank statement		1,343
Add: deposits in transit	1,400		Add: deposits in transit		3,500
	986		Less: checks issued #344	(84)	
		2,386	#348	(440)	
Less: debit card transactions	(245)		#349	(622)	
	(1,682)		#350	(847)	
	(361)				(1,993)
	(894)		Balance per reconciliation		2,850
	(278)				
		(3,460)	Balance per balance sheet		2,850
Balance per reconciliation		4,349			
			Difference		–
Balance per balance sheet		4,295			
Difference		54			

B. Investments An increasingly popular way to hold cash is amid a money market account managed by an investment company. Investment companies have started offering features similar to what a regular bank offers, including check and debit card services. A money market account could be presented as a cash equivalent on the balance sheet, but the nature of this type of account more closely resembles an investment. Money market funds place customer deposits into short-term financial instruments, such as United States Treasury bills or commercial paper issued by larger corporations. A certificate of deposit (CD) purchased through a bank should also be treated as an investment since the bank typically invests the underlying funds in similar financial instruments.

Stocks and bonds fit the classical description of an investment. A stock certificate allows an investor to obtain equity ownership in another company. A bond represents a formal lending document between an investor and a company—the company borrowing the money usually sets the terms. An organization might trigger unwanted tax code provisions if it holds too many investments. These provisions try to limit ordinary businesses from acting as investment funds.

> Investment instruments are discussed in greater detail in Chapter 15.

TAX TREATMENT

Rules related to the presentation of investments for tax purposes can be quite extensive. Consult a tax professional if your organization holds a substantial investment portfolio or ownership in other private businesses.

C. Accounts Receivable An account receivable represents an amount owed to an organization by an external party, normally a patient who has received services. The *cash* method of accounting does not normally make use of accounts receivable. Even if patients owe money to an organization, nothing is ever reported on the balance sheet. Revenue and cash are recorded by a journal entry when money is received. An organization using the cash method will still want to keep track of amounts owed to it. Instead of viewing accounts receivable directly on the balance sheet, information on amounts owed are stored behind the scenes in the accounting system.

The cash method only uses a receivables account to handle unique items. Prepaying a credit card would be considered an account receivable and could be labeled separately as *credit card receivable* to clarify why the account resides on the balance sheet. Giving employees a payroll advance to prepay a business trip or to help them meet personal bills should be presented distinctly as an *employee receivable* or *employee advance*. In both situations, cash has simply been withdrawn from a bank account in anticipation of a future economic event, such as a credit card transaction or business trip, but withdrawing cash and placing it elsewhere does not automatically give rise to a valid business expense.

> Health care organizations may use a practice management software program to keep track of patient receivables apart from a standard accounting program.

Under the *accrual* method, a patient receivable is established once an organization renders services or sells products regardless of whether cash has traded hands. The accrual method looks at the *economic substance* of an event to determine if a transaction occurred and not merely if cash was exchanged. If a business exchange takes place that results in an organization earning the right to receive money, an account (patient) receivable would be used to *describe* the status of cash. This type of record-keeping activity involves the origination of two description accounts wherein the account receivable will eventually be reversed once the actual cash is collected. Figure 7.4 shows the difference in journal entries between both methods.

> The term "economic substance" refers to the circumstances of a particular transaction that are used to determine if a business exchange has truly occurred.

FIGURE 7.4 Cash vs. Accrual Method

Cash Method	Debit	Credit	
Cash	250		→ Balance Sheet
Revenue		250	→ Income Statement
To record the receipt of payment for prior services rendered.			
Accrual Method	**Debit**	**Credit**	
Accounts Receivable	250		→ Balance Sheet
Revenue		250	→ Income Statement
To record payment due for services rendered.			
Cash	250		→ Balance Sheet
Accounts Receivable		250	→ Balance Sheet
To record the receipt of payment on an account receivable.			

The net effect is the same with either method. The accrual method of accounting simply adds an additional step in order to capture the proper timing of the actual business exchange. The accrual method provides a straightforward approach to keeping a detailed list of amounts owed to an organization through the accounts receivable balance. With either accounting method, an organization will want to establish a *subsidiary ledger* or similar record in order to keep tabs on what each patient owes. In addition, the accounting system should contain notes regarding any collection efforts. Good notes will ensure that patients are sent accurate invoices at appropriate intervals. Excessive billing efforts or inaccurate invoices will easily sour the patient experience. Many organizations use a separate practice management software program to keep detailed records over what patients owe because of the unique nature of health care. For example, a practice management software program may provide for the inclusion of insurance codes and unique payment terms when establishing the details of patient receivables or when constructing invoices.

Estimated Bad Debts

When following the accrual method, an organization needs to reduce the balance of receivables according to an estimate of uncollectible amounts. Notice on the sample balance sheet in Figure 7.1 how the word *net* appears after accounts receivable. Suppose that on average 5% of accounts receivable are never collected from patients. If accounts receivable total $100,000, then the balance sheet would report a net total of $95,000 reflecting an estimated $5,000 of bad debts. The percentage used to calculate the estimate for bad debts is usually based on historical experience or specific assumptions about the future.

D. Inventory Many health care organizations sell small-scale products as a side benefit to patients and as a means to boost revenue. Any unsold items being held by an organization are viewed as inventory. However, products are never *capitalized* and reported as inventory on the balance sheet under the *cash method*. The purchase of products using cash would give rise to an automatic expense. For example, the purchase of $200 worth of products for resale would give rise to a $200 expense that would be reported on the income statement. If a vendor does not request payment immediately, then an organization will report neither an expense nor inventory under the cash method. The name given to this particular expense account is **cost of goods sold (COGS)**.

Cost of Goods Sold (COGS): The total amount of inventory that is expensed in relation to the quantity of items sold or purchased.

In contrast, the *accrual method* attempts to match revenue against the underlying expenses used to generate revenue. Purchasing products for resale does not give rise to an immediate expense. The cost of products is capitalized on the balance sheet as inventory and treated as an expense only if corresponding revenue activity occurs. The process involved with formulating the expense starts with an inventory count. An organization will want to count the products it has on hand at the beginning of the year and again at the end of the year.

Various rules exist to assign value to the products on hand, such as **last-in-first-out (LIFO), first-in-first-out (FIFO),** or specific identification. For example, the LIFO method of inventory valuation requires that the last item purchased by an organization represent the first item to be expensed. Consider buying a product for $55 and then another one two months later for $58. According to LIFO, if only one item sells in the current time period, the $58 item would be expensed while the $55 item would remain capitalized on the balance sheet as inventory. Per the FIFO method, the opposite would occur wherein the expense would equal $55 and ending inventory would equal $58. An organization could also use the specific identification method and choose which item to expense and which to capitalize as inventory. Figure 7.5 presents an expanded example of the LIFO and FIFO methods of inventory valuation using the purchase of five different items.

Last-in-first-out (LIFO): An inventory counting method whereby the last item placed into stock is expensed first.

First-in-first-out (FIFO): An inventory counting method whereby the first item placed into stock is expensed first.

Capitalization involves placing an expense temporarily on the balance sheet to control the time period in which the expense is placed on the income statement.

FIGURE 7.5 Inventory Methods (accrual basis)

Three items were sold in the current period and two were retained as inventory.

Purchases		LIFO		FIFO	
May 9	55		55	55	
May 12	57		57	57	
May 18	62	62		62	
May 22	60	60			60
May 24	65	65			65
		187	112	174	125
		COGS	Ending Inventory	COGS	Ending Inventory

LIFO

LIFO is a method for valuing inventory whereby the *last* item that came into the organization forms the basis for calculating how much expense should be matched against revenue activity. Given multiple unsold items in stock, each one might have been purchased at a different cost, yet the amount paid for the *last* one acquired will be taken out of inventory first and reported as an expense. This treatment often results in a larger expense being reported, causing net profit to appear lower.

FIFO

FIFO is a method for valuing inventory whereby the *first* item that came into the organization forms the basis for calculating how much expense should be matched against revenue activity. Given multiple unsold items in stock, each one might have been purchased at a different cost, yet the amount paid for the *first* one will be taken out of inventory first and reported as an expense. This treatment often results in a smaller expense being reported, causing net profit to appear higher.

Cost of Goods Sold (COGS)

Products are expensed under the accrual method of accounting if products are sold in the current period. The amount of expense (COGS) to take is reflected by the change in beginning and ending inventory numbers from manual inventory counts. The calculation of COGS involves the change in inventory values along with purchases made throughout the time period under consideration as shown in Figure 7.6.

> COGS under the cash method simply equals what an organization purchased for resale in the current time period regardless if products actually sold.

FIGURE 7.6 Calculation of Cost of Goods Sold (COGS)

This calculation process is only necessary when following the accrual method of accounting.

Inventory at beginning of year	221	
Plus: purchase of new products	736	
Total inventory during year	957	
Less: inventory at end of year	(377)	⟶ Balance Sheet
Cost of goods sold	580	⟶ Income Statement

Inventory Impairment

In certain situations, an organization may find that an item held in stock has declined in value. An *impairment* might need to be recorded if an organization is required to present inventory at either the lower of historical cost or current market value. Once an inventory item has been impaired, it will remain at the reduced value until sold or abandoned.

TAX TREATMENT

An organization that uses the cash method of accounting may still be required to accrue inventory for tax-reporting purposes. These rules apply if revenues exceed certain thresholds over an extended timeframe. The typical health care organization should meet the criteria for an exception and avoid having to match COGS with revenues in accordance with the accrual method. An integrated health care clinic might generate revenues in excess of specified thresholds, thus invoking the accrual method of accounting for inventory reporting. Consult a licensed tax professional to verify that your organization meets an exception.

The cash method does not generally make use of the prepaid expense account.

E. Prepaid Expenses The *accrual method* of accounting requires that a payment made in advance be placed on the balance sheet if the economic substance of the underlying transaction has not been fully concluded. Imagine an organization pays $600 for a 12-month malpractice insurance contract. A portion of the contract applies to each of the next 12 months whereby the monthly allocation equals $50 ($600 ÷ 12). As insurance coverage provides malpractice protection each month, amounts would be transferred to the income statement as an expense. If four months of the contract still remain as of the balance sheet date, $200 ($50 × 4) of uncompleted economic value must be presented as an asset.

TAX TREATMENT

U.S. tax regulations require prepayments to be capitalized if the economic substance of a transaction cannot be completed within 12 months—even when using the cash method. See IRS Publication 535 for more information.

A valid loan agreement should always be established whenever amounts are borrowed or lent even by a family member or business owner.

F. Notes Receivable Lending money to an external party will give rise to a note receivable. The total amount is separated on the balance sheet under both the current and long-term asset sections in order to highlight the division of when amounts are due. As the current portion becomes satisfied at the end of a specific time period, a new portion is taken from the long-term notes receivable section and *reclassified* to the current section. Figure 7.7 shows the treatment of a $12,000 loan extended by an organization that is due in equal increments over the next four years. This treatment applies to both the cash and accrual methods assuming that payments are received on time.

FIGURE 7.7 Note Receivable Schedule

Pay attention to how $3,000 of the note receivable presented in the long-term section of the balance sheet is reclassified to the current section each year.

	2012	2013	2014	2015
Current portion of note receivable	3,000	3,000	3,000	3,000
Note receivable	9,000	6,000	3,000	–
Total	12,000	9,000	6,000	3,000

G. Fixed Assets If an expense (or multiple related expenses) is large in nature and has a useful life beyond one year, the total amount should be capitalized on the balance sheet under fixed assets. In addition to the actual fixed asset, the cost to ship or install equipment might be added to the total amount capitalized. The typical small to midsized health care organization will want to capitalize amounts over $500 to $1,000 depending upon its *capitalization policy*. An organization should review any unclear situations with a licensed professional who has more experience pinpointing the type of expenses to capitalize. Capitalizing an expense maintains its value on the balance sheet over multiple time periods. A portion of the value is removed from the balance sheet each period and allocated to the income statement as *depreciation expense*. The amount removed is tracked separately on the balance sheet using the *accumulated depreciation* account. Readers of the balance sheet will always see the full historical cost of fixed assets the organization possesses but will also find a **contra account** comprised of accumulated depreciation at the bottom of the fixed assets section. Accumulated depreciation is one of the few instances where a credit balance is shown on the asset side of the balance sheet.

Contra Account: An account that offsets the balance in another account, such as bad debts, accumulated depreciation, or product returns.

The *cash method* and *accrual method* carry the same accounting treatment in relation to depreciation expense and accumulated depreciation, especially since these accounts represent noncash activity.

The amount of depreciation expense to be reported each period is based on an asset's estimated useful life along with any salvage value available upon disposal of the asset. These estimations of useful life and salvage value involve subjective assessments based on the particular set of circumstances surrounding how an asset will be used by an organization. For example, two identical printers could have different useful lives and salvage values if an organization uses one more than the other.

A piece of equipment held on the balance sheet might undergo major repairs or an overhaul. For instance, office chairs might be reupholstered. If modifications are large and greatly extend an asset's useful life, costs related to the modification could become capitalized together with the original asset. An organization would then need to modify estimates of the asset's useful life and salvage value and then recalculate the amount of depreciation expense to take in future periods.

A major overhaul of a building or piece of land is often capitalized and depreciated as a separate *improvement* with a completely different useful life than the original building or piece of land. Land improvements are subject to depreciation even though land itself is perceived to have an infinite life and is not subject to depreciation. If land is purchased together with other assets, an organization must apply a reasonable formula to separate the cost of land apart from such other assets in order to properly calculate depreciation expense.

> The cost of a fixed asset remains on the balance sheet until disposed of.

Depreciation Methods

Various methods exist to calculate the amount of depreciation to take each period. The *straight-line method* simply divides the total cost of a fixed asset—less salvage value—by an asset's useful life and allocates an equal amount of depreciation expense to each period under consideration. Some variation might occur between beginning and ending time periods based on the month an asset was placed into service.

The other key way of calculating depreciation expense involves a *declining-balance method*. The term *declining balance* refers to how the value of an asset is reduced by depreciation expense from prior periods before applying the preset depreciation rate. The rate of depreciation applied is normally 150% or 200% greater than the rate used under the straight-line method. Declining-balance methods are rooted in the idea that an asset will provide the most economic benefit in the first few years of service, thus depreciation expense should be greater in the beginning.

Figure 7.8 provides an example of the straight-line method, 200% declining-balance method, and 150% declining-balance method in relation to a piece of office equipment that cost $5,000 without any salvage value and has a useful life of five years.

The depreciation expense is constant each year relative to the straight-line method. The depreciation rate equals 20% since the equipment is depreciated over five years (100% ÷ 5 = 20%). This depreciation rate is multiplied by the base amount of $5,000 to derive the total amount of depreciation to take. The accumulated depreciation account would grow by $1,000 ($5,000 × 20%) each year, but this does not impact the base amount used to calculate the depreciation expense for the following year.

In contrast, the two declining-balance methods report different amounts of depreciation expense each period. The straight-line rate of 20% is multiplied by either 200% or 150% to derive the declining-balance rates of 40% and 30%, respectively. The individual declining-balance rates are multiplied by the base amount of $5,000 at first. For example, the depreciation expense under the 200% declining-balance method would equal $2,000 ($5,000 × 40%) in the first year. The $2,000 of depreciation expense from the first year reduces the base amount used to calculate depreciation in the second year. The declining-balance rate of 40% is again multiplied by the asset's *new* net value—now equal to $3,000—to obtain $1,200 ($3,000 × 40%) of depreciation expense. In subsequent years, the base amount used to calculate depreciation expense reflects the amount of accumulated

> Although additional depreciation methods exist beyond the ones presented in this book, they normally do not apply to a small or midsized health care organization.

FIGURE 7.8 Depreciation Methods

Straight Line	Rate	Base Amount	Expense	Net Value
Year 1	20%	5,000	1,000	4,000
Year 2	20%	5,000	1,000	3,000
Year 3	20%	5,000	1,000	2,000
Year 4	20%	5,000	1,000	1,000
Year 5	20%	5,000	1,000	—
200% Declining	**Rate**	**Base Amount**	**Expense**	**Net Value**
Year 1	40%	5,000	2,000	3,000
Year 2	40%	3,000	1,200	1,800
Year 3	40%	1,800	720	1,080
Year 4	40%	1,080	432	648
Year 5	40%	648	648 (plug)	—
150% Declining	**Rate**	**Base Amount**	**Expense**	**Net Value**
Year 1	30%	5,000	1,500	3,500
Year 2	30%	3,500	1,050	2,450
Year 3	30%	2,450	735	1,715
Year 4	30%	1,715	515	1,200
Year 5	30%	1,201	1,201 (plug)	—

depreciation from all prior years. This cycle repeats until reaching an asset's final useful year wherein the depreciation expense is typically a *plug number* that removes any remaining net value (except salvage value).

Remember that treatment of fixed assets under the cash and accrual methods is normally the same.

Journal Entries

The following journal entries illustrate how capitalized assets are posted to the accounting system and then depreciated. Notice how the journal entry used to record depreciation in Figure 7.9 does not impact the office equipment account. This $5,000 amount remains on the balance sheet untouched until the related office equipment is sold or abandoned.

FIGURE 7.9 Capitalization and Depreciation

Account	Debit	Credit	
Office Equipment	5,000		→ Balance Sheet
Checking Account — General		5,000	→ Balance Sheet
To record purchase of network system, including four computers.			
Depreciation Expense	1,200		→ Income Statement
Accumulated Depreciation		1,200	→ Balance Sheet
To record depreciation in Year 2 using the 200% declining-balance method.			

The original cost of an asset less accumulated depreciation represents the *net value* of the asset. Any difference between an asset's net value and eventual sales price would be reported as either a gain (credit) or loss (debit) at the bottom of the income statement. Suppose this same $5,000 asset is sold for $3,000 in the fifth year before depreciation expense for that year is recorded. The journal entry shown in Figure 7.10 illustrates how a gain on the sale of the equipment would be recorded assuming that accumulated depreciation equals $4,352 at that point.

FIGURE 7.10 Sale of Capitalized Asset

Account	Debit	Credit	
Checking Account — General	3,000		⟶ Balance Sheet
Accumulated Depreciation	4,352		⟶ Balance Sheet
Office Equipment		5,000	⟶ Balance Sheet
Gain on Sale of Office Equipment		2,352	⟶ Income Statement
To record sale of network computer system for $3,000.			

TAX TREATMENT

A health care organization will typically want to follow tax rules when computing depreciation in order to minimize bookkeeping. Tax authorities may have specific rules or guidelines that outline when to capitalize or expense items. The month in which an asset is actually placed in service can also impact the rate of depreciation in the first year. U.S. tax code does not allow for the inclusion of salvage value. Internal Revenue Service (IRS) Code Section 179 may allow a business owner to immediately expense the full amount of a capitalized asset. IRS Publication 946 provides information on how to depreciate property for federal tax purposes. Many assets fall within the **Modified Accelerated Cost Recovery System (MACRS)**, which specifies an asset's exact depreciation treatment. Table 7.1 contains a list of the most common types of assets that a health care organization would generally possess along with the corresponding useful life and depreciation method prescribed by U.S. tax code.

Modified Accelerated Cost Recovery System (MACRS): The system of depreciation prescribed by U.S. tax code.

TABLE 7.1	**IRS Depreciation Rules**	
Type of Asset	**Useful Life**	**Method**
Office machinery	5 years	200% declining
Computer and peripheral equipment	5 years	200% declining
Automobiles	5 years	200% declining
Office furniture and fixtures	7 years	200% declining
Land improvements	15 years	150% declining
Leasehold improvements	39 years	Straight line
Nonresidential buildings	39 years	Straight line

In terms of automobiles, depreciation expense should be adjusted for any personal use. Taxpayers can also choose to forego depreciation on automobiles and calculate a general expense based on a *standard mileage rate*. The standard mileage rate can take the place of depreciation as well as other costs related to operating and repairing an automobile. A taxpayer should keep a mileage log to maintain documentation on personal versus business use of a vehicle. Additional limits may apply if an automobile is considered luxurious.

It is important to note that depreciation begins when an organization actually places a fixed asset into service. The cost of an asset might be placed on the balance sheet in one period, but depreciation may not begin until an economic benefit is derived in a later time period. The purchase of a fruit tree illustrates this point since it might take several years before a fruit tree can grow large enough to produce fruit (economic benefit). Depreciation expense will not be taken in the interim. An organization can use this concept to its advantage when tax planning by waiting to place assets into service.

H. Intangibles Capitalized assets that have no physical existence are classified separately as intangibles. The terminology also shifts to the word *amortization* in place of depreciation. The cash and accrual methods treat amortization of intangibles in the same manner. Journal entries and balance sheet presentation parallel what the treatment of depreciation involves. In order for an intangible to become capitalized and qualify for amortization, it must have been *purchased* by an organization. Amounts spent to *produce* an intangible from scratch are expensed in the current period. Table 7.2 lists the common types of intangible property an organization can purchase.

TABLE 7.2	Intangible Property
Type	**Description**
Copyright	Legal rights over written work
Patent	Legal rights over an invention or process
Trademark	Legal rights over a unique business symbol
Goodwill	The price of a business in excess of its market value
Covenant not-to-compete	Restrictions placed on the seller of a business
Business files	Normally involves customer records
Business start-up costs	Amounts used to initiate business operations
Organizational costs	Legal expenses related to forming a new business

TAX TREATMENT

IRS rules allow amortization of intangibles to be taken over a period equal to or greater than 15 years using the straight-line method. Most of the intangible property recognized by the IRS is listed under code section 197. More information can be found in IRS Publication 535, Chapter VIII.

Liabilities

The liability section of the balance sheet lists the future obligations of an organization. Satisfying a liability will reduce an organization's cash balance, but doing so will reduce *financial risk* as well. It is common for organizations to take on financial risk in an effort to seek out profitable ventures that can generate more money than was originally invested. A commonly accepted order in which to present liability accounts is based on when amounts will generally come due. Amounts due within one year, including portions of long-term liabilities, are listed as current. All remaining liabilities are reported as noncurrent or long term. Finally, the equity section is presented separately after liabilities. There is no distinction between current and noncurrent accounts in relation to equity.

Figure 7.11 reflects the liability and equity side of a sample balance sheet under the accrual method of accounting. The total from this side of the balance sheet must always equal the corresponding asset side. The accounts listed in Figure 7.11 are referenced throughout the next part of this chapter as a way to exemplify concepts. A cash-method balance sheet would not contain all the accounts shown.

FIGURE 7.11 Sample Balance Sheet (liability and equity side)

The alphabetic values I through P correspond to the explanation of liability and equity accounts.

	Balance Sheet — Accrual Method **For the year ending December 31**		
	Liabilities and stockholder's equity		**2012**
	Current liabilities		
I	Accounts payable	3,295	
I	Payroll payable	2,450	
I	Credit card payable	486	
J	Accrued interest	500	
K	Unearned revenues	1,200	
L	Current portion of long-term debt	15,964	
M	Current portion of capital lease obligations	2,970	
	Total current liabilities		26,865
	Long-term debt		
L	Equity line of credit	47,046	
L	Bank loan payable	155,686	
	Total long-term debt		202,732
M	**Obligations under capital lease**		6,905
	Total liabilities		236,502
	Stockholder's equity		
N	Common stock, $1 par value, 800 shares authorized, 500 shares issued and outstanding	500	
O	Additional paid-in capital	14,500	
P	Retained earnings	14,039	
	Total stockholder's equity		29,039
	TOTAL LIABILITIES AND STOCKHOLDER'S EQUITY		265,541

I. Accounts Payable Under the *cash* method, an expense is not recorded until an organization hands over currency, places a check in the mail, or has a charge card swiped. A list of bills that an organization needs to pay would be tracked separately, apart from the balance sheet. Accounting programs offer the ability to keep track of invoices and other amounts owed using some type of ledger or report.

Certain unique payable items may be reported on the balance sheet even under the cash method. A postdated check acts as an account payable since cash has not been officially handed over to an external party. Any bank account with a negative balance should be shown on the liability side of the balance sheet as a bank overdraft. Credit card transactions should be posted using the individual dates listed on the credit card statement and any unpaid balance functions as a short-term loan. Figure 7.12 reflects the journal entry used to record a $2,000 payment for credit card charges in contrast to a balance due of $2,486.

FIGURE 7.12 Posting Credit Card Charges

Account	Debit	Credit	
Computer Expense	265		→ Income Statement
Meals and Entertainment	422		→ Income Statement
Repairs and Maintenance	1,052		→ Income Statement
Advertising	747		→ Income Statement
Checking Account — General		2,000	→ Balance Sheet
Credit Card Payable		486	→ Balance Sheet
To record charges listed on the December credit card statement.			

The *accrual* method requires the establishment of an account payable anytime a business exchange has occurred and an organization owes money. This treatment describes what must be done with cash sometime in the future. It is common for the balance sheet to present different categories of accounts payable using separate naming conventions, such as for payroll, credit cards, and taxes. Accounts payable specifically refer to amounts owed to external vendors. A vendor will often send an *invoice* that contains payment terms. An organization should attempt to make payment on an invoice by the final due date but take note of any discounts offered for early payment.

J. Accrued Expenses An accrued expense resembles an account payable but normally involves amounts that will not be owed to an external party until a specific point in the future. Suppose an organization makes loan payments every six months on a bank loan. As each month passes, an obligation to pay interest on the loan would accrue. The accumulation of interest charges would be reported on the balance sheet as an accrued expense. As the corresponding loan payment is made at each six-month interval, the accrued expense would be removed with an offsetting entry to cash. This treatment attempts to allocate the economic substance of the loan to the appropriate time periods. Imagine if the interest charges equal $1,200 every six months but an organization reports balance sheet activity after four months. Two-thirds (4 months ÷ 6 months) of the interest charges would apply to the current time period. As such, $800 ($1,200 × 2/3) would be reported on the balance sheet as accrued interest with an offsetting entry to interest expense on the income statement.

> The cash method does generally not make use of the accrued expense account.

K. Unearned Revenues Under the *accrual* method, if patients prepay before receiving services, amounts are credited to a current liability account instead of revenue. The liability signifies that the organization has an obligation to render services in the future (not pay money). This accounting treatment might appear a little odd since most liabilities involve an obligation to pay money but the objective is to place revenue in the period in which an economic event occurs. When an organization finally renders the prepaid services, the liability will be reversed and a credit to revenue will be made.

> The cash method does not generally make use of the unearned revenue account.

L. Long-Term Debt The *cash* and *accrual* methods apply the same accounting treatment to long-term debt. Acquiring long-term debt is common in order to purchase equipment, land, a practice, or building. Although long-term debt generally constitutes a noncurrent liability, the **principal** portion due in the coming year should be reclassified to the current liabilities section of the balance sheet.

The total amount of loan payments set to be paid over the life of a loan do not equal the loan principal shown on the balance sheet since loan payments also include interest charges. A portion of each loan payment is treated as interest expense and the remaining portion is used to reduce the current loan balance (principal). Standard bank loans

> **Principal:** The total amount of borrowed funds or remaining balance thereof that is expected to be repaid to the lender (excluding interest charges).

slowly allocate more of each loan payment to principal and less to interest expense over the course of time. In the early stages of a standard loan, the loan balance will not decrease substantially, keeping financial risk high.

Assume that at year's end a health care organization enters into a $200,000 bank loan for 10 years at an interest rate of 8%. Payments would equal $2,427 (calculation not shown) each month and total $29,118 for a full 12-month period. In the first year, the total interest expense would equal $15,508 (calculation not shown) and the remaining $13,610 ($29,118 – $15,508) would go toward reducing the loan's principal balance. By the second year, the amount treated as interest would equal $14,378 (calculation not shown) and the remaining $14,740 ($29,118 – $14,378) would again reduce the principal balance. The loan payments remain the same each year, but the amount treated as interest and principal changes. The journal entries listed in Figure 7.13 would be used to record activity for the *first* year of the loan. Note how the amount of principal set to be paid in the second year is reclassified to the current liabilities section of the balance sheet. This reclassification process would be performed every year until the loan is fully satisfied.

> The various types of loans available to a health care organization are covered in Chapter 14.

> The allocation of loan payments to interest and principal is discussed in greater depth in Chapter 11.

FIGURE 7.13 Long-Term Debt

Account	Debit	Credit	
Cash	200,000		→ Balance Sheet
Bank Loan Payable		200,000	→ Balance Sheet
To record proceeds of a new long-term bank loan.			
Bank Loan Payable	13,610		→ Balance Sheet
Interest Expense	15,508		→ Income Statement
Cash		29,118	→ Balance Sheet
To record 12 months of loan payments on the long-term bank loan.			
Bank Loan Payable	14,740		→ Balance Sheet
Current Portion of Long-Term Debt		14,740	→ Balance Sheet
To reclassify the current portion of long-term debt to current liabilities.			

TAX TREATMENT

An *impairment* can also occur with long-term debt wherein the lender forgives part or all of a loan. This type of situation occurs more frequently whenever a family member loans money and does not require repayment. A bank loan might be reduced as part of a bankruptcy settlement as well. Per U.S. tax regulations, any amount of liability impairment would be considered revenue to the taxpayer and subject to income taxes.

M. Obligations under Capital Leases Many health care organizations rent or lease office space and equipment. Lease payments generally flow directly to the income statement as rental or lease expense. The actual value of the property being leased does *not* become capitalized on the balance sheet since ownership does not change hands. For example, imagine that a $15,000 piece of equipment is leased for five years at a cost of $4,000 per year and will be returned to the original vendor at the end of the lease agreement. The balance sheet will not reflect the $15,000 value or any related accumulated depreciation since the organization does not take ownership of the equipment. The $4,000 payments would be reported as an **operating lease** expense on the income statement each year. This treatment would apply to both the *cash method* and *accrual method*.

> **Operating Lease:** A lease agreement that results in a normal lease exchange in which case amounts are directly expensed on the income statement.

In instances where a lease agreement has the appearance of a loan or the leased equipment will not revert back to the original vendor at the end of the lease period, an organization might be required to capitalize the asset's value on the balance sheet and record depreciation. A **capital lease** occurs anytime an organization triggers reporting criteria set forth by an external party, such as a tax authority. These criteria attempt to prevent an organization from sidestepping a capitalization policy related to fixed assets and directly expensing equipment costs. Following along this example, treatment as a capital lease would require the organization to capitalize the $15,000 asset on the balance sheet and establish an artificial loan within the obligations under capital leases account. Instead of recording the $4,000 lease payments directly, the organization would report varying amounts of depreciation expense and *imputed* interest charges each year. Depreciation and interest expense would not equal what is paid on the lease each year but, over the life of the lease, either treatment would result in expenses totaling $20,000 as shown in Figure 7.14.

The amount for depreciation expense shown in Figure 7.14 has been calculated using MACRS rules as set forth in IRS Publication 946, *How to Depreciate Property*. Beyond just taking depreciation expense each year, the organization will also formulate an artificial loan schedule and allocate the $4,000 annual lease payments to both principal and interest. The artificially constructed loan balance presented in the obligations under capital leases account would be reduced each year until reaching zero in the final year.

The journal entries used to record information related to a capital lease can be challenging to understand. In this particular example, $15,000 would be debited initially to the fixed asset account on the balance sheet with an offsetting $15,000 credit to the obligations under capital leases account. The annual lease payments of $4,000 would reduce the obligations under capital leases account (debit), be treated as interest expense (debit), and reduce cash (credit). Over the course of five years, the imputed interest charges would total only $5,000. In order to reflect the full $20,000 in capital lease expenses, the capitalized asset must be depreciated each year, leading to total depreciation expense (debit) and accumulated depreciation (credit) of $15,000. The capitalized asset would appear on the balance sheet until sold or abandoned, but the accumulated depreciation account would offset the value shown for fixed assets.

Capital Lease: A lease agreement that acts as a loan or transfers substantial rights of ownership leading to treatment of the leased item as a fixed asset.

Consult a tax professional to verify whether a lease should be treated as an operating or capital lease. Various complex rules apply to this assessment.

The formula used to calculate the imputed interest expense each year is explained in Chapter 11.

FIGURE 7.14 Capital and Operating Lease Schedule

| | Operating Lease | Capital Lease | | |
	Lease Expense	Depreciation Expense	Interest Expense	Total
Year 1	$4,000	$3,000	$1,565	$4,565
Year 2	4,000	4,800	1,310	6,110
Year 3	4,000	2,880	1,030	3,910
Year 4	4,000	1,728	720	2,448
Year 5	4,000	1,728	375	2,103
Year 6	0	864	0	864
Total	$20,000	$15,000	$5,000	$20,000

TAX TREATMENT

Information related to capitalizing leases can be found in IRS Publication 946. A lease may be subject to reporting as a capital lease per U.S. tax regulations under the following circumstances:

1. The lessee gains some form of ownership interest or title to the property.
2. The lessee is responsible for maintaining the property or incurs risk from any potential decrease in the property's value.
3. The lessee has the right to obtain the property at substantially less than its market value.

Equity

Equity represents the value that business owners possess in an organization. Equity accounts on the balance sheet are presented in accordance with accounting rules and do not reflect the true market value of equity. Except for retained earnings, the *cash* and *accrual* methods generally result in the same presentation of equity accounts. The presentation of retained earnings may differ as a result of revenues, expenses, gains, losses, and owner distributions being reported differently.

N. Owner's Equity The owner's equity account reports the amount of *capital* contributions made by a business owner. Making a change to this account usually accompanies a change in ownership stake. A partnership may refer to this account as partner capital or partner interest. A corporation uses the term "shareholder's equity" and includes detail about the nature of **common stock** ownership. For example, a corporation will list the number of shares **authorized**, **issued**, and **outstanding** as well as the **par value** of those shares. **Treasury stock** refers to common stock that has been issued but was bought back by the issuing corporation and is no longer outstanding.

Stock is a legal document used to assert ownership in a corporation, but the rules surrounding stock are loosely defined. A corporation can formulate any number it wants in terms of the total amount of shares authorized as well as the par value of those shares. The par value usually equals an amount far less than the stock's actual market value yet it sets a minimum value for exchange. A corporation is prevented from issuing stock for less than the par value it has set; the par value might be considered relevant in a bankruptcy proceeding.

The number of shares held by a business owner means nothing in isolation. The number of shares held by each individual owner must be compared to the total amount of stock outstanding. Owning 20% of 1 million outstanding shares affords the same rights as owning 20% of 1,000 outstanding shares.

In instances where a business owner constantly makes contributions without any subsequent transfer of ownership stake, such activity should be reported on the statement of retained earnings as an offset to distributions (to the extent possible). This treatment occurs whenever a business owner pays for an item using personal funds yet needs to record a business expense. The related journal entry would debit an expense account and credit either owner distributions or owner's equity (instead of cash).

O. Additional Paid-In Capital This account summarizes all amounts paid for stock over its par value. A corporation can set the par value at its own discretion and may even disregard setting a par value altogether. Suppose a business owner decides to set par value at $1 and allows the corporation to authorize 800 shares. The owner then inserts $15,000 of capital into the corporation in exchange for 500 shares. Only $500 (500 shares × $1 par value) would be reported under owner's equity. The remaining $14,500 ($15,000 − $500) would appear under the additional paid-in capital account. This account does not exist for other business forms, such as a partnership or sole proprietorship.

P. Retained Earnings This account involves amounts carried over from the income statement and statement of retained earnings—specifically the accumulated totals of net income (or loss) and owner distributions. The *cash* and *accrual* methods may result in different amounts being reported in the retained earnings account based on when revenues, expenses, gains, losses, and owner distributions are reported. Since the retained earnings account summarizes a significant amount of accounting data, the balance in this account should be verified from one time period to the next. If the *ending* retained earnings balance of one time period does not match the *beginning* balance in the next time period, then an error exists somewhere in the accounting system—and the hunt begins to find it. This search can be daunting since the retained earnings account contains a multitude of transactions involving all the income statement and statement of retained earnings accounts.

Assets
− Liabilities
= Equity

Capital is a fancy term for money. A capital contribution can also be referred to as a financial contribution.

Stock is often referred to as shares or equity. For example, the terms *stockholder*, *shareholder*, and *equityholder* mean the same.

Common Stock: The general class of stock offered by most corporations providing for ownership rights and access to owner distributions.

Authorized: The amount of stock a corporation could potentially transfer to owners.

Issued: The amount of stock in total that has been transferred to owners.

Outstanding: The amount of stock that owners still currently hold.

Par Value: The minimum value stated on a stock certificate for which it can be issued.

Treasury Stock: Shares that have been issued and were once outstanding but have since been repurchased.

Net Income
− Owner Distributions
= Retained Earnings

Summary

A health care organization should perform a bank reconciliation often to verify information contained in the accounting system is correct. An organization should also keep strict controls over cash to prevent errors and fraud. Based on the timing of when amounts will be received or paid, the balance sheet will list items as either current or noncurrent. Certain accounts may apportion amounts to both the current and noncurrent sections. In total, assets will equal liabilities plus equity.

Most health care organizations will follow the cash method of accounting and attempt to incorporate elements of the tax code. Tax law can result in very complex modifications being made to the cash method and reliance on a licensed professional is expected. When using the cash method, an organization will not record amounts until cash is exchanged. Amounts due from patients or owed to vendors must be tracked behind the scenes using a ledger or reported separately from the balance sheet.

The accrual method requires that all amounts be reported on the balance sheet as soon as a business exchange occurs or an economic benefit accrues. This section has covered many of the rules that apply to the accrual method, but others exist, especially if an organization must follow GAAP.

7.2   Income Statement

The main section of the income statement presents revenues and expenses related to an organization's customary operating activity. Amounts placed on the income statement will often differ according to whether the *cash* or *accrual* method is followed, but the types of accounts used are generally the same. Revenue includes inflows of cash or value into an organization whereas expenses represent outflows that support the production of revenue.

Certain expenses become capitalized on the balance sheet because of their unique nature. The expenses that are most often capitalized include lease payments that function as long-term debt (capital lease), significant property that has value beyond one year (fixed assets), and significant nonphysical property that an organization purchased (intangibles). A portion of a capitalized expense is allocated to the income statement across multiple time periods based on a relevant depreciation or amortization method.

Gains and losses refer to nonstandard activity and are presented toward the bottom of the income statement. Figure 7.15 reflects a sample income statement under the *accrual* method of accounting. A cash-method income statement would contain the same accounts shown—except for bad debts—but may present a different amount in cases where cash has not yet been exchanged. The bad debts account represents an estimate of accounts receivable that an organization feels will not be collected.

Revenues

A revenue account captures the inflow of cash or value derived from extending services or selling products in a standard manner. According to the *cash* method, revenue should be reported using the date an organization receives cash or cash equivalents in the mail or in person. It is customary practice to use the date listed on a bank or credit card statement when posting charge card transactions. The *accrual* method specifies that revenue should be reported when a business exchange occurs, even if money has not yet been exchanged. An account receivable would be established to note that money is due, but the account receivable will eventually be reversed once cash or a cash equivalent is received.

Any reimbursement of revenue made to a patient or third-party payor should be reported within the returns and allowances account. This account functions as a *contra account* under revenues and can be referred to simply as refunds.

FIGURE 7.15 Sample Income Statement

Income Statement — Accrual Method
For the year ending December 31

			2012
a	Revenue		
	Primary revenue	148,611	
	Secondary revenue	14,935	
	Product revenue	872	
b	Refunds	(1,652)	
	Net revenue		162,766
	Expenses		
	Advertising	3,922	
c	Bad debts	720	
	Charitable contributions	200	
d	Computer expense	1,965	
	Continuing education	350	
e	Cost of goods sold	580	
	Depreciation and amortization	12,824	
	Dues and subscriptions	128	
	Insurance	8,540	
	Legal and professional	4,881	
	Meals and entertainment	2,916	
	Office expense	2,234	
	Office supplies	1,782	
	Postage and delivery	1,321	
	Repairs and maintenance	2,763	
f	Salaries and wages	65,000	
g	Taxes and licenses	9,650	
	Travel expense	978	
	Utilities	4,266	
	Miscellaneous	389	
	Total expenses		125,409
	Net profit (loss) from operations		37,357
	Interest expense		(18,562)
	Interest income		745
	Gains and losses		(822)
	Net profit (loss)		18,718

a. Revenue accounts have been segregated to give management better insight into the sources of revenue.
b. Refunds is a contra revenue account and is not treated as an expense.
c. The bad debts account reflects the estimate of uncollectible accounts receivable.
d. Certain expense accounts should be reviewed to ensure all items have been properly capitalized.
e. COGS = beginning inventory + purchases − ending inventory.
f. An owner of a corporation who works for the corporation must earn a reasonable wage.
g. Payroll taxes are often combined with other business-related taxes.

Expenses

Tax authorities and GAAP rules specify that an expense must have a *reasonable* business purpose. Otherwise, the amount should be shown as an owner distribution instead of an expense. The definition of what constitutes reasonable is generally assessed in relation to the customary operating activity of the business in question. Buying $1,000 worth of baking soda would be practical for a baker, but probably not for a health care organization. Taxpayers often try to claim that property used personally serves a reasonable business purpose or they might make an extravagant purchase when a more practical option exists. Tax authorities have been involved in many disputes with taxpayers over the definition of the word *reasonable*. Tax law does not provide clear guidance, forcing taxpayers to make a judgment call or request a special ruling to obtain a determination about the reasonability of an expense. Writing to a tax authority proactively is recommend in lieu of paying back taxes on an expense that a tax authority later deems invalid. The following are two examples of expenses that may not serve a reasonable business purpose.

> Writing to the IRS rarely occurs because tax professionals have the experience to make judgment calls.

EXAMPLE A

Placing a business logo on a personal boat does not automatically convert the boat into business property. Capitalizing the boat and taking depreciation expense would subject an organization to the risk of paying back taxes. Although the circumstances would need to be assessed by a qualified professional, an organization might be able to expense the cost of placing signage on the boat—but not the boat itself.

EXAMPLE B

Buying dinner for a friend who also comes in as a patient would not constitute a valid business expense if the conversation centered on personal matters. The IRS allows taxpayers to deduct one-half of the total cost of meals and entertainment that serve a reasonable business purpose. The business purpose of the dinner should be noted on the back of the receipt.

In order to simplify tax reporting, an organization could arrange the *chart of accounts* according to the general account structure prescribed by the IRS as listed in Table 7.4. An organization may need to include additional *acceptable* categories beyond the ones

TABLE 7.4	Categories of Expense Accounts

Standard IRS Categories		Acceptable Categories
Advertising	Legal and professional	Bank charges
Automobile expense	Meals and entertainment	Computer expense
Charitable contributions	Office expense (general)	Consulting fees
Compensation of officers	Office supplies	Continuing education
Contract labor	Rent expense	Dues and subscriptions
Cost of goods sold	Repairs and maintenance	Internet service
Depreciation and amortization	Retirement plan expense	Landscaping
Employee benefit programs	Salaries and wages	Marketing supplies
Insurance	Taxes and licenses	Postage and delivery
Interest expense	Travel expense	Telephone expense
Lease expense	Utilities	Miscellaneous

prescribed by the IRS in order to describe the nature of all expenses properly. An expense account should have a name that reasonably describes the nature of transactions being recorded within it. Expense accounts are normally listed in alphabetical order on the income statement.

Gains and Losses

Inflows and outflows of cash or value from transactions related to nonstandard business exchanges are referred to as gains and losses. These transactions normally comprise balance sheet items that are sold or abandoned. Suppose an organization purchases chairs for the waiting room at a cost of $1,500. The organization fully depreciates them over seven years according to MACRS rules. The organization then decides to purchase new chairs for the waiting room and sells the old chairs for $300. Since the chairs were fully depreciated and had a net value of zero on the balance sheet, the entire $300 would be considered a gain. The journal entry to remove the old chairs appears in Figure 7.16. The name used to describe the gain or loss often references the account through which the gain or loss originated—in this case office equipment.

FIGURE 7.16 Recording a Gain

Account	Debit	Credit	
Cash	300		→ Balance Sheet
Accumulated Depreciation	1,500		→ Balance Sheet
Office Equipment		1,500	→ Balance Sheet
Gain on Sale of Office Equipment		300	→ Income Statement
To record the sale of fully depreciated chairs for $300.			

The reverse occurs if an asset sells for less than its net value reported on the balance sheet. An organization would record a loss represented as a debit in this situation.

Summary

Under the *cash* method, amounts related to standard operating activity are recorded as either revenue or an expense when cash is exchanged. The *accrual* method requires that amounts be recorded when business activity occurs and when cash is exchanged. A gain or loss is recorded anytime a transaction involves nonstandard business activity. The definition of what constitutes a standard and reasonable business expense varies based on what an organization customarily does. The IRS prescribes certain expense categories for use in tax reporting. An organization has the ability to create any categorization schema it chooses for internal purposes but may find what the IRS prescribes works best. The IRS does not provide a comprehensive list of expense categories; thus additional accounts may be needed according to the nature of expenses.

7.3 Statement of Retained Earnings

The income statement is closed each period and account balances are reset to zero. Amounts are rolled into a net earnings figure, which is then transferred to the statement of retained earnings. The net earnings figure is further reduced by any distributions made to owners. The amount of net earnings that remains represents what business owners retain for future business purposes. This final amount of *retained* earnings is transferred onto the balance sheet and placed within the equity section. The statement of retained earnings might also show activity related to other equity accounts to clarify what is occurring in

The retained earnings account summarizes countless historical transactions together; that is, revenues, expenses, gains, losses, and owner distributions.

the equity section of the balance sheet overall. For example, owner contributions could be presented in a separate area on the statement of retained earnings. Figure 7.17 reflects a sample statement of retained earnings under the *accrual* method of accounting. The statement would be structured the same under the *cash* method but will most likely present a different amount of retained earnings.

FIGURE 7.17 Sample Statement of Retained Earnings

Statement of Retained Earnings — Accrual Method
For the year ending December 31

Retained earnings

Balance at beginning of year	1,321
Net profit (loss)	18,718
Stockholder distributions	(6,000)
Balance at end of year	14,039
Common stock, $1 par value, 800 shares authorized, 500 shares issued and outstanding	500
Additional paid-in capital	14,500
Total stockholder's equity	29,039

Be careful paying for business expenses with personal funds. This might damage the legal liability protections afforded to you by the form of business you operate under.

In some instances, an owner might continuously make cash or indirect personal contributions without a corresponding change in ownership stake. A common example is when an owner pays for items with personal funds yet wants to claim a business expense. This type of contribution should be offset against owner distributions if possible instead of being added to owner's equity.

Summary

The statement of retained earnings provides a crucial link between the income statement and balance sheet. Amounts reported on the income statement are packaged together as net earnings and transferred to the statement of retained earnings. Distributions made to owners are then deducted to derive an amount of *retained* earnings. This final retained earnings figure is presented within the equity section of the balance sheet.

CHAPTER ASSIGNMENT

Working in a group of three to four students or fellow professionals, complete the following items.

1. The month-end bank statement reports a cash balance of $2,954. An organization member recently dropped off a cash deposit in the amount of $498 but this does not yet appear on the statement. Three recent checks in the amounts of $84, $276, and $1,645 reported in the accounting system did not appear on the bank statement either.

Calculate the cash balance that should be reported on the balance sheet based on the bank statement and reconciling items.

2. Describe the difference between the cash and accrual methods of accounting. Under the cash method, why would the amounts owed to an organization not be reported on the balance sheet? How might an organization keep track of such information?

3. Go online to irs.gov and search for Publication 946. Using the MACRS tables in the appendix, calculate what the depreciation expense would be each year for a $6,000 piece of office furniture. Pay attention to the asset class. How much depreciation could be taken in the first year under Code Section 179 assuming the organization qualifies?

4. The normal straight-line depreciation rate for a 15-year asset is 6.67%. What would the 150% declining-balance rate be? Assuming that the full amount of depreciation expense is taken in the first year on an asset that cost $20,000, how much depreciation expense would be taken in the second year according to the 150% declining-balance method?

5. Complete the following journal entry.

Sale of Capitalized Asset	Debit	Credit	
Checking Account — General	(a)		→ Balance Sheet
Accumulated Depreciation	8,425		→ Balance Sheet
(b)	(c)		(d)
Medical Equipment		19,000	→ Balance Sheet
To record sale of x-ray machine for $6,500.			

6. Explain why a portion of long-term debt should be reclassified each period to current liabilities. What other asset and liability accounts invoke this same treatment?

7. Review the criteria set forth by U.S. tax code that require an organization to capitalize a lease. List the different accounts used for an operating lease in contrast to a capital lease. How much interest expense would be reported over the life of a capital lease if the underlying asset has a value of $19,000 and the lease agreement requires eight payments of $3,000 each?

8. How is owner's equity presented on the balance sheet of a corporation? Is there a specific amount of stock that a corporation must authorize and should the stock have a specific par value?

Segmentation
Opportunity Cost
Variance
Variable Expenses
Fixed Expenses

Sensitivity Analysis
Breakeven Analysis
Contribution Margin
Ad Hoc Report

Business Analysis

AUTHOR'S NOTE

Mastering the concepts in Chapters 6 and 7 puts you in the driver's seat of the accounting system. An understanding of accounting is essential to perform management functions. Segmenting accounts into distinct categories makes it easier to analyze specific activity. Consider having organization members track their time using job codes as wages tend to be the largest expense that an organization has. You may want to create financial ratios apart from the 20 listed in this chapter in order to track important activity. Learning how to prepare a cash budget is essential because even profitable organizations need to guard against cash shortfalls. A business plan will normally include the three forms of profitability analysis shown in this chapter.

Compiling accounting information can do more than simply satisfy tax or lending institution requirements. A savvy entrepreneur will know how to read the numbers and incorporate accounting information into the decision-making process. Even if an entrepreneur never personally compiles accounting records, understanding how to derive accounting information can clarify what the numbers mean.

Structuring the accounting system around the needs of external parties may not provide an organization with the information it needs for internal purposes. The chart of accounts should be framed according to the nature of operations, especially where an organization operates distinct service lines. Internal control measures and proper training of bookkeeping personnel will help ensure that amounts are recorded in the correct accounts. Journal entries must also contain an accurate explanation of what an activity involves. Accounting information that is inaccurate or lacks detail will not properly support the decision-making process.

Imagine that an organization serves two distinct groups of patients and begins tracking the profitability of each. Expenses are allocated to each service line based on how they support the production of revenue; however, an organization member mistakenly posts all depreciation expense to the first service line, artificially inflating the profit on the second service line and decreasing the profit shown for the first service line. What would happen if the business owner concludes that the first service line delivers very little value for the organization and decides to terminate it?

The *accrual* method of accounting often provides the best information when conducting business analysis. For example, various financial ratios presented in this chapter use accrual-basis accounts that do not exist under the *cash* method. Activity recorded using the *accrual* method is less susceptible to manipulation because it captures the actual time period in which a business transaction takes place. An organization that follows the *cash* method may need to temporarily switch information to the *accrual* method. Luckily, accounting software programs make this process incredibly simple.

8.1 Account Segmentation

Segmentation: The process of delineating information contained in an account or multiple accounts into distinct categories.

How an organization records a transaction will greatly affect its ability to perform meaningful business analysis. The **segmentation** of accounts into subcategories enables an organization to isolate specific activity according to what is determined significant. Segmenting accounts can increase administrative time and the potential for errors. It would not benefit an organization to maintain a complex accounting system beyond what the decision-making process truly necessitates. Still, software programs have greatly simplified the process of recording accounting information.

Knowing the best way to segment revenue accounts requires insight into what drives revenue along with the types of costs that accompany a revenue source. The segmentation of revenue accounts could be based on service lines, time of day, type of payor, marketing campaigns, and so forth. Did a new patient decide to use your services as the result of a referral source, coupon book, or sales luncheon? Answering this type of question empowers an organization to expend resources in a highly efficient manner. Expense accounts can be segmented the same way as revenue accounts in an attempt to calculate the profit associated with a particular activity. Expense accounts can be categorized in other meaningful ways if their segmentation according to revenue activity is not possible. Isolating expense activity allows an organization to consider ways of reducing or replacing expenses.

Table 8.1 provides an example of how an organization can segment accounts. Revenues have been divided based upon their source. An assessment can be made regarding which payor type generates the most revenue as well as personal satisfaction for organization members. Instead of categorizing revenues and expenses in the same manner, expense accounts have been segmented according to the type of employee. The organization can examine the costs of hiring part-time versus full-time workers and compare those costs to job performance and work output. Since part-time workers do not qualify for employee benefits, the account segmentation schema found in Table 8.1 ignores retirement plan expenses and employee benefit programs for such workers.

TABLE 8.1	Example Account Segmentation
As Required by Tax Regulations	**As Structured for Internal Decision-Making**
Revenues	Revenue from insurance companies
	Revenue from car accident claims
	Revenue from cash payors
Refunds and allowances	Refunds and allowances—insurance
	Refunds and allowances—accidents
	Refunds and allowances—cash payors
Expenses:	
Compensation of officers	Compensation of officers
Salaries and wages	Salaries and wages—full time
	Salaries and wages—part time
Taxes and licenses	Payroll taxes—officers
	Payroll taxes—full time
	Payroll taxes—part time
Employee benefit programs	Employee benefit programs—officers
	Employee benefit programs—full time
Retirement plan expense	Retirement plan expense—officers
	Retirement plan expense—full time

An accounting system should evolve as information is collected and as activity changes. The chart of accounts creates a general and flexible outline of where to record amounts. Accounting programs provide for the use of *subaccounts* in order to segment the chart of accounts. Software programs also contain filter and search options in order to isolate transactions for review. The explanation given in a journal entry serves as a reminder of what a specific transaction involved. Giving each transaction a proper explanation can prove valuable down the road if a random problem surfaces and research must be conducted.

CASE STUDY

Account Segmentation

Suppose a health care organization receives three bills each month for three different phones: a standard land line and two cell phones. After six months, the office manager notices that phone charges seem excessive and wants to evaluate the need to (1) switch phone carriers or (2) completely eliminate a particular phone line. Imagine that the office manager opens the general ledger for the telephone expense account and sees each charge labeled *phone bill*. This generic explanation would not provide any specific information useful for business analysis. It would prove helpful if each explanation referenced the respective phone and month in question, such as *Cell Phone 1—May*. The office manager could then analyze the expense account according to the unique explanations and examine the charges related to each phone.

Suppose the charges for Cell Phone 2 are found to be two times greater than the charges for Cell Phone 1. An inquiry could be made as to why this particular cell phone costs more to operate. The solution might involve setting limits on cell phone use, changing to another plan, changing to another carrier, or eliminating the phone altogether. Does this cell phone support the production of revenue? The decision-making process is supported by concise access to relevant information.

Summary

To conduct business analysis, a health care organization needs access to the correct information. The chart of accounts outlines the main account structure and should direct you to where information can be recorded and found. The chart of accounts could be structured according to the needs of external parties or in a way that supports business analysis internally. For internal management purposes, an organization might want to segment accounts according to what drives revenues or expenses. Many software programs provide for *subaccounts* in order to segment accounts in this manner. Writing detailed explanations in journal entries simplifies the process of searching through accounting information and isolating activities later.

8.2   Financial Ratios

A template that contains some of these ratios can be found online at remedybooks.com under the *Students* tab.

After compiling the financial statements for a set time period, an organization can put together a spreadsheet containing financial ratios. An organization member can be placed in charge of updating these ratios at set intervals as a way of maintaining information useful for decision making. Certain financial ratios do not provide meaningful information as stand-alone figures. These ratios have meaning when compared to the ratios of competitors or when changes are tracked over time. The direction and magnitude of a ratio's change must be considered when making this assessment. Pay attention to how an increase of one ratio might signal a positive trend whereas an increase to another ratio may signify problems exist.

The ratios contained in this chapter have been constructed using the *accrual* method financial statements from Chapter 7. An organization might want to convert cash-basis amounts to the accrual method since several ratios are formed using accrual accounts. Many accounting software programs have the ability to easily switch back and forth between cash and accrual method reports by a mere click of the mouse.

Debt Ratios

Debt ratios as shown in Table 8.2 put debt levels into perspective and examine an organization's ability to make payments on time. Among school, personal, and practice loans, a health care provider can amass a heavy debt load. Apart from business debt, an amount for personal debt and personal interest expense could be included on the spreadsheet used to calculate financial ratios since the total amount borrowed can often be substantial and income from operations will ultimately be needed to service personal loans.

TABLE 8.2	Debt Ratios			
1 Times Interest Earned 50,104 ÷ 18,562 = 2.70	Increase Good Decrease Bad	18,718 18,562 12,824	Net Profit Interest Expense Depreciation and Amortization	
		50,104 18,562	Total Cash Interest Expense	
2 Debt Ratio 236,502 ÷ 265,541 = 0.89	Increase Bad Decrease Good	236,502 265,541	Total Liabilities Total Assets	
3 Long-Term Debt to Total Assets Ratio 209,637 ÷ 265,541 = 0.79	Increase Bad Decrease Good	202,732 6,905	Long-Term Debt Obligations under Capital Leases	
		209,637 265,541	Total Long-Term Debt Total Assets	

1. TIMES-INTEREST EARNED

(Net Profit + Interest Expense + Depreciation + Amortization)/Interest Expense

An organization will want to ensure that it can at least cover the interest charges on its debt. This ratio takes net profit and adds back interest expense in order to figure the total cash available for interest payments. Depreciation and amortization are added back as well because they are noncash deductions. The total amount of cash on hand before making interest payments is divided over the interest expense to formulate a multiplier. In the example shown in Table 8.2, a multiplier of 2.7 means that the approximate cash earned throughout the year is 2.7 times more than what is needed to cover interest charges. Interest related to education and personal loans could be included in this ratio to review the total encumbrance on business cash.

2. DEBT RATIO

Total Liabilities/Total Assets

This ratio attempts to show the extent to which liabilities could be covered if all assets were suddenly sold. Lenders will care significantly about this ratio because they want to make certain that assets could be converted into cash in order to cover any remaining loan balance if operations cease or prove deficient. The use of historical asset balances in the denominator usually results in a more conservative figure. Under the *cash* method, the balance sheet does not contain amounts owed to vendors or due from patients. These amounts should be added to the balance sheet since they could have a material impact on this ratio. The standard debt ratio can also be constructed using the balance for equity instead of total assets since these three major sections of the balance sheet are all interconnected.

3. LONG-TERM DEBT TO TOTAL ASSETS RATIO

(Long-Term Debt + Obligations under Capital Leases)/Total Assets

This ratio isolates the risks surrounding long-term debt since an organization tends to have less flexibility in terms of when payment on long-term debt must occur; in addition, lending institutions have more power to force a company into bankruptcy. Even when operating under the corporate form of business, a lending institution may require the borrower to sign away personal protections, increasing the risks emanating from long-term debt.

Liquidity Ratios

The liquidity ratios shown in Table 8.3 clarify the amount of cash—currently on hand or soon to be collected—that an organization could use to satisfy current liabilities. Whereas debt ratios look at the capacity to service loan obligations, liquidity ratios target an organization's ability to continue operations for another year. A low liquidity ratio means that an organization could face challenges in maintaining a sustainable business.

TABLE 8.3	Liquidity Ratios			
4 Current Ratio	Increase Good	21,624		Current Assets
$21,624 \div 26,865 = 0.80$	Decrease Bad	26,865		Current Liabilities
5 Acid Test Ratio	Increase Good	350		Petty Cash
$18,047 \div 26,865 = 0.67$	Decrease Bad	4,295		Checking Account—General
		2,850		Checking Account—Payroll
		1,588		Investments
		8,964		Accounts Receivable, net
		18,047		Current Assets (select)
		26,865		Current Liabilities

4. CURRENT RATIO

Current Assets/Current Liabilities

Current assets represent the expected inflows of cash or value over the course of the next year that could be used to cover current liabilities owed over the same time period. The current ratio includes the current portion of long-term liabilities and notes receivable. A high ratio demonstrates that an organization can support operations for at least another year.

5. ACID TEST (QUICK) RATIO

(Cash and Cash Equivalents + Investments + Accounts Receivable)/Current Liabilities

This ratio specifically targets the extent to which highly liquid current-asset accounts could cover all current liabilities over the next year. This represents a highly conservative approach toward ensuring that enough funds will be available to support continued operations. Inventory, prepaid expenses, and the current portion of notes receivable are excluded from this ratio since there is less certainty that these items could be converted into cash for the purpose of covering current liabilities.

Profitability Ratios

Profitability ratios as shown in Table 8.4 capture the overall efficiency of how resource expenditures have been used. A high profitability ratio signifies that an organization expends money wisely in its effort to generate revenue.

TABLE 8.4	Profitability Ratios			
6 Net Profit Margin $18{,}718 \div 162{,}766 = 11\%$	Increase Good Decrease Bad	18,718 162,766	Net Profit Net Revenue	
7 Return on Equity $18{,}718 \div 29{,}039 = 64\%$	Increase Good Decrease Bad	18,718 29,039	Net Profit Total Equity	
8 Return on Assets $18{,}718 \div 265{,}541 = 7\%$	Increase Good Decrease Bad	18,718 265,541	Net Profit Total Assets	

6. NET PROFIT MARGIN

Net Profit/Total Revenue

Net profit takes into account all revenues, expenses, gains, and losses. This financial ratio mainly provides insight into how well expenses support the production of revenue. Profit levels could decline if revenue levels are negatively impacted by a reduction in supporting expenses. An organization needs to find the right balance between expenses and revenues in order to reach optimal profitability. Conducting this analysis may require the use of segmented accounts in order to isolate business activity. Since gains and losses usually refer to the sale of assets, the net profit margin also provides some feedback on the turnover occurring with assets. A low net-profit margin may signify that an organization has purchased unproductive equipment or the actual sales effort of outdated equipment is deficient.

7. RETURN ON EQUITY

Net Profit/Total Equity

Equity involves the capital that an owner has contributed to an organization as well as amounts of retained earnings (profit). This financial ratio illustrates how well an organization has used a business owner's money to generate profit. A low number might signify that an owner has incurred an **opportunity cost** as a result of putting capital into a particular organization—as opposed to a more profitable venture elsewhere.

Opportunity Cost:
An implied cost that results from having foregone other more valuable opportunities in order to continue along a current course of action (or inaction).

8. RETURN ON ASSETS

Net Profit/Total Assets

This ratio looks at the overall value derived from investing in operations and fixed assets (capitalized expenses). Assets tied to an *operating lease* can be included in this ratio's denominator. For example, a leased office space may not be reported on the balance sheet, but an organization may want to assess how well leased office space is used to generate profit. Of course, a *capital lease* automatically results in a leased asset being reported on the balance sheet. A health care organization should strive to use assets in the most effective way possible.

Billing Ratios

Billing ratios as presented in Table 8.5 demonstrate an organization's ability to collect outstanding balances from patients or third-party payors. Using the *cash* method makes formulating billing ratios more difficult because only *accrual* accounts describe the status of unpaid amounts. A cash-method financial statement will only show a record of transactions once cash has traded hands in contrast to what external parties owe in total (accounts receivable). When using an accounting software program, outstanding balances can be housed behind the scenes and brought forth when calculating these ratios.

TABLE 8.5	Billing Ratios			
9 Bad Debts Ratio	Increase Bad	162,766		Net Revenue
$720 \div 182,964 = 0.4\%$	Decrease Good	720		Bad Debts
		19,478		Total Discounts [assumed]
		182,964		Total Charges [assumed]
10 Charge Discounts Ratio	Increase Bad	162,766		Net Revenue
$19,478 \div 182,964 = 11\%$	Decrease Good	720		Bad Debts
		19,478		Total Discounts [assumed]
		182,964		Total Charges [assumed]
11 Accounts Receivable Turnover	Increase Good	162,766		Net Revenue
$162,766 \div 9,718 = 16.7$	Decrease Bad	10,472		Beginning Accounts Receivable [assumed]
		8,964		Ending Accounts Receivable
		19,436		Total Accounts Receivable
			$\div 2 = 9,718$	Average Accounts Receivable
12 Average Collection Rate	Increase Bad	365		Calendar Days
$365 \div 16.7 = 22$ days	Decrease Good	16.7		Accounts Receivable Turnover
Alternative Expression		365		Calendar Days
$365 \times 9,718 \div 162,766 = 22$ days	Increase Bad	9,718		Average Accounts Receivable
	Decrease Good	162,766		Net Revenue

9. BAD DEBTS RATIO

Bad Debts/Total Billable Charges

A high percentage of bad debts (as compared to billable charges) means collection efforts are deficient. Collection efforts should be improved or patients could be required to pay upfront at time of service to reduce bad debts. The overall patient experience should be considered part of this assessment. If using the *cash* method, an estimate of bad debts may need to be specially prepared for this ratio. The denominator of this ratio reflects the total amount of valid charges.

Bad debts represent valid charges that patients fail to pay.

10. CHARGE DISCOUNTS RATIO

Total Discounts/Total Billable Charges

Charge discounts represent billable charges that an organization is unable to recuperate because of third-party restrictions or *price incentives*. The actual charges submitted to third-party payors are often reduced per contract terms. An organization might discount charges in an effort to attract new patients. An organization should measure what would be earned if patients paid full price for all services. This ratio can be used to assess the practicality of a cash practice or no longer working with a particular group of patients.

Net Revenue
+ Total Discounts
+ Bad Debts
= Total Billable Charges

11. ACCOUNTS RECEIVABLE TURNOVER

Net Revenue/Average Accounts Receivable

This financial ratio shows how quickly unpaid balances are collected. A health care organization can experience a low turnover rate if third-party payors take a long time to process patient charges. This lag impacts an organization's ability to turn around and expend resources with the goal of producing *future* revenues. In order to calculate the denominator of this ratio, take the accounts receivable balance at the beginning of the period, add the accounts receivable balance from the end of the period, and divide both by two. Reduce accounts receivable for any estimated bad debts since this ratio should only include amounts that an organization can reuse in future periods.

12. AVERAGE COLLECTION RATE

365/Accounts Receivable Turnover

Alternative Expression: (365 × Average Accounts Receivable)/Net Revenue

The average collection rate represents a more intuitive way of thinking about the speed of accounts receivable turnover. This specific format shows the average number of days it takes to receive payment. An accounts receivable turnover rate of 16.7 means that it takes 22 days (365 days ÷ 16.7) on average to collect amounts from patients and third-party payors. A low number means that charges are being collected quickly. An alternative expression is provided to show another method of calculating this ratio.

Operating Ratios

The operating ratios as shown in Table 8.6 isolate an organization's standard business activity and ignore nonstandard activity, such as gains, losses, interest expense, or interest income. Since gains and losses relate to the disposal of assets, this activity is not considered customary for a health care organization. The interest costs related to a loan and interest income from investments are ignored by these ratios because they are not viewed as having a role in standard operating activity either.

TABLE 8.6	Operating Ratios				

13 Operating Ratio
$125,409 \div 162,766 = 77\%$

Increase Bad
Decrease Good

125,409   Operating Expenses
162,766   Net Operating Revenue

14 Operating Margin
$37,357 \div 162,766 = 23\%$

Increase Good
Decrease Bad

37,357   Net Profit from Operations
162,766   Net Operating Revenue

15 Worker Productivity Ratio
$73,450 \div 162,766 = 45\%$

Increase Bad
Decrease Good

65,000   Salaries and Wages
8,450   Payroll Taxes [assumed]
73,450   Payroll Expenses
162,766   Net Operating Revenue

16 Marketing Ratio
$7,479 \div 162,766 = 5\%$

Increase Bad
Decrease Good

3,922   Advertising
2,916   Meals and Entertainment
641   Office Expense [assumed]
7,479   Marketing Expenses
162,766   Net Operating Revenue

13. OPERATING RATIO

Operating Expenses/Net Operating Revenue

Operating revenue is calculated net of any returns and allowances.

This ratio explains how well an organization uses operating-specific expenses to generate operating-specific revenue. Nonstandard activity should be ignored. For example, idle cash might be placed into a money market account to draw interest income. The passive interest income derived from a money market account along with any associated maintenance fees would not represent standard operating activity for a health care organization.

14. OPERATING MARGIN

Net Profit from Operations/Net Operating Revenue

This expression looks at operating performance from a bottom-up perspective, comparing net profit from operations to net operating revenue after deducting operating expenses.

15. WORKER PRODUCTIVITY RATIO

(Payroll Expenses + Temporary Labor)/Net Operating Revenue

Payroll expenses normally represent the greatest cost to a service organization. Workers must remain productive throughout the day in order to optimize profit margins. A low ratio means that organization members have consistent workloads and the work supports the production of operating revenue. This ratio will increase if organization members have no work, work is performed inefficiently, or work does not relate to the production of revenue. An organization can use temporary labor to deal with times of abnormally high workloads or for special projects. Depending on the nature of the work performed, an organization may want to include the cost of independent contractors in the numerator.

16. MARKETING RATIO

Marketing Expenses/Net Operating Revenue

With proper account segmentation and journal entry explanations, an organization can determine how well marketing efforts support the production of revenue. An expense that relates to marketing may become buried within an account requiring an organization member to sift through the general ledger before formulating this ratio. An organization could formulate an *opportunity cost* related to the time and energy involved with marketing and add that amount to the ratio as well. For example, spending two hours per day to support $20,000 in annual revenue does not appear as efficient as spending one hour per day to generate $30,000 in annual revenue. Time could be converted into an equivalent hourly rate and added to the ratio's numerator.

Patient Ratios

Patient ratios as illustrated in Table 8.7 often involve data that are separate from the accounting system. An organization should keep track of patient and visit counts in order to assess patient retention. These ratios may alert to problems occurring with the patient experience and clarify the value lost from a bad experience. Suppose an organization eliminates one service line and then profitability across the board subsequently declines. The organization may have failed to realize that patients came in more frequently, spent more on average, and referred others more often as a result of the abandoned service line.

Employee bonuses can be based on financial or patient ratios.

TABLE 8.7	Patient Ratios		
New Patients 421	Continuing Patients 361	Total Patients 782	Total Visits 6,541
17 Retention Ratio $361 \div 782 = 46\%$	Depends Depends	361 782	Continuing Patients Total Patients
18 Visit Turnover $6,541 \div 782 = 8.4$	Increase Good Decrease Bad	6,541 782	Total Visits Total Patients
19 Patient Margin $162,766 \div 782 = \$208$	Increase Good Decrease Bad	162,766 782	Net Revenue Total Patients
20 Visit Margin $162,766 \div 6,541 = \$25$	Increase Good Decrease Bad	162,766 6,541	Net Revenue Total Visits
Alternative Expression $208 \div 8.4 = \$25$	Increase Good Decrease Bad	208 8.4	Patient Margin Visit Turnover

17. RETENTION RATIO

Continuing Patients/Total Patients

The retention ratio looks at how many new patients from a prior period continued care in the current period. The number of current new patients could be substituted in the numerator. This ratio does not refer to the number of visits of each individual patient nor does it encompass former patients who will renew care later. An increase in this ratio may signal that patients perceive the experience as positive. Trends among new patients must be reviewed in comparison because this same increase could also be the result of declines in new patient recruitment.

18. VISIT TURNOVER

Total Visits/Total Patients

This ratio examines how many visits each individual patient has made on average within a given time period. A low visit turnover rate could result if patients see rapid improvements to their health or if patient retention is low. This ratio should be compared to the retention ratio to determine if a problem might be occurring. The visit turnover ratio does not capture how the current group of patients will make appointments in future periods.

19. PATIENT MARGIN

Net Revenue/Total Patients

This ratio calculates how much the average patient has spent within the current time period. Net profit could be substituted in the numerator. This ratio does not refer to the historical amount of patients who have been seen in the past nor does it include the number of visits made. The current group of patients may spend more or less on average sometime in the future.

20. VISIT MARGIN

Net Revenue/Total Visits

Alternative Expression: Patient Margin/Visit Turnover

The patient or visit margin may use either net revenue or net profit in the numerator.

The visit margin provides an estimate of how much each patient spends on average per visit. This ratio has significance when trying to establish prices and service lines. Imagine that a health care organization offers three services priced at $20, $40, and $54. The average price of these three services, if consumed in equal proportions, would equal $38. When the visit margin differs significantly from this mark, an organization can assume that patients favor one service line over the others. In this example, a visit margin of $25 means that most patients gravitate toward the $20 service line. The organization could then look at the profit potential of the $20 service line to determine if any modifications should be made to price rates or service offerings. An alternative expression is provided to show another method of calculating this ratio.

Summary

An organization should review different financial ratios as a form of business analysis. An organization that follows the *cash* method of accounting may need to switch to the *accrual* method in order to gather meaningful data. The debt and liquidity ratios look at the ability to cover obligations using profit levels or current assets. Profitability and operating ratios examine how well expenses and equity capital are used to support the production of revenue. Billing ratios cover the extent to which amounts due from patients are collected in total. Finally, the organization will want to review patient and visit activity in order to assess the patient experience.

8.3   Budgeting

A budget outlines what an organization hopes will take place financially in the future and sets limits on resource expenditures. A budget could serve to inspire better performance by listing ideal targets as opposed to outlining expected activity. The scope of a budget may involve a week, month, quarter, year, or several years depending on the situation. Several types of budgets exist, but they often focus on operating, financial, and cash activity.

Together, the operating and financial budgets estimate what the value of all accounts should be at a future moment in time. Once that future moment has passed, the actual account values are compared against the earlier budgeted amounts to assess the **variance** between estimated and actual performance. A *positive* variance reflects an outcome that was better than expected, whereas a *negative* variance results when revenue or expense activity proves worse than expected. Variance analysis is used to highlight any inefficient activity that is taking place. A cash budget is used to confirm that an organization has enough money to pay expenses and make crucial investments in fixed assets without the cash balance becoming negative at some point.

An organization will need to forecast future activity to formulate a budget. Historical trends serve as a good starting point when formulating assumptions about the future. Current trends and marketing efforts could be used to establish or refine assumptions further.

Variance: Difference between amounts budgeted at the beginning of a time period and the actual account activity over the entire time period.

Forecasting principles are discussed in the finance section of this textbook. The terms *estimated* and *projected* are synonymous with the word *forecasted*.

Operating Budget

An operating budget normally covers all *income statement* accounts, including interest expense, gains, and losses. The best starting point for the entire budgeting process involves formulating revenue assumptions and estimating future revenue levels. Historical trends, current economic conditions, and marketing efforts influence this assessment. Various expense accounts can be estimated based on the forecasted revenue levels. For example, there might be a strong relationship between revenues and office expenses. An expense might bear no relationship to revenue levels whereupon other factors must be considered. For instance, a tax professional may charge a flat annual fee or rent expense might already be established in a lease contract. Every income statement account must be analyzed separately to understand what drives activity.

The variance between estimated and actual activity must be assessed at the end of each time period. Figure 8.1 uses the same income statement from Chapter 7, but adds budgeted and actual amounts for the subsequent year. The positive and negative variances shown in the last column should be examined to determine what went wrong during the year and what could be improved.

Financial Budget

An organization can also prepare a financial budget that seeks to estimate *balance sheet* activity. Estimated net profit calculated from the operating budget can flow to the equity section of the financial budget. Estimated revenue and expense levels can shape estimates for accounts receivable, inventory, and accounts payable. The estimated value of cash from the cash budget (seen in Figure 8.2) can be placed in the financial budget as well. Assumptions can be formulated in order to estimate the remaining balance sheet accounts. The purchase and sale of fixed assets should be based on growth projections plus any estimated replacements. Accumulated depreciation can be configured using an organization's estimated fixed asset needs. A loan schedule will specify a loan's estimated balance plus the amount that should be reclassified to current liabilities. The remainder of the financial budget must be properly estimated according to what the individual accounts involve. The variance between estimated and actual activity must be assessed at the end of each time period.

Either the cash or accrual method is acceptable for compiling the operating and financial budgets.

An example financial budget is not shown. A financial budget has the same format as an operating budget, but relates to balance sheet accounts.

FIGURE 8.1 Sample Operating Budget

Operating Budget—Accrual Method
For the period ending December 31

	Prior 2012	Actual 2013	Budget 2013	Variance 2013
Revenues				
Primary revenue	148,611	135,211	160,000	(24,789)
Secondary revenue	14,935	16,197	15,000	1,197
Product revenue	872	2,865	1,000	1,865
Refunds	(1,652)	(965)	(1,000)	35
Net revenue	162,766	153,308	175,000	(21,692)
Expenses				
Advertising	3,922	4,527	4,000	(527)
Bad debts	720	843	800	(43)
Charitable contributions	200	200	200	–
Computer expense	1,965	864	1,200	336
Continuing education	350	395	375	(20)
Cost of goods sold	580			–
Depreciation and amortization	12,824	10,425	10,425	–
Dues and subscriptions	128	134	130	(4)
Insurance	8,540	9,461	8,800	(661)
Legal and professional	4,881	3,486	4,000	514
Meals and entertainment	2,916	3,357	3,000	(357)
Office expense	2,234	1,942	2,300	358
Office supplies	1,782	1,538	1,900	362
Postage and delivery	1,321	1,277	1,400	123
Repairs and maintenance	2,763	846	2,500	1,654
Salaries and wages	65,000	65,000	70,000	5,000
Taxes and licenses	9,650	9,578	9,700	122
Travel expense	978	645	1,300	655
Utilities	4,266	4,397	4,300	(97)
Miscellaneous	389	86	300	214
Total Expenses	125,409	119,001	126,630	7,629
Net profit (loss) from operations	37,357	34,307	48,370	(14,063)
Interest expense	(18,562)	(17,642)	(17,642)	–
Interest income	745	523	600	(77)
Gains and losses	(822)	–	–	–
Net profit (loss)	18,718	17,188	31,328	(14,140)

Cash Budget

An organization needs cash on a consistent basis to meet liability obligations. Even a highly profitable organization can run into cash flow problems if expenses are not properly matched against the timing of revenue. Suppose a printer breaks and is immediately replaced. A day later, payroll checks are sent to employees and not enough funds are available. Bouncing payroll checks can greatly frustrate employees, lead to overdraft fees, and cause government authorities to assess penalties for submitting payroll taxes late. *Meeting payroll expenses will present a continual challenge for a health care organization.*

> Consider using a payroll service to ensure payroll obligations are paid on time.

In the example cash budget shown in Figure 8.2, amounts have been categorized into operating, investing, and financing activities. The purchase or sale of capitalized assets is

FIGURE 8.2 Example Cash Budget

		Budgeted Amounts			
		Current Month	**Next Month**	**Month 2**	**Month 3**
	Beginning cash balance	7,495	9,879	4,100	6,381
	Cash from operating activity				
A	Collections	13,564	12,840	14,900	14,900
B	Payroll expenses	(6,121)	(6,121)	(6,121)	(6,121)
B	Insurance	(712)	(712)	(712)	(712)
B	Utilities	(356)	(356)	(356)	(356)
C	Capitalized lease payments	(333)	(333)	(333)	(333)
D	Priority expenses	(1,942)	(548)	(642)	(73)
D	General expenses	(389)	(1,622)	(1,528)	(2,097)
	Total cash from operations	3,711	3,148	5,208	5,208
	Cash from investing activity				
E	Sales	1,600	–	–	–
E	Purchases	–	(6,000)	–	–
	Total cash from investing	1,600	(6,000)	–	–
	Cash from financing activity				
	Contributions	–	–	–	–
	Distributions	(500)	(500)	(500)	(500)
	New loan proceeds	–	–	–	–
F	Loan payments	(2,427)	(2,427)	(2,427)	(6,927)
	Total cash from financing	(2,927)	(2,927)	(2,927)	(7,427)
G	Ending cash balance	9,879	4,100	6,381	4,162

The alphabetic values A through G correspond to the explanation of activity that follows.

A. Based on current billable charges and general revenue assumptions, collections are expected to decline in the coming month. In the months thereafter, historical trends are used to generate an estimate of future collections.

B. These expenses show little fluctuation and must be paid on time. These three expenses represent two-thirds of the total budget for expenses.

C. Although the organization capitalized a lease and reports depreciation and interest expense on the income statement, the cash budget reflects the actual monthly lease payment of $333, which totals $4,000 per year. Imputed interest expense and noncash depreciation related to the capital lease are not part of the cash budget.

D. The remaining expenses are divided into two categories: priority and general. Most expenses are deemed a priority in the current month, but expenses set to occur in later months are not considered a priority yet. If a negative cash balance was projected to occur, the organization could postpone general expenses (and perhaps priority expenses) if necessary.

E. The organization sold some furniture for $1,600 and a search is underway for replacement furniture that will cost an estimated $6,000. The cash budget shows that the organization has enough funds to cover this nonstandard activity.

F. The organization would like to decrease its bank loan in an effort to reduce interest charges. After three months, the cash budget shows that a $4,500 payment could occur without generating a negative cash balance.

G. The ending cash balances each month appear to provide a sufficient cushion against an overdraft occurring. If the organization attempted to buy furniture and pay down its loan within the next month, a cash shortfall might occur.

listed under investing activity. The inflow and outflow of capital from investors is considered financing activity. This framework does not have to be followed when arranging your own cash budget.

Only the *cash* method of accounting should be used to compile a cash budget. A cash budget should continuously roll forward covering the next three to four one-month time periods. As one month ends, a new month is added to the budget. Variances are not used with a cash budget, meaning actual performance is not compared to budgeted amounts. If a negative cash balance is projected, an organization must decide which bills to postpone paying. Relationships and penalties should be considered when making this decision.

Vendors will often invoice an organization after rendering services. An invoice will stipulate the general terms of payment. A cash budget should take into account the final due date listed on invoices since vendors will become agitated or assess penalties if bills are paid late. In a close-knit community, vendors may be a good source of referrals and should be treated with utmost consideration. An organization needs to understand how much flexibility it has to withhold payment until cash becomes available.

The assumptions used to create the operating and financial budgets can apply to the cash budget. Modification may be needed since a cash budget normally covers a shorter time period. Accounts receivable or outstanding patient balances can foreshadow what the estimated rate of collections might be over the next several months. Payroll expenses can be time sensitive and should be reported in isolation. The remaining expenses can be listed individually or grouped together in terms of priority. Cash flows related to long-term debt or lease obligations may already be established per a contract. Noncash items, such as depreciation and amortization, should not be placed in a cash budget. The remaining budget for expenses can be constructed using invoices already received or based on assumptions about future activity.

Summary

The budget process is used to estimate account values as part of planning for a future time period. A variance represents the difference between budgeted and actual amounts. An operating budget encompasses the *income statement* whereas a financial budget covers the *balance sheet*. A cash budget presents the balance of cash at given points in time, usually monthly. A negative cash balance can occur—even for an organization that is highly profitable—if cash inflows are not properly matched against outflows.

8.4   Profitability Analysis

An organization needs to clearly understand the relationship between revenues and expenses in an effort to maintain healthy profit levels. A negative cash balance can cause problems for an organization, but insufficient levels of profit can result in business failure. Before initiating operations, a health care provider should conduct a profitability analysis as part of a business plan to ensure that a newfound organization can generate sufficient levels of profit to fairly compensate for the time and energy involved with starting and running the venture. An established organization should conduct a profitability analysis to ensure profit levels will remain sufficient and to consider ways of boosting profit levels further.

Sensitivity Analysis

Variable Expenses: Outflows of cash or value that vary in direct relation to revenue levels.

It becomes important to distinguish between variable and fixed expenses when conducting business analysis. **Variable expenses** fluctuate in direct relation to revenue levels whereas **fixed expenses** bear a weak relationship to revenue activity. Office supplies, advertising, and overtime pay are examples of expenses that may increase or decrease in step with revenue levels. Most health care organizations face a high degree of fixed expenses encompassing office rent, loan payments, payroll expenses, utilities, and so forth. On a monthly basis, fixed expenses will not fluctuate much (by definition) yet revenue levels can vary significantly.

An organization should conduct a **sensitivity analysis** to review the degree of influence expenses have on profit levels. Figure 8.3 shows what happens to profit levels when revenues decline in the face of high fixed expenses. Note how both revenues and variable expenses decline by the same rate of 20%. This 20% decline has resulted in a 29% decline in overall profitability. Increasing the percentage of fixed expenses would further amplify this impact on profitability. An organization that worries about profit levels falling too low should attempt to maintain a higher percentage of variable expenses. For example, instead of hiring a permanent, full-time staff member, a temporary or part-time worker could be employed.

Fixed Expenses:
Outflows of cash or value that bear little or no relationship to revenue activity and which tend to remain constant over time.

Sensitivity Analysis:
An examination of how economic variables impact each other.

FIGURE 8.3 Sensitivity Analysis

Note how fixed expenses cause net profit to fall 29% when revenue declines by 20%.

	Estimated	20% Decline	Change
Revenue	$150,000	$120,000	20%
Fixed expenses	(40,000)	(40,000)	0%
Variable expenses	(20,000)	(16,000)	20%
Net profit	$90,000	$64,000	29%

Breakeven Analysis

A business plan should include a **breakeven analysis** that shows exactly how much revenue is needed to cover all expenses. The breakeven point reveals where net profit equals zero. Pinpointing the breakeven point becomes difficult since variable expenses move in tandem with revenue levels. The net balance of revenues less variable expenses is called the **contribution margin**. This combined margin needs to exceed the total for fixed expenses. In Figure 8.4, variable expenses represent 20% of this organization's total expenses. A minimum contribution margin of $40,000 is needed before the organization can cover fixed expenses according to this percentage rate.

Breakeven Analysis:
An examination of the approximate revenue level needed to cover all fixed and variable expenses.

Contribution Margin:
The amount of profit existing after deducting variable expenses from revenue.

FIGURE 8.4 Breakeven Analysis

Various contribution margin figures are shown as of way of demonstrating exactly where the breakeven point occurs. The breakeven point reflects a net profit level of zero.

	Breakeven				
Revenues	30,000	40,000	50,000	60,000	70,000
Variable expenses	(6,000)	(8,000)	(10,000)	(12,000)	(14,000)
Contribution margin	24,000	32,000	40,000	48,000	56,000
Fixed expenses	40,000	40,000	40,000	40,000	40,000
Net profit (or loss)	(16,000)	(8,000)	–	8,000	16,000

Marketing Analysis

An analysis of marketing efforts should be conducted to specify the most efficient allocation of marketing resources. A well-structured accounting system enables an organization to keep track of marketing expenditures. Segmenting accounts or explaining journal entries in detail helps identify the transactions that serve a marketing purpose.

To determine how marketing efforts support the production of revenue, new patients should fill out a questionnaire to determine (1) how they heard about the organization and (2) what compelled them to come in as a new patient (or renew care). Imagine that a health care organization spent $8,000 to produce a radio commercial and 24 patients listed the commercial as the primary reason for initiating care. Over time, the original 24 patients referred an additional 36 patients as noted on subsequent questionnaires. Further review showed that these 60 (36 + 24) patients made 480 visits in total, resulting in revenue of $24,000. Imagine that an additional $2,000 in other expenses were allocated to this radio campaign, leading to net profit of $14,000 ($24,000 − $8,000 − $2,000). The organization could review the overall success of the radio campaign using patient ratios as shown in Table 8.8 and contrast the results against other marketing efforts.

TABLE 8.8	Marketing Analysis		
Direct Patients 24	Indirect Patients 36	Total Patients 60	Total Visits 480
Visit Turnover	8	480	Total Visits
		60	Total Patients
Patient Margin	$233	$14,000	Net Profit
		60	Total Patients
Visit Margin	$29	$14,000	Net Profit
		480	Total Visits

Net revenue or net profit can be used in the numerator of the patient or visit margin.

Summary

An organization needs to be mindful of the relationship between revenues and expenses in order to remain sufficiently profitable. A profitability analysis can be conducted as part of a business plan or to assess the ongoing operations of an existing business. A sensitivity analysis clarifies the impact fixed expenses have on profit levels by a given change in revenue activity. A contribution margin represents the net amount of revenues minus variable expenses. The breakeven point specifies the total contribution margin needed to cover fixed expenses. In order to efficiently allocate marketing resources, the amount spent on a marketing campaign must be matched with the revenue generated from patients who reacted to the marketing campaign, either directly or indirectly.

8.5   Ad Hoc Reporting

Ad Hoc Report: An unconventional report meant to explore the circumstances of an atypical situation.

The term "ad hoc" refers to any unconventional type of report. Information needed to compile an **ad hoc report** derives mainly from the accounting system but both qualitative and quantitative data apart from the accounting system can be incorporated. In order to illustrate what ad hoc reporting entails, the following case study involves a hypothetical request for information regarding apparent scheduling problems.

CASE STUDY

Ad Hoc Reporting

A health care provider has asked staff members to produce two separate ad hoc reports before the next monthly staff meeting. Staff members subsequently prepare the reports and provide an assessment to help direct the meeting's discussion.

Report #1

The health care provider wants to know how many missed appointments occurred in the preceding month, how much those visits represented in lost revenue, and how many visits were recaptured. The health care provider asked for a written overview of what took place when the missed visits were rescheduled.

Tabulation of Missed Visits			Total	Per Patient
Missed visits	14	Potential revenue	$952	$68
Recaptured visits	11	Actual revenue	594	54
Lost visits	3	Lost revenue	$358	

Staff Assessment

Each patient was called and attempts were made to reschedule after a missed visit occurred. Our charge policy concerning missed visits was communicated. Eleven patients rescheduled, but the average visit margin was only $54 as compared to the organization's normal average of $68. Patients who miss visits do not seem to spend as much as other patients. We lost approximately $358 in revenue along with valuable staff time as a result of this patient group. The staff assessment concludes that we should discover more about the source of these patients and redirect marketing resources.

Report #2

The lack of availability on the appointment schedule has been an issue voiced by patients. The health care provider wants to learn more about the impact this is having on the patient experience. A questionnaire was assembled and presented to 40 patients at random, of which 25 replied. The health care provider wants to see the questionnaire results along with a staff assessment.

Questionnaire Results

Can you always schedule an appointment at the time you want?
Strongly Agree: 6   Agree: 5   Neutral: 3   Disagree: 7   Strongly Disagree: 4

Do you feel that your appointments take place during a convenient time?
Strongly Agree: 11   Agree: 8   Neutral: 2   Disagree: 3   Strongly Disagree: 1

Specific Inconveniences Mentioned

One patient mentioned traffic and two patients mentioned having to wait too long.

Staff Assessment

The schedule normally contains a limited number of current openings and many patients must schedule weeks in advance. Around 40% of our patients leave without making a next appointment. Per the questionnaire results, it appears that patients remain satisfied with the appointment times that are made. This does not mean that the scheduling process is easy, and calls must be placed to patients who do not reschedule at the time of their appointment. The staff assessment concludes that the organization should consider extending its operating hours or acquiring another health care provider to assist with the patient load.

Summary

An ad hoc report seeks to address unconventional issues that traditional financial reports do not cover. The issue could involve both quantitative and qualitative data. After reviewing an ad hoc report, further analysis may be needed to determine the cause of a problem or to find an effective solution.

CHAPTER ASSIGNMENT

Working in a group of three to four students or fellow professionals, complete the following items.

1. How could understanding accounting concepts help with management decision making? How might better decision making allow more time to be spent with patients instead of dealing with administrative issues or marketing?

2. Define segmentation. What importance does it hold for an organization with several distinct service lines? What are ways that information can be segmented in the accounting system?

3. List the six categories of financial ratios and explain the role that each has in business analysis.

4. What financial ratios would you want to see increase over time? What ratios signal that a problem might be occurring if they increase?

5. Define variance. What financial statements correspond to the operating and financial budgets, respectively?

6. What is the main purpose of a cash budget? In what ways could a cash budget be structured?

7. Why is it important to closely manage payroll expenses?

8. If variable expenses average 18% of revenue and fixed expenses equal $38,000 per year, how much annual revenue would an organization need in order to reach its breakeven point?

Taxation

AUTHOR'S NOTE

Focus on the tax rules related to S corporations and what it means to earn a reasonable wage as a corporation owner. Because of strict requirements on how distributions must be made by corporations, two or more business owners working together may want to operate as a partnership or limited liability corporation. Pay close attention to what business owners must do in order to uphold a corporation's status as a separate entity. Estimated tax payments are a way of life for most small business owners. Have a tax professional ensure that estimated tax payments are sufficient throughout the year and consider paying more than the bare minimum in order to avoid a large year-end tax payment. Finally, get in the habit of keeping good records on expense items and clearly specifying their business purpose.

Taxes are a way of life for organizations operating for profit. Navigating the rules on how to file tax returns correctly can be overwhelming. An organization can attempt to base its internal accounting system around the tax code in order to simplify the process of reporting tax information. In most cases, tax professionals will make adjustments to an organization's accounting records to correct any improperly recorded transactions. Understanding the basic structure of the tax code and filing requirements allows organization members to carry on a better conversation with tax professionals and minimize the costs associated with filing returns. This chapter covers the tax filing requirements for organizations operating in the United States. Tax authorities with jurisdiction outside of the United States could set forth substantially different tax filing requirements.

An organization must decide on the optimal business form before initiating business activity. Not only will the business form define tax policy, but it will also have legal implications as well. A corporate form of business usually grants all business owners a fair degree of protection against personal liability for business debts. *A lending institution can circumvent this protective shield by requiring a borrower to sign over personal assets to cover a loan in case of default.* The U.S. tax code establishes two different approaches toward taxing corporations. A corporation could face a corporate-level tax on earnings and an additional individual-level tax on any **dividend** distribution. Or, a corporation could file an informational return at the corporate level and pay only an individual-level tax on corporate activity reported on an owner's personal tax return. The latter approach permits a corporation to face one level of taxation instead of two and represents the most desirable business form for most small business owners. Since the related set of rules is contained under Subchapter S of the U.S. tax code, this business form is referred to as an S corporation.

Dividend: A distribution of stock or money made to an owner of a corporation.

Payroll taxes must be paid promptly on behalf of all employees no matter the business form. The use of a payroll service is advised since filing requirements occur frequently throughout the year and can involve a high degree of complexity. A health care organization will most likely face additional taxes at the state and local levels. An organization must pay attention to all of these different filing requirements and keep good records to support amounts reported on tax forms. Websites administered by tax authorities maintain a large collection of forms, instructions, and publications that cover most inquiries. Ask a tax professional when in doubt and encourage the use of a *letter ruling* when no clear answer is available. Letter rulings are quite rare since they require high fees and tax professionals can usually figure out the appropriate treatment of tax matters based on available information and general experience.

9.1 Business Forms

The individual states in the United States are responsible for granting legal authority to a business form. The state agency that governs business forms is normally called the **Secretary of State**. The tax filing requirements at the federal, state, and local levels are based on the business form permitted by state law. There are three broad approaches to taxation that apply to businesses as outlined in Table 9.1. Among the first type, a business owner must place revenue and expense activity on Form 1040 Schedule C as well as supporting tax forms. This approach involves only one layer of taxation at the individual level. The second approach requires an informational tax return at the business level. Business information then flows to Form 1040 Schedule E as well as supporting tax forms at the individual level where taxes are then assessed. The final approach involves paying a corporate-level tax liability on earnings along with another layer of taxes at the individual level on any dividend distribution (of earnings) giving rise to **double taxation**.

> **Secretary of State:** The statewide government department in charge of authorizing businesses.
>
> **Double Taxation:** An approach to taxation where earnings are taxed at the corporate level and again at the individual level when distributed to owners.

TABLE 9.1	Taxation Approaches	
	Business Level	**Individual Level**
First Approach	No filing requirement	Business filing and tax liability
Second Approach	Informational return only	Business filing and tax liability
Third Approach	Business filing and tax liability	Tax liability on distributions

A business form must be properly selected according to the desired taxation approach and legal conditions that apply. Table 9.2 lists the main variables to consider in regard to the main business forms available in the United States.

> S corporations can offer distinct tax and legal advantages. Pay strict attention to how payroll taxes are assessed when operating as an S corporation.

TABLE 9.2	Business Forms			
	Legal Protection	**Corporate Tax Liability**	**Individual Tax Liability**	**Payroll Liability**
Sole Proprietorship	None	None	Total profits	Total profits
General Partnership	None	None	Total profits	Total profits
Limited Parternship	Limited partner	None	Total profits	Total profits
Limited Liability Partnership	All partners	None	Total profits	Total profits
Limited Liability Corporation	All members	None	Total profits	Total profits
C Corporation	All shareholders	Total profits	Distributions and wages	Wages only
S Corporation[1]	All shareholders	Rare	Profits and wages	Wages only

[1]S corporation owners must pay taxes at the individual level on all profits, whether distributed or not.

Sole Proprietorship

By default, an individual will operate as a sole proprietorship if nothing is done to establish a different business form. A state or local tax authority may require a general business license or another fee to be paid along with submission of proper documentation. In certain jurisdictions, having a valid health care license might be enough to start operations legally as a sole proprietorship.

Legal The lack of personal protection from creditors represents the biggest drawback to operating as a sole proprietorship. In a bankruptcy proceeding, personal assets would be taken into account when evaluating the ability to satisfy business debts. A bankruptcy proceeding involving a business will usually start with a **Chapter 11** business reorganization

> **Chapter 11:** An initial bankruptcy filing that attempts to keep a business solvent by reorganizing debts and setting forth a plan to meet future obligations.

Chapter 7: A bankruptcy filing that results in liquidation of a business (or personal assets) in satisfaction of debts resulting in conclusion of business activity.

Personal assets will not be accessible in a bankruptcy proceeding if the business form grants personal protection.

filing. The debtor will confirm a plan to satisfy obligations with creditors and continue to engage in business activity. If a plan under Chapter 11 becomes unachievable, the bankruptcy proceeding could progress to a **Chapter 7** filing wherein business and personal assets will be liquidated until either (1) debts are fully satisfied or (2) the debtor would not have enough to survive properly.

Taxes A sole proprietorship files business activity on Form 1040 Schedule C at the individual level along with supporting forms. This represents the easiest way to file a business tax return and can minimize filing costs. Most of the business information is placed directly on the Schedule C. The reporting of auto expenses, depreciation, amortization, and the sale of assets are areas that receive special treatment and are normally reported on supporting forms first.

General Partnership

When two or more individuals combine ownership stakes, the business form automatically defaults to a general partnership. Under this scenario, the business owners share assets and liability obligations as set forth in a partnership agreement or as stipulated by state law. Most states require that a general partnership submit a business application that includes a signed partnership agreement. Lending institutions will often want to see a partnership agreement before opening a related business bank account.

Legal Sharing ownership with another person inserts various risks into the equation. A soured relationship or disagreements over how to manage operations can result in dissolution of the business or increased stress and tension along the way. Money can easily change how people behave and sharing ownership should come with many strict conditions set forth in a well-structured partnership agreement. A partnership agreement has incredible significance if a business dissolves since assets belong to all business partners unless otherwise noted. A general partnership does not provide any personal protection from creditors. Owners have responsibility for all the liabilities of the partnership and may be forced to settle the debts of other partners, especially in instances where one partner seeks protection under bankruptcy laws.

A partnership may refer to owner's equity as partner's capital.

Taxes A partnership files Form 1065 and supporting forms. This represents an informational return and does not give rise to a partnership-level tax liability. Form 1065 includes a section to reconcile differences between accounting methods and another section used to track partner's capital. The partners take their portion of tax information and place it on their respective individual tax returns using Form 1040 Schedule E and supporting forms. Business information is commingled with other personal information leading to an individual-level tax only.

Limited Partnership

In order to minimize risks and create protection from creditors, states allow the formation of a limited partnership wherein two classes of ownership exist: general and limited. A limited partnership itself must have at least one general and one limited partner. A health care provider may consider this business form instead of a general partnership in order to protect a passive outside investor, such as a family member, wanting to help contribute capital. Although this business form provides legal protection to a limited partner, a general partner would not enjoy this same protection.

Legal A general partner can openly participate in the management of the partnership but must assume more risk by not receiving any creditor protection. A general partner faces personal liability for all partnership debts. The second class of ownership involves a limited partner who is prohibited from participating in management affairs. A limited partner takes a passive investor role and assumes no personal responsibility for the partnership's debts as a result. The only potential loss equals the amount of investment placed into the organization, but nothing beyond that amount. If a limited partner *does* participate in management of the business, this protective status could be lost whereby the investor would be treated as a general partner.

Taxes A *limited* partnership would file tax information in the same manner as a *general* partnership using Form 1065 and supporting forms. Tax information would be passed along to each partner based on the percentage of ownership or as prescribed in a partnership agreement. Partners would pay tax at the individual level after placing their portion of the partnership's tax information on their respective Form 1040 Schedule E and supporting forms.

Limited Liability Corporation

An *individual* who is incorporated as a limited liability corporation (LLC) can file tax forms in the same manner as a *sole proprietorship* using Form 1040 Schedule C and supporting forms. In contrast, an LLC with two or more *members* would file tax information using Form 1065 in the same manner as a *partnership*. Unlike a sole proprietorship or partnership, an LLC offers legal protection against creditors to every owner without regard to ownership class. The advent of the LLC has removed nearly all advantages of operating as a sole proprietorship or partnership. An LLC is not a default business form, meaning a state will not grant authority to an LCC without submission of a proper business application.

> Owners of an LLC are referred to as members, not partners.

A less common business form is the limited liability partnership (LLP), which faces almost the same legal and tax conditions as a multimember LLC. Since the discussion here also applies to an LLP (for the most part), this business form is not reviewed in isolation.

Legal An LLC affords personal protection from creditors to every owner. The personal affairs of a business owner will not be factored into a bankruptcy filing unless the business form was improperly administered per state law. Personal protection could be lost if an owner does not treat the LLC as a separate entity. Commingling personal assets with business assets as in a bank account could give creditors the ammunition they need to **pierce the corporate veil**. Not holding regular corporate meetings, not paying state incorporation fees, not submitting an annual report to the state, or not performing other duties necessary to maintain the corporate structure increases the potential risk of creditors gaining access to an owner's personal assets. *Corporate governance* represents the steps a business owner must take to maintain the corporate business form as reflected in Table 9.3. Even if the corporate structure remains intact, a corporation does not afford protection against liabilities arising from illegal activities. A lending institution can also circumvent the corporate veil by having a borrower sign over personal assets as part of extending a loan.

> **Pierce the Corporate Veil:** A situation where creditors gain access to personal assets as a result of owners improperly administering the corporate structure.

TABLE 9.3	Corporate Governance

The corporate business form must be maintained by engaging in certain activities:

1. Holding regular corporate meetings
2. Paying state incorporation fees
3. Submitting an annual report to the state
4. Keeping business activity separate from personal activity
5. Performing other duties as necessary

Taxes Even though an LLC functions as a corporation per state law, the tax reporting requirements parallel those of a sole proprietorship or partnership. By default, a single-member LLC has the same tax reporting requirements as a sole proprietorship. Business information is placed on Form 1040 Schedule C and supporting tax forms at the individual level only. This spares a business owner from having to file an additional business-level tax return. When an LLC involves two or more members, business information is placed on partnership Form 1065 and supporting forms first and then is passed along to the respective members at the individual level. An LLC has the choice to be taxed as a corporation, but this rarely occurs. Many states place restrictions on the types of business forms available to health care providers. Check with a licensed professional to make sure your state allows a single-member LLC or professional service LLC if this business form is desired.

C Corporation

A standard corporation falls under Subchapter C of the U.S. tax code. This business form treats an organization as a separate legal and tax entity. The state will grant authority to a corporation after proper submission of a corporate application. Major companies usually operate under this type of corporate structure, allowing investors to buy and sell ownership stakes without any personal liability for corporate debts. Investors can lose the amount of money or property contributed to a corporation, but nothing beyond this amount. A C corporation will pay taxes on earnings and investors must pay an additional tax on the distribution of these same earnings (dividends). Owners will receive dividend distributions according to their exact percentage of ownership. In contrast, owners of a partnership or LLC have the flexibility to distribute profits per any formula as set forth in a partnership agreement. Most small business owners favor other business forms that provide creditor protection without the burden of double taxation or these strict distribution rules.

An LLC may not need to maintain a board of directors depending on state law.

Legal An organization will want to ensure that the corporate structure is being maintained properly through strong corporate governance. The state will require submission of an annual report and incorporation fees. Personal and business assets should not be commingled in any fashion. A corporation should also hold annual meetings, which usually involve legal counsel being present.

The investors of a major corporation may be completely removed from the actual management of a company. In order to provide oversight on managers who run the company, investors elect a **board of directors** to work on their behalf. Board members serve the investors of a company by providing management oversight on major issues. The board of directors typically sets management pay and makes decisions about hiring and firing management. Board members meet infrequently and generally receive very little compensation.

Board of Directors: An elected body that oversees a company's management team on behalf of owners.

With a small corporation, one person might be an owner, board member, and manager all at once. A corporation will need to have these roles performed even if only one person fulfills all the duties. A business owner could lose personal protection against creditors if a board of directors is not maintained. Check with a licensed professional to verify if your state will allow a one-owner corporation (if applicable).

Taxes A corporation files Form 1120 and supporting forms in accordance with Subchapter C of the U.S. tax code. A corporate-level tax is assessed based on the taxable income of the corporation. The board of directors can declare and pay a distribution of earnings (dividend). Owners face an additional tax liability on such distributions at the individual level, thus resulting in double taxation.

Corporate tax code requires that managers of a corporation earn a *reasonable* salary. The definition of reasonable is vague, but the amount should compare to what employees in similar positions make within the marketplace. Using wages as a tax strategy can be difficult and may lead to a confrontation with tax authorities. Tax authorities consider excessive wages to be an indirect owner distribution and have the power to recharacterize these amounts. Part of the wages paid to an owner could be reversed on the corporate tax return, causing an increase to the corporation's taxable income. The decrease in wages would reverse some of the individual-level tax liability for the time being—perhaps offsetting some or all of the increased corporate tax liability—but the owner would face more taxes when trying to make a dividend distribution of the recharacterized corporate earnings. In order to avoid a dispute with tax authorities, a licensed professional should be consulted when establishing the reasonability of owner wages.

A C corporation may trigger criteria that would cause it to be defined as a personal service corporation (PSC). A flat 35% tax rate may apply to all corporate profits in cases where individuals performing personal services, including in the field of health, own 95% of the stock. Instead of the graduated tax rates that start much lower and then slowly build in increments over different ranges of taxable income, only one tax rate would apply to a PSC resulting in a much larger tax liability. A health care organization that operates as a C corporation can easily trigger PSC rules resulting in a highly unfavorable tax environment.

> Consult a tax professional to determine if PSC rules apply to your corporation (if applicable).

S Corporation

Owners of a C corporation can elect to be taxed under Subchapter S of the U.S. tax code. One of the most preferred business forms has become the S corporation because it does not provoke double taxation. A corporate-level tax is not assessed in this situation. Business information is passed along to the respective owners whereby corporate earnings are subject to individual-level taxes only. An S corporation offers an additional tax advantage in relation to payroll taxes. An owner of a sole proprietorship, partnership, or LLC does not receive a wage resulting in payroll taxes being assessed on all earnings. Payroll taxes are not assessed on the earnings of a C, S, or personal service corporation, rather only on the wages that an owner might earn. Unlike all other business forms, an S corporation provides an owner the unique ability to avoid double taxation *and* encounter payroll taxes only on wages.

One drawback of operating as an S corporation involves the distribution of earnings (or retained earnings) per the exact percentage of ownership. Owners of a partnership or LLC have the flexibility to distribute amounts per a different distribution formula if set forth in a partnership agreement.

Legal   A state may impose limitations on business owners who want to operate as an S corporation. Check with a licensed professional to make sure that your state will allow a single-owner S corporation or a professional service S corporation. As with any other corporate form of business, an S corporation owner can lose creditor protection if the corporate structure is not properly maintained. An S corporation must have a board of directors, even if only one person fulfills this and other roles.

Taxes   After filing the proper documents with the state, an organization will receive an official date of incorporation. An organization then has two months and 15 days to file Form 2553 with the IRS to elect treatment under Subchapter S of the corporate tax code. Failing to file within this deadline could make it extremely difficult to become an S corporation later. Although IRS rules place restrictions on the ability to form an S corporation, most small health care organizations should qualify for Subchapter S status unless state law determines otherwise.

If granted an S election by the IRS, an organization would report tax information on Form 1120S and supporting forms. Tax information would then flow to each owner's Form 1040 Schedule E and supporting forms at the individual level. There is no corporate tax liability on profits of an S corporation even where the corporation qualifies as a personal service corporation. An S corporation can distribute its earnings without the burden of double taxation—and without invoking payroll taxes either. Operating as an S corporation becomes advantageous from a tax standpoint after considering not only corporate and individual taxes on income, but payroll taxes as well.

> A few rare instances will give rise to a corporate-level tax when operating as an S corporation.

A health care provider who operates as a sole proprietorship, general partnership, limited partnership, or LLC will pay *both* payroll and income taxes on all earnings without the benefit of reducing net earnings with wage payments. In contrast, an S corporation allows an owner to distribute profits directly to the individual level without being subject to payroll taxes. Only the wages that an S corporation owner must reasonably earn are subject to both payroll and income taxes. This denotes the main advantage to operating as an S corporation. *Corporate-level taxes are virtually never assessed and payroll taxes are only assessed on wages.* With all other business forms, the overall tax liability tends to be higher as a result of how corporate, payroll, and individual taxes are levied in total.

The IRS pays strict attention to the wages and distributions of an S corporation because of this tax advantage. The IRS will levy back payroll taxes if it feels that the wages paid to an owner were excessively low. An owner who works for a corporation must earn a reasonable salary in terms of the work performed. This notion of reasonable may refer to what similar health care providers in the marketplace earn, an organization's historical level of profit, or the amount of profit that other organization members help produce. A health care provider operating alone without any employees would have a hard time justifying a low wage because all profits derive from just one person's efforts. In order to avoid a dispute with tax authorities, a tax professional should be consulted when establishing the reasonability of owner wages.

Summary

A debtor will first attempt to seek protection under Chapter 11 of the bankruptcy code. A debtor will confirm a plan of reorganization with creditors and continue operations if allowed. If a debtor cannot adhere to the plan, then the bankruptcy may proceed to a Chapter 7 liquidation. The corporate structure can offer personal protection against creditors if properly maintained. If creditors pierce the corporate veil or a business owner operates as a partnership or sole proprietorship, personal assets might be used to fulfill business debts. Lending institutions will often require corporate owners to secure a loan using personal assets to circumvent the corporate veil.

Profits reported by an owner of an LLC, partnership, or sole proprietorship are subject to payroll and individual-level taxes. The profits of an S corporation are only subject to individual-level taxes, escaping both payroll and corporate taxes. An owner of an S corporation who also works for the business must earn a reasonable wage. Payroll and individual taxes are only assessed on wages, thus allowing an owner of an S corporation to face a smaller tax liability compared to all other business forms. Check with a tax professional to verify if a particular wage appears reasonable and if limitations exist on operating under a certain business form.

9.2 Payroll Taxes

Payroll taxes and related tax forms typically need to be submitted on a monthly, quarterly, and annual basis. An organization must obtain an employer identification number (EIN) before submitting federal payroll forms. Apart from employment activity, a business operating as a partnership or corporation must obtain an EIN in order to submit general tax forms. Applying for an EIN can be done online through the Internal Revenue Service website, toll-free over the phone, or by downloading and submitting Form SS-4. Seek the advice of a licensed tax professional to determine if you need an EIN or if questions exist about how to file the form correctly.

Apply for an EIN online at irs.gov.

An organization will need to alert the state's labor department before engaging in employment activity. Giving notice of intent to engage in employment activity is often done indirectly as part of filing business forms with the Secretary of State's office. Business applications often ask about employment activity and then forward related information to the appropriate state agency. As a result of the time sensitivity related to filing federal and state payroll forms along with making payroll tax payments, *a small health care organization should hire a payroll service.* A payroll service comes in handy when trying to administer employee benefit programs, such as a retirement plan, and usually costs very little overall.

Federal Payroll Taxes

Payroll taxes at the federal level include unemployment insurance as set forth in the Federal Unemployment Tax Act (FUTA). The federal base rate for FUTA equals .8% of gross wages and this amount is paid by the employer only. The Federal Insurance Contributions Act (FICA) involves the shared payment of Social Security and Medicare taxes between an employer and employee. The current FICA rate equals 15.3% of which one-half equals 7.65%. This amount is levied on the total amount of gross wages, including the reasonable wages that a C, S, or personal service corporation owner earns. An owner of a sole proprietorship, partnership, or LLC would be subject to FICA taxes on all earnings. A limited partner would not be subject to any payroll taxes.

> The Social Security portion of the FICA tax is not levied on wages over $110,000 in 2012. This wage base will increase in future years.

State Payroll Taxes

An organization might experience a higher FUTA rate if the state unemployment insurance rate as set forth in the State Unemployment Tax Act (SUTA) is not high enough. The SUTA rate will vary by state, but it is usually much larger than the FUTA rate. The exact amount levied may also vary based on the type of industry an organization operates within and the unemployment history of the organization itself. A state might require an employer to carry worker injury and disability insurance, or *worker's compensation* as it is sometimes called. For example, if an employee runs an errand and gets into an auto accident, the individual's automobile insurance will most likely refuse to cover any injuries. The employer's worker's compensation insurance would provide coverage instead since the employee had the accident while on the job. Some states provide worker's compensation insurance directly, but other states force organizations to obtain an insurance policy from a third-party vendor. States may assess other payroll taxes, but SUTA and worker's compensation represent the most common ones required.

Independent Contractors

An independent contractor performing services for an organization does not constitute an employee for whom payroll taxes would apply. Treating an employee as an independent contractor in an effort to avoid payroll taxes could result in a lawsuit or an assessment of back payroll taxes by a tax authority. If a worker does not meet the standards of an independent contractor, an organization must treat the worker as a regular employee. The determination is based largely on the amount of control that can be exerted over a person's work. Table 9.4 provides a general overview of what distinguishes an independent contractor from an employee.

TABLE 9.4 Determination of Worker Status	Independent Contractor	Regular Employee
Activity Control		
Does the organization dictate how to perform a task, including what supplies or equipment to use?	No	Yes
Do the tasks performed relate to a specific project or could they continue for an indeterminate amount of time?	Project	Indeterminate
Is there a contract that defines the tasks?	Yes	No
Financial Control		
Must the worker pay for supplies or equipment without the right of reimbursement?	Yes	No
Does the organization pay by the hour or in accordance to a flat fee?	Flat Fee	Hourly
Does the worker offer services to other organizations?	Yes	No

More information
about determining a
worker's status can be
found in Chapter 18.

More information related to payroll matters can be found in IRS Publications 15 and 15A. Consult a licensed professional if the status of an independent contractor seems questionable. If the status of a worker appears unclear, an organization can file IRS Form SS-8, Determination of Worker Status. When in doubt, an organization should treat a worker as an employee in order to avoid a lawsuit or back taxes. Table 9.5 presents a general list of IRS publications useful to a small business.

TABLE 9.5	IRS Publications
Publication 15	Circular E, Employer's Tax Guide
Publication 15A	Employer's Supplemental Tax Guide
Publication 334	Tax Guide for Small Business (Schedule C)
Publication 505	Tax Withholding and Estimated Tax
Publication 535	Business Expenses
Publication 541	Partnerships
Publication 542	Corporations
Publication 583	Starting a Business and Keeping Records
Publication 946	How to Depreciate Property
Publication 1518	IRS Tax Calendar for Small Businesses and Self-Employed

Summary

The process of filing payroll tax forms and submitting tax payments can overwhelm a small business. A payroll service can handle such matters for a small monthly fee. An organization will need to pay FICA and FUTA taxes at the federal level. The state will most likely impose SUTA and worker's compensation taxes. An organization does not have to pay taxes for an independent contractor. This can lead an organization to improperly treat an employee as an independent contractor. An organization needs to evaluate the amount of activity and financial control being exerted to properly determine a worker's status. Read IRS publications 15 and 15A and consult a licensed professional if a worker's status seems questionable.

9.3   State and Local Taxes

State and local tax authorities will most likely assess several types of business taxes or a licensing fee. The most common forms of state taxes are assessed on income, personal property, gross receipts, or consumption activity.

Income Tax

A state income tax is levied on business profits at the corporate or individual level depending on the type of business form. A state's corporate or individual income tax system may imitate U.S. tax code but with slight modifications. Seven states do not levy an income tax.

Personal Property Tax

The total amount of an organization's applicable capitalized assets may be subject to a personal property tax. *Personal property* refers to equipment in contrast to *real property* that involves buildings and land. States maintain their own capitalization policies governing which expenses to capitalize.

Gross Receipts Tax

A gross receipts tax is levied on net revenue ignoring all business expenses. This contrasts with an income tax that is assessed on net profit after consideration of expenses.

Consumption Tax

A consumption (sales) tax is levied on the sale of products and usually ignores service revenue. An organization will remit the tax even though it might be directed at the consumer. A use tax might be imposed on products that came free of sales tax originally, but would otherwise have been subject to a sales tax if purchased within the state or under normal circumstances. The state may impose a flat consumption tax rate, to which local tax authorities can assess additional amounts, resulting in different combined rates throughout the state.

Apart from what the state collects, a city or county might impose a business tax or licensing fee. A licensing fee could equal a flat rate or reflect a percentage of income. Local taxes might be part of a multicity or multicounty tax agreement. Contact a tax professional to find out what state and local tax requirements exist in your area.

Summary

A health care organization will need to consider taxes levied by state and local authorities. Common examples include income, personal property, gross receipts, and consumption taxes. Each marketplace differs and an organization will need to contact a tax professional to figure out what reporting requirements apply at the state and local level.

9.4   Tax Planning

An organization following the *cash* method of accounting should try to manage the timing of revenues and expenses toward the end of a tax year in order to place net profit in a time period with a favorable **marginal** or **effective tax rate**. The *cash* method provides more flexibility in terms of controlling when revenues and expenses can be reported in contrast to the *accrual* method. Two factors will determine the best time period in which to place revenue and expense activity: (1) to what extent will tax rates change and (2) what is the estimate of future taxable income?

An organization will want to consider revenues and expenses separately when figuring out the best time period in which to report activity. If tax rates or estimated revenue levels are expected to increase, an organization may want to postpone paying certain expenses until the next time period. Caution should be used since vendors might impose penalties or grow frustrated by late payments. Billing efforts could be intensified to collect more patient revenue in the current period when tax rates are currently lower.

If revenue levels or tax rates are expected to decline in the future, an organization should pay expenses or consummate purchases in the current time period. Tax authorities usually limit a deduction for prepaid expenses that cover more than one year. For example, prepaid malpractice insurance is only deductible if payments apply to coverage over the next twelve months. A tax deduction is not available for prepaying a credit card. An organization could slow billing efforts in an attempt to postpone collections until the next tax period.

> **Marginal Tax Rate:** The tax rate imposed upon a specific layer of taxable income.

> **Effective Tax Rate:** The average percentage of tax imposed upon taxable income after application of marginal rates.

> Depending on an organization's overall level of taxable income, some marginal tax rates may not be triggered.

Estimated Tax Payments

Once the tax period closes, a taxpayer will need to remit tax liabilities before the filing deadline of the corresponding tax return even if an extension is made. If tax documents cannot be filed before the filing deadline, a taxpayer should submit an estimate of the taxes owed. A taxpayer may be assessed fees and penalties if the filing deadline passes and a large underpayment remains.

A self-employed taxpayer will often need to make sufficient **estimated tax payments** throughout the year or face penalties and fees. A proper approach to tax planning involves estimating the *annual* tax liability at each due date of the estimated tax payments to confirm that each payment will be sufficient. Most tax professionals will present a taxpayer with

> **Estimated Tax Payments:** Payments made to a tax authority incrementally, usually quarterly, in an effort to satisfy a projected year-end tax liability.

Estimated tax payments may be required if taxes are not submitted by another source, such as an employer.

estimated tax payment coupons at the first of the year that reflect the minimum amount required by tax authorities. Once the year is complete, the actual tax liability may greatly exceed these minimum payments that were originally required. A taxpayer could face an enormous tax bill by approaching estimated tax payments in this manner. Consider making estimated tax payments that reflect an estimate of the total amount to be owed for the year instead of merely paying the bare minimum.

Summary

An organization that uses the *cash* method of accounting can attempt to shift revenues or expenses into a time period with more favorable tax rates. A taxpayer should make calculations throughout the year in order to verify that estimated tax payments can sufficiently cover all year-end tax liabilities instead of paying the bare minimum as many tax professionals will recommend. Once the tax period closes, a taxpayer should again make a proper estimate of any potential tax liability to ensure enough is paid before the original filing deadline.

9.5   Record Keeping

Federal, state, and local tax authorities will insist that an organization maintain proper accounting records, especially on amounts claimed as deductions. A *qualified* expense will have a reasonable business purpose in terms of an organization's standard business activity and be supported with documentation. Unless an expense can be substantiated with supporting documentation, it should not be reported on a tax form. A tax professional may need to ask that proper documents exist before preparing a tax return.

Receipts can be kept in a big brown bag with the year marked on the outside.

A mileage log should be kept on a vehicle used for business purposes if automobile expenses are computed using the standard mileage rate, especially if a vehicle is used personally as well. Request a receipt when making purchases and write a brief description about the transaction's business purpose on the back of the receipt. Noting information right away makes bookkeeping much easier than having to later remember what an item entailed.

In cases where an organization is *audited* by a tax authority, the presence of detailed documents will help to quickly prove amounts. Auditors will never comb through every receipt, but if a problem does exist in one situation, the inaccuracy that is found can be statistically applied to an account or the entire accounting system, resulting in an imputed amount of invalid deductions. For example, the IRS will often estimate the amount of back taxes it feels fully captures the correct tax liability instead of picking through all the tax detail to properly calculate what the tax liability should be—the IRS simply does not have time to perform an exact calculation. The taxpayer would then have to defend a lower amount by sifting through the accounting system and proving the real tax liability.

A tax authority will often send a letter requesting clarification on a matter. In other situations, a tax authority will automatically make corrections per documents received from a third party. A more in-depth audit may be launched if a tax authority feels that an organization has not properly reported tax information or if an organization is selected at random for a full audit. In each of these cases, a taxpayer would need proper documentation to defend amounts reported on tax documents.

In terms of payroll matters, an organization needs to keep a record of each employee's worker eligibility status by retaining a Form I-9 on each employee. The Department of Homeland Security has taken over responsibility for managing Form I-9. Certain payroll forms ask for the number of hours employees worked within a specific time period. Employees should fill out timecards to document hours worked and confirm that they engaged in productive activities throughout the day. Form W-4 provides a worksheet permitting employees to calculate the amount to withhold from each paycheck for their own personal tax liabilities. The number listed on this form is used to specify tax withholding at the state level as well. Table 9.6 contains a list of documentation that a business should maintain for at least *six years* from the filing deadline of the corresponding tax return.

TABLE 9.6	Business Documentation

1. Bank statements
2. Credit card statements
3. Processed checks
4. Expense receipts with their reasonable business purpose written on back
5. Invoices sent from third-party vendors
6. Car mileage log if using the standard mileage rate
7. Employee timecards and Forms W-4 and I-9
8. Forms 1098 or 1099 supplied by other businesses
9. Anything else deemed important

Summary

An organization should keep documentation proving amounts reported on tax forms. Organization members can write notes on the back of receipts, keep a vehicle mileage log, or maintain other records to provide clear evidence of expenses. Proper documentation will help prove that a lower tax liability applies in situations where a tax authority has audited an organization and revised the tax liability upward. Keeping good documentation also applies to payroll matters, such as with Forms W-4 and I-9.

Federal Employment Forms		
Form I-9	uscis.gov	Employment Verification Worksheet
Form W-4	irs.gov	Employee's Withholding Allowance Certificate

CHAPTER ASSIGNMENT

Working in a group of three to four students or fellow professionals, complete the following items.

1. How would an individual-member LLC report tax information? What would happen to the filing requirements if a new member joined the LLC?

2. Explain how an owner of an S corporation avoids double taxation and might not be faced with the same level of payroll taxes as other business forms. What might prevent a health care organization from operating as an S corporation?

3. What must an owner of a corporation do to ensure that the corporate structure remains intact and that personal protection against the claims of creditors are not *pierced*?

4. Describe the two general categories of payroll taxes levied at the federal and state levels. What happens if a state requires worker's compensation insurance but does not provide coverage directly?

5. Log onto your state's Department of Revenue website and research if the tax system contains an income, personal property, gross receipts, or consumption tax.

6. A health care organization uses the *cash* method of accounting and usually receives payment on 80% of its invoices within 30 days. What should this organization do if tax rates in the next tax period are expected to decrease? How could the organization manage expenses and fixed asset purchases?

7. Go online to irs.gov and review Chapter 2 of Publication 505, Tax Withholding and Estimated Tax. What are the four estimated tax payment deadlines?

8. Why might an organization want to pay more in estimated taxes than the minimum amount that is required by a tax authority?

9. Go online to irs.gov and review Publication 583, Starting a Business and Keeping Records. How long should a taxpayer retain accounting information? What are examples of acceptable forms of documentation?

Appendix II Review of Tax Forms

This section begins with a review of 2011 tax forms starting with Form 1120S, Form 1120S, which is used to report information pertaining to an S corporation. Form 1065, used to report information for a multimember LLC, general partnership, LP, or LLP, closely resembles Form 1120S and will not be covered as a result. Because single-member LLCs generally report tax information in the same way as a sole proprietorship, this section includes a review of Form 1040 Schedule C. The discussion in this appendix ignores the filing requirements for a C corporation, which calculates taxes at the corporate level. Various supporting forms are reviewed later in this appendix, but these represent only a key selection of the total possible forms that might need to be filed. This discussion does not cover all topics that might be relevant to an organization. It serves only to highlight certain key issues to help when setting up the accounting system and while working with a tax professional.

Form 1120S, Page 1

An S corporation files Form 1120S as an informational return. Only a few rare situations would give rise to tax liability at the corporate level. All income and expense information passes through to the individual level. Form 1120S is simply used to report the total activity of an organization before information flows to each owner.

Line A and G Is the corporation electing to be an S corporation beginning with this tax year? If *Yes*, attach Form 2553 if not already filed. It is important to remember that an organization must file Form 2553 federally within two months and 15 days of becoming a confirmed corporate entity by the state's licensing division.

Line D The taxpayer will need to file Form SS-4 on paper or online in order to obtain an Employer Identification Number (EIN) if not already done.

Income The total operating revenues minus any returns or allowances are reported across line 1. A health care organization might have cost of goods sold related to product sales. Form 1125-A (not shown) contains a worksheet for calculating cost of goods sold that then flows into line 2 of this section. Net gain from Form 4797 seen on line 4 refers to gains or losses on the sale of capitalized assets, such as medical equipment.

Deductions An owner who works for a corporation must earn a reasonable salary. This amount is reported on line 7 whereas other employee salaries are reported on line 8. In order to simplify preparation of this entire section, an organization's chart of accounts can already include the various expense accounts mentioned herein. Line 19 involves the remaining operating expenses that fit into other categories. An organization can develop relevant titles for these expense categories or use some of the standard titles as presented in Chapter 7.

Tax and Payments An S corporation will most likely *not* have to pay taxes despite the bottom section referencing tax items. These items pertain to highly irregular situations.

U.S. Income Tax Return for an S Corporation

Form **1120S**

Department of the Treasury
Internal Revenue Service

▶ Do not file this form unless the corporation has filed or is attaching Form 2553 to elect to be an S corporation.
▶ See separate instructions.

OMB No. 1545-0130

2011

For calendar year 2011 or tax year beginning _____ , 2011, ending _____ , 20_____

A S election effective date	TYPE OR PRINT	Name	D Employer identification number
B Business activity code number *(see instructions)*		Number, street, and room or suite no. If a P.O. box, see instructions.	E Date incorporated
C Check if Sch. M-3 attached ☐		City or town, state, and ZIP code	F Total assets *(see instructions)* $

G   Is the corporation electing to be an S corporation beginning with this tax year? ☐ Yes ☐ No   If "Yes," attach Form 2553 if not already filed

H   Check if: **(1)** ☐ Final return **(2)** ☐ Name change **(3)** ☐ Address change **(4)** ☐ Amended return **(5)** ☐ S election termination or revocation

I   Enter the number of shareholders who were shareholders during any part of the tax year . . . . ▶

Caution. *Include only trade or business income and expenses on lines 1a through 21. See the instructions for more information.*

Income

1a	Merchant card and third-party payments. For 2011, enter -0- . . .	1a	
b	Gross receipts or sales not reported on line 1a (see instructions) . .	1b	
c	Total. Add lines 1a and 1b	1c	
d	Returns and allowances plus any other adjustments (see instructions)	1d	
e	Subtract line 1d from line 1c	1e	
2	Cost of goods sold (attach Form 1125-A)	2	
3	Gross profit. Subtract line 2 from line 1e	3	
4	Net gain (loss) from Form 4797, Part II, line 17 *(attach Form 4797)*	4	
5	Other income (loss) *(see instructions—attach statement)* . . .	5	
6	**Total income (loss).** Add lines 3 through 5 . . . . ▶	6	

Deductions *(see instructions for limitations)*

7	Compensation of officers	7	
8	Salaries and wages (less employment credits)	8	
9	Repairs and maintenance	9	
10	Bad debts	10	
11	Rents	11	
12	Taxes and licenses	12	
13	Interest	13	
14	Depreciation not claimed on Form 1125-A or elsewhere on return *(attach Form 4562)* . .	14	
15	Depletion **(Do not deduct oil and gas depletion.)**	15	
16	Advertising	16	
17	Pension, profit-sharing, etc., plans	17	
18	Employee benefit programs	18	
19	Other deductions *(attach statement)*	19	
20	**Total deductions.** Add lines 7 through 19 . . . . ▶	20	
21	**Ordinary business income (loss).** Subtract line 20 from line 6 . . .	21	

Tax and Payments

22a	Excess net passive income or LIFO recapture tax (see *instructions*) . .	22a	
b	Tax from Schedule D (Form 1120S)	22b	
c	Add lines 22a and 22b *(see instructions for additional taxes)* . . .	22c	
23a	2011 estimated tax payments and 2010 overpayment credited to 2011	23a	
b	Tax deposited with Form 7004	23b	
c	Credit for federal tax paid on fuels *(attach Form 4136)*	23c	
d	Add lines 23a through 23c	23d	
24	Estimated tax penalty *(see instructions)*. Check if Form 2220 is attached . . . . ▶ ☐	24	
25	**Amount owed.** If line 23d is smaller than the total of lines 22c and 24, enter amount owed . .	25	
26	**Overpayment.** If line 23d is larger than the total of lines 22c and 24, enter amount overpaid . .	26	
27	Enter amount from line 26 **Credited to 2012 estimated tax** ▶ _____ **Refunded** ▶	27	

Sign Here

Under penalties of perjury, I declare that I have examined this return, including accompanying schedules and statements, and to the best of my knowledge and belief, it is true, correct, and complete. Declaration of preparer (other than taxpayer) is based on all information of which preparer has any knowledge.

▶ _____ _____
  Signature of officer   Date

▶ _____
  Title

May the IRS discuss this return with the preparer shown below (see instructions)? ☐ Yes ☐ No

Paid Preparer Use Only

Print/Type preparer's name	Preparer's signature	Date	Check ☐ if self-employed	PTIN
Firm's name ▶			Firm's EIN ▶	
Firm's address ▶			Phone no.	

For Paperwork Reduction Act Notice, see separate instructions.   Cat. No. 11510H   Form **1120S** (2011)

Form 1120S, Page 2

Schedule B, Other Information   Under line 1 of Schedule B, the accounting method reported will be either the cash or accrual method. The accrual method might be required in some instances, adding greater complexity to reporting functions. Line 2 displays the type of business industry and the main type of revenue producing activity. The IRS has predetermined categories for both. An amount for accumulated retained earnings is highlighted on line 7.

Schedule K, Shareholders' Pro Rata Share Items   The final section toward the bottom (Schedule K) begins the process of showcasing various items that receive different tax treatment at the individual level. Because this form represents an informational return only and amounts will flow to Form 1040 and supporting forms, each owner must be able to take business information and report it on the appropriate individual forms. Many of the items on this page refer to investment or passive activity unrelated to operations. However, the net profit from operations as calculated using the cash or accrual method is listed on line 1.

Form 1120S (2011)

Page **2**

			Yes	No
Schedule B	**Other Information** (see instructions)			

1 Check accounting method: **a** ☐ Cash **b** ☐ Accrual **c** ☐ Other (specify) ▶ _____

2 See the instructions and enter the:

a Business activity ▶ _____ **b** Product or service ▶ _____

3 At the end of the tax year, did the corporation own, directly or indirectly, 50% or more of the voting stock of a domestic corporation? (For rules of attribution, see section 267(c).) If "Yes," attach a statement showing: **(a)** name and employer identification number (EIN), **(b)** percentage owned, and **(c)** if 100% owned, was a qualified subchapter S subsidiary election made? . . . .

4 Has this corporation filed, or is it required to file, **Form 8918,** Material Advisor Disclosure Statement, to provide information on any reportable transaction? . . . .

5 Check this box if the corporation issued publicly offered debt instruments with original issue discount . . . . ▶ ☐

If checked, the corporation may have to file **Form 8281,** Information Return for Publicly Offered Original Issue Discount Instruments.

6 If the corporation: **(a)** was a C corporation before it elected to be an S corporation **or** the corporation acquired an asset with a basis determined by reference to the basis of the asset (or the basis of any other property) in the hands of a C corporation **and (b)** has net unrealized built-in gain in excess of the net recognized built-in gain from prior years, enter the net unrealized built-in gain reduced by net recognized built-in gain from prior years (see instructions) . . . . ▶ $ _____

7 Enter the accumulated earnings and profits of the corporation at the end of the tax year. $ _____

8 Are the corporation's total receipts (see instructions) for the tax year **and** its total assets at the end of the tax year less than $250,000? If "Yes," the corporation is not required to complete Schedules L and M-1 . . . .

9 During the tax year, was a qualified subchapter S subsidiary election terminated or revoked? If "Yes," see instructions .

10a Did the corporation make any payments in 2011 that would require it to file Form(s) 1099 (see instructions)? . . . .

b If "Yes," did the corporation file or will it file all required Forms 1099?. . . . .

			Total amount	
Schedule K	**Shareholders' Pro Rata Share Items**			
Income (Loss)	**1** Ordinary business income (loss) (page 1, line 21)	**1**		
	2 Net rental real estate income (loss) (attach Form 8825)	**2**		
	3a Other gross rental income (loss)	**3a**			
	b Expenses from other rental activities (attach statement) . . .	**3b**			
	c Other net rental income (loss). Subtract line 3b from line 3a	**3c**		
	4 Interest income	**4**		
	5 Dividends: **a** Ordinary dividends	**5a**		
	b Qualified dividends	**5b**			
	6 Royalties	**6**		
	7 Net short-term capital gain (loss) (attach Schedule D (Form 1120S))	**7**		
	8a Net long-term capital gain (loss) (attach Schedule D (Form 1120S))	**8a**		
	b Collectibles (28%) gain (loss)	**8b**			
	c Unrecaptured section 1250 gain (attach statement)	**8c**			
	9 Net section 1231 gain (loss) (attach Form 4797)	**9**		
	10 Other income (loss) (see instructions) . . . Type ▶	**10**		

Form **1120S** (2011)

Form 1120S, Page 3

Schedule K, Shareholders' Pro Rata Share Items (continued) Breaking apart different elements of revenue and expenses that might receive different treatment at the individual level continues on page 3 of Form 1120S. Line 11 summarizes the Section 179 deduction, which refers to an allowance for immediate depreciation taken in the current year instead of over the normal class life prescribed by MACRS. Line 12 lists any charitable contributions made. These two lines report items that receive different tax treatment at the individual level, namely that the individual taxpayer faces limitations on deductible amounts. Finally, line 17c under the section *Other Information* is where owner distributions are reported. This amount will lower the retained earnings balance. Apart from these three lines, the other sections of Schedule K contain unique tax items that most small businesses do not encounter on a regular basis.

		Shareholders' Pro Rata Share Items (continued)		Total amount	
Deductions	**11**	Section 179 deduction (*attach Form 4562*)	**11**		
	12a	Contributions	**12a**		
	b	Investment interest expense	**12b**		
	c	Section 59(e)(2) expenditures **(1)** Type ▶ _____ **(2)** Amount ▶	**12c(2)**		
	d	Other deductions (*see instructions*) . . . Type ▶	**12d**		
Credits	**13a**	Low-income housing credit (section 42(j)(5))	**13a**		
	b	Low-income housing credit (other)	**13b**		
	c	Qualified rehabilitation expenditures (rental real estate) (*attach Form 3468*)	**13c**		
	d	Other rental real estate credits (*see instructions*) Type ▶ _____	**13d**		
	e	Other rental credits (*see instructions*) . . . Type ▶ _____	**13e**		
	f	Alcohol and cellulosic biofuel fuels credit (*attach Form 6478*)	**13f**		
	g	Other credits (*see instructions*) . . . . . Type ▶	**13g**		
Foreign Transactions	**14a**	Name of country or U.S. possession ▶ _____			
	b	Gross income from all sources	**14b**		
	c	Gross income sourced at shareholder level	**14c**		
		Foreign gross income sourced at corporate level			
	d	Passive category	**14d**		
	e	General category	**14e**		
	f	Other (*attach statement*)	**14f**		
		Deductions allocated and apportioned at shareholder level			
	g	Interest expense	**14g**		
	h	Other	**14h**		
		Deductions allocated and apportioned at corporate level to foreign source income			
	i	Passive category	**14i**		
	j	General category	**14j**		
	k	Other (*attach statement*)	**14k**		
		Other information			
	l	Total foreign taxes (check one): ▶ ☐ Paid ☐ Accrued	**14l**		
	m	Reduction in taxes available for credit (*attach statement*)	**14m**		
	n	Other foreign tax information (*attach statement*)			
Alternative Minimum Tax (AMT) Items	**15a**	Post-1986 depreciation adjustment	**15a**		
	b	Adjusted gain or loss	**15b**		
	c	Depletion (other than oil and gas)	**15c**		
	d	Oil, gas, and geothermal properties—gross income	**15d**		
	e	Oil, gas, and geothermal properties—deductions	**15e**		
	f	Other AMT items (*attach statement*)	**15f**		
Items Affecting Shareholder Basis	**16a**	Tax-exempt interest income	**16a**		
	b	Other tax-exempt income	**16b**		
	c	Nondeductible expenses	**16c**		
	d	Distributions (*attach statement if required*) (*see instructions*)	**16d**		
	e	Repayment of loans from shareholders	**16e**		
Other Information	**17a**	Investment income	**17a**		
	b	Investment expenses	**17b**		
	c	Dividend distributions paid from accumulated earnings and profits	**17c**		
	d	Other items and amounts (*attach statement*)			
Reconciliation	**18**	**Income/loss reconciliation.** Combine the amounts on lines 1 through 10 in the far right column. From the result, subtract the sum of the amounts on lines 11 through 12d and 14l	**18**		

Form 1120S, Page 4

Schedule L, Balance Sheets per Books This last page provides space to present the balance sheet for the current and previous years. Inclusion of the balance sheet helps ensure all business information has been placed on the tax return. Failure to include all debits and credits will cause the balance sheet to fall out of *balance*.

Schedule M-1, Reconciliation of Income (Loss) The Schedule M-1 section provides an opportunity to highlight any differences between what is presented using the cash or accrual method internally and what a taxpayer is forced to report per the income tax method.

Schedule M-2, Analysis of Accumulated Adjustments Account Schedule M-2 keeps track of the retained earnings account in accordance with the income tax method. The term *accumulated adjustments* refers to retained earnings.

Form 1120S (2011)

Page **4**

Schedule L — Balance Sheets per Books

	Assets	Beginning of tax year (a)	(b)	End of tax year (c)	(d)
1	Cash				
2a	Trade notes and accounts receivable				
b	Less allowance for bad debts	( )		( )	
3	Inventories				
4	U.S. government obligations				
5	Tax-exempt securities (*see instructions*)				
6	Other current assets (*attach statement*)				
7	Loans to shareholders				
8	Mortgage and real estate loans				
9	Other investments (*attach statement*)				
10a	Buildings and other depreciable assets				
b	Less accumulated depreciation	( )		( )	
11a	Depletable assets				
b	Less accumulated depletion	( )		( )	
12	Land (net of any amortization)				
13a	Intangible assets (amortizable only)				
b	Less accumulated amortization	( )		( )	
14	Other assets (*attach statement*)				
15	Total assets				
	Liabilities and Shareholders' Equity				
16	Accounts payable				
17	Mortgages, notes, bonds payable in less than 1 year				
18	Other current liabilities (*attach statement*)				
19	Loans from shareholders				
20	Mortgages, notes, bonds payable in 1 year or more				
21	Other liabilities (*attach statement*)				
22	Capital stock				
23	Additional paid-in capital				
24	Retained earnings				
25	Adjustments to shareholders' equity (*attach statement*)				
26	Less cost of treasury stock		( )		( )
27	Total liabilities and shareholders' equity				

Schedule M-1 — Reconciliation of Income (Loss) per Books With Income (Loss) per Return

Note. Schedule M-3 required instead of Schedule M-1 if total assets are $10 million or more—see instructions

1	Net income (loss) per books		5	Income recorded on books this year not included on Schedule K, lines 1 through 10 (itemize):	
2	Income included on Schedule K, lines 1, 2, 3c, 4, 5a, 6, 7, 8a, 9, and 10, not recorded on books this year (itemize) _____		a	Tax-exempt interest $ _____	
3	Expenses recorded on books this year not included on Schedule K, lines 1 through 12 and 14l (itemize):		6	Deductions included on Schedule K, lines 1 through 12 and 14l, not charged against book income this year (itemize):	
a	Depreciation $ _____		a	Depreciation $ _____	
b	Travel and entertainment $ _____				
			7	Add lines 5 and 6	
4	Add lines 1 through 3		8	Income (loss) (Schedule K, line 18). Line 4 less line 7	

Schedule M-2 — Analysis of Accumulated Adjustments Account, Other Adjustments Account, and Shareholders' Undistributed Taxable Income Previously Taxed (see instructions)

		(a) Accumulated adjustments account	(b) Other adjustments account	(c) Shareholders' undistributed taxable income previously taxed
1	Balance at beginning of tax year			
2	Ordinary income from page 1, line 21			
3	Other additions			
4	Loss from page 1, line 21	( )		
5	Other reductions	( )	( )	
6	Combine lines 1 through 5			
7	Distributions other than dividend distributions			
8	Balance at end of tax year. Subtract line 7 from line 6			

Form **1120S** (2011)

Form 1040 Schedule C, Page 1

A single-member LLC or sole proprietorship would file Form 1040 Schedule C and supporting forms at the individual level by default. A multimember LLC would file a partnership return Form 1065 and supporting forms, which resembles the tax filing process for an S corporation. Schedule C filings are much easier to complete since they do not involve multiple layers of tax documents or balance sheet accounts. Still, a taxpayer should track balance sheet information separately in order to ensure that all debit and credit accounts indeed balance together.

Lines A through J The first section containing letters A through H asks for much of the same general business information as Form 1120S or Form 1065. However, a taxpayer may not need to file Form SS-4 in order to obtain an Employer Identification Number (EIN). A Schedule C filer can usually use a personal social security number, unless the business has employees. Items I and J ask about Forms 1099, which are discussed later in this appendix.

Part I, Income In Part I, total operating revenues are reported on line 1 minus returns and allowances, which are placed on line 2. Any cost of goods sold is calculated on page 2 of Schedule C and then transferred to line 4.

Part II, Expenses Under deductions in Part II, an organization may want to arrange the chart of accounts to include these expense categories in order to group information for tax reporting purposes. Amounts for lines 9 and 13 are usually first calculated elsewhere. Deductible meals and entertainment on line 24 are normally limited to 50%. Other categories of expenses are listed separately and then summarized on line 27.

Line 30 references business use of the home. A home-based business would normally qualify for this deduction, but a taxpayer *cannot* make this claim if another business location exists where work could be performed. Simply doing work from home does not count. The deduction represents a percentage of home expenses in relation to the square footage of the home used for business purposes.

SCHEDULE C
(Form 1040)

Department of the Treasury
Internal Revenue Service (99)

Profit or Loss From Business
(Sole Proprietorship)

▶ **For information on Schedule C and its instructions, go to** *www.irs.gov/schedulec*
▶ **Attach to Form 1040, 1040NR, or 1041; partnerships generally must file Form 1065.**

OMB No. 1545-0074

2011

Attachment
Sequence No. **09**

Name of proprietor

Social security number (SSN)

A Principal business or profession, including product or service (see instructions)

B Enter code from instructions
▶

C Business name. If no separate business name, leave blank.

D Employer ID number (EIN), (see instr.)

E Business address (including suite or room no.) ▶
City, town or post office, state, and ZIP code

F Accounting method: **(1)** ☐ Cash **(2)** ☐ Accrual **(3)** ☐ Other (specify) ▶

G Did you "materially participate" in the operation of this business during 2011? If "No," see instructions for limit on losses .   ☐ Yes ☐ No

H If you started or acquired this business during 2011, check here .   .   .   .   ▶ ☐

I Did you make any payments in 2011 that would require you to file Form(s) 1099? (see instructions) .   .   .   .   .   ☐ Yes ☐ No

J If "Yes," did you or will you file all required Forms 1099?   .   .   .   .   ☐ Yes ☐ No

Part I   Income

1a	Merchant card and third party payments. For 2011, enter -0- . . .	1a
b	Gross receipts or sales not entered on line 1a (see instructions) . .	1b
c	Income reported to you on Form W-2 if the "Statutory Employee" box on that form was checked. **Caution.** See instr. before completing this line	1c
d	**Total gross receipts.** Add lines 1a through 1c	1d
2	Returns and allowances plus any other adjustments (see instructions)	2
3	Subtract line 2 from line 1d	3
4	Cost of goods sold (from line 42)	4
5	**Gross profit.** Subtract line 4 from line 3	5
6	Other income, including federal and state gasoline or fuel tax credit or refund (see instructions) . . .	6
7	**Gross income.** Add lines 5 and 6 . . . . ▶	7

Part II   Expenses

Enter expenses for business use of your home only on line 30.

8	Advertising	8	**18**	Office expense (see instructions)	18
9	Car and truck expenses (see instructions). . . .	9	**19**	Pension and profit-sharing plans .	19
			20	Rent or lease (see instructions):	
10	Commissions and fees .	10	**a**	Vehicles, machinery, and equipment	20a
11	Contract labor (see instructions)	11	**b**	Other business property . . .	20b
12	Depletion	12	**21**	Repairs and maintenance . . .	21
13	Depreciation and section 179 expense deduction (not included in Part III) (see instructions). . . .	13	**22**	Supplies (not included in Part III) .	22
			23	Taxes and licenses	23
			24	Travel, meals, and entertainment:	
14	Employee benefit programs (other than on line 19) . .	14	**a**	Travel	24a
15	Insurance (other than health)	15	**b**	Deductible meals and entertainment (see instructions) .	24b
16	Interest:		**25**	Utilities	25
a	Mortgage (paid to banks, etc.)	16a	**26**	Wages (less employment credits) .	26
b	Other	16b	**27a**	Other expenses (from line 48) . .	27a
17	Legal and professional services	17	**b**	**Reserved for future use** . . .	27b

28	**Total expenses** before expenses for business use of home. Add lines 8 through 27a . . . . . ▶	28
29	Tentative profit or (loss). Subtract line 28 from line 7	29
30	Expenses for business use of your home. Attach **Form 8829.** Do **not** report such expenses elsewhere . .	30
31	**Net profit or (loss).** Subtract line 30 from line 29.	

- If a profit, enter on both **Form 1040, line 12** (or **Form 1040NR, line 13**) and on **Schedule SE, line 2.**
If you entered an amount on line 1c, see instr. Estates and trusts, enter on **Form 1041, line 3.**

- If a loss, you **must** go to line 32.

32 If you have a loss, check the box that describes your investment in this activity (see instructions).

- If you checked 32a, enter the loss on both **Form 1040, line 12,** (or **Form 1040NR, line 13**) and on **Schedule SE, line 2.** If you entered an amount on line 1c, see the instructions for line 31. Estates and trusts, enter on **Form 1041, line 3.**

- If you checked 32b, you **must** attach **Form 6198.** Your loss may be limited.

31	

32a ☐ All investment is at risk.
32b ☐ Some investment is not at risk.

For Paperwork Reduction Act Notice, see your tax return instructions.   Cat. No. 11334P   Schedule C (Form 1040) 2011

Form 1040 Schedule C, Page 2

Part III, Cost of Goods Sold Any cost of goods sold is calculated using beginning and ending inventory counts and then transferred to page 1 of Schedule C.

Part IV, Information on Your Vehicle Information on a vehicle used for business purposes is reported in Part IV. A taxpayer might have to complete additional supporting forms related to the use of a vehicle. Instead of taking actual automobile expenses as a deduction, a taxpayer could elect to use the standard mileage rate based on the total number of business miles driven in the year. A mileage log provides the documentation necessary to calculate the number of miles to report.

Part V, Other Expenses Part V includes other categories of expenses that have not been provided for on page 1 of Schedule C. An organization can develop relevant expense categories or use some of the basic types of categories as presented in Chapter 7.

Part III **Cost of Goods Sold** (see instructions)

33   Method(s) used to value closing inventory: **a** ☐ Cost   **b** ☐ Lower of cost or market   **c** ☐ Other (attach explanation)

34   Was there any change in determining quantities, costs, or valuations between opening and closing inventory?
If "Yes," attach explanation . . . . ☐ Yes ☐ No

35	Inventory at beginning of year. If different from last year's closing inventory, attach explanation . . .	35
36	Purchases less cost of items withdrawn for personal use	36
37	Cost of labor. Do not include any amounts paid to yourself	37
38	Materials and supplies	38
39	Other costs	39
40	Add lines 35 through 39	40
41	Inventory at end of year	41
42	**Cost of goods sold.** Subtract line 41 from line 40. Enter the result here and on line 4	42

Part IV   **Information on Your Vehicle.** Complete this part **only** if you are claiming car or truck expenses on line 9 and are not required to file Form 4562 for this business. See the instructions for line 13 to find out if you must file Form 4562.

43   When did you place your vehicle in service for business purposes? (month, day, year) ▶ _____ / _____ / _____

44   Of the total number of miles you drove your vehicle during 2011, enter the number of miles you used your vehicle for:

   a Business _____   **b** Commuting (see instructions) _____   **c** Other _____

45   Was your vehicle available for personal use during off-duty hours? . . . . ☐ Yes ☐ No

46   Do you (or your spouse) have another vehicle available for personal use?. . . . . ☐ Yes ☐ No

47a   Do you have evidence to support your deduction? . . . . ☐ Yes ☐ No

   b If "Yes," is the evidence written? . . . . ☐ Yes ☐ No

Part V   **Other Expenses.** List below business expenses not included on lines 8–26 or line 30.

--	
--	
--	
--	
--	
--	
--	
--	

48	Total other expenses. Enter here and on line 27a	48

Form 4562, Page 1

Supporting forms provide more detail on specific items listed on Forms 1120, 1120S, 1065, or Schedule C, such as depreciation, amortization, and the sale of business assets. If a supporting form is filled out at the corporate or partnership level, it will most likely need to be filled out at the individual level as well. Form 4562 is used to report the depreciation expense related to capitalized assets.

Part I, Election to Expense Certain Property Under Section 179   Part I covers Section 179 of the U.S. tax code, which allows an organization to fully depreciate an asset placed into service in the current year. This special depreciation amount is taken in addition to amounts allowed under MACRS. The rules regarding Section 179 deductions are highly complex requiring consultation with a tax professional.

Part II, Special Depreciation Allowance and Other Depreciation   As a result of weak economic conditions, an additional depreciation allowance is available for qualified property. Consult a tax professional to determine the proper calculation of special depreciation.

Part III, MACRS Depreciation   Part III covers the basic amount of depreciation permitted by the IRS. In most situations, the depreciation of assets will follow MACRS rules as set forth in Publication 946, How to Depreciate Property. MACRS rules impose a predetermined useful life and depreciation rate according to the type of asset. Section A refers to the total amount of depreciation from assets placed into service in prior years. An organization will have to keep track of this number separately. Section B covers the current year additions of capitalized assets, which must be organized per their useful life. In terms of tax planning, an organization could buy an asset in one period when cash flows are high and then wait to place the asset into service until a later period where the tax deduction would be more favorable.

Form **4562**	**Depreciation and Amortization** (Including Information on Listed Property)	OMB No. 1545-0172
Department of the Treasury Internal Revenue Service (99)	▶ See separate instructions. ▶ Attach to your tax return.	**2011** Attachment Sequence No. **179**

Name(s) shown on return | Business or activity to which this form relates | Identifying number

Part I   Election To Expense Certain Property Under Section 179

Note: *If you have any listed property, complete Part V before you complete Part I.*

1	Maximum amount (see instructions)	**1**
2	Total cost of section 179 property placed in service (see instructions)	**2**
3	Threshold cost of section 179 property before reduction in limitation (see instructions)	**3**
4	Reduction in limitation. Subtract line 3 from line 2. If zero or less, enter -0-	**4**
5	Dollar limitation for tax year. Subtract line 4 from line 1. If zero or less, enter -0-. If married filing separately, see instructions	**5**

6	**(a)** Description of property	**(b)** Cost (business use only)	**(c)** Elected cost

7	Listed property. Enter the amount from line 29 . . . . **7**	
8	Total elected cost of section 179 property. Add amounts in column (c), lines 6 and 7	**8**
9	Tentative deduction. Enter the **smaller** of line 5 or line 8	**9**
10	Carryover of disallowed deduction from line 13 of your 2010 Form 4562	**10**
11	Business income limitation. Enter the smaller of business income (not less than zero) or line 5 (see instructions)	**11**
12	Section 179 expense deduction. Add lines 9 and 10, but do not enter more than line 11	**12**
13	Carryover of disallowed deduction to 2012. Add lines 9 and 10, less line 12 ▶ **13**	

Note: *Do not use Part II or Part III below for listed property. Instead, use Part V.*

Part II   Special Depreciation Allowance and Other Depreciation (Do not include listed property.) (See instructions.)

14	Special depreciation allowance for qualified property (other than listed property) placed in service during the tax year (see instructions)	**14**
15	Property subject to section 168(f)(1) election	**15**
16	Other depreciation (including ACRS)	**16**

Part III   MACRS Depreciation (Do not include listed property.) (See instructions.)

Section A

17	MACRS deductions for assets placed in service in tax years beginning before 2011	**17**
18	If you are electing to group any assets placed in service during the tax year into one or more general asset accounts, check here . . . . ▶ ☐	

Section B—Assets Placed in Service During 2011 Tax Year Using the General Depreciation System

(a) Classification of property	(b) Month and year placed in service	(c) Basis for depreciation (business/investment use only—see instructions)	(d) Recovery period	(e) Convention	(f) Method	(g) Depreciation deduction
19a 3-year property						
b 5-year property						
c 7-year property						
d 10-year property						
e 15-year property						
f 20-year property						
g 25-year property			25 yrs.		S/L	
h Residential rental property			27.5 yrs.	MM	S/L	
			27.5 yrs.	MM	S/L	
i Nonresidential real property			39 yrs.	MM	S/L	
				MM	S/L	

Section C—Assets Placed in Service During 2011 Tax Year Using the Alternative Depreciation System

20a Class life					S/L	
b 12-year			12 yrs.		S/L	
c 40-year			40 yrs.	MM	S/L	

Part IV   Summary (See instructions.)

21	Listed property. Enter amount from line 28	**21**
22	**Total.** Add amounts from line 12, lines 14 through 17, lines 19 and 20 in column (g), and line 21. Enter here and on the appropriate lines of your return. Partnerships and S corporations—see instructions	**22**
23	For assets shown above and placed in service during the current year, enter the portion of the basis attributable to section 263A costs **23**	

For Paperwork Reduction Act Notice, see separate instructions.   Cat. No. 12906N   Form **4562** (2011)

Form 4562, Page 2

Part V, Listed Property Part V covers several types of equipment that are often used for personal use. The IRS wants these items listed separately in order to force the taxpayer to note the percentage of business use. Sections B and C provide space to cover more topics on the use of vehicles specifically. A taxpayer or employee provided with a vehicle should keep a log of business and personal miles. Most taxpayers provide a rough guess, but the IRS may deny taxpayers this deduction as a result.

Part VI, Amortization Part VI provides space to report amortization expense on intangibles, such as legal expenses related to starting a business.

Form 4562 (2011)
Page **2**

Part V Listed Property (Include automobiles, certain other vehicles, certain computers, and property used for entertainment, recreation, or amusement.)

Note: *For any vehicle for which you are using the standard mileage rate or deducting lease expense, complete only 24a, 24b, columns (a) through (c) of Section A, all of Section B, and Section C if applicable.*

Section A—Depreciation and Other Information (Caution: *See the instructions for limits for passenger automobiles.***)**

24a Do you have evidence to support the business/investment use claimed? ☐ Yes ☐ No 24b If "Yes," is the evidence written? ☐ Yes ☐ No

(a) Type of property (list vehicles first)	(b) Date placed in service	(c) Business/ investment use percentage	(d) Cost or other basis	(e) Basis for depreciation (business/investment use only)	(f) Recovery period	(g) Method/ Convention	(h) Depreciation deduction	(i) Elected section 179 cost

25 Special depreciation allowance for qualified listed property placed in service during the tax year and used more than 50% in a qualified business use (see instructions) . | **25** |

26 Property used more than 50% in a qualified business use:

		%						
		%						
		%						

27 Property used 50% or less in a qualified business use:

		%			S/L –			
		%			S/L –			
		%			S/L –			

28 Add amounts in column (h), lines 25 through 27. Enter here and on line 21, page 1 . | **28** |

29 Add amounts in column (i), line 26. Enter here and on line 7, page 1 . . . . | **29** |

Section B—Information on Use of Vehicles

Complete this section for vehicles used by a sole proprietor, partner, or other "more than 5% owner," or related person. If you provided vehicles to your employees, first answer the questions in Section C to see if you meet an exception to completing this section for those vehicles.

	(a) Vehicle 1	(b) Vehicle 2	(c) Vehicle 3	(d) Vehicle 4	(e) Vehicle 5	(f) Vehicle 6
30 Total business/investment miles driven during the year (**do not** include commuting miles) .						
31 Total commuting miles driven during the year						
32 Total other personal (noncommuting) miles driven						
33 Total miles driven during the year. Add lines 30 through 32						
34 Was the vehicle available for personal use during off-duty hours?	Yes No	Yes No	Yes No	Yes No	Yes No	Yes No
35 Was the vehicle used primarily by a more than 5% owner or related person? . . .						
36 Is another vehicle available for personal use?						

Section C—Questions for Employers Who Provide Vehicles for Use by Their Employees

Answer these questions to determine if you meet an exception to completing Section B for vehicles used by employees who **are not** more than 5% owners or related persons (see instructions).

	Yes	No
37 Do you maintain a written policy statement that prohibits all personal use of vehicles, including commuting, by your employees?		
38 Do you maintain a written policy statement that prohibits personal use of vehicles, except commuting, by your employees? See the instructions for vehicles used by corporate officers, directors, or 1% or more owners		
39 Do you treat all use of vehicles by employees as personal use?		
40 Do you provide more than five vehicles to your employees, obtain information from your employees about the use of the vehicles, and retain the information received?		
41 Do you meet the requirements concerning qualified automobile demonstration use? (See instructions.) . . .		

Note: *If your answer to 37, 38, 39, 40, or 41 is "Yes," do not complete Section B for the covered vehicles.*

Part VI Amortization

(a) Description of costs	(b) Date amortization begins	(c) Amortizable amount	(d) Code section	(e) Amortization period or percentage	(f) Amortization for this year

42 Amortization of costs that begins during your 2011 tax year (see instructions):

| | | | | | |
| | | | | | |

43 Amortization of costs that began before your 2011 tax year . . . . | **43** | |

44 **Total.** Add amounts in column (f). See the instructions for where to report . . . . | **44** | |

Form **4562** (2011)

Form 4797, Page 1

Part I, Most Property Held More Than 1 Year Part I deals with the sale of general business assets that were held one year or longer. By holding onto assets at least one year, lower capital tax rates will apply. It becomes important to keep good records on the date each specific capitalized asset was purchased as well as the purchase price. For example, by referencing a group of common assets only as *chairs*, it may become difficult to pinpoint the original price and purchase date of one particular chair.

Part II, Ordinary Gains and Losses In contrast, Part II references the sale of assets held for less than one year. Ordinary tax rates apply to such sales. Again, good record keeping helps when determining whether capital or ordinary tax rates will apply.

Form **4797**	**Sales of Business Property** (Also Involuntary Conversions and Recapture Amounts Under Sections 179 and 280F(b)(2)) ▶ Attach to your tax return. ▶ See separate instructions.	OMB No. 1545-0184

Department of the Treasury
Internal Revenue Service   (99)

2011
Attachment Sequence No. **27**

Name(s) shown on return | Identifying number

---

1   Enter the gross proceeds from sales or exchanges reported to you for 2011 on Form(s) 1099-B or 1099-S (or substitute statement) that you are including on line 2, 10, or 20 (see instructions) . . . . | **1** |

Part I   Sales or Exchanges of Property Used in a Trade or Business and Involuntary Conversions From Other Than Casualty or Theft—Most Property Held More Than 1 Year (see instructions)

2	(a) Description of property	(b) Date acquired (mo., day, yr.)	(c) Date sold (mo., day, yr.)	(d) Gross sales price	(e) Depreciation allowed or allowable since acquisition	(f) Cost or other basis, plus improvements and expense of sale	(g) Gain or (loss) Subtract (f) from the sum of (d) and (e)

3 Gain, if any, from Form 4684, line 39	**3**	
4 Section 1231 gain from installment sales from Form 6252, line 26 or 37	**4**	
5 Section 1231 gain or (loss) from like-kind exchanges from Form 8824	**5**	
6 Gain, if any, from line 32, from other than casualty or theft	**6**	
7 Combine lines 2 through 6. Enter the gain or (loss) here and on the appropriate line as follows:	**7**	

Partnerships (except electing large partnerships) and S corporations. Report the gain or (loss) following the instructions for Form 1065, Schedule K, line 10, or Form 1120S, Schedule K, line 9. Skip lines 8, 9, 11, and 12 below.

Individuals, partners, S corporation shareholders, and all others. If line 7 is zero or a loss, enter the amount from line 7 on line 11 below and skip lines 8 and 9. If line 7 is a gain and you did not have any prior year section 1231 losses, or they were recaptured in an earlier year, enter the gain from line 7 as a long-term capital gain on the Schedule D filed with your return and skip lines 8, 9, 11, and 12 below.

8 Nonrecaptured net section 1231 losses from prior years (see instructions)	**8**	
9 Subtract line 8 from line 7. If zero or less, enter -0-. If line 9 is zero, enter the gain from line 7 on line 12 below. If line 9 is more than zero, enter the amount from line 8 on line 12 below and enter the gain from line 9 as a long-term capital gain on the Schedule D filed with your return (see instructions)	**9**	

Part II   Ordinary Gains and Losses (see instructions)

10   Ordinary gains and losses not included on lines 11 through 16 (include property held 1 year or less):

11 Loss, if any, from line 7	**11**	( )
12 Gain, if any, from line 7 or amount from line 8, if applicable	**12**	
13 Gain, if any, from line 31	**13**	
14 Net gain or (loss) from Form 4684, lines 31 and 38a	**14**	
15 Ordinary gain from installment sales from Form 6252, line 25 or 36	**15**	
16 Ordinary gain or (loss) from like-kind exchanges from Form 8824.	**16**	
17 Combine lines 10 through 16	**17**	

18   For all except individual returns, enter the amount from line 17 on the appropriate line of your return and skip lines a and b below. For individual returns, complete lines a and b below:

a   If the loss on line 11 includes a loss from Form 4684, line 35, column (b)(ii), enter that part of the loss here. Enter the part of the loss from income-producing property on Schedule A (Form 1040), line 28, and the part of the loss from property used as an employee on Schedule A (Form 1040), line 23. Identify as from "Form 4797, line 18a." See instructions . . | **18a** |

b   Redetermine the gain or (loss) on line 17 excluding the loss, if any, on line 18a. Enter here and on Form 1040, line 14 | **18b** |

For Paperwork Reduction Act Notice, see separate instructions.   Cat. No. 13086I   Form **4797** (2011)

Form 4797, Page 2

Part III, Gain from Disposition of Property Under Sections 1245, 1250, 1252, 1254, and 1255 Part III covers several unique asset and transaction categories that require special treatment under the tax code. In most situations, an asset held more than one year will receive preferential tax treatment. Per the tax code sections mentioned in this page's title, a portion of capital gains may be characterized as ordinary gains despite the fact that an asset was held more than one year. The rules are complex and a tax professional can help clarify what might trigger this contrary treatment.

Form 4797 (2011)

Part III Gain From Disposition of Property Under Sections 1245, 1250, 1252, 1254, and 1255 (see instructions)

19	(a) Description of section 1245, 1250, 1252, 1254, or 1255 property:	(b) Date acquired (mo., day, yr.)	(c) Date sold (mo., day, yr.)
A			
B			
C			
D			

	These columns relate to the properties on lines 19A through 19D. ▶		Property A	Property B	Property C	Property D
20	Gross sales price (**Note:** See line 1 before completing.)	20				
21	Cost or other basis plus expense of sale	21				
22	Depreciation (or depletion) allowed or allowable	22				
23	Adjusted basis. Subtract line 22 from line 21	23				
24	Total gain. Subtract line 23 from line 20	24				
25	**If section 1245 property:**					
a	Depreciation allowed or allowable from line 22	25a				
b	Enter the **smaller** of line 24 or 25a	25b				
26	**If section 1250 property:** If straight line depreciation was used, enter -0- on line 26g, except for a corporation subject to section 291.					
a	Additional depreciation after 1975 (see instructions)	26a				
b	Applicable percentage multiplied by the **smaller** of line 24 or line 26a (see instructions)	26b				
c	Subtract line 26a from line 24. If residential rental property **or** line 24 is not more than line 26a, skip lines 26d and 26e	26c				
d	Additional depreciation after 1969 and before 1976	26d				
e	Enter the **smaller** of line 26c or 26d	26e				
f	Section 291 amount (corporations only)	26f				
g	Add lines 26b, 26e, and 26f	26g				
27	**If section 1252 property:** Skip this section if you did not dispose of farmland or if this form is being completed for a partnership (other than an electing large partnership).					
a	Soil, water, and land clearing expenses	27a				
b	Line 27a multiplied by applicable percentage (see instructions)	27b				
c	Enter the **smaller** of line 24 or 27b	27c				
28	**If section 1254 property:**					
a	Intangible drilling and development costs, expenditures for development of mines and other natural deposits, mining exploration costs, and depletion (see instructions)	28a				
b	Enter the **smaller** of line 24 or 28a	28b				
29	**If section 1255 property:**					
a	Applicable percentage of payments excluded from income under section 126 (see instructions)	29a				
b	Enter the **smaller** of line 24 or 29a (see instructions)	29b				

Summary of Part III Gains. Complete property columns A through D through line 29b before going to line 30.

30	Total gains for all properties. Add property columns A through D, line 24	30	
31	Add property columns A through D, lines 25b, 26g, 27c, 28b, and 29b. Enter here and on line 13	31	
32	Subtract line 31 from line 30. Enter the portion from casualty or theft on Form 4684, line 33. Enter the portion from other than casualty or theft on Form 4797, line 6	32	

Part IV Recapture Amounts Under Sections 179 and 280F(b)(2) When Business Use Drops to 50% or Less (see instructions)

			(a) Section 179	(b) Section 280F(b)(2)
33	Section 179 expense deduction or depreciation allowable in prior years	33		
34	Recomputed depreciation (see instructions)	34		
35	Recapture amount. Subtract line 34 from line 33. See the instructions for where to report	35		

Form **4797** (2011)

Form 1099

Form 1099 is an informational return used to summarize amounts paid to specific third parties. There are different versions of Form 1099 depending on the nature of the transaction involved. An organization might also receive a Form 1099 from another entity if engaged in certain activity. A taxpayer will send a copy of Form 1099 to the IRS, thus giving the IRS a tool to screen for reporting inaccuracies made by the different parties. In order to ensure that an organization has accurate information when preparing Form 1099, the accounting system should keep track of certain transactions separately.

As seen on Form 1099-MISC, an organization will report amounts on line 7 for work performed by certain independent contractors. An erroneous amount reported on this line could cause tax problems for an independent contractor. In addition to Form 1099, an organization will need to submit Form 1096, which summarizes amounts from all Forms 1099 sent to the IRS.

□ VOID □ CORRECTED		
PAYER'S name, street address, city, state, ZIP code, and telephone no.	**1** Rents $	OMB No. 1545-0115
	2 Royalties $	**2011** Form **1099-MISC** — Miscellaneous Income
	3 Other income $	**4** Federal income tax withheld $
PAYER'S federal identification number / RECIPIENT'S identification number	**5** Fishing boat proceeds $	**6** Medical and health care payments $ — Copy 1 For State Tax Department
RECIPIENT'S name	**7** Nonemployee compensation $	**8** Substitute payments in lieu of dividends or interest $
Street address (including apt. no.)	**9** Payer made direct sales of $5,000 or more of consumer products to a buyer (recipient) for resale ▶ □	**10** Crop insurance proceeds $
City, state, and ZIP code	**11**	**12**
Account number (see instructions)	**13** Excess golden parachute payments $	**14** Gross proceeds paid to an attorney $
15a Section 409A deferrals $ / **15b** Section 409A income $	**16** State tax withheld $	**17** State/Payer's state no.	**18** State income $

Form **1099-MISC**   Department of the Treasury - Internal Revenue Service

TYPES OF FORM 1099

1099-C	Cancellation of debt, $600 or more
1099-DIV	Dividends and distributions, $10 or more
1099-INT	Interest income, $10 or more
1099-MISC	Proceeds paid to attorneys, $600 or more
1099-MISC	Payments to independent contractors, $600 or more

CHAPTER

10

Accounting System

AUTHOR'S NOTE

As part of the goal of maintaining strong relationships with community members, you must ensure that the accounting system is error free. The decision-making process and efforts to build community can be undermined if the accounting system contains inaccurate information. Imagine how frustrated a patient would become if overbilled or blindsided with a surprise charge. An error could frustrate a vendor or organization member if it results in underpayment. Tight internal controls will ensure that the accounting system presents account balances correctly. The vast majority of small health care organizations use Quickbooks to maintain their accounting systems. Take note of how this software program does not differentiate between the accrual and cash methods when transactions are recorded. An organization will select an accounting method only when running reports.

The *accounting system* holds all the numeric data regarding financial transactions. An *accounting information system* refers to the process of recording data properly, generating reports, and analyzing activity. The decision-making process might produce erroneous conclusions if accounting information contains inaccuracies. Organization members must possess a strong understanding of accounting concepts in order to evaluate what reports mean. Posting transactions properly and generating reports holds little value if organization members cannot draw conclusions or find ways to better manage the organization.

Internal control measures protect the integrity of information entering the accounting system, ensuring all amounts are placed into appropriate accounts. *All cash flows must pass through a bank account or appear on a credit card statement to generate third-party verification.* Each bank or credit card statement should be reconciled to the accounting system providing assurance that all transactions have been recorded. Job duties should be divided so that one person handles cash while a separate individual posts transactions to the accounting system. Use of an external bookkeeper can create this segregation of duties, prevent interoffice **collusion**, and insulate private information—such as what organization members earn. An organization that maintains accounting records in-house must undertake sufficient training. The training should encompass how to post journal entries to the correct accounts and how to provide a detailed explanation of what a transaction involves. An auditor, tax professional, or organization member wanting to conduct historical research or review accounting information might waste time or derive false conclusions if the purpose of a transaction is unclear.

Collusion: Two or more organization members working together to commit fraud despite the existence of internal controls.

An organization needs to prepare financial statements and budgets using accurate accounting information. Such information can be used to conduct a profitability analysis, prepare an *ad hoc* report, or calculate financial ratios. Evaluating financial statements and reports will greatly enhance the decision-making process, resulting in better allocation of resources. Recording and analyzing accounting information can be supported with the use of an accounting software program. This chapter presents an overview of Quickbooks by Intuit, an accounting software program that is heavily used among small businesses. The first part of this overview provides instructions on how to set up a new file. The second part highlights key functionality related to standard bookkeeping tasks.

10.1   Internal Controls

Internal controls were first mentioned in Chapter 6 in relation to bookkeeping activities.

An owner of a health care organization can assume that at some point a staff member will steal or be tempted to steal. Staff members can easily make errors when posting transactions to the accounting system as well. Internal controls work to prevent or reveal instances of error or fraud.

Revenue Controls

Patient revenue represents the greatest potential area for theft. Imagine a situation where a patient unexpectedly drops in, receives treatment, and then pays at the front desk in cash. Without the proper internal control structure, the staff member taking receipt of the cash might have the power to pocket the money without posting the activity. To prevent the theft of cash or cash equivalents, job duties must be segregated and monitored. In this example, an organization member apart from the staff member receiving cash could examine patient cards and a daily sign-in sheet to confirm that the proper amount of billable charges was posted for all patients—even unexpected drop-ins. A proper record of billable charges supports the effort to record all payments. The ultimate control over cash and cash equivalents involves reconciling cash balances to a bank or credit card statement, but accounting detail and such statements will not bring attention to missing revenue that has never been deposited *and* recorded. An organization must ensure that cash is always deposited *or* recorded by making use of internal controls. As long as a bank or credit card company processes all inflows and outflows of cash and cash equivalents, a bank or credit card statement will protect the accuracy of accounting information by providing a parallel record of transactions.

If needed, patients could be asked to confirm their payment history to verify revenue, but this process should be handled with delicacy to prevent an organization from appearing disorganized.

> **DIALOGUE**
>
> Provider: Hello. I'm contacting you today because I wanted to make sure you were not overcharged.

Expense Controls

A staff member could steal by way of paying a bogus expense to an interconnected vendor. The external vendor would receive payment and share the proceeds with the dishonest staff member. A staff member with the authority to write checks should be prevented from adding new vendors to a software system whereas a staff member with the power to add vendors should not be allowed to write checks. An organization should place strict limitations over the ability to write checks. Do not allow the same individual who records transactions, such as an external bookkeeper, to also sign checks. Although one organization member could be allowed to make small purchases using a charge card or check, ensure that charge cards have a low credit limit and material check purchases require prior approval. For example, a banking institution could have account features preventing checks over $500 from being processed unless two signatures are present. Review the general ledger on occasion or when compiling financial statements to confirm that all vendors are legitimate and the amounts paid to each appear reasonable.

Certain expenses occur at set periods throughout the year. An internal control measure over expenses involves adding the number of related transactions and affirming that the individual amounts appear reasonable. For instance, a utility bill may arrive monthly and range between $30 and $40. If a review of the accounting system indicates that only 11 transactions were recorded throughout the year or one amount appears unreasonably large, an investigation must determine if a recording error was made. This review process is a normal part of compiling financial statements and involves combing through the general ledger.

An organization that has work performed by an independent contractor must send a copy of Form 1099 to both the IRS and the independent contractor detailing how much was paid. An organization will create tax problems for an independent contractor if amounts posted to the *contract labor account* are wrong, resulting in the submission of an incorrect Form 1099. Maintain a separate record of invoices received from an independent contractor and review them against what the accounting system reports at year's end. Documents that support the amounts reported in the accounting system should always be kept and marked with appropriate notes. Receipts, invoices, processed checks, a mileage log, and other documents provide evidence that an external party could review. An organization should conduct a physical count of items meant for resale (inventory) along with fixed assets and office supplies to confirm account balances and ensure property does not go missing.

Certain account balances can be verified using specific third-party documentation. For example, a lending institution is required to submit Form 1098 listing how much interest an organization paid within the tax period. Table 10.1 shows the common types of documents an organization can use to confirm account balances. An organization can also contact vendors directly to confirm what was paid and that no outstanding balance remains.

TABLE 10.1   **Third-Party Verification**

Documents from external sources can be used to verify information in the accounting system.

Account	Document
Cash	Bank statements
Investments	Investment statements
Credit card payable	Credit card statements
Long-term debt	Loan statements
Salaries and wages	Payroll service documents and timecards
Charitable contributions	Letters from non-profit organizations
Interest expense	Forms 1098 and loan statements
Expense accounts	Credit card and bank statements

Trend Analysis

Trend Analysis:
Reviewing the balances shown for a particular account across multiple time periods to spot patterns or unusual activity.

Current year activity can be displayed next to the prior year account balances when compiling a budget or the financial statements. Large *variances* found between time periods or in contrast to estimated amounts shown on a budget should be examined in more detail. This type of **trend analysis** can also provide useful information in the decision-making process. Does a pattern exist over time in relation to the balances reported for a particular account? An unusual trend may allude to a problem whereas a strict pattern can prove useful when forecasting future amounts.

Summary

Errors in the accounting system can undermine meaningful business analysis. Theft can deplete resources and cause significant disruptions when discovered. It should be assumed that at some point a staff member will steal or attempt to steal resources. An organization can keep control over inflows and outflows of cash and cash equivalents by having a banking institution or credit card company maintain a parallel set of records. Patient revenue must be deposited into a bank account *and* be recorded in the accounting system. Segregation of duties regarding the handling of cash as well as a review of patient cards and a sign-in sheet can minimize error or fraud occurring with inflows of cash and cash equivalents. Limitations on check writing, a review of the general ledger, trend analysis, and third-party documentation can further protect the accounting system.

10.2   Quickbooks® 2011

This section is an independent learning module and is not affiliated with, nor has it been authorized, sponsored, or otherwise approved by Intuit, Inc. Information presented in the screenshots may have been added by the author of this work. Intuit® and Quickbooks® are a

This chapter provides guidance on one of the most commonly used accounting software programs used by small businesses: Quickbooks. Most health care organizations use Quickbooks to maintain their general accounting system. Almost all health care organizations use a separate program or manual process to keep track of patient activity apart from Quickbooks. An organization has many options to weigh before deciding what programs or manual processes to implement.

The following overview by no means captures all the capabilities of Quickbooks. This overview should not be construed as a recommendation to use or buy Quickbooks. The following screenshots are only meant to illustrate how an accounting software program can facilitate the administration of an accounting system. The reader of this software overview should properly assess the appropriateness of a particular accounting program.

> The use of software programs to manage patient activity is discussed in Chapter 20.

Interview Guide for New Company

When creating a new company file, an interview guide walks you through setting up key elements of the accounting system. Click on *Start Interview* to bring up the screen shown in Figure 10.1 and then input basic contact information and make your industry selection: *Medical, Dental or Health Service.*

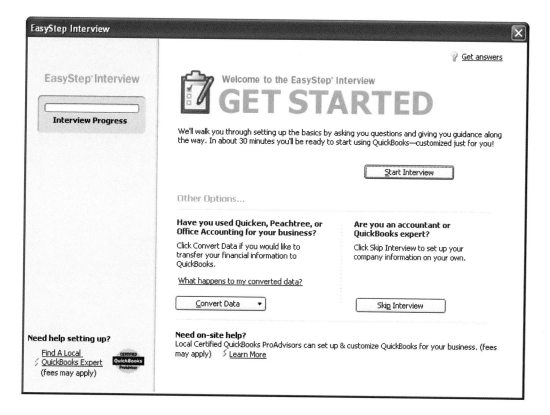

FIGURE 10.1
Interview Guide

The third screen on the interview guide as shown in Figure 10.2 asks about how the organization operates. Each of these business forms was mentioned in Chapter 9. Note how the LLC has different selections depending on the number of members. In order to operate as an S corporation, an election must be made by submitting Form 2553 to the IRS within 2 months and 15 days of incorporation.

The interview guide will continue with several more input screens asking for general information, such as an administrator password and file location. Continue answering questions about what you sell and take note of what answers are recommended. If you decide to use a practice management software program to track patient billing activity,

FIGURE 10.2
Business Forms

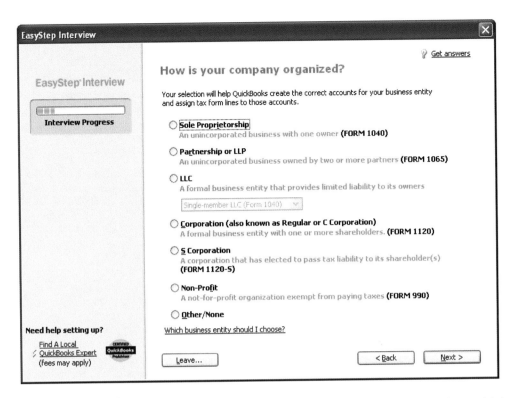

then respond *no* to the question about billing statements as illustrated in Figure 10.3. Unless noted, interview screens that are not shown in this chapter should almost always be marked as recommended. Still, the particular circumstances of your organization must be considered when making selections.

FIGURE 10.3
Billing Statements

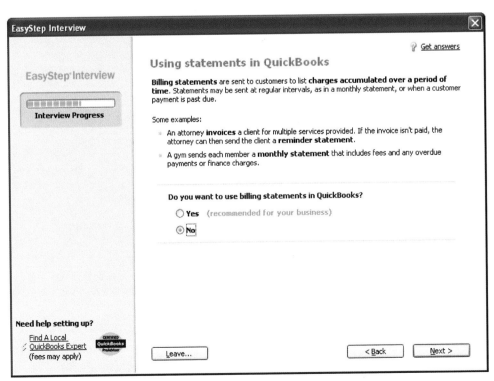

Although tracking time is not recommended by the input screen presented in Figure 10.4, an organization should decide if tracking time would provide useful information for the decision-making process. Requiring all organization members to keep track of their time can prevent waste and improve productivity.

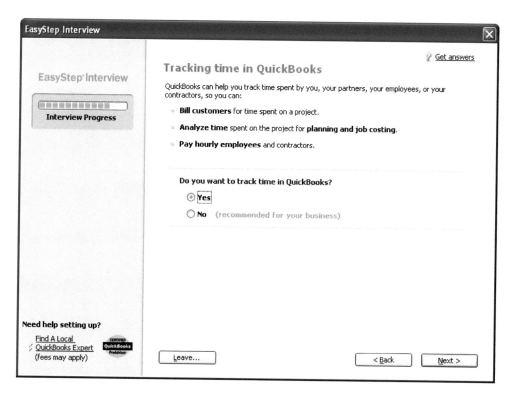

FIGURE 10.4
Job Tracking

The next screen in the interview guide asks about the types of workers an organization uses. A *W-2 employee* as listed in Figure 10.5 refers to IRS Form W-2, Wage and Tax Statement, which an organization uses to report payroll information (including tax withholdings) to an employee. An organization should consider using an external payroll service to manage payroll matters. An independent contractor would receive Form 1099 in which case an organization would *not* be responsible for submitting payroll taxes and payroll forms. An organization must examine the level of control exerted over a worker to determine the worker's proper status. Treating a valid employee as an independent contractor improperly could result in a legal hassle and a subsequent assessment of back payroll taxes.

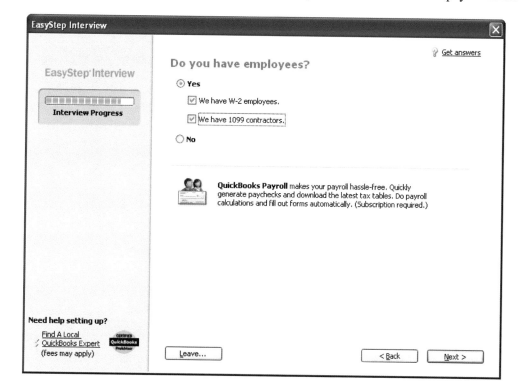

FIGURE 10.5
Worker Status

The next several screens beginning with the one presented in Figure 10.6 address the need to configure the chart of accounts. One of the screens asks for bank account information. An organization that operates as a corporation should maintain at least one business account and refrain from using an owner's personal bank account. The chart of accounts can be formulated using the general categories prescribed by the IRS (as listed in Chapter 7) and later evolve as information needs become clearer.

FIGURE 10.6
Chart of Accounts

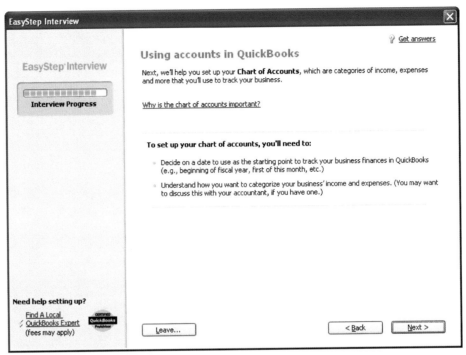

Quickbooks provides a recommended list of accounts, as shown in Figure 10.7, that relate specifically to the health care profession. The suggested account titles can be changed according to the needs of your organization. Run through the entire list and click *on* and *off* accounts to activate only those that will be used initially. Make certain to click on any relevant subaccounts as well. After this screen, the interview guide will ask for some additional contact information as well as a file-specific password before concluding.

FIGURE 10.7
Recommended
Accounts

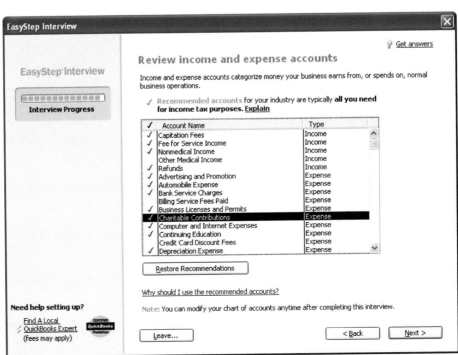

Bookkeeping Functions

This overview will now examine the normal everyday features of Quickbooks. Under the *Lists* tab as illustrated by Figure 10.8, a user has access to the chart of accounts. Other lists indicated on the drop-down menu are meant to track information related to fixed assets, products, and services. Information contained within a list can be quickly applied to a transaction or tax form.

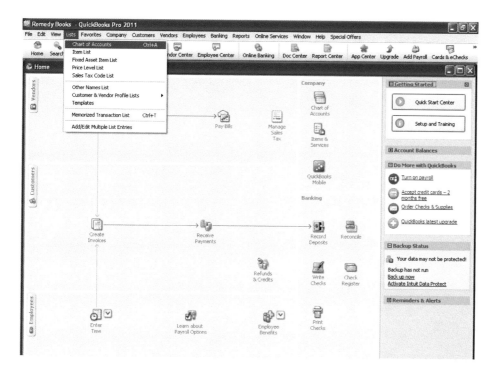

FIGURE 10.8
Lists Tab

Under the *Company* tab, a user can change contact information or access general tasks. This tab provides another link to the chart of accounts. The link highlighted in Figure 10.9 allows organization members to input odometer readings and produce a mileage report. The

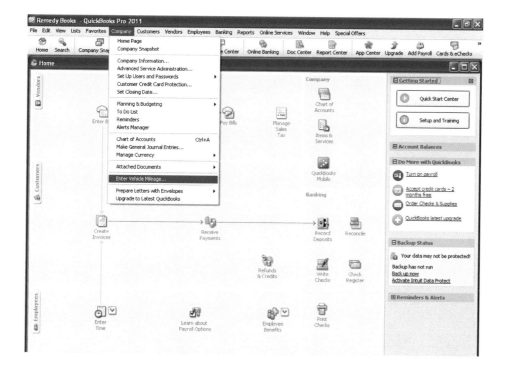

FIGURE 10.9
Company Tab

IRS is becoming very strict about businesses maintaining a mileage log when the standard mileage rate is used as an expense deduction. Employees must be reimbursed according to the standard mileage rate if they used their personal vehicle for an approved business purpose. The planning and budgeting link shown on the drop-down menu brings up an option to create either a combined operating and financial budget or a cash budget (as mentioned in Chapter 8).

On the *Company* drop-down menu (shown previously), clicking on the *Make General Journal Entries* link will bring up the screen appearing in Figure 10.10. Note the format of how a journal entry is made and the space provided to write an explanation of the transaction. Journal entries made here are normally reserved for special transactions, adjusting journal entries, or noncash items (depreciation). An organization will make very few journal entries in this fashion. Most transactions will be posted through other input screens.

FIGURE 10.10
General Journal Entry

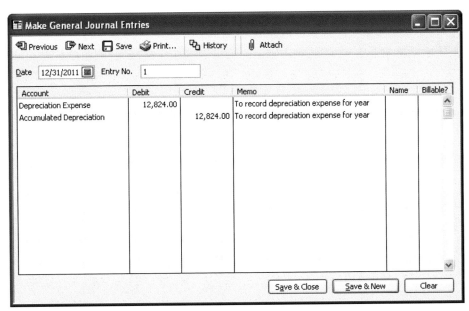

On the *Company* drop-down menu (shown previously), clicking on the link called *Set up Users and Passwords* will bring up a series of screens as illustrated by Figure 10.11. The organization member who was specified as the system administrator on the interview guide can limit the program functions available to other software users. For example, an

FIGURE 10.11
Segregation of Duties

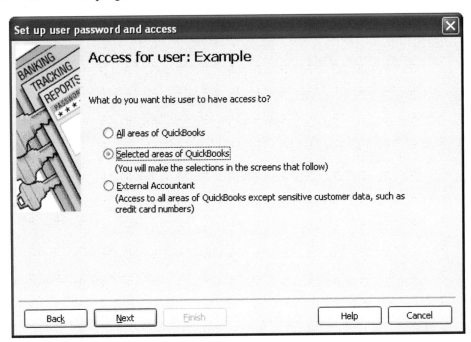

administrator could prevent staff members from setting up a new vendor, thus limiting the risk of a fraudulent check being written. This feature can help segregate job duties by specifying that one organization member has the ability to record certain transactions whereas another organization member has only the authority to review the related transactions.

Clicking on *Credit Cards* from the main ribbon will bring up the introductory screen shown in Figure 10.12. Quickbooks can provide the support needed to process charge cards and track amounts upon registering with a charge card company and purchasing related equipment.

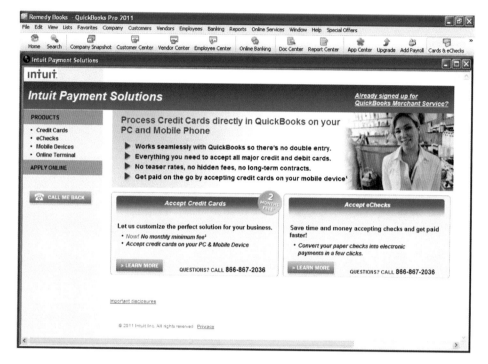

FIGURE 10.12
Charge Card Acceptance

Clicking on *Vendors* and then following the *Vendor Center* link on the drop-down menu brings up the directory presented in Figure 10.13 meant to keep track of vendor information. Information contained in this directory can be used to automatically populate other

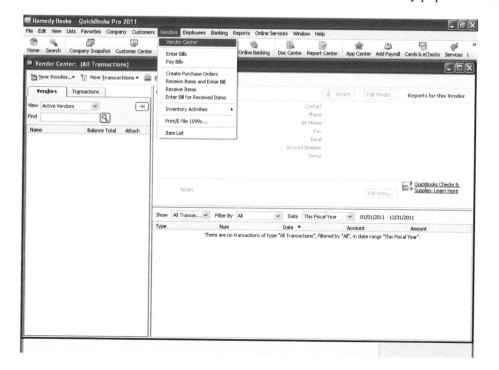

FIGURE 10.13
Vendors Tab

payment screens. This framework creates an internal control over staff members being able to pay fraudulent expenses. An organization has space to keep notes on the vendor relationship as well.

The screen shown in Figure 10.14 is accessible under the *Banking* tab after clicking on the *Write Checks* link on the drop-down menu. A separate menu on this screen will provide a list of vendors already placed in the system. System limitations should prevent new vendors from being added by an unauthorized person. This screen acts like a journal entry where information reported here posts to a designated expense account (debit) as well as a cash account (credit). A user should include any reference number presented on a vendor's invoice in order to help the vendor understand what the check relates to when payment is submitted. Quickbooks allows for efficient check printing by using a standard template that contains a stub that vendors can use to reference your account number or balance.

FIGURE 10.14 Check Writing

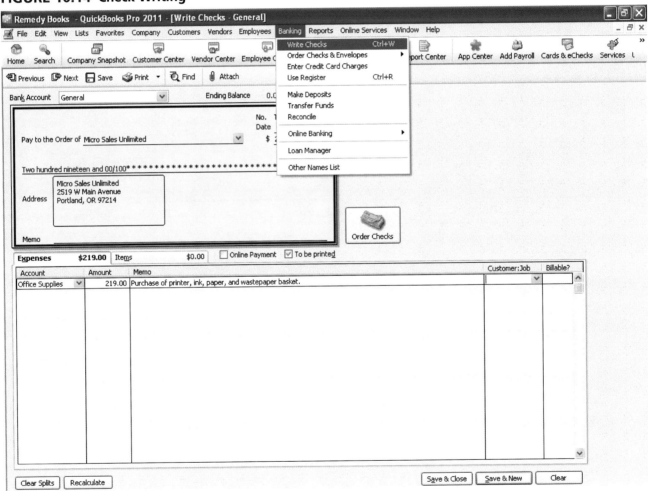

The *Employees* tab contains a link on the drop-down menu called *Enter Time*. From there, a user can access the *Use Weekly Timesheet* link to bring up the screen presented in Figure 10.15. It is important for employees to keep track of their hours in order to compute payroll and complete certain payroll-related tax forms. Employees should also enter job codes to track their productivity.

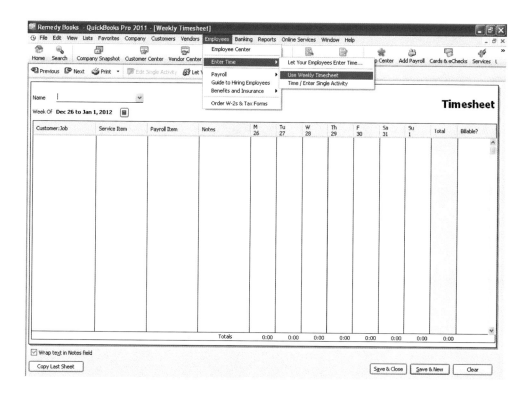

FIGURE 10.15
Employee
Timesheet

Clicking on the *Edit* tab and then *Preferences* will cause the box presented in Figure 10.16 to appear. This screen provides various options to modify how Quickbooks operates. Within the *Tax:1099* field listed in the left-hand column, an organization can click on the *Yes* radio button and then select accounts using a separate drop-down menu in order to associate those accounts with Form 1099. This selection process provides an internal control to ensure correct amounts are reported to independent contractors.

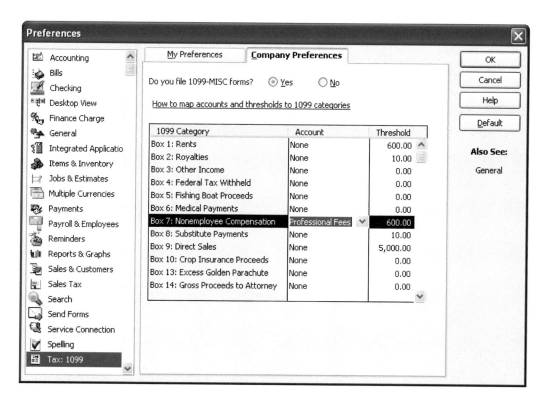

FIGURE 10.16
General
Preferences

Under the *Banking* tab, clicking on the *Make Deposits* link will bring up the screen listed in Figure 10.17, which acts as a journal entry for cash and check deposits. An entry here would post information to a designated revenue account (credit) and a cash account (debit). An entry must be made here when using a separate program to manage patient activity. Charge card transactions involve a separate input screen as long as an organization uses a charge card service offered through Quickbooks.

FIGURE 10.17 Recording Collections

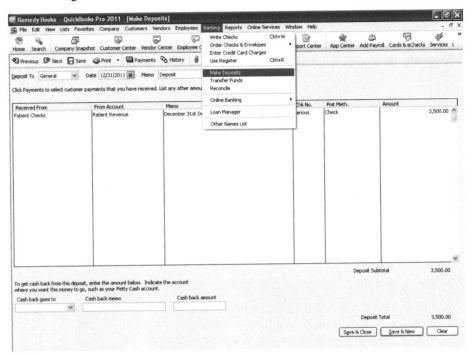

Under the *Banking* tab, the *Reconcile* link brings up the screen illustrated in Figure 10.18 used to perform a bank reconciliation. Enter a bank statement's cash balance on the initial pop-up screen that appears and then click continue. Place a checkmark next to amounts that are listed if they are also reported on the bank statement. The difference between what the accounting system reports and what the bank statement shows must equal all *unchecked* items. An amount shown in the bottom right-hand corner represents an error that must be researched. Any item that remains unchecked for an extended time

FIGURE 10.18 Bank Reconciliation

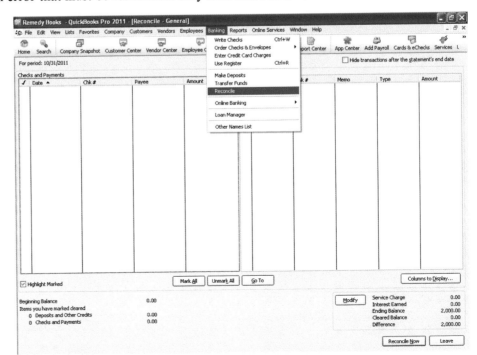

period must also be researched since amounts should clear the bank within a relatively short time. For example, a vendor may need to be contacted to determine if a check was lost and to prevent the vendor from thinking one was never sent.

The *Reports* tab lists a wide selection of reports as listed in Figure 10.19 that can be automatically generated. The *Company & Financial* link displays all the main financial statements, including the income statement (Profit & Loss) and the balance sheet. The default report that first appears after clicking on any of these links can be modified and then saved under *Memorized Reports* for future use.

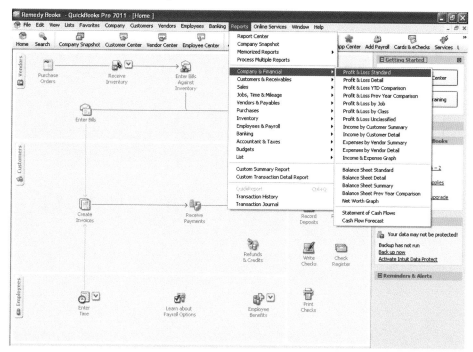

FIGURE 10.19
Financial Statements

The menu appearing in Figure 10.20 allows a user to modify a report. The report date range isolates only those transactions occurring within a designated time period. Instead of following either the *cash* or *accrual* method specifically, Quickbooks gives the option to automatically switch back and forth between either method through this screen within

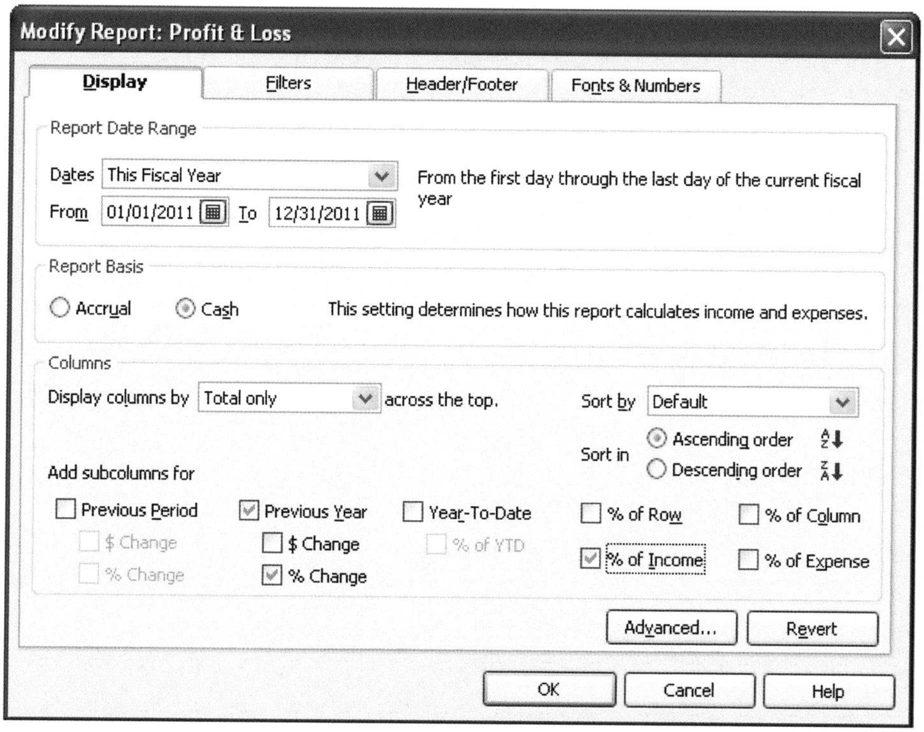

FIGURE 10.20
Editing Reports

the *Report Basis* field. This capability is possible since activity is normally recorded in Quickbooks when a business exchange occurs or when cash trades hands. Accrual-type activity entered into Quickbooks is stored in the background and can be either accessed or ignored when running reports depending on the selection made. *Note how this question about accounting methods was never posed during the initial interview guide.*

A few additional buttons on this menu can be clicked to further modify reports. Previous periods can be viewed alongside the current time period as a way of conducting a trend analysis. Looking at amounts within a particular time period as a percentage of income is also a helpful business analysis tool.

CHAPTER ASSIGNMENT

Working in a group of three to four students or fellow professionals, complete the following items.

1. What internal control measures could be used to ensure that all inflows of cash are deposited in a bank account? What internal control measures could be used to ensure that all outflows of cash have a legitimate business purpose?

2. How could an organization quickly verify that expenses reoccurring on a monthly basis were recorded properly?

3. Which items could be verified using third-party documentation? Which ones could be verified with a physical count?

4. Why does Quickbooks only require the user to input one side of an otherwise dual-sided journal entry when posting revenue and expense activity?

5. List some ways that Quickbooks establishes internal controls. Consider vendors and segregation of duties in your response.

6. Why should organization members record their hours worked along with job codes in a timesheet?

7. Explain how a bank reconciliation works within Quickbooks. What do the *unchecked* items represent?

8. Why doesn't Quickbooks ask an organization to select an accounting method during the initial interview guide? Since an organization always needs to keep a record of accounts receivable and accounts payable, what happens to this information if a report is run under the *cash* method?

Mathematical Finance

AUTHOR'S NOTE

The concept of net present value is at the core of finance. Cash flows projected into the future do not have the same intrinsic value as current-day cash flows. To assess cash flows occurring over multiple time periods, a modification must be made for differences in *risk* and *inflation* faced by cash flows of different time periods. Adjusting future cash flows for both risk and inflation converts them into a present-day equivalent. The total of all adjusted cash flows reset into a present-day equivalent equals their combined net present value. If you struggle with understanding concepts found in the next three chapters, remember what is trying to be accomplished: The concepts are meant to establish future cash flows and then adjust them for differences in risk and inflation. You are welcome to skip ahead to Chapter 14 if these concepts prove difficult initially.

Option A: $60,000 −
$30,000 = $30,000

Option B: $90,000 −
$50,000 = $40,000

A firm understanding of accounting principles allows a health care organization to perform a deeper analysis of inflows and outflows of money. For instance, imagine that a health care provider needs a new x-ray machine. Option A will cost $30,000 whereas Option B will cost $50,000. Looking at costs alone, Option A appears to be a better deal, but what is the overall profitability of each option? Suppose the organization forecasts future revenues and finds that Option A will generate revenues of $60,000 whereas Option B will generate revenues of $90,000. How has estimating future revenue streams altered the decision-making process? The organization forecasts it can bring in $40,000 ($90,000 − $50,000) in net profit under Option B representing $10,000 more in net profit than with Option A. The cost of Option B is more, but the profit potential is much greater. This type of *profitability analysis* should be conducted prior to expanding operations, purchasing capital assets, or taking over another health care provider's business.

Financial concepts pinpoint the value that money has by removing any element of risk or inflation.

Inflation: An increase in general price levels within an economy due to the presence of excess money beyond what is needed to purchase all the products and services available in an economy.

What happens if amounts that have been estimated do not materialize as planned? Unlike the profitability analyses seen in Chapter 8, the concepts here involve *future* cash flows that must be modified to reflect uncertainty. The organization in the example above that wants to buy a new x-ray machine should adjust the two revenue forecasts for both risk and **inflation**. This process would convert the future revenue streams into a present-day equivalent from which the current cost to purchase an x-ray machine could be deducted. Converting all cash flows into a present-day equivalent provides a better understanding of the true *value* associated with a particular business transaction.

The value of money is not static; it changes over time, impacting one's purchasing power.

The mathematical side of finance contains formulas used to adjust estimated future cash flows for risk and inflation. The risk and inflation factors exist for different reasons. Inflation reflects how the *purchasing power* of money declines due to an excess amount of money circulating through an economy beyond what is needed for commerce. Looking back 30 years, $100 could purchase more in total products and services than $100 could today. It's the same *absolute* quantity of money, but its *relative* value has changed over time. A risk exists that events could take place within an economy, marketplace, or specific organization that prevent cash flows from being received as estimated.

An organization should choose the most profitable option given cash flow forecasts that are adjusted for risk and inflation. Once a transaction has been examined financially, an organization will want to explore funding options to meet any capital requirements. This initial chapter looks at the mathematical foundation needed to perform financial calculations. Later chapters explore how to create assumptions for use in estimating future activity. Chapter 14 then looks at the funding options available when needing to raise capital to initiate a venture or sustain a period of cash shortfalls.

11.1   Discount Rate

A discount rate combines the mathematical concepts of risk and inflation into a single quantitative form. This combined rate facilitates the process of adjusting future cash flows into a present-day equivalent. Applying a discount rate will remove any estimated amounts of risk and inflation from future cash flow streams, thus making all cash flows comparable in terms of the *value* of money. The true value of a venture that involves cash flows occurring over multiple time periods cannot be properly evaluated unless all the cash flows are equilibrated. For instance, an x-ray machine may boost revenues by an estimated $90,000 but what will the purchasing power of $90,000 be in the future and could unforeseen circumstances result in less than the full $90,000 being received? This future sum should be discounted for risk and inflation to determine how much **present value** the x-ray machine will actually contribute. Take note of how the term "discount rate" goes by various other names as listed in Table 11.1. These are all a combined reflection of risk and inflation regardless of the name used.

> Inflation
> + Risk Premium
> = Discount Rate

Present Value: The approximate amount of current-day money that a future cash flow would equal upon consideration of differences in risk and inflation.

TABLE 11.1	Discount Rate Aliases
The discount rate goes by different names, which are all a combined reflection of risk and inflation.	

Interest rate	Cost of debt
Rate of return	Cost of equity
Return on equity	Cost of capital
Return on debt	

Inflation

A relationship exists between the total amount of products and services an economy makes available and the total amount of money circulating within that economy. Any imbalance between these two factors can lead to a change in the purchasing power of money. This relationship does not refer to supply and demand forces. An economy has a finite ability to make products and services available to consumers and money is the instrument used to facilitate the exchange of such products and services. Placing money into an economy beyond what the current level of economic activity allows will simply empower consumers to bid up price levels and drive down the value of money. Inflation sets in as money circulates through an economy without having a functional use.

Disinflation refers to any time range where the rate of inflation decreases from one period to the next. An economy may experience a period of **deflation** where price levels decline. The value of money will increase in a deflationary environment due to the scarcity of money in relation to the available product and service levels.

This relationship between money and economic activity also tends to provide insights into the business cycle. Inflationary forces tend to rise sharply toward the peak of a business cycle and can foreshadow a coming recession. An organization should know the approximate stage of the business cycle before launching a new venture and also adjust cash flow estimates and the discount rate accordingly. For example, buying a practice at the peak of a business cycle may lock a health care provider into a higher-than-average interest rate at a time when economic activity is expected to decline. A savvy entrepreneur will wait until the trough of a business cycle to initiate business activity when lending rates are at their lowest and economic activity will not decline further. Despite consumers feeling a great amount of fear at the trough of a business cycle, a savvy entrepreneur knows that economic activity will soon improve.

Disinflation: The overall rate of inflation decreases from one time period to the next.

Deflation: A decrease to general price levels within an economy due to the lack of money in relation to what is needed to purchase all the products and services available in an economy.

Information related to the business cycle can be found in Chapter 1.

Risk Premium

Various factors may prevent an organization from receiving future cash flows as estimated. These factors form the risk premium of a discount rate. Risk components may vary depending on the timing of a cash flow. However, the discount rate used to modify a future cash flow stream tends to be applied uniformly in order to simplify the calculation process.

Risk Premium = Systematic Risk + Operating Risk + Leverage Risk + Model Risk

Systematic Risk An event that impacts the entire economic *system* is considered a systematic risk. For example, the business cycle has a major influence over the general level of economic activity. Persistent inflation can erode the purchasing power of all consumers. A government entity may pass legislation altering regulations or the tax system. War, natural disasters, and consumer trends can pose a risk to all organizations operating in an economy.

Operating Risk An event is deemed an operating risk if it can directly impact an organization's revenue or expense activity. For instance, patient revenues could decline if negative word of mouth about an organization spreads. A change to price levels or the service mix could alter consumption patterns. A health care provider estimating the value of a practice may want to include *rapport risk* into the calculation to account for patients who will leave once the practice transition is made.

A vendor may increase prices leading to higher expenses. The bankruptcy of a vendor may force an organization to purchase products or services elsewhere at a higher cost. A new expense might surface as a result of employee turnover, a lawsuit, equipment breakage, and so forth. An organization should also consider the level of *fixed* versus *variable* expenses.

Leverage Risk An organization will face a specific set of risks related to its debt level and type of debts. A fixed obligation due at set intervals will force an organization to maintain a continual stream of money to cover payments. Health care providers often emerge from school with significant education loans. Adding other personal loans, a practice loan, or fixed asset loans makes servicing debt more challenging. A lending institution can circumvent corporate bankruptcy protections indirectly by requiring a borrower to secure a commercial loan using personal property. *Leverage* refers to the association between debt levels and the various resources a business has, such as income or assets. A highly leveraged organization will possess a relatively small amount of resources in comparison to debt levels.

Model Risk A degree of risk is involved with assembling a cash flow projection itself. The estimated cash flows or discount rate might be based on faulty assumptions or a projection might contain calculation errors. Model risk accounts for any shortfall in skill or expertise on the part of the individual putting together a projection.

Summary

A discount rate is applied to a future cash flow stream, modifying it for risk and inflation. The forecasting process is often simplified by applying one discount rate to all cash flows. In terms of the purchasing power of money, any imbalance between money and production within a country can lead to inflation, disinflation, or deflation. The current level of inflation can foreshadow changes to the business cycle. The risk that cash flows might not occur as expected can derive from the assumptions used in the financial model itself or from systematic, operating, or leverage risk factors.

11.2   Weighted Average Cost of Capital

Constructing a discount rate by way of quantifying risks and estimating inflation can be extremely difficult and may increase model risk. The weighted average cost of capital (WACC) represents a formulaic approach to generating a discount rate using the current *market* cost of debt and equity. The current expectations of risk and inflation within the investment community shape what providers of debt and equity capital want to earn. Using the WACC formula ensures that an organization will produce enough profit to properly compensate debt and equity investors for risk and inflation. A health care provider will often obtain debt financing through a lending institution and use personal funds as a source of equity.

$$\text{WACC} = \% \text{ Debt} \times \text{Interest Rate} \times (1 - \text{Tax Rate}) + \% \text{ Equity} \times \text{Cost of Equity}$$

WACC Formula

The *percentage* of debt and equity used in the WACC formula normally reflects a target ratio set by an organization itself (not the market). Because interest charges are tax deductible, the market interest rate on debt is multiplied by *1-Tax Rate* to find the **after-tax interest rate**. Consult a licensed tax professional to obtain a tax rate to apply in the WACC formula.

> **After-Tax Interest Rate:** The net cost of debt that reflects the benefit derived from deducting interest charges on a tax return.

    The interest rate on a *new* loan represents the current market rate of debt and should be placed in the formula. The cost of debt financing tends be lower than the cost of equity, but leverage risk precludes an organization from deriving 100% of its capital from debt sources. A lending institution will generally require a down payment, thus preventing 100% debt financing as well.

    A business owner's equity contribution must generate a rate of return that properly compensates the business owner for risk and inflation. The same expectation pertains to a venture funded through retained earnings. Finding the appropriate *market* cost of equity can be difficult for a small health care organization. The expected rates of return on small publically traded companies might provide insights. The market rate of equity could be found by asking other health care professionals what they would want to earn if their money was placed at risk. A business owner may simply want to determine the cost of equity based on experience or per a desired rate of return.

> An organization should always review the tax savings it derives from interest charges even apart from the WACC formula.

CASE STUDY

WACC Formula

A health care provider intends to purchase an established practice for $100,000. A lending institution will provide a new loan at an interest rate of 7.5% but will require a 28% down payment. A licensed tax professional believes that the interest charges are tax deductible at a marginal rate of 20%. A survey of other local health care providers indicates that they would want to earn a 25% rate of return on equity contributions. What would the WACC be that applies to a business valuation involving the future cash flows of the established practice?

    Percentage debt = 72% (100% − 28%)

    Percentage equity = 28%

    Cost of debt = 7.5%

    Marginal tax rate = 20%

    Cost of equity = 25%

→ WACC = [72% × 7.5% (1 − 20%)] + [28% × 25%]

→ WACC = 4.3% + 7.0%

→ WACC = 11.3%

The future cash flows projected for the business valuation would all be discounted by 11.3% *annually*. The discount process ensures that this health care provider will generate enough profit to cover the costs of debt and equity capital. These costs of capital reflect the risk and inflation that investor money is exposed to over time. Note how an organization cannot just be profitable. An organization must earn enough profit to cover the additional risk and inflation costs associated with funding a business or venture.

Summary

The weighted average cost of capital (WACC) provides a formulaic approach to constructing a discount rate. The calculation normally combines the current *market* rates of debt and equity financing. The interest rate on debt is reduced by *1-Tax Rate* to reflect how interest charges are deductible for tax purposes. The *percentages* of debt and equity used in the formula usually reflect ideal targets set by an organization. A smaller health care organization might benefit from using the WACC when a venture is partially financed with outside loans and partially with personal funds. This often happens when large fixed assets are purchased, such as a building or practice.

11.3 Compound Growth

The notion of compound growth is illustrated by how a savings account accumulates funds. Suppose an investor deposits $500 into an interest bearing account that earns a fixed 4% per annum. After year one, the bank will pay interest income of $20 ($500 × 4%) into the account. As a result of holding $520 in Year 2, the bank would pay $20.80 in interest, leaving a balance of $540.80 ($520 × 4%). The additional 80 cents in Year 2 reflects 4% earned on the $20 of interest income from Year 1. Figure 11.1 shows how the $500 will compound over a five-year time frame at a *quadratic* (increasing) rate.

FIGURE 11.1 Compound Interest

Compound interest reflects how past interest payments earn interest in future time periods, adding to the overall account balance.

	Year 1	Year 2	Year 3	Year 4	Year 5
Beginning balance	500.00	520.00	540.80	562.43	584.93
Interest rate	4%	4%	4%	4%	4%
Interest payment	20.00	20.80	21.63	22.50	23.40
Ending balance	520.00	540.80	562.43	584.93	608.33

The effect of compounding has importance when establishing future cash flow streams and discounting them for risk and inflation. Both the inflation rate and discount rate behave in a compounding manner. For example, suppose a computer currently costs $1,000, but the rate of inflation will grow at 3% per annum. Ignoring any compound growth would result in $30 ($1,000 × 3%) being added to the price of the computer each year. Assuming that nothing else changes, the computer would cost $1,150 in five years. However, the inflation rate compounds, resulting in the 3% being applied to a new price level each year. The price of the computer would total $1,159 after five years as illustrated in Figure 11.2 because of how the inflation rate compounds.

FIGURE 11.2 Compound Inflation

Compound inflation reflects how prices increase at an increasing rate.

	Year 1	Year 2	Year 3	Year 4	Year 5
Beginning price	1,000	1,030	1,061	1,093	1,126
Inflation rate	3%	3%	3%	3%	3%
Price increase	30	31	32	33	34
Ending price	1,030	1,061	1,093	1,126	1,159

The amount of interest earned on an investment equals the **stated interest rate**. However, when amounts compound within a one-year time period, the theoretical rate of interest is greater than the stated rate. The **effective interest rate** reflects how interest received before year's end can earn even more interest by being reinvested. For example, an annual *stated* interest rate of 8% on an investment would earn an *effective* rate of 8.16% if payments were made biannually (every six months). The interest payment made after six months could be taken and invested elsewhere, allowing an investor to theoretically earn .16% more in interest. However, the *actual* interest rate for the year may differ if cash flows cannot be reinvested at the original investment's stated rate.

Stated Interest Rate: The amount of interest a financial product will cost or earn.

Effective Interest Rate: The theoretical amount of interest a financial product will cost or earn based on the ability to retain cash flows in a separate financial product before year's end.

Summary

Compound growth reflects how amounts accumulate over time at a *quadratic* (increasing) rate. This concept applies to an inflation rate, discount rate, or amounts retained in a savings account. Compound growth also occurs when amounts received from one investment are reinvested elsewhere before year's end.

11.4   Present Value

A series of cash flows set to occur over multiple time periods cannot be compared because they each possess a different degree of risk and inflation. In order to make future or even historical cash flows comparable, they must be reset into a common time period—the most common time period used is the present. Removing risk and inflation from future cash flows will automatically convert them into a present-day equivalent. It's important to note that not all cash flows are exposed to risk, especially if they occurred in the past.

Imagine that a health care organization sees a furniture promotion where no payment is expected for two years. The organization selects $1,000 worth of products. What is the true cost of this purchase if the expected rate of inflation equals 4% in the coming year and 5% in the year thereafter? Figure 11.3 demonstrates how the $1,000 cash flow would be discounted for inflation alone.

FIGURE 11.3 Present Value

Paying $1,000 in two years would be the same as paying $915.75 today according to the inflation rates shown.

Transaction		Year 1		Year 2
$915.75	$\times\ 1 + 4\% =$	$952.38	$\times\ 1 + 5\% =$	$1,000

To get a better sense of the economic consequences of this transaction, the $1,000 payment is divided by *1+Inflation Rate* in each of the years under consideration. The organization will make a $1,000 payment in two years, but that amount will be equivalent to $915.75 in terms of the present value of money. By waiting two years to make the furniture payment, the value of money changes by 9.2% or $84.25. Since inflation erodes the value of money over time, waiting two years to *pay* $1,000 has less impact than if done currently.

The inflation rate or discount rate used in analysis is normally applied uniformly to a cash flow stream to simplify the calculation process. Consider a situation where an annual payment of $2,000 will be made over the next five years as listed in Figure 11.4. The rate of inflation over this time period is expected to average 3.75% *per annum*. The organization will make $10,000 in total payments, but each cash flow has a different value when observed in present value terms as a result of inflation. For example, note how the cash flow occurring in Year 2 is modified twice by the estimated inflation rate of 3.75% because it is exposed to inflation for two time periods (not just one).

FIGURE 11.4 Present Value Calculation

Each future cash flow is discounted per the estimated rate of inflation converting each amount into a present-day equivalent.

Present	Year 1	Year 2	Year 3	Year 4	Year 5
	$2,000	$2,000	$2,000	$2,000	$2,000
	$\div$	$\div$	$\div$	$\div$	$\div$
	$(1.0375)^1$	$(1.0375)^2$	$(1.0375)^3$	$(1.0375)^4$	$(1.0375)^5$
1,927.71					
1,858.03					
1,790.88					
1,726.15					
1,663.76					
$ 8,966.52	Present value				

Cash flows are exposed to more inflation as time progresses, resulting in the inflation rate being raised to the power of n, where n represents the time period under consideration. Since the cash inflows are viewed as an end-of-year event in this example, the n exponent equals the year in question. The inflation rate compounds over time, causing later cash flows to become increasingly discounted. When adjusted for inflation, the actual cost of the loan will equal $8,966.52.

A full discount rate that combines risk and inflation (not just inflation) is generally applied to a future cash flow stream. The use of a risk premium applies in situations where future cash flows may not be received as estimated. Suppose a health care organization believes it can increase revenue $4,000 per year for five years by purchasing a $16,000 piece of equipment. In this example, risks may include low demand, equipment defects, staffing issues, and so forth. A *net* present value calculation would be performed since cash outflows are being subtracted from cash inflows. Due to the potential risks estimated at 7% and an estimated inflation rate of 3%, a total discount rate of 10% is applied to all future cash flows in this example. Figure 11.5 shows the undiscounted revenue stream being discounted by 1.1 (1 + 10%). The original equipment cost of $16,000 is not discounted because it already occurs in the present moment. The amount is made with 100% certainty and bears no impact from inflation.

If the discounting process were ignored, the project would generate an estimated $20,000 in revenue for an initial cost of $16,000, providing net profit of $4,000. After removing risk and inflation from the revenue projection, the *net present value* of the venture reflects a loss of $837. This transaction may generate more or less than this amount, but chances are greater that this venture will result in failure. This venture should be rejected because it does not properly compensate the organization for the estimated level of risk and inflation. *Only ventures showing a positive net present value should be accepted.*

FIGURE 11.5 Net Present Value Calculation

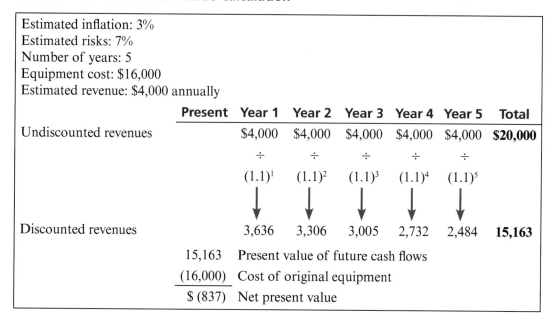

Estimated inflation: 3%
Estimated risks: 7%
Number of years: 5
Equipment cost: $16,000
Estimated revenue: $4,000 annually

	Present	Year 1	Year 2	Year 3	Year 4	Year 5	Total
Undiscounted revenues		$4,000	$4,000	$4,000	$4,000	$4,000	**$20,000**
		÷	÷	÷	÷	÷	
		$(1.1)^1$	$(1.1)^2$	$(1.1)^3$	$(1.1)^4$	$(1.1)^5$	
		↓	↓	↓	↓	↓	
Discounted revenues		3,636	3,306	3,005	2,732	2,484	**15,163**

15,163	Present value of future cash flows
(16,000)	Cost of original equipment
$ (837)	Net present value

Summary

A present value calculation places all future (or historical) cash flows into the context of today's money. Future cash flows should be discounted to reflect the decrease of value from risk and inflation, especially when considering *net* cash flows. Only transactions with a positive *net present value* will provide a sufficient level of return to compensate investors for estimated levels of risk and inflation.

11.5   Future Value

A future value calculation takes the opposite approach to adjusting cash flows. It tries to predict the dollar amount of a future transaction based on present amounts already known. Imagine a health care student has two more years of school and expects to work for two years thereafter. The student has four years before starting a practice and would like to *budget* for the future costs. If the student expects to purchase equipment that currently costs $15,000, how much will the price of the equipment be in four years when the transaction is actually made? The student calls the manufacturing company and discovers that it intends on raising prices to keep pace with inflation. The rate of inflation has averaged 1% every year for the past four years, but the economy is starting to emerge from a recession. The student conducts research and finds that economists predict inflation will rise by 3% on average in the future. Figure 11.6 shows the calculation process wherein the equipment cost is multiplied by *1 + Inflation Rate*. The inflation rate compounds over four time periods resulting in 1.03 (1 + 3%) being raised to the power of 4.

> Note how the future value calculation involves *multiplying* the cash flow by a discount rate and the present value calculation involves *dividing* the cash flow by a discount rate.

FIGURE 11.6 Future Value Calculation

Estimated inflation: 3%
Number of years: 4
Equipment cost: $15,000

Future value ⟶ $15,000 × 1.03^4 = $16,883

This student would need $16,883 to purchase this piece of equipment in four years according to the future value calculation. Inflation compounds over time, leading to a price increase of $1,883. Approximating future cash flows may influence the student's budget and create the need to find additional sources of capital financing.

Future Cash Flow

A future cash flow stream is first established using the future value calculation and then it becomes discounted using the present value calculation.

The future cash flows related to a venture or business will seldom resemble the corresponding present-day cash flows unless fixed by a contract—such is the case with a bank loan or lease agreement. Most cash flows will be impacted by inflation or some other variable causing a change to occur in the future. For example, a particular type of computer costing $1,000 today could drop in price due to technological advancements. Analysis should reflect the estimated amount of a cash flow in its future form—not how the cash flow appears currently. Once a future cash flow stream is established, it must always be further discounted into present value terms to remove risk and inflation.

Suppose that a health care organization wants to compile a net present value calculation regarding a new venture involving a $10,000 piece of equipment. The equipment manufacturer recommends changing parts every five years. The health care organization asked about any future price changes and the manufacturer stated that it intends to keep prices in line with inflation. Further research shows that economists estimate inflation will increase 3% on average. If parts cost $1,000 today, these same parts will cost an estimated $1,159 ($1,000 $\times$ 1.03^5) in five years, as listed in Figure 11.7. Revenues that start at an estimated $3,000 are also adjusted for inflation. Note how the revenues in Year 2 equal $3,090 ($3,000 $\times$ 1.03). The *net* cash flows are then discounted into present value terms using a combined discount rate of 10% to remove both risk and inflation. This calculation shows that the venture will produce positive net present value of $1,288.

FIGURE 11.7 Cash Flow Projection

Step 1: Estimate future cash flows

	Present	Year 1	Year 2	Year 3	Year 4	Year 5
Projected revenues		$3,000	$3,090	$3,183	$3,278	$3,377
Projected expenses						(1,159)
Projected net profit		3,000	3,090	3,183	3,278	2,218

Step 2: Discount future cash flows for risk and inflation

		Year 1	Year 2	Year 3	Year 4	Year 5
Projected net profit		3,000	3,090	3,183	3,278	2,218
		$\div$	$\div$	$\div$	$\div$	$\div$
		$(1.1)^1$	$(1.1)^2$	$(1.1)^3$	$(1.1)^4$	$(1.1)^5$
		$\downarrow$	$\downarrow$	$\downarrow$	$\downarrow$	$\downarrow$
Discounted net profit		2,727	2,554	2,391	2,239	1,377

11,288	Net present value of future cash flows
(10,000)	Cost of original equipment
$1,288	Total net present value

Summary

The calculation of future value resembles the calculation of present value, but the process works inversely. A future value calculation involves making adjustments to current prices according to the rate of inflation or another relevant variable in order to estimate what a cash flow will look like in the future. Once the estimated future amounts have been established, the *net* cash flow for each year needs to be discounted into present value terms to remove risk and inflation.

11.6   Loan Schedules

Lending institutions provide various types of loans, including student, practice, and building loans. A loan can be forged with an acquaintance or directly with the seller of an asset. A lease might trigger criteria causing it to be capitalized on the balance sheet whereby an artificial loan would be added to the liability section of the balance sheet corresponding to this capitalized amount. An **amortization schedule** provides a listing of how the loan payments will be applied to either *principal* or interest in each time period.

Consider a $100,000 student loan consolidated over 30 years with payments due monthly. Assuming an annual interest rate of 6%, each monthly payment would equal roughly $600 [calculation not shown]. Part of each individual payment of $600 is viewed as both principal and interest in varying amounts as show in Table 11.2. The amount of interest charged after one month would equal $500 ($100,000 × 6% ÷ 12 months). The division by 12 months sets the interest rate into a monthly equivalent. The $100 ($600 − $500) paid in addition to the interest charge is considered principal and would reduce the overall loan balance to $99,900. The interest charge for the second month would equal $499.50 ($99,900 × 6% ÷ 12 months). The principal portion from the second payment would total $100.50 ($600.00 − $499.50) and the loan balance would be reduced again to $99,799.50.

> Note the correct spelling is principal and not principle!
>
> **Amortization Schedule:** A detailed listing of how each loan payment is applied to interest charges and the principal balance.

TABLE 11.2   Amortization Schedule

Month	Beginning Balance	Monthly Interest*	Interest Portion	Total Payment	Principal Portion	Ending Balance
January	$100,000.00	0.5%	500.00	600.00	100.00	$99,900.00
February	$ 99,900.00	0.5%	499.50	600.00	100.50	$99,799.50
March	$ 99,799.50	0.5%	499.00	600.00	101.00	$99,698.50
April	$ 99,698.50	0.5%	498.49	600.00	101.51	$99,596.99
May	$ 99,596.99	0.5%	497.98	600.00	102.02	$99,494.97
June	$ 99,494.97	0.5%	497.47	600.00	102.53	$99,392.45
July	$ 99,392.45	0.5%	496.96	600.00	103.04	$99,289.41
August	$ 99,289.41	0.5%	496.45	600.00	103.55	$99,185.86
September	$ 99,185.86	0.5%	495.93	600.00	104.07	$99,081.79
October	$ 99,081.79	0.5%	495.41	600.00	104.59	$98,977.20
November	$ 98,977.20	0.5%	494.89	600.00	105.11	$98,872.08
December	$ 98,872.08	0.5%	494.36	600.00	105.64	$98,766.44

*The monthly interest rate can be found by dividing 6% by 12 months.

In each subsequent month, the loan balance would be multiplied by the *monthly* interest rate to derive the interest charge. The portion of each loan payment *not* treated as interest represents principal; the amount treated as principal reduces the loan balance further. As the principal balance on the loan decreases, the amount of each loan payment characterized as interest declines, causing a larger portion of each $600 loan payment to reduce the principal balance. At the end of the 30-year time horizon, the last payment would officially pay down any remaining loan balance.

The term "amortization" used in finance differs from the amortization of intangibles seen in accounting.

Table 11.3 illustrates the amortization process related to a standard loan arrangement. Other types of loans exist that may amortize amounts differently, but such loans are rare. Microsoft Excel or a financial calculator can assist with setting up a loan amortization schedule.

TABLE 11.3	Amortization Process
1. Loan balance × interest rate = interest charge
2. Loan payment − interest charge = principal portion
3. Loan balance − principal portion = new loan balance

The portion of loan payments treated as interest charges begins to decrease in size while the principal portion slowly increases in size. Over the life of a loan, the principal portion of each payment will continue to increase until the final loan payment is made. Figure 11.8 illustrates the relationship between interest and principal over the course of a standard loan. Since a loan's principal balance declines very slowly, *leverage risk* will remain fairly static until later stages of a loan when more of each payment will be applied to the principal balance.

FIGURE 11.8 Treatment of Loan Payments

Note how a $600 loan payment is applied differently to interest and principal over time.

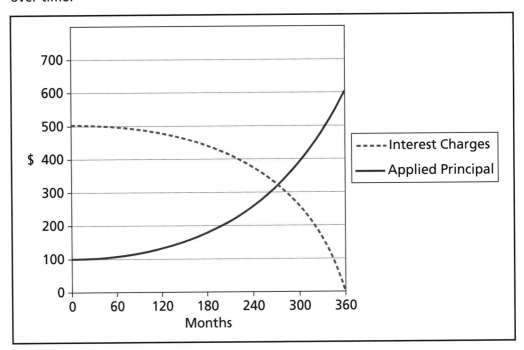

Summary

A loan payment is divided between principal and interest in varying proportions over time. An amortization schedule shows the breakdown of principal and interest according to each loan payment. The amortization process begins by multiplying the current loan balance by the relevant interest rate (often a monthly equivalent). The amount of calculated interest is deducted from the loan payment. The remainder of the loan payment is used to reduce a loan's principal balance further. This calculation sequence repeats until the loan balance reaches zero.

CHAPTER ASSIGNMENT

Working in a group of three to four students or fellow professionals, complete the following items.

1. A country has produced products and services worth $8 trillion in the current year. Would the economy experience inflation or deflation if the total money supply equaled $8.5 trillion? What would happen if the money supply contracted to less than $8 trillion?

2. What are the two main components of the discount rate?

3. Suppose that an organization wants to fund a $200,000 project. A bank will loan $144,000 of the capital needed at an 8% cost of debt (interest rate). The business owner will contribute the remaining $56,000 using personal funds, but will want to generate a 15% rate of return on personal money (cost of equity). A tax professional was contacted and believes that interest on the bank loan will be tax deductible at a 35% marginal tax rate. What discount rate would the organization use for this project?

4. Explain what compound growth means and how it applies to a period of continuous inflation.

5. What does it mean to set future cash flows into *net present value* terms? How does a discount rate factor into this process?

6. Calculate the net present value of the following cash flow stream given a discount rate of 12%.

Year 0	Year 1	Year 2	Year 3
(10,000)	3,500	3,500	3,500

7. What will an $800 printer cost in two years if economists estimate the rate of inflation will be 3.5% and 4.5% per annum, respectively?

8. Imagine a $100,000 loan has been paid down and now has a current balance of $83,439. Each fixed *monthly* loan payment is $974 and the *annual* interest rate is 8%. What portion of the next loan payment would be treated as interest expense versus principal?

Corporate Finance

AUTHOR'S NOTE

This chapter is comprised of case studies offering insight into how a business owner should *think*. Conducting financial calculations as shown is not always necessary, but a business owner must think holistically before making business decisions. Pay special attention to how *future* cash flows are established using assumptions and then discounted into *present value* terms. Hopefully, some of the concepts in this chapter regarding statistics and Microsoft Excel were covered elsewhere during your education. Take note of the financial and statistical functions inside the *Insert Function* toolbox in Microsoft Excel. These premade functions can greatly simplify any calculation and circumvent the need to learn extravagant formulas. An entrepreneur must at least understand what the calculation results mean.

The mathematical concepts learned in the last chapter are used to calculate the financial *value* of a business venture. For example, the decision to buy new equipment or change fees can be assessed using the future value and present value calculation processes. These same financial calculations can operate on a larger scale to formulate the value of a health care practice. No matter what type of venture, assumptions about expected future activity are used to configure projected cash flows. The *net* future cash flows are then always converted into present value terms in order to remove any risk and inflation.

The net present value (NPV) calculation represents one of the most important management tools used to evaluate the value of a business venture. A venture must provide a positive NPV in order to generate enough profit to cover the costs of capital (debt and equity). Other evaluation techniques provide more insight into the nature of a venture's cash flows and value proposition. The **internal rate of return (IRR)** formula looks at the *annualized* rate of return a venture will generate. The IRR must be greater than the discount rate to ensure that a venture will return enough profit to cover the costs of capital. The **payback period** looks at the length of time needed to recuperate the initial amounts used to fund a project. A long payback period exposes capital funding to risk and inflation longer and it forces a business owner to wait before reusing such funds in other capacities. A venture can be further evaluated by compiling *financial ratios* or a *cash budget*. An organization must ensure that any cash shortfalls brought about by a venture will be covered.

This chapter ends with a general overview of Microsoft Excel because of the role it plays in performing calculations and managing cash flow streams. An organization can use Excel to assist with marketing, accounting, and management tasks as well. Take time to understand this program in sufficient depth to properly manage all the quantitative aspects of your organization.

> More information about formulating assumptions for use in valuing a practice can be found in Chapter 13.

> **Internal Rate of Return:** The overall rate of profit that a cash flow stream provides on an annualized basis.

> **Payback Period:** The time until any capital investment in a venture is recovered through the generation of future net cash flows.

12.1 Financial Projections

A health care provider will face countless decisions over the course of time. Each situation contains a unique set of circumstances, requiring a thoughtful and holistic reflection on what should be incorporated into the decision-making process. Financial tools enable an evaluation of those circumstances in terms of their quantitative aspects. A financial projection looks specifically at the quantitative activity that has not yet occurred. The estimated cash inflows of a projection are netted against cash outflows before being modified by a discount rate. A discount rate can be constructed using the weighted average cost of capital (WACC) formula or through a direct estimation of risk and inflation. *The discount rate applied to a venture's net cash flow stream should never be less than an organization's WACC.* Adding together all discounted net cash flows results in a single net present value (NPV) figure. A venture with a negative NPV should be rejected; a venture with a positive NPV should be evaluated in full, using various evaluation techniques before being accepted. The following case studies demonstrate how financial tools can be used to evaluate various business transactions. The case studies build in complexity throughout this chapter.

Marketing Campaign

A survey of new patients revealed that very few responded to an organization's telephone book ad. Most new patients made appointments as a result of being referred. Getting the telephone book ad published required an immaterial amount of administrative time. The ad cost of $8,000 is considered the only relevant expense as listed in Figure 12.1. By removing the telephone book ad, the organization expects patient revenues of $200,000 to decline by 3% ($6,000). The business owner would like to use a discount rate of 15% for this situation based on personal preference.

FIGURE 12.1 **Telephone Advertisement**

Present	Year 1	
	$8,000	Ad savings
	(6,000)	Lost revenue from ad removal
	2,000	
NPV = $ 1,739		

By removing the telephone book ad, the organization expects to save an estimated $1,739 on a risk and inflation adjusted basis.

Hiring an Associate

An organization is considering hiring an associate to develop the practice further and offer additional service lines. The estimated payroll expenses for the new associate shown in Figure 12.2 total $58,650 per year including benefits and payroll taxes. This organization expects revenues to increase to $165,000 in the coming year with help from the associate. In order to support this level of revenue, administrative costs are expected to increase by $10,000. All other expenses should remain fixed and will not increase after the inclusion of an associate. The business owner would like to use a discount rate of 25% based on discussions with other small businesses.

FIGURE 12.2 **Hiring an Associate**

Present	Year 1	
	$165,000	Expected revenues
	(58,650)	Payroll expenses—associate
	(30,000)	General administrative costs
	(10,000)	Increased administrative costs
	66,350	Net profit
NPV = $ 53,080		

The organization believes it can generate profit of $60,000 [calculation not shown] next year without an associate. This financial projection shows net profit increasing by $6,350 ($66,350 − $60,000) after hiring an associate. However, the *value* of this venture on a risk and inflation adjusted basis is only $53,080, leading to a potential loss of $6,920 ($60,000 − $53,080). This estimated level of net profit does not properly compensate the business owner for the risk and inflation related to this venture. Could the organization increase value through an unrelated venture or by hiring a different associate? Would projecting net profit beyond one year produce significantly different results?

A financial projection should rarely go beyond five years due to the high degree of model risk involved with projecting cash flows so far into the future.

Purchase of New Equipment

A discount rate can reflect the capital costs of a particular venture as long as it is higher than the capital costs of the organization as a whole.

An organization purchased a basic computer system when it opened three years ago. Since the patient base has grown dramatically, the organization now requires a more advanced system. Research into new computer systems revealed two prospective options that could provide enough functionality for an estimated five years. The organization would like to rely on its WACC of 13% [calculation not shown] to capture the risk and inflation of this venture. This WACC has been calculated based on the organization's overall capital costs.

Option A Purchase three new computers along with a standard billing software program. The computers and software would cost $2,500 and $3,000, respectively. The new computer system is not expected to increase revenues, but the health care provider should save approximately 25 hours per year of administrative time at an equivalent hourly rate of $95 totaling $2,375 ($95 × 25 hours). Figure 12.3 demonstrates that this first option will produce NPV of $2,853.

FIGURE 12.3 Standard Computer System

Option A	Present	Year 1	Year 2	Year 3	Year 4	Year 5
		$2,375	$2,375	$2,375	$2,375	$2,375
Time saved	8,353 ←					
Computers	(2,500)					
Biling software	(3,000)					
NPV =	$2,853					

Note how all projected cash flows are static and have not been adjusted per inflation or other relevant variables—the future cash flow streams may not be correctly formulated!

Option B Purchase three new computers, a high-end billing software program, and digital tablets to take notes in the treatment rooms. The computers would cost $2,500 and the billing system would cost $8,500. The tablets would cost an additional $4,000. This setup should save the health care provider approximately 40 hours in administrative time each year at an equivalent hourly rate of $95 totaling $3,800 ($95 × 40). The tablets' attractive appearance and improvements to the patient experience should increase positive word of mouth and patient retention. The organization believes that revenues will increase by approximately $2,000 per year as a result. Figure 12.4 demonstrates that this second option will generate NPV of $5,400.

FIGURE 12.4 Advanced Computer System

Option B	Present	Year 1	Year 2	Year 3	Year 4	Year 5
		$3,800	$3,800	$3,800	$3,800	$3,800
Time saved	13,365 ←					
		2,000	2,000	2,000	2,000	2,000
Increased revenues	7,034 ←					
Computers	(2,500)					
Billing software	(8,500)					
Tablets	(4,000)					
NPV =	$5,400					

Opportunity Cost: A theoretical loss incurred from engaging in a specific activity as opposed to a more profitable one.

An **opportunity cost** exists anytime resources are not allocated to the most productive activity possible. The time saved under both system options is represented as revenue in this analysis because the health care provider believes more patients could be seen if less time is spent on administrative matters. This revenue provision may not be appropriate if a health care provider cannot fill this time with revenue producing activities—no opportunity cost would exist. Option B has a higher net present value, meaning it would offer a greater amount of profit after considering the organization's capital costs (risk and inflation). Option B should be selected over Option A purely as a result of providing $2,547 ($5,400 − $2,853) more in NPV.

Forecasting Beginning Revenues

A recent graduate has an opportunity to rent space in an established health care clinic and build a practice from scratch. The other providers in the clinic expect to refer at least five patients per month because of the nature of the association. During school, the recent graduate put together a comprehensive marketing plan and *territory worksheet* listing ways to connect with market participants. The recent graduate started contacting close network participants and confirmed that seven individuals will become new patients. Fifteen others expressed some interest in receiving care, but only five of these are predicted to become new patients.

The recent graduate has set forth various marketing campaigns involving roughly 100 people each month and believes 1% of these individuals will become new patients within the first year. As a result of maintaining relationships, more people from this group should decide to become patients at a rate of 2% in the second year. Further contact with another 1,200 (100 × 12 months) people in the second year through ongoing marketing campaigns will generate 12 (1,200 × 1%) new patients as well. Some of these 2,400 people contacted over this two-year period will become referral sources and recommend services to yet others using dialogue *applications* provided by the recent graduate. The referrals should result in one new patient per month in the first year and two new patients each month in the second year.

Health care providers at the clinic claim patients obtain approximately $1,000 in health care services on average. The recent graduate estimates a lower *patient margin* during the initial year of operations equal to $600. The average amount of revenue per patient is expected to increase to $800 in the second year as the patient experience improves. Figure 12.5 presents all the revenue assumptions and calculates the discounted revenue values for the first and second years of operation using an assumed discount rate of 25%.

FIGURE 12.5 Forecasting Beginning Revenues

Projected revenues are calculated by multiplying the estimated new patient total by the estimated patient margin for each year. The projected revenues of $57,600 and $96,000 have been discounted for one and two time periods, respectively.

Patient Source	New Patients: Year 1		New Patients: Year 2	
	Monthly	Annualized	Monthly	Annualized
Integrated clinic	5	60	5	60
Marketing campaigns	1	12	3	36
Network referrals	1	12	2	24
Network participants:				
Seven certain		7		
Fifteen uncertain		5		
Total new patients		96		120
Patient margin		$ 600		$ 800
Projected revenues		$57,600		$96,000
Discounted revenues		$46,080		$61,440

The recent graduate will need to project expenses and discount them in order to formulate the NPV of this venture. The NPV must be sufficiently large to cover the recent graduate's personal living expenses. Other opportunities should be explored to find the one with the highest NPV.

Summary

A financial projection is designed after thoughtful and holistic consideration of both financial and nonfinancial matters. The related cash flows should be projected for each respective time period—normally up to five years. Projected revenues are then netted together with projected expenses before being discounted for risk and inflation. The discount rate can reflect an organization's WACC or be constructed through an estimation of risk and inflation. Adding together all discounted net cash flows results in one net present value figure. An organization should consider a venture only if it offers positive net present value.

12.2   Project Evaluation

The net present value calculation represents the most important tool used to evaluate a venture. An organization should never engage in activities that offer a *negative* net present value because the costs of debt and equity financing—specific to the venture or the entire organization—will not be covered. A venture offering *positive* net present value produces enough revenue to cover both the expenses of the venture *and* financing costs. Other problems may exist with a particular venture and an organization should review other metrics, including the financial ratios discussed in Chapter 8, before committing resources.

Internal Rate of Return

The internal rate of return (IRR) calculation indicates how much a venture will earn on average when looking at its net *undiscounted* cash flows. The IRR represents an annualized rate of return in relation to a venture's funding costs, but the exact rate of return earned in a given year may differ from the IRR. Making this calculation is not straightforward and generally requires a spreadsheet program or financial calculator.

A project must earn enough to cover the costs associated with using debt and equity financing. These costs reflect the risk and inflation faced by the sources of such capital. An organization should select ventures with the highest IRR first in an effort to maximize what is available to cover financing costs. An IRR less than the discount rate or WACC means that an organization will not earn enough profit to pay its financing costs potentially leading to bankruptcy (debt) or a dissatisfied business owner (equity). A large spread between the IRR and discount rate is desired because it allows more room for error in terms of the discount rate being used. Table 12.1 presents the general criteria to use when deciding to accept or reject a venture.

TABLE 12.1	IRR Evaluation		
	IRR > discount rate	⟶	Accept the venture
	IRR = discount rate	⟶	Accept the venture
	IRR < discount rate	⟶	Reject the venture

Payback Period

An organization should assess the timing of cash flows to identify any negative cash balances and determine how long will it take to fully recuperate the capital invested in a venture. Normally, a venture will initially involve a large capital outflow followed by a long period of positive net inflows. The payback period calculation shows the point at which the accumulative inflows and outflows of cash finally equal zero. The calculation can involve either discounted or undiscounted cash flows. The payback period can also reveal periods of cash shortfalls that may need to be covered through other means. For example, a venture may generate losses for the first several years, requiring additional sources of funding.

General Project

A health care organization wants to take $40,000 from savings to expand an outside parking lot and begin charging neighboring businesses a user fee. Initial revenue from the fees is estimated at $11,000 and will increase in subsequent years according to a projected inflation rate of 2.5% as seen in Figure 12.6. The organization feels that risk levels should be quantified at 20% based on the lack of experience with parking lot ventures. The combined discount rate equals 22.5% (20% + 2.5%). According to these assumptions, the venture will result in a $7,558 loss of value.

Note how the inflation rate influences the cash flow projection and the discount rate.

FIGURE 12.6 General Project Evaluation

	Present	Year 1	Year 2	Year 3	Year 4	Year 5
Projected revenues		$11,000	$11,275	$11,557	$11,846	$12,142
		$\div$	$\div$	$\div$	$\div$	$\div$
		$(1.225)^1$	$(1.225)^2$	$(1.225)^3$	$(1.225)^4$	$(1.225)^5$
	8,980					
	7,514					
	6,287					
	5,261					
	4,402					
Total present value	32,442					
Original investment	(40,000)					
Net present value	$ (7,558)					

The *undiscounted* payback period needed to recuperate the original $40,000 investment equals three years and seven months. The revenue stream during the first three years totals $33,832. If monthly parking lot revenue remained constant in the fourth year, it would take seven more months to earn the remaining $6,168 ($40,000 − $33,832).

The *undiscounted* cash flow stream would generate a 13.43% IRR [calculation not shown]. Since the discount rate is 22.5%, this venture would not properly compensate the health care organization for risk and inflation—meaning the financing costs would not be covered. The actual cash flows of this venture may differ substantially from projected amounts, but the organization faces a strong possibility of incurring actual losses. The parking lot should not be expanded since the related IRR is less than the discount rate and the venture offers a negative NPV.

6,168
÷ 11,846
× 12 months
= 7 months (rounded)

Functions in Microsoft Excel were used to perform the IRR calculation.

Complex Project

A health care provider is considering vacating a leased office space and purchasing a $100,000 building. A commercial lender is offering a $75,000 five-year loan at 6% interest with a required down payment of $25,000. The down payment would come from personal savings and the loan payments would equal roughly $1,933.28 each month [calculation not shown]. The health care provider wants to use the WACC formula to derive the discount rate. Based on conversations with small business owners in the area, the required return on equity is estimated at 20%. A tax professional recommends using a marginal tax rate of 28% for the projection. These variables produce a discount rate of 8.2% when using the WACC formula as listed in Figure 12.7.

FIGURE 12.7 Weighted Average Cost of Capital

Percentage debt = 75% ($75,000 ÷ $100,000)
Percentage equity = 25% ($25,000 ÷ $100,000)
Cost of debt = 6.0%
Marginal tax rate = 28%
Cost of equity = 20%

⟶ WACC = [75% × 6.0% (1 − 28%)] + [25% × 20%]
⟶ WACC = 3.2% + 5.0%
⟶ WACC = 8.2%

The health care provider currently pays $1,000 per month on a lease, but lease payments adjust according to the rate of inflation each year. Inflation is expected to increase by 2% over the next five years. The health care provider would save $12,000 ($1,000 × 12) in the first year by ending the lease agreement, and an increasing amount in each subsequent year as adjusted for inflation. Commercial loan payments would replace the lease payments and amount to $23,200 ($1,933.28 × 12) in each of the next five years. The health care provider anticipates selling the building in five years. Figure 12.8 lists all of the cash flows related to this transition.

FIGURE 12.8 Complex Project Evaluation

	Present	Year 1	Year 2	Year 3	Year 4	Year 5	
Lease savings		$12,000	$12,360	$12,731	$13,113	$13,506	Line 1
Down payment	$(25,000)						Line 2
Loan payments		(23,200)	(23,200)	(23,200)	(23,200)	(23,200)	Line 3
Building expenses		(2,000)	(2,000)	(2,000)	(2,000)	(2,000)	Line 4
Building proceeds						121,665	Line 5
Tax consequences		2,105	1,800	1,476	1,132	(4,845)	Line 6
	(25,000)	(11,095)	(11,040)	(10,993)	(10,955)	105,126	
		÷	÷	÷	÷	÷	
		$(1.082)^1$	$(1.082)^2$	$(1.082)^3$	$(1.082)^4$	$(1.082)^5$	
Year 1 discounted	(10,250) ←						
Year 2 discounted	(9,423) ←						
Year 3 discounted	(8,669) ←						
Year 4 discounted	(7,981) ←						
Year 5 discounted	70,757 ←						
NPV =	$9,434						
IRR =	12.60%						

Line 1 reflects the savings generated by avoiding lease payments of $12,000 in the first year and as adjusted for inflation thereafter. The personal capital contribution of $25,000 presented on *Line 2* would not be impacted by risk or inflation because it occurs in the present moment with 100% certainty. The fixed loan payments totaling $23,200 per year are reflected on *Line 3*. Additional costs related to estimated building repairs and maintenance are shown on *Line 4*. Included at the end of *Line 5* is the anticipated sales price of the building after five years. Assumed in this calculation is that the building's value will grow at 2% above inflation reaching a *future value* of $121,665.

Deducting interest charges and building expenses has produced a tax benefit as shown on *Line 6*. The tax savings in *Year 5* are offset by taxes owed on the sale of the building. The original cost of the building less accumulated depreciation presents a net book value of $84,258 ($100,000 − $15,742). Depreciation expense of $15,742 was calculated using rules pertaining to nonresidential real property found in IRS Publication 946. The tax liability generated from the sale of the building totals $5,611 [($121,665 − $84,258) × 15%] based on the capital gains tax rate of 15%. Note how the estimated sales price of $121,665 was reduced by the building's net book value to determine the amount subject to capital gains tax.

See IRS Publication 544 for more information on capital gains taxes.

Transitioning from a leased office space into a building would offer net present value of $9,434 on a risk and inflation adjusted basis. The IRR of 12.6% has been calculated using functions in Microsoft Excel. This venture is projected to cover the costs of debt and equity financing since the IRR is more than the WACC.

Although the IRR and NPV figures make the venture appear viable, the payback period does not occur until the fifth year. The health care provider will not recuperate the full personal investment of $25,000 until the building is sold—assuming that the sales price will be sufficient and the building will sell immediately. Negative cash flows occurring in the first four years must be covered by other financing sources. Will this influence the health care provider's willingness to put personal money at risk for so many years? What financial ratios could the organization apply in this example to further examine whether to accept the venture or reject it?

Summary

Only ventures that offer positive net present value should be considered. An organization must still look at other metrics to determine if a venture with positive NPV contains other drawbacks. The internal rate of return (IRR) reflects the annualized percentage of profit that a venture will earn. A venture's IRR must be greater than its discount rate (WACC) to ensure the costs of capital (risk and inflation) will be covered. The payback period shows how long capital financing will be exposed to risk and inflation. A long payback period means that any initial outflow of capital will not be recuperated quickly. An organization can employ other business analysis tools, such as financial ratios, to evaluate the overall merits of a venture.

12.3   Econometrics

Econometrics refers to the body of statistical concepts used within the field of economics and business. Finding patterns amid quantitative data is important when forecasting future activity or making management decisions. This overview touches on the most common econometric concepts. The calculation process related to econometrics often involves a spreadsheet program.

Data Set: The complete list of numeric values under consideration.

Data Set

Statistical calculations are often performed with an available **data set** that contains numeric values categorized into different **arrays** (columns). Certain information can be converted

Array: A specific list of numeric values categorized together within a data set.

into a data set by assigning numeric values to qualitative terms. Consider a short questionnaire asking patients to provide feedback about the care they received in the past.

Do you believe that the care you received has led to an improvement in your health?

Strongly Agree	Agree	No Change	Disagree	Strongly Disagree	N/A

Imagine that the organization received 57 responses to this survey and arranged a numeric value system as shown in Figure 12.9 in order to capture the relevance of each qualitative term. For example, a response of *strongly disagree* could correspond to high patient turnover or negative word of mouth; thus an assumed metric of -10 best reflects the potential consequences of such a response. In contrast, a response of *strongly agree* receives an assumed metric of $+7$ because of what it means in terms of patient retention and positive word of mouth.

FIGURE 12.9 Questionnaire Results

Questionnaire responses have been converted into quantitative terms

	Response Rate		Metric		Total Value
Strongly agree	18	$\times$	$+7$	$=$	126
Agree	13	$\times$	$+4$	$=$	52
No change	6	$\times$	-3	$=$	-18
Disagree	9	$\times$	-7	$=$	-63
Strongly disagree	3	$\times$	-10	$=$	-30
N/A	8	$\times$	0	$=$	0
	57				67

In relation to the number of responses, the average point of value equaled $+1.175\,(67 \div 57)$ in contrast to a maximum possible value of $+7$. The survey results appear to signify that patients have not experienced tremendous improvements to their health. The organization can hand this same questionnaire to patients at a later time to see if this rate improves or worsens.

Correlations

Assume in the previous example that the organization researched how many times respondents came in for treatment. The total number of visits per each response category is reported in Figure 12.10 next to the number of respondents. The average number of visits is then calculated and reported next to the value system created before. The relationship between this value system and quantity of average visits is assessed statistically using the **correlation** function in Excel.

Correlation: A formula used to determine the approximate relationship between two arrays.

FIGURE 12.10 Example Correlation

A correlation statistic is run to assess the relationship between the average number of visits set by a specific group of survey respondents and a quantitative metric formulated to represent each respondent group's impact on an organization's success.

	Respondents	Total Visits	Average Visits	Metric
Strongly agree	18	252	14	7
Agree	13	156	12	4
No change	6	30	5	−3
Disagree	9	36	4	−7
Strong disagree	3	6	2	−10
N/A	8	48	6	0
	57	528	Correlation =	95.9%

A correlation shows how the numbers in two different arrays correspond to one another. Two arrays containing numbers that increase or decrease in perfect tandem would result in a correlation of 100%. A correlation of 95.9% between health outcomes and average patient visits illustrates that a very strong relationship exists. How would the organization interpret this correlation? Patients will come in more frequently if the care they receive improves their health; or patients see improvements to their health if they come in more frequently. Organization members should discuss this issue with patients to arrive at a proper conclusion.

Positive Correlation: Activity in one array moves in tandem with another array. For example, an expense would be considered variable if it shared a close relationship with patient revenue.

No Correlation: The data contained in two different arrays are **spurious** and do not show a relationship. For example, a fixed expense remains static even when patient revenue changes.

Negative Correlation: An inverse relationship exists between arrays. For example, uncollectible bad debts may decline as collection efforts increase.

Spurious: Amounts that appear random across time periods and lack any clear pattern.

The **coefficient of determination** identifies the extent to which activity in one array *causes* movement in another array. This calculation entails squaring the correlation figure (correlation²). In the previous example, 95.9% × 95.9% would produce a 92.0% coefficient of determination. This number signifies that 92.0% of the perceived health outcomes are directly linked to the average number of visits being set whereas 8.0% of the relationship between the two arrays is spurious.

Coefficient of Determination: A formula that more specifically isolates how one array influences (or does not influence) another.

Linear Regression Line

A linear **regression line** shows the general change in one variable based on changes in another variable. The regression formula enables the prediction of an *unknown* variable in one array based on a *known* variable from the other array. The regression formula is represented by the equation $y = mx + b$, where m = slope and b = the y-intercept. This formula requires at least two arrays whereby the x column denotes the independent variable and the y column specifies the dependent variable. The x value will influence the y value, but not vice versa. In instances where $x = 0$, the value for y will equal the value for b.

Suppose an organization wants to understand if amounts spent on marketing have an influence over revenue levels and approximately how much needs to be spent on marketing to reach a monthly revenue goal of $15,000. The correlation between these arrays as presented in Figure 12.11 equals 96.8% according to the correlation function in Excel. The

Regression Line: A linear pattern established between an independent array and a dependent one that can be used to predict an unknown value in one of the arrays.

coefficient of determination—representing the squared correlation—equals 93.8%. Both of these statistical calculations show that a strong relationship exists between the two arrays, thus confirming that a regression formula built using this data set would provide useful information. A weaker correlation would suggest that other factors drive revenue besides marketing expenses. In the real world, a health care provider might find that the number of hours spent talking with people has the highest correlation with patient revenue.

FIGURE 12.11 Example Data Set

	x Marketing Expense	*y* Revenue
January	50	7,917
February	75	8,083
March	116	8,665
April	108	9,000
May	145	9,415
June	158	9,830
July	179	9,750
August	195	10,081
September	175	10,500
October	200	10,750
November	213	11,120
December	225	11,310

The correlation and regression formula can be calculated using functions in Excel as explained later in this chapter.

The regression formula in this example is found to equal $y = 19.6x + 6,700$ [calculation not shown]. The organization can now forecast how much to spend on marketing (independent variable) to reach revenues of $15,000 (dependent variable).

Step 1: $15,000 = 19.6x + 6,700$

Step 2: $8,300 = 19.6x$

Step 3: $x = \$423$

The organization should spend roughly $423 on marketing each month to reach a revenue level of $15,000 according to the pattern found between the arrays.

Multiple Regression Line

Activity may contain multiple independent factors (*x* variables) that influence one dependent variable (*y* variable). A **multiple regression line** would be formulated to predict an unknown variable given a set of known variables. The type of independent variables that could influence revenue activity overall may include the number of hours spent marketing, the type of marketing campaign initiated, and the amount of marketing expenses.

Multiple Regression Line: A linear pattern established between more than one independent array and only one dependent array that can be used to predict an unknown value in one of the arrays.

MULTIPLE REGRESSION FORMULA

$y = m_1x_1 + m_2x_2 + m_3x_3 + b$

Quadratic Regression Line

Quadratic Regression Line: A quadratic pattern established between one or more independent array(s) and a dependent array that can be used to predict an unknown value in one of the arrays.

Often, two arrays move in approximately the same direction, but at an increasing rate (not linear). The compound growth of inflation demonstrates how patterns are not always uniform across time. Calculation of an increasing (quadratic) growth pattern requires a different formula not shown. Microsoft Excel has functions that enable the calculation of a **quadratic regression line**.

Summary

Statistics play a key role in forecasting future amounts, especially when a strong historical relationship is present between two arrays of data. Qualitative terms must be converted into numeric values before analysis is possible using statistical tools. A correlation describes the relationship between arrays. The coefficient of determination takes the square of the correlation value and more precisely identifies how one array influences another. The regression formula $y = mx + b$ takes the association of variables in a data set and predicts the value for an *unknown* variable. Multiple independent variables can be used to predict one dependent variable. A linear or quadratic relationship may exist between arrays.

12.4 Microsoft® Excel®

This section is an independent learning module and is not affiliated with, nor has it been authorized, sponsored, or otherwise approved by Microsoft Corporation. Microsoft® and Excel® are registered trademarks of Microsoft Corporation in the United States and/or other countries. Microsoft product screenshots reprinted with permission from Microsoft Corporation. Information presented in the screenshots has been added by the author of this work.

A good working knowledge of Excel can eliminate the need to perform complex calculations by hand. The following overview provides general instruction on how the program operates, especially in relation to financial calculations. Excel opens with a worksheet view containing vertical columns labeled alphabetically and horizontal rows labeled numerically. The boxes outlined with a light grey border through the worksheet in Figure 12.12 are called *cells*. Each cell can be referred to by an alphabetic and numeric value, such as E2 or F8.

FIGURE 12.12 Excel Basics

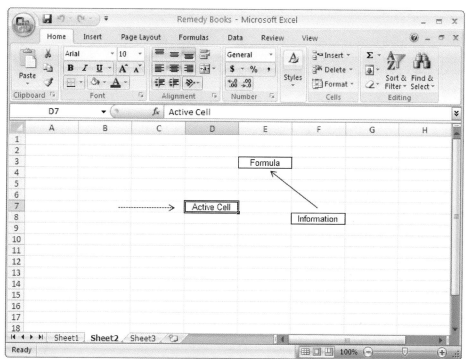

Excel allows a user to form lines of communication among cells populated with information and formulas. For instance, one cell (E3) could contain a formula that references another cell (F8). Information placed in cell F8 would flow automatically to cell E2 and alter the formula result. Notice how cell D7 is currently selected. The column and row headings are highlighted and the contents of cell D7 appear in the *formula bar* directly above the worksheet area.

To begin a formula within a cell, an equal (=) sign must be entered first. In the example shown in Figure 12.13, a basic formula is placed in cell E4 and has no lines of communication with any other cell. As the formula is typed into cell E4, the same formula also appears above the main worksheet area in the formula bar next to the *fx* button.

FIGURE 12.13 Basic Calculation

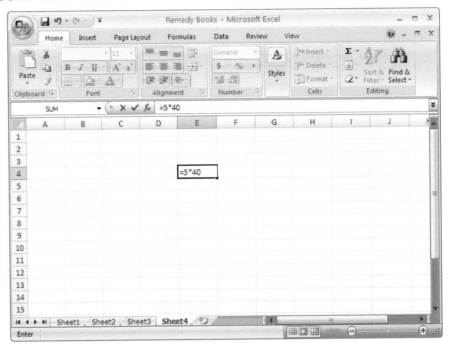

The result of a calculation will appear once the cell is deselected by activating a different cell (enter key). The user can return to a cell and view its exact contents from looking at the formula bar above the main worksheet area. Notice in Figure 12.14 how =5*40 appears in the formula bar while the formula result (200) is shown in the cell itself.

FIGURE 12.14 Calculation Result

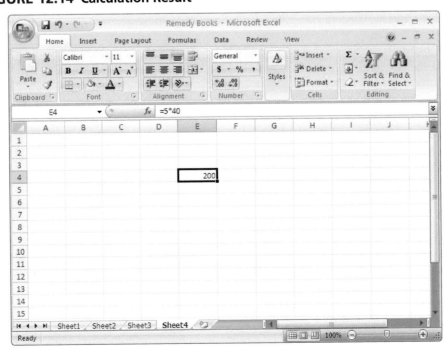

This same calculation could be made by forming lines of communication among multiple cells. The formula typed into cell E6 as shown in Figure 12.15 references two other cells: E3 and E4. The formula result in cell E6 is dependent on information placed into these two other cells. Changing the amounts placed in these cells would produce a different formula result. This exchange among cells facilitates the calculation process when working with a large data set.

FIGURE 12.15 Linked Calculation

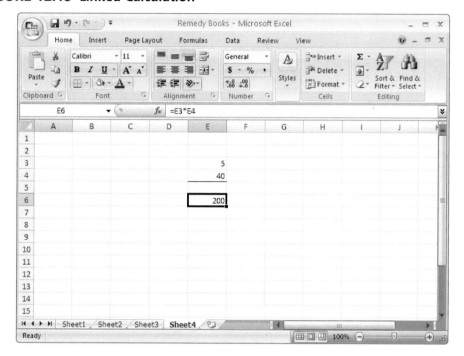

Consider a more complex example of a cash flow forecast as illustrated in Figure 12.16. The unadjusted cash flow stream shown is growing each year by the rate of inflation. If the initial cash flow equals $20,000, the value for the next year could be found by multiplying the initial cash flow in cell D9 by the inflation rate in cell D4. Notice how the formula =D9*(1+D4) is shown above the worksheet area in the formula bar.

Add 1 to the inflation rate for calculation purposes.

FIGURE 12.16 Financial Projection

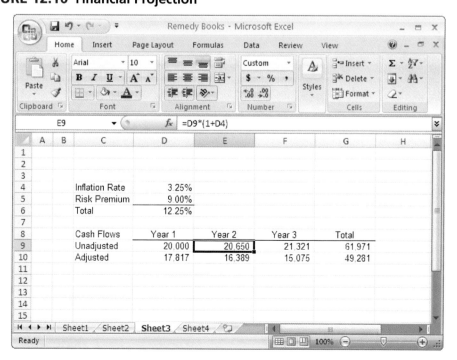

The user can switch views as demonstrated in Figure 12.17 to see the entire formula structure of the worksheet.

FIGURE 12.17　Formula View

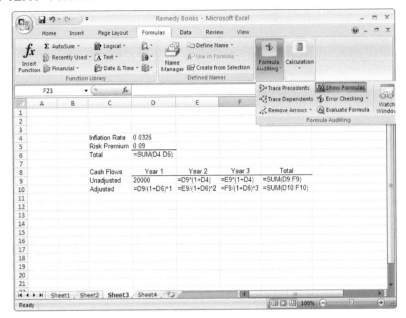

1. Cell D6 combines the inflation rate (0.0325) and risk premium (0.09) using the summation function. Various functions are discussed next.
2. Cells E9 and F9 take the initial $20,000 cash flow and compound it at the rate of inflation as noted by the reference to cell D4.
3. The formulas in cells D10 through F10 discount the unadjusted cash flows by dividing each one by cell D6. The discount rate is raised to the power of n, where $n =$ years that discounting will occur. Notice how the formula in Year 3 is raised to the power of 3.
4. The two summation functions in column G add together the unadjusted and adjusted cash flow streams, respectively.

By clicking on the *fx* button on the left side of the formula bar as illustrated in Figure 12.18, the user can insert a premade formula (called a function) into the active cell. A function can also be placed into the active cell by typing the function name directly.

FIGURE 12.18　Insert Function

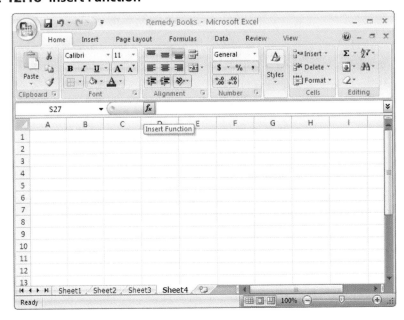

After clicking the *fx* button, a menu appears with a list of functions as shown in Figure 12.19. A broad range of functions can be found through the search box or from the category drop-down list. Calculations are greatly simplified by finding the appropriate function in the menu and referencing the cells that house the data set. Some common statistical and financial functions are presented in Table 12.2.

FIGURE 12.19 Function Menu

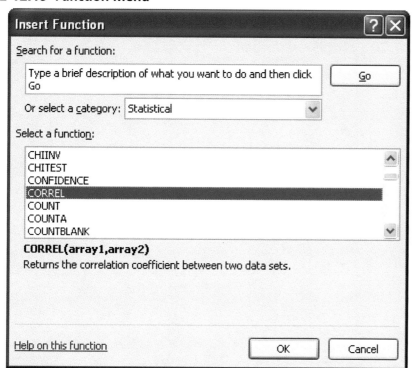

TABLE 12.2	Excel Functions

Statistical Functions		Financial Functions	
=AVERAGE	Sums numeric values and divides them by the number of instances to find an average value.	=FV	Computes the future value of an amount using an estimated growth rate, number of time periods, payments (if applicable), and present value.
=CORREL	Finds the correlation between two arrays.		
=INTERCEPT	Calculates the linear regression between two arrays and returns the *y*-intercept coefficient.	=PV	Computes the present value of an amount using known values for the discount rate, number of time periods, payments (if applicable), and projected future value.
=SLOPE	Calculates the linear regression between two arrays and returns the slope coefficient.	=NPV	Computes the net present value of a series of projected cash flows using a known discount rate.
=TREND =FORECAST	Calculates a linear regression line and finds the next unknown value in one array based on a known value from another array.	=IRR	Computes the annualized rate of return for a series of projected cash flows.
		=PMT	Figures the periodic loan payment using known values for the interest rate, number of time periods, and original loan balance.
=GROWTH =LOGEST	Considers any quadratic shape to the regression line and finds the next unknown value in one array based on a known value from another array.	=RATE	Figures the interest rate on a loan using known values for the periodic loan payment, number of time periods, and original loan balance.

Imagine that a health care organization wants to know if overtime hours worked by staff members are related to the number of patient visits. The data set listed in Figure 12.20 was compiled in order to calculate the correlation between these two arrays. The formula bar shows the correlation function entered into cell G6. The correlation was calculated as −27.0%, representing a weak inverse relationship. This negative correlation means that overtime hours actually decreased as patient visits increased. This organization should look for other variables that influence overtime hours in an effort to reduce payroll costs.

FIGURE 12.20 Correlation Function

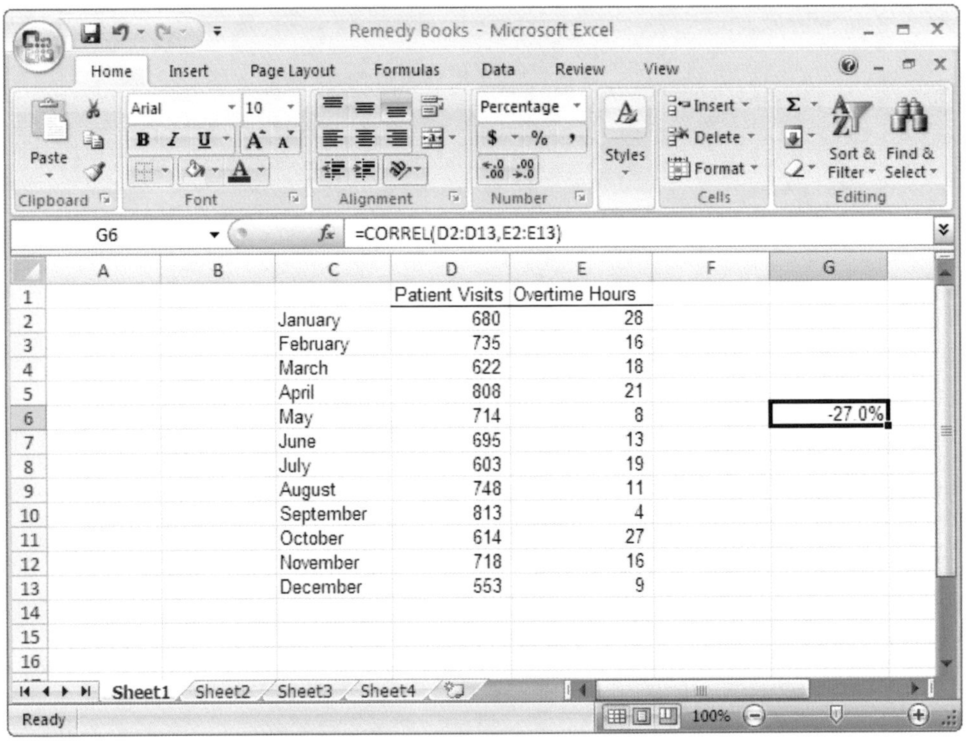

	C	D	E	F	G
1		Patient Visits	Overtime Hours		
2	January	680	28		
3	February	735	16		
4	March	622	18		
5	April	808	21		
6	May	714	8		-27.0%
7	June	695	13		
8	July	603	19		
9	August	748	11		
10	September	813	4		
11	October	614	27		
12	November	718	16		
13	December	553	9		

CHAPTER ASSIGNMENT

Working in a group of three to four students or fellow professionals, complete the following items.

1. Why would future cash flows be discounted into net present value terms while initial cash flows occurring in the present moment remain undiscounted?
2. Under what conditions would a health care provider insert an artificial cost (equivalent hourly rate) for time and energy into a financial calculation?
3. Suppose a health care organization has the option of using a professional bookkeeper who charges $40 per hour versus hiring an internal employee to maintain accounting information. The market rate for employees with technical bookkeeping skills is $16 per hour. What are some assumptions that should be considered when setting up a net present value calculation to see which option would provide the most value?
4. An organization member has found that local businesses report an average sales growth of 5% after advertising with a particular coupon book. Assume that current revenue equals $150,000 and the coupon ad will cost $2,200 to run annually. Also, it will take six hours of time at an equivalent rate of $55 per hour to put the ad together

initially. Find the internal rate of return for this venture across two time periods using a spreadsheet program, such as Microsoft Excel, to perform the calculation.

5. Calculate the payback period for the following cash flow streams. How does finding the payback period differ from calculating the NPV? What would the NPV and IRR be for this data set? What other issues should an organization bear in mind when reviewing these cash flows?

	Year 0	Year 1	Year 2	Year 3	Year 4	Year 5
Unadjusted	(16,000)	5,000	5,000	5,000	5,000	5,000
Discounted	(16,000)	4,545	4,132	3,757	3,415	3,105
Note: Input amounts into a spreadsheet program and run the calculations.						

6. How does the calculation of a correlation differ from the coefficient of determination? What do both of these calculations attempt to accomplish in regards to two arrays in a data set?

7. Why would it be important to understand whether a regression line follows a *linear* or *quadratic* pattern? What functions in Excel could be used to determine the shape of a regression line along with the regression line formula.

8. Describe *two* functions in Excel that could be used to calculate amounts related to a loan.

Business Valuations

AUTHOR'S NOTE

The concepts in this chapter apply whether a person starts a business from scratch or buys an existing practice. A financial projection should be assembled to determine the estimated *net present value* of future business activity. A lending institution may want to see a business plan that includes this type of financial projection, even when loan proceeds are used to buy equipment. *The most important notion to bear in mind is that a financial projection should be highly personalized.* The assumptions should correspond to what will most likely take place in the future as a result of *your* managing a particular organization. The assumptions should keep separate the value that you will personally contribute and the value that other business owners will contribute to the organization. You never want to pay another individual for value that you can personally generate. Spend money on value that would be inaccessible unless created and sold by someone else. A case study in Appendix III illustrates the process of putting together a personally relevant business valuation.

A financial projection that looks at the value of an entire business is normally more complex than the ones explored in the last two chapters. Despite there being more complexity with a business valuation, the general calculation process is the same. The valuation process begins with a forecast of future cash flow streams. Those cash flows are netted together in each time period and then discounted on a risk and inflation adjusted basis into net present value terms. A business valuation tends to require a greater range of *assumptions* about how the future will unfold. A health care provider could compile a business valuation for any number of reasons, including changing locations, merging with another provider, buying a practice, or starting a brand new one.

Remember that the terms *estimation*, *projection*, and *forecast* can be used interchangeably.

The amounts used in a business valuation should follow the *accrual* method of accounting. The *cash* method may not properly capture all relevant business activity and accounting information can be manipulated to make a business appear more profitable. Having reliable accounting information helps when trying to predict the future with a high degree of certainty. Where accounting information is only available under the *cash* method, make certain no one has made attempts to manipulate the timing of cash flows. Throughout this chapter, assume that account values have been calculated based on the *accrual* method.

Where a valuation attempts to compute the sales price of an existing business, amounts should reflect the net present value of all estimated future cash flows that originated somehow from the *seller's* actions. Would it make financial sense to pay someone else for a patient base that you could put together yourself? Revenue derived from patients you could attract without the help of the seller's existing business structure should not be reflected within the calculated sales price. Isolating cash flows according to their source may require a host of assumptions related to the particular circumstances of a business arrangement.

The buyer of a business needs to thoroughly examine all material cash flows and make a determination about the value a business *personally* offers. The same business may hold a completely different value proposition for another buyer. Very few finance and accounting professionals have a background in putting together a formal business valuation. Moreover, these same professionals rarely understand the distinct value that you can produce using the community, assets, reputation, human resources, and patient base of an existing business. The person that has direct experience with a business is in the best position to formulate assumptions. A health care provider should spend time working with an organization before compiling a business valuation—and before spending a large sum of money.

Buying a practice does not preclude a health care provider from marketing. An organization must always take steps to attract and retain new patients. By working through the process of gaining enough skills to take over a practice, a patient base should already be forming. If skill levels are deficient, buying a practice is contraindicated. When working in an associate position, retain all legal rights to patients who have been attracted through personal efforts. Keeping control of patients creates the option of transitioning into a personal practice instead of needing to build one completely from scratch or buying one. Forge legal documentation with an employer outlining such rights and clarify what constitutes a personally attracted patient.

13.1   Business Risk Premium

A risk premium reflects all of the estimated risk that an organization faces. The following discussion expands upon the same risk components listed in Chapter 11. Examining these risks directly and quantifying them in a meaningful way can be tremendously difficult. The weighted average cost of capital (WACC) formula is often used to estimate risk and inflation levels using the current market cost of debt and equity. The WACC formula relies on the entire investment community (the market) to quantify risk and inflation. An analysis of risk is still a crucial part of formulating cash flow assumptions.

> Systematic Risk
> + Operating Risk
> + Leverage Risk
> + Model Risk
> = Risk Premium

Systematic Risk

A business valuation begins with a **top-down analysis** of systematic risks that could impact the underlying business. It is necessary to determine the current stage of the business cycle to clarify how historical activity will compare with future activity. If the economy is nearing a peak, then forecasts should reflect the possibility of a recession. Emerging from an economic trough might require assumptions about future cash flows and the discount rate to reflect increased inflation. Before starting a business valuation, review (leading) macroeconomic indicators and gauge the health of the overall economy. What parts of the business cycle will the economy encounter over the next five years? Find estimated rates of inflation using recognized economic sources. Will any other events impact the entire economic system, such as wars, changes in tax policy, new government leadership, or natural disasters?

> **Top-Down Analysis:**
> A review of macroeconomic, microeconomic, and marketplace forces that could impact a cash flow analysis.

> Review Chapter 1 to learn more about conducting macroeconomic research.

After considering this top macroeconomic level, the next phase of a valuation involves an assessment of the overall industry. How might the health care industry evolve going forward, especially over the next five years? Potential legislation could help or hinder a practice sometime in the future. A random event in the marketplace could potentially alter consumer behavior. Contact your respective state association to learn about legislative activity and read local newspapers to keep tabs on consumer trends.

A top-down analysis of systematic risks should conclude with the potential impact of events within an applicable marketplace. A valuation should consider competitive pressures or the availability of *substitutes*. A marketplace might not provide enough profitability to keep all health care providers happy or competition within a specific target market could hamper an organization's *differentiation* strategy. Compile a detailed *territory worksheet* to understand what is occurring within your marketplace.

Operating Risk

Operating risks involve events that could impact an organization directly. The hardest part of a business valuation involves the estimation of future revenues. A new organization being formed may not have much historical activity to analyze. An existing practice might show a clear historical pattern in terms of revenues, but that pattern could change once a new health care provider takes over. A patient base could easily shrink because of a difference in rapport (rapport risk), treatment approach, or communication style. A beginning health care provider or someone new to an area might have difficulty gaining membership on insurance panels. Patients will probably discontinue care if an organization is suddenly forced to stop accepting their insurance. Inexperience with collection efforts could lead to an increase in bad debts as well.

When determining the sales price of an existing organization, what value the seller contributes should be considered. If a business seller stops marketing in anticipation of retirement, revenues might decline soon after transitioning the practice to the buyer. Taking over a practice requires skill in recruiting and retaining new patients. The buyer should work alongside the business seller beforehand and gauge the value that an existing business will actually offer in the future. Working with a particular patient base can expose any concerns about rapport and provide proof that the buyer has enough expertise to manage an organization and continue to recruit and retain new patients.

On the cost side, taking over an organization typically means that all marketing materials will need to be updated. Other expenses could arise that were not present within the former organization. The inclusion of a practice loan will automatically cause interest charges and debt levels to increase. The individual costs for insurance, legal services, officer wages, automobile use, and so forth can easily change. Problems with employee management could lead to higher employee turnover, training costs, or administrative inefficiencies. Not managing internal processes effectively can cause expenses to rise or the patient experience to worsen. Having a trial period where the buyer works within the organization being sold can greatly reduce the risk of taking over an ill-suited business.

A valuation related to forming a new business must rely on assumptions about the level of business activity that can be derived from a health care provider's personal network and recent marketing efforts. A beginning health care provider might have very little experience recruiting and retaining patients, making it difficult to forecast precisely how the patient base will grow over time. Figuring out the expenses that a new organization will encounter can require a lot of delicate assumptions as well.

Leverage Risk

By assuming a new practice loan, the borrower will automatically increase leverage risk for a business. Personal or student loans will place additional demands on an organization's future profit levels. A lending institution could *pierce the corporate veil* and force a borrower to put personal assets up for collateral. Leverage risk can remain high over the short and medium terms because of how slowly loans amortize the principal balance. Most of the loan payments will be characterized as interest during the first few years causing debt *leverage* to remain fairly static in the beginning.

Model Risk

The complexity involved with ordinary financial projections can easily introduce the possibility for error. A business valuation can entail an even higher degree of complexity because of the number and types of assumptions. Based on a person's experience with conducting financial projections, the discount rate should be modified in consideration of the risk that the cash flow projection could contain errors or faulty assumptions.

Summary

Systematic risks impact all organizations in an economy, industry, or marketplace indirectly. A review of macroeconomic indicators can pinpoint where the economy is in the business cycle. Competition will naturally occur in a marketplace and should not influence a business valuation unless competitive pressures threaten to materially impact revenue estimates. Other large-scale events, including legislative changes and consumer trends, can also disturb an organization's cash flows.

Events that directly impact an organization's future revenue and expense levels could easily take place, introducing a high degree of operating risk. Differences in rapport with a patient base or overall inexperience can lead to problems with the recruitment and retention of patients. Use of a practice loan will automatically increase leverage risk by placing demands on profit levels. Since loans slowly paydown their principal balance, leverage risk can remain high over the near term. Putting together a business valuation involves tremendous complexity and a discount rate should reflect the risk that a projected cash flow model contains errors or faulty assumptions.

13.2 Income Statement Projection

The main goal of putting together a business valuation involves projecting future net profit levels. Forecasting each income statement account separately is necessary because each one displays different behavior over time. Various transactions within an account might behave differently, requiring that one particular account be divided into multiple subaccounts. For instance, the wages of some employees may vary according to revenue activity whereas other payroll expenses may remain fixed.

Historical patterns need to be reviewed in light of any top-down analysis to determine the extent to which patterns will remain going forward. For example, a company that has experienced recent growth in sales might encounter a decline in revenue levels if the economy enters into a recession. Information derived from both the top-down analysis and historical review is used to draft assumptions about future cash flow activity. The projected cash flows that are based on these assumptions are netted together for each time period before being discounted into net present value terms.

> Review the difference between the cash flow projection in Appendix III and at the end of Chapter 15.

Step 1: Review Historical Activity

The past may not be the best indication of what will occur in the future, but it serves as a foundation when trying to project cash flows. Even a health care provider who wants to form a new practice may have a small patient base already. Activity related to this patient base could guide the formation of assumptions about the future. If acquiring an existing business, get permission to look at historical accounting records and study the details in each account in order to isolate transactions that display different behaviors. Ideally, historical accounting records will exist for the previous *five years* in order to observe annual cash flow patterns. If five years of data are not available, historical behavior should be examined in biannual, quarterly, or monthly segments. Historical activity should be examined in an effort to determine which of the following three behaviors apply.

Trend A **trend** reflects how cash flows follow an established pattern from one period to the next. Calculation of a regression line will show if a historical trend exists in an upward, downward, or level pattern and whether the trend follows a linear or quadratic shape. A regression line can be calculated using functions in Microsoft Excel. A determination must be made to project future cash flows using observed historical patterns or overlook such patterns because of how future activity is expected to differ according to the findings of the top-down analysis.

> Trend: An observable pattern seen across multiple time periods.

Spurious When account behavior appears *spurious* (random), then no clear trend that can be followed exists. Future cash flows can be established by taking an average of spurious amounts or they can be constructed using specific assumptions about future activity.

Specific   An organization may face a new type of cash flow where historical activity or a top-down analysis would provide no insights. A new practice loan, malpractice insurance policy, or employment activity could require specific assumptions about the future.

Even where amounts are best projected using a trend line or an average of spurious account balances, specific adjustments can be made to modify a historical or future cash flow stream. Adjustments can be made directly to historical data to remove unique items that should not influence the projection of future cash flows. Or, a cash flow stream could be projected and then modified for unique items expected to take place in the future. For instance, if an organization knowingly intends on replacing a specific piece of equipment in three years, the future value of that equipment could be placed into the cash flow projection for that year after the fixed asset account has already been projected.

Step 2: Draft Assumptions Regarding Future Revenues

How much revenue can a business generate in the future and whose efforts will produce that revenue? Forming revenue assumptions takes tremendous skill, especially when a valuation relates to a business with little or no historical activity. A valuation related to an existing business should isolate revenue attributable to the business *seller*. Because a valuation of an existing business involves determining its sales price, the buyer will want to exclude revenue that can be generated *personally*.

> Do not pay someone else for revenue that you can generate yourself!

General Decline   Patients recruited as an associate or purchased from an existing organization may not all transition to a newfound organization. Changing office locations may lead to a general decline of the patient base as well. Communicating with patients before making a business transition can reveal the extent to which the patient base may contract. Imagine a patient is willing to drive a long distance to see a distinguished health care provider, but would rather switch to someone closer if the practice is sold. A health care provider wanting to buy an existing practice needs to understand that differences in rapport can cause fairly rapid turnover of the patient base. Some patients will simply discontinue care if an incoming health care provider uses a different treatment approach or communication style. If a business transition is expected to result in a general decline of patients, assumptions must designate how much revenue will be lost.

New Patients   The *buyer* of an existing business needs to look beyond the current patient base and communicate with the business *seller's* network and referral system. These discussions can allude to the quantity and timing of new patients. The sales price of an existing practice should reflect the extent to which the buyer can generate new patients from the seller's community. If the business seller has let relationships fade in anticipation of retirement, the current rate of new patients may not be a strong indicator of what patient levels will be soon after the business is sold. The flow of new patients might slow considerably as a result of a deficiency in earlier marketing efforts or a lack of generating rapport.

> Remember the marketing pendulum! Current marketing efforts generate future patient activity.

A health care provider who buys a practice cannot make the mistake of believing that patient levels will remain static without the need for continual marketing efforts. The patient base of an existing practice is only temporary, causing its value over time to be limited. A network and referral system must be developed and maintained in order to support a patient base into the future. The value stemming from a personal community should be kept separate from the value produced from a business seller's community when setting the sales price of an existing business. A personal community can be assessed in terms of size, rapport quality, referral history, and marketing activity. Such features of a personal community can be used to forecast revenues for a brand new practice.

Returning Patients   Former and current patients will often reinstitute care at a later time when a future need arises. The greatest percentage of revenue for an organization can easily come from repeat business. Because patients tend to want familiarity in their health care experience, they will often restart care with the same organization or health care provider.

CASE STUDY

New Patient Assumptions

Suppose a health care provider wanting to buy an existing business conducts a random survey of 100 patients to determine the source of such patients. The survey revealed that 60% of these patients maintain ties to community organizations that the business seller has frequented in the past. An additional 30% represent referrals from business professionals who have formed long-term relationships with the existing organization. The remaining 10% learned about the organization through marketing campaigns directed at a target market.

The buyer wanted to determine the extent to which patients could be pulled from each of these sources in the future. The buyer expressed very little interest in frequenting these same community organizations and felt that generating strong rapport with community organization members would be difficult. It was noted that the business professionals currently referring patients are nearing retirement age and may not be in a position to refer much longer. Finally, the buyer noted a lack of expertise to properly service the organization's target market. Assumptions formulated for the business valuation should reflect how the business seller's community would contribute very few new patients in the future. The buyer would need to rely heavily on a personal network and referral system causing the desired purchase price of the business to be set very low.

An evaluation of the loyalty and appointment patterns of patients can help form assumptions about how many of these patients will return for care and when.

Accessing a long-standing patient base constitutes a key value when buying an existing business. The buyer must have a realistic notion of (1) how many former patients will return and (2) if these patients will remain with the organization far into the future. The buyer does not want to pay for patients who will not use the newfound organization. The value proposition that an existing business affords should be adjusted downward if the buyer does not view the patient base as loyal or in need of related health care services again. For example, a pediatrician may not encounter a lot of former patients wanting to restart care as patients may want to access a different type of health care provider as they grow older.

> Former patients should be sent marketing materials to alert them of a change in location or the sale of a practice in order to ensure that they are informed about what is taking place.

Patient Margin Patients will remain under care for various lengths of time and spend a certain amount of money each visit. The patient margin shows how much each patient generates in revenue on average. This ratio will often decline after a major transition due to higher patient turnover or reduced amounts of revenue obtained per visit. The patient margin could also improve if patients have access to better service lines or the patient experience comes under better management.

> Net Revenue
> ÷ Total Patients
> = Patient Margin

Terminal Activity A business valuation that includes cash flows estimated beyond five years is normally viewed with suspicion because of the high degree of uncertainty regarding activity beyond this point. A **terminal value** placed in the *sixth year* is used to capture activity that extends over all remaining time periods. A business valuation assumes that after five years, cash flows will closely resemble long-term industry or economic trends. The formula used to calculate the terminal value uses a so-called infinite time horizon. Since a discount rate causes cash flows further along the time horizon to continually diminish until reaching an immaterial amount, the discounting process eventually ignores cash flows occurring far into the future—it does not actually capture an infinite number of time periods. Working through the discounting process will occur later in this chapter.

> **Terminal Value:** The last time period used in a cash flow projection meant to fully capture any persisting value from all future time periods thereafter.

In relation to the purchase of an existing practice, few new patients will come from a business seller's historic community after five years. The value of a business will largely reflect the patient base formed by the buyer over such time. Terminal activity can be formulated by understanding the consumption patterns of current patients as well as a health care provider's ability to encourage former patients to return again for care in the future.

Step 3: Draft Assumptions Regarding Future Expenses

A health care organization can face many *fixed* expenses that remain fairly static over time and do not vary according to revenue levels. *Variable* expenses by definition move in relation to revenue levels. Subaccounts may be used if expenses behave differently within a particular account itself. For example, the meals and entertainment account could be split based on sales luncheons that support the production of revenues (variable) and meals that are served at monthly staff meetings (fixed).

A business valuation should take note of expenses that behave in materially different ways. Assumptions should consider trends, spurious amounts, and specific items related to historical and future activity. A cash flow projection could include a *time* or *energy* component to capture the effort required to manage a particular organization. Experience working with an organization can provide an opportunity to better understand expense behavior and management requirements.

Costs arising from a new practice loan can be factored in at the very end of the valuation process.

A health care provider forming a new organization should examine other businesses to identify types of expenses. A cash flow projection involving the purchase of an existing business will need to account for *specific* expenses expected to change once the transition to the buyer occurs. A one-time event that will not be repeated could be removed from an expense account to avoid ascribing such amounts to future time periods; or a unique event set to occur in the future could be specifically placed into the cash flow projection. Vendors should be contacted directly in an attempt to get a quote on prices. For example, an insurance company may charge different rates to a newfound organization for business-related insurance products.

Step 4: Project Future Revenues and Expenses

Assumptions drafted at this point should outline exactly how to set up the projection of future cash flows. The projected cash flows should be adjusted according to the estimated rate of inflation where applicable. Certain amounts may remain completely fixed (by contract) and not adjust according to inflation, such as loan payments, lease obligations, or rent expense. Certain expenses may change according to other variables, such as advancements in technology or supply limitations. Excel provides a range of functions and spreadsheet capabilities useful in structuring all the numeric data.

Allocating fixed expenses is not necessary when compiling a business valuation on a brand new health care organization.

All the projected expenses related to a newly formed organization should be used in a business valuation. A valuation involving an existing business must isolate the value stemming from the seller's efforts. A buyer does not want to pay for value that could have been generated personally apart from the existing business. Assumptions must identify how much revenue can be generated from the seller's community, business assets, reputation, human resources, and patient base already in existence. An appropriate amount of expenses must then be allocated against the projected revenue stream. Variable expenses will naturally correlate with revenue activity and can be directly configured. Fixed costs do not bear a close relationship with revenue levels and must be designated using an *allocation method*.

Allocation Method A   Combine revenue projections for both the buyer and seller to arrive at a total for how much the newfound organization is expected to generate in revenue. Take the percentage of the seller's projected revenues over the organization's total projected revenues to derive an allocation rate for fixed expenses. Apply the resulting percentage rate to each fixed expense account unless specific amounts will be used (see Method C).

Allocation Method B A revenue projection could be made that examines what would occur if the seller never sold the organization. These hypothetical revenue levels could be compared to what the seller's efforts are projected to provide to the newfound organization. Take the percentage of the seller's projected revenues over the total hypothetical revenues to derive an allocation rate for fixed expenses. Apply the resulting percentage rate to each fixed expense account unless specific amounts will be used (see Method C).

Allocation Method C The buyer could examine factors driving fixed expenses and report specific amounts in the projected cash flow stream. For example, if the buyer expects to spend $500 mailing letters to the seller's former patients, this marketing campaign is only taking place as a result of purchasing a business. The total amount of this expense should be specifically included in the projected cash flow stream.

Summarize net profit for each year after removing the revenues and expenses that the buyer of an existing business will contribute. The projected stream of net profit must be further adjusted in order to isolate cash flows available to either debt or equity holders. The next section looks at what these adjustments involve. The cash flows can then be modified for risk and inflation using an appropriate discount rate.

Summary

A business valuation involves a review of historical revenue and expense behavior along with a top-down analysis to derive assumptions about the future. Assumptions are used to project cash flows for each individual account (or subaccount). Cash flows may follow a set trend over time, appear spurious, or involve specific activity unique to one or more time periods. Projected cash flows may adjust according to the estimated rate of inflation. The cash flows of an existing business must then be modified to isolate the value contributed by the seller's community, business assets, reputation, human resources, and patient base. The buyer should never purchase value that could be personally derived without help from the seller's resources. A business valuation usually encompasses five years but adds a sixth year to capture any residual (terminal) value. Functions in Microsoft Excel greatly facilitate the establishment of a cash flow projection.

13.3   Free Cash Flows

A projected income statement must be modified to isolate the value offered to either debt or equity holders. Since net profit can include noncash items and certain balance sheet obligations can place constraints on cash, a business valuation should attempt to isolate available (free) cash flows. **Free cash flow to equity (FCFE)** represents the value available to equity owners of a business in contrast to **free cash flow to the firm (FCFF)**, which presents the value available to debt and equity holders. Following the *accrual* method of accounting is considered desirable for a free cash flow projection.

> **Free Cash Flow to Equity (FCFE):** Amount of net cash flow available to equity owners of a business.
>
> **Free Cash Flow to the Firm (FCFF):** Amount of net cash flow available to both debt and equity holders of a business.
>
> The FCFF adjustments are similar to the ones used to produce the times-interest earned ratio listed in Chapter 8.

Free Cash Flow to the Firm

A borrower who includes a FCFF calculation in a financial plan will provide a lending institution with important financial information and appear more knowledgeable on business matters. A lending institution will want to see the free cash flows available to both debt and equity holders when assessing the financial strength of a future or existing organization. A FCFF calculation shows the cash flow level of an organization before loan payments are ever made. The projected net profit stream should be adjusted to remove any interest charges as a result. The principal portion of a loan payment is already excluded from the net profit stream and does not require a specific adjustment. Tax payments are not available to debt or equity holders and should reduce the FCFF stream.

Free Cash Flow to Equity

Traditionally, the calculation of FCFE leaves out all payments made to debt holders and tax authorities because they are not available for distribution to equity holders. Such payments would include both the interest and principal portions of loans. A business valuation done for a small health care organization should not follow this same process because payments related to a land or building loan require special treatment. A plot of land or a building represents *real property* that contains value separate from a business organization. Loan payments related to real property do not necessarily cause a direct reduction in business value; in fact, the principal portion of such loans will allow a borrower to build equity ownership in the assets. Any interest expense on such loans should not be deducted to compute net profit.

The only loan payments that should be deducted from net profit when calculating the FCFE stream include ones made on a practice, equipment, or operating loan. Table 13.1 shows the free cash flow adjustments as proposed for a small health care organization.

TABLE 13.1	**Free Cash Flow Adjustments**
Free Cash Flow to the Firm	**Free Cash Flow to Equity**
Projected net profit	Projected net profit
A Plus: Interest expense	A Plus: Interest expense (select)
B Less: Tax liability	B Less: Tax liability
C Less: Capital expenditures	C Less: Capital expenditures
C Plus: Depreciation	C Plus: Depreciation
D Less: Increases to working capital	D Less: Increases to working capital
D Plus: Decreases to working capital	D Plus: Decreases to working capital
	E Plus: Operating loan proceeds
	E Less: Operating loan payments
= Free cash flow to the firm	= Free cash flow to equity

Despite the complex terminology and convoluted formulas in this section, these adjustments are fairly benign. Many adjustments reverse over time or have no material impact on a business valuation.

A. Interest expense reflected in net profit must always be removed from the FCFF stream whereas the FCFE calculation normally requires interest expense to be included in net profit. This adjustment shown in Table 13.1 involves only *select* items: any interest paid on a land or building. Any interest paid on an operating or equipment loan should reduce projected net profit as part of the FCFE calculation. *The interest expense related to a practice loan will be deducted during a later stage of the valuation process.*

B. Federal or state *income* taxes are typically assessed on net profit. An adjustment for interest expense should be made before calculating an organization's tax liability with either free cash flow method. A tax professional can help sort through business and personal activity to determine an appropriate tax rate to apply.

C. Many small businesses make use of *Section 179* of the U.S. tax code, which allows all depreciation to be taken within the year an asset is placed into service. The total adjustment for capital expenditures and deprecation would net to zero if Section 179 is invoked. Otherwise, the cash flow projection would reflect a fixed asset purchase in the year it was placed into service and depreciation expense would be removed from net profit in future time periods. This treatment would also apply to the purchase of intangibles and related noncash amortization expense. A fixed asset purchased *on loan* does not result in an immediate cash flow adjustment since the true cash outflow does not occur until an organization makes the underlying loan payments.

D. **Working capital** is found by subtracting current liabilities from current assets—in contrast to noncurrent liabilities and noncurrent assets. Common working capital accounts include accounts receivable, inventory, prepaid expenses, accounts payable, accrued expenses, and unearned revenue. These accounts are generally used only under the *accrual* method of accounting. The cash account will be present under both the cash and accrual methods.

An organization will often need to increase product levels or delay making payment to vendors in preparation for rapid growth. Working capital when compared to a prior time period will subsequently increase as a result. A business valuation should include the *change* in working capital to capture an organization's *investment in current assets*. Since a change in working capital usually reverses over time, this adjustment is not always material.

In regard to the purchase of a health care practice, the seller usually retains accounts receivable in effect before the business transition. The seller is also responsible for satisfying existing accounts payable. As a result, the working capital of the seller is not typically sold as part of a business. The beginning balances in the working capital accounts for the buyer will most likely be zero. A business valuation should reflect the *change* in working capital accounts taking place in subsequent years.

E. A business may borrow money in order to finance daily operations (working capital loan). A working capital loan would place cash directly into a bank account that equity holders could then access. In contrast, loan proceeds used to purchase assets or the business itself are never deposited into an organization's bank account—they go directly to the asset seller. A special adjustment to the FCFE calculation must be made for either the proceeds or payments related to an operating (working capital) loan.

> **Working Capital:** The net amount after subtracting current liability accounts from current asset accounts.

> This change in working capital traditionally forms part of the free cash flow calculation. Do not be too concerned with projecting this change, especially since it normally reverses over time.

Discounting Process

The final step of the valuation process involves discounting free cash flows to their net present value. The process resembles what has occurred with other financial projections except terminal year activity is now introduced and it must be discounted in a slightly different way. Ordinarily, each cash flow would be divided by $(1 + DR)^n$, where DR represents the discount rate and n represents the time period under consideration. The terminal free cash flow needs to be discounted first by an infinite time horizon as represented by the formula $DR - g$ where DR equals the discount rate and g reflects the rate of growth that will occur across this so-called infinite time horizon. The long-term growth rate of the economy can be used for g since the growth rate of a business will usually coincide with the general economy over time.

After discounting the *terminal cash flow* by its infinite time horizon, it must be further discounted by the five preceding time periods before it will be fully reset into present value terms. First, review the *incorrect* methods of calculating net present value for a hypothetical cash flow stream as shown in Figure 13.1.

In both of these methods, the terminal free cash flow was improperly discounted. In the first method, it was discounted by $n = 6$ periods which would not capture the infinite

> The infinite time horizon does not really span an infinite amount of time. Cash flows occurring in the distant future become immaterial since they are heavily discounted.

FIGURE 13.1 Incorrect Discounting Methods

	Year 1	Year 2	Year 3	Year 4	Year 5	Terminal Year
Free cash flows	$71,537	$67,631	$56,447	$50,230	$29,025	$11,724
INCORRECT Method 1	$(1 + DR)^1$	$(1 + DR)^2$	$(1 + DR)^3$	$(1 + DR)^4$	$(1 + DR)^5$	$(1 + DR)^6$
INCORRECT Method 2	$(1 + DR)^1$	$(1 + DR)^2$	$(1 + DR)^3$	$(1 + DR)^4$	$(1 + DR)^5$	$(DR - g)$

time horizon. In the second incorrect method, the terminal free cash flow successfully captured the infinite time horizon, but the resulting figure was not reset into present value terms. However, take note of how the terminal free cash flow has already been discounted in the *sixth* time period as a result of the formula $DR - g$.

Assume that a buyer wants to use a discount rate of 18% that captures risks of 14.75% and estimated inflation of 3.25% whereas the long-term growth rate of the overall econom is expected to average 2%. Figure 13.2 shows how the terminal cash flow must undergo two steps in order to be properly reset into present value terms. The *correct* calculation of NPV discounts the terminal cash flow by $DR - g$ to account for the infinite time horizon and then by $(1 + DR)^{n-1}$ to capture the previous *five* time periods. Thus, the terminal year cash flow is first discounted to reflect an infinite time horizon and then the result of that calculation ($73,275) is further discounted into present value terms.

All of the cash flows in *Step 2* are discounted and combined into one net present value figure. This business valuation demonstrates that $214,176 of value will be made available on a risk and inflation adjusted basis. A lending institution will want to review this figure before extending a loan. If a practice loan is used to gain access to this free cash flow stream, the overall value proposition offered to an equity holder will decrease. The cost of a practice loan must be taken into account when calculating the value of the FCFE stream.

Practice Loan Adjustment   Cash flows related to a practice loan must be removed from the FCFE stream. An equity holder will want to value the cash flows that remain after making payments on a practice loan. Imagine that an established health care provider wants $160,000 for an existing practice including equipment. How much value would accrue to the buyer if a lending institution required a 25% down payment on a ten-year loan charging 8% interest? The actual loan would total $120,000 ($160,000 × 75%) as a result of the 25% down payment.

Since the buyer will want to account for tax savings on interest payments, finding a loan's *present value* involves (1) drafting an amortization schedule, (2) modifying the cash flow stream to reflect a tax deduction for interest charges, and (3) discounting the *after-tax* cash flow stream. A borrower should make certain that leverage and model risk stemming from a practice loan are adequately reflected in the discount rate used. This overall process would result in a loan value of $73,903 [calculation not shown] using a discount rate of 18% and an estimated tax rate of 22%.

A shorter method exists that can produce reasonably accurate results. More information related to this shorter method can be found in Appendix III. First, the interest rate is modified for tax savings estimated in this example to be 22%. Using the =PMT function in

> Assuming that a bank requires a 25% down payment, how easily could a buyer use the WACC formula to establish a discount rate?

FIGURE 13.2 Correct Discounting Methods

The calculation of each discounted free cash flow is shown underneath each formula result within the numeric view.

		Year 1	Year 2	Year 3	Year 4	Year 5	Terminal Year
Free cash flows		$71,537	$67,631	$56, 447	$50,230	$29,025	$11,724
Formula view:	Step 1						$(DR - g)$
	Step 2	$(1 + DR)^1$	$(1 + DR)^2$	$(1 + DR)^3$	$(1 + DR)^4$	$(1 + DR)^5$	$(1 + DR)^5$
Numeric view:	Step 1						73,275
							11,724/(.16)
	Step 2	60,625	48,572	34,355	25,908	12,687	32,029
		71,537/(1.18)^1	67,631/(1.18)^2	58,447/(1.18)^3	50,230/(1.18)^4	29,025/(1.18)^5	73,275/(1.18)^5
	NPV = $214,176						

Excel, the monthly loan payments are found to equal $1,346.75 using the *after-tax* interest rate. The monthly after-tax loan payment stream of $1,346.75 must then be discounted into present value terms using an appropriate discount rate. If a discount rate of 18% is applied, the 120 monthly payments would equal $74,743 using the =PV function in Microsoft Excel. This shorter method would only differ by $840 ($74,743 − $73,903) representing an immaterial amount.

> A licensed tax professional should determine the estimated tax rate to use for a business valuation.

Final Net Present Value Funding this transaction with $120,000 of debt would decrease the net present value available to equity holders to $140,273 ($214,176 − $73,903) on a risk and inflation adjusted basis. Although the sale price currently stands at $160,000, the buyer has a strong chance of *losing* $19,727 ($140,273−$160,000) through this arrangement. Since actual results could vary significantly from what has been estimated, the buyer must be comfortable with the cash flow projection and the discount rate used. The buyer may try to move forward with the transaction despite not being properly compensated for risk and inflation. The buyer should attempt to negotiate a smaller purchase price, which would change the practice loan value. The final net present value figure could easily be updated since the practice loan calculation was made separately. The buyer should attempt to purchase the business at an amount equal to or less than the final net present value figure.

> The ultimate funding sources—debt and equity—may influence the discount rate or weighted average cost of capital formula.

Summary

After projecting income statement accounts, adjustments are made to isolate the cash flows that are *free* (available) to debt and equity holders. The free cash flow to equity (FCFE) calculation identifies the value specific to equity holders whereas the free cash flow to the firm (FCFF) calculation shows what both debt and equity holders have available. Either calculation method should adjust for cash outflows due to taxes, the future purchase of fixed assets, and changes in working capital. The FCFE method traditionally involves an adjustment for all loan payments, but a FCFE calculation related to a small health care organization should only take into account cash flows related to an operating, equipment, or practice loan.

Free cash flows are discounted using the formula $(1 + DR)^n$, where DR equals the discount rate and $n =$ the time period under consideration. Terminal year activity is first discounted over the current and infinite time horizon using the formula $DR - g$ where g equals a constant growth rate. The result is then discounted for the previous *five* time periods using the formula $(1 + DR)^{n-1}$. The net present value of the business calculated thus far must be reduced by the present value of a practice loan. A short method exists whereby the loan value can be estimated using the =PMT and =PV functions in Excel.

13.4 Relative Valuation

A **relative valuation** makes use of metrics applied to a specific historical cash flow stream of a business to determine an approximate business value. These metrics should never replace a full net present value calculation using free cash flows since a relative valuation ignores any unique financial matters specific to the buyer. The historical cash flow streams used for a relative valuation often involve net profit, revenue, or some close variant. These amounts can be adjusted for material nonrecurring items specific to the past.

> **Relative Valuation:** Use of industry metrics in relation to adjusted historical cash flow streams of a business to establish a sales price.

In the example shown in Figure 13.3, a $3,500 miscellaneous expense in Year 2007 has been removed from net profit because of its unique nature. A review of the historical data demonstrates that the remaining expenses are considered reasonable. The amounts of adjusted net profit for each period do not evenly compare as a result of changes in the value of money (inflation). The historical figures need to be adjusted for inflation setting them into present value terms. Historical rates of inflation are already known and do not need to be forecast.

FIGURE 13.3 Relative Valuation (net profit)

Historical Inflation

2007: 3.50%

2008: 4.00%

2009: 3.50%

2010: 4.25%

Example calculation: $113,463 × 1.035 × 1.04 × 1.035 × 1.0425 = $131,778.

	2006	2007	2008	2009	2010
Historical revenue	219,223	220,478	225,210	239,069	243,838
Historical expenses	(105,760)	(128,687)	(121,625)	(128,993)	(135,236)
Historical net profit	113,463	91,791	103,585	110,076	108,602
Adjustments	—	3,500	—	—	—
Adjusted net profit	113,463	95,291	103,585	110,076	108,602
Present value of net profit	131,778	103,003	111,767	114,754	108,602

After resetting the historical cash flow stream into present value terms, the buyer can average these amounts or take other steps to create a fair representation of the business's value. For example, the Year 2006 cash flow appears disproportionately large and may not represent general or even current trends. Suppose the buyer perceives the Year 2006 cash flow as highly unusual and removes it from the relative valuation. Averaging the remaining cash flows produces an average present value of $109,532 as listed in Figure 13.4.

FIGURE 13.4 Average Net Profit

The 2006 cash flow has been excluded from the calculation of average net profit because it has been deemed abnormal.

	2006	2007	2008	2009	2010	Average
Adjusted present value	Excluded	103,003	111,767	114,754	108,602	**109,532**

Multiplier: A standard ratio multiplied against a numeric figure meant to derive the expected value of another numeric figure.

To complete the relative valuation, the buyer needs to find a proper net profit **multiplier** that corresponds to industry norms. A proper multiplier might be obtained from a valuation reference guide, management consultant, licensed professional, or the known sales price of other health care organizations. If a standard multiplier is not published or known, the buyer must choose a reasonable multiplier based on preference. Suppose that health care organizations normally sell at a rate 1.5 times average net profit. This multiplier would set the organization's value at $164,298 ($109,532 × 1.5). The buyer would know that a sales price of $160,000 appears reasonable based on this relative valuation and that other buyers will find this deal appealing.

A relative valuation can encompass other cash flow streams of the business including historical revenue levels. Again, the revenue stream should be adjusted if necessary and reset into present value terms using historical rates of inflation as demonstrated in Figure 13.5.

FIGURE 13.5 Relative Valuation (revenue)

Historical Inflation

2007: 3.50%

2008: 4.00%

2009: 3.50%

2010: 4.25%

Example calculation: $219,223 × 1.035 × 1.04 × 1.035 × 1.0425 = $254,610.

	2006	2007	2008	2009	2010
Historical revenue	219,223	220,478	225,210	239,069	243,838
Adjustments	—	—	—	—	—
Adjusted revenue	219,223	220,478	225,210	239,069	243,838
	↓	↓	↓	↓	↓
Present value of revenue	254,610	247,409	242,999	249,229	243,838

Since the revenue stream appears reasonable, the buyer decides to average all years together as represented in Figure 13.6. Assume that industry norms place the value of health care organizations at .75 times average revenues. Using this multiplier would generate a relative value of $185,713 ($247,617 × .75). This number provides another point of comparison in terms of the business value.

EBIT and EBITDA are common cash flow streams used for a relative valuation. They are calculated using earnings before interest and taxes (EBIT) and the latter also removes depreciation and amortization (EBITDA).

FIGURE 13.6 Modified Revenue Stream

	2006	2007	2008	2009	2010	Average
Adjusted Patient Revenue	254,610	247,409	242,999	249,229	243,838	**247,617**

If the example business is worth $185,713 according to average revenue levels, yet that value is reduced to $164,298 after taking into account expenses, this organization might contain a high degree of inefficiency when compared to other health care organizations. The business produces a high level of revenue, but high expenses are driving down net profit. The buyer could potentially capture a tremendous amount of value if this organization's expenses can be better managed.

The free cash flow model should be given the most weight in the decision-making process. Free cash flows should never be modified to fall more closely in line with relative metrics. Although the sales price of a business might appear fair when compared to relative metrics, the buyer may be somehow limited to a lower free cash flow value due to unique circumstances surrounding a venture. *The buyer should reject a venture where the sales price is more than the net present value of all future free cash flows.*

The free cash flow model is the only court-approved method of valuing a business.

Summary

A relative valuation applies a standard multiplier to amounts for net profit, revenue, or some variant cash flow stream. Such accounting figures should be adjusted for nonrecurring items and set into present value terms to make historical cash flows comparable.

The outcome of the relative valuation should help the buyer make an informed decision about whether to proceed with a transaction or continue exploring other options. A complete business valuation involving free cash flows should always be conducted and relied on most heavily.

13.5   Valuing Capital Assets

A business valuation typically looks at the free cash flows that can be generated from a patient base and business organization. Upon taking over a practice, a health care provider may come into possession of fixed assets, such as equipment, land, or a building.

Fixed assets are best valued using the services of a licensed appraiser. The market value of fixed assets must be carefully reviewed when a certified appraisal is not possible. The market value might be derived from deliberate negotiations between the buyer and seller. A rough price range might exist based on a general review of classified advertisements. The current sales price of assets with similar features could serve to clarify market value. A buyer could also ask other organizations what they would pay for a particular asset. Considering that fixed assets held by an existing business might be old, the replacement cost for such assets might serve to determine their value.

The value assigned to equipment will ultimately be used to reduce a business valuation. Equipment represents an expense to a business; thus any related outflow of cash will not be made available to debt or equity holders, as would any other type of expense. A cash flow projection for a business should include the cost of equipment to be purchased after the business is sold. Any *current* purchases made with cash should directly reduce the value of a business. The cost of equipment currently purchased on loan is reflected within the cash flows of a practice or equipment loan—and by virtue of removing depreciation expense from net profit.

Any cash flows related to a land or building purchase should be removed if embedded in a business valuation. The payments on a land or building loan do not necessarily reduce the value of a business. The *principal* portion on these loans enables the buyer to build equity in real property; thus the outflow of cash leads to a direct increase in building or land value. The *interest* portion may not necessarily cause the buyer to lose value overall if the building or land appreciates in market value over time. The buyer should consider applying a portion of interest charges to a business valuation if the interest rate on a land or building loan is greater than the expected rise in market value. For example, assume a building's value is expected to grow by 2% each year, but the interest rate on a related loan is 6%. The buyer could allocate 4% (6% − 2%) of the interest charges to the cash flow projection of the business since this portion of interest provides no value to the buyer. A building may be needed to support the production of revenue, but many of the building's associated costs provide their own type of value separate from the business itself. Costs that do not provide any separate value should reduce the business valuation.

> The eventual sales price of equipment could be placed in the cash flow projection, thus increasing the business value.

Summary

A health care provider will most likely obtain other fixed assets in combination with the purchase of a patient base and business organization. A licensed appraiser can value cash flows related to land or a building. The value of equipment is usually determined based on market prices for assets with similar features or by direct negotiations. Otherwise, the buyer may need to review classified advertisements, figure replacement costs, or contact other organizations to find an asset's market value.

CHAPTER ASSIGNMENT

Working in a group of three to four students or fellow professionals, complete the following items.

1. How might taking over an existing health care organization be problematic because of the need to always recruit and retain new patients?

2. What is the main goal of conducting a review of historical activity? How might macroeconomic, industry, and marketplace forces influence the review of historical activity?

3. Explain the four components of the risk premium.

4. List the four steps to follow when projecting an income statement. How might these steps differ for someone forming a new organization versus buying an existing one?

5. What are the five main categories of revenue assumptions to examine?

6. What is the importance of isolating the value that a seller's community, business assets, reputation, human resources, and patient base offer? Why would a health care provider not want to pay for value that could otherwise be generated through personal efforts apart from the existing business?

7. How does the FCFE calculation differ from the FCFF calculation? In what way do these methods address the value available to debt versus equity holders differently?

8. How does discounting terminal activity differ from discounting the main cash flow stream occurring across the preceding time periods?

9. What is the importance of resetting historical cash flows into present value terms when conducting a *relative* valuation?

10. How could a buyer configure an appropriate multiplier in order to review the estimated sales price of a business?

11. If a buyer has the opportunity to purchase a practice and building together, why would valuing each asset separately benefit the buyer's attempt to clarify the value of each?

12. Why does equipment reduce the value of a business instead of adding value to it?

13. Go online to remedybooks.com and find the business valuation assignment under the *Teachers* tab. Use the Excel spreadsheet found under the *Students* tab to project cash flows and derive a net present value figure. If correct, the spreadsheet will let you know.

Appendix III Example Business Valuation

Overview

The following case study incorporates the concepts learned in Chapter 13. Please refer to Chapter 13 for more information on each section. This *hypothetical* scenario involves a health care provider wanting to purchase an existing health care organization. The buyer has reviewed several economic reports and finds that the estimated average rate of inflation will be 3.25%. Macroeconomic data reveal that the business cycle is midway through an expansionary phase and economic growth should remain fairly stable over the next five years. The professional society does not expect any legislative changes that could materially impact the business.

TABLE A	Historical Revenues					
		2007	2008	2009	2010	2011
A	Patient revenue	218,243	219,863	224,198	238,647	243,019
B	Product revenue	980	615	1,012	422	819
		219,223	220,478	225,210	239,069	243,838

1. Review Historical Revenue Activity

The business seller supplied the historical revenue data shown in Table A in accordance with the *accrual* method of accounting.

A. Patient revenue shows a clear uptrend that could be calculated using functions in Microsoft Excel. These amounts appear material and most likely influence multiple expense categories.

B. Product revenue appears spurious with no clear trend. Amounts are immaterial and probably do not influence cost behavior in any significant way. Amounts will be reintroduced later after expenses have been projected.

As noted in the formula bar of Figure A, the =LOGEST function of Microsoft Excel calculates that patient revenue has grown at a compound rate of 1.03 or 3%. This growth rate of 3% reflects that revenue growth is quadratic and has been rising at an increasing rate. A growth rate of 3% could be the result of inflationary pressures, especially if the business seller has changed prices historically according to the rate of inflation.

FIGURE A Historical Revenue Trends

2. Draft Assumptions Regarding Future Revenues

The following assumptions attempt to isolate the value offered by the business seller and remove any value that the buyer could generate personally without the help from the business seller's community, assets, reputation, human resources, and patient base.

A. General Decline The buyer believes that 5% of the existing patients will discontinue care upon the sale of the practice.

B. New Patients The business seller has reduced marketing expenses over the last two years. As such, 15% of new patients normally derived from these marketing efforts will be lost. Fifty percent of new patients will come from the business seller's direct personal network and referral system. Based on conversations with network participants and referral sources, the buyer believes that this amount will steadily decline until reaching 5% in the *terminal year*. The remaining 35% of new patients will come from indirect word of mouth stemming from the business seller's community. The buyer wishes to assume that word of mouth will generate 5% fewer new patients in Years 1 through 3 and then 10% fewer thereafter until reaching zero. Overall, patients who are completely new to the organization represent 25% of annual revenues.

C. Returning Patients Returning patients constitute 75% of annual revenues in contrast to 25% from new patients. The rate at which the seller's former patients will return for care should remain high based on the results of a survey sent to a sample group. After five years, the buyer believes that the portion of returning patients somehow tied to the former organization will gradually decline to 45%.

D. Patient Margin The business seller has a strong ability to effectively communicate with patients. The buyer believes that patients will probably end treatment sooner on average because of weaker communication skills. Patient turnover should decline by an estimated 10% after the transition, but then increase 5% each year as communication skills improve.

E. Terminal Activity After five years, an estimated 20% of the historical patient base will still return for care. An additional 5% of new patients will have had some interaction with the former organization, but will never have made a purchase decision until the terminal period.

3. Project Future Revenues

The buyer has decided to project future revenues using the same compound rate of 3% that was observed in relation to the historical revenue stream.

As shown in Figure B, the projected revenue stream has been calculated using a 3% compound growth rate in each successive period. The dollar signs ($) in the =GROWTH function shown in the formula bar are used to lock the alphanumeric references onto the historical numbers, causing related parts of the formula to not change when the formula is applied to the other cells.

This projected revenue stream reflects estimated activity of the existing business. The revenue stream must be adjusted based on assumptions A through E outlined previously to remove any personally generated value. The business valuation should not include any value that the buyer could produce separate from this business. Table B presents the total projected amounts for patient revenue stemming from the business seller.

FIGURE B Projected Patient Revenue

Note how using dollar signs locks the formula onto the range of cells C4 to G4 and C5 to G5. These cell ranges will not change when the formula is applied to other cells.

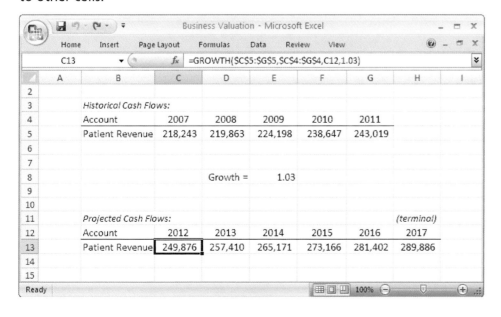

TABLE B	Adjusted Patient Revenue					

The adjustments made for new and returning patients represent only 25% and 75% of the total projected patient revenue stream, respectively.

	2012	2013	2014	2015	2016	Terminal
Projected patient revenue	249,876	257,410	265,171	273,166	281,402	289,886
Instant decline	−5%	−5%	−5%	−5%	−5%	−5%
	(12,494)	(12,871)	(13,259)	(13,658)	(14,070)	(14,494)
New patients (25%)	—	−15%	−15%	−15%	−15%	−15%
	−9%	−18%	−27%	−36%	−45%	−45%
	−5%	−10%	−15%	−25%	−35%	−35%
	(8,746)	(27,672)	(37,787)	(51,902)	(66,833)	(68,848)
Returning patients (75%)	—	−5%	−15%	−30%	−55%	−80%
	—	(9,653)	(29,832)	(61,462)	(116,078)	(173,932)
Patient turnover	−10%	−5%	—	—	—	—
	(24,988)	(12,871)	—	—	—	—
Adjusted patient revenue	203,649	194,345	184,294	146,144	84,421	32,612

4. Review Historical Expense Activity

The detail of each expense account was reviewed for the past five years to understand cost behavior as listed in Table C. In terms of this business valuation, payroll expenses were observed to behave differently. Payroll accounts have been divided into fixed and variable subaccounts as a result.

TABLE C	Historical Expenses				

	2007	2008	2009	2010	2011
1 Salaries and benefits—variable	22,190	22,840	23,462	25,219	27,814
2 Salaries and benefits—fixed	37,000	38,500	47,000	49,820	49,820
3 Advertising	416	678	784	604	208
4 Dues and subscriptions	250	250	274	284	306
5 Insurance	1,012	1,047	1,089	1,127	1,175
6 Lease payments	20,000	20,700	21,528	22,228	23,172
7 Legal and professional services	2,035	2,127	2,345	2,684	6,540
8 Meals and entertainment	1,850	1,425	1,684	2,018	1,940
9 Miscellaneous	125	4,178	819	207	389
10 Office supplies	3,257	3,488	3,126	3,894	4,120
11 Payroll taxes—variable	2,885	2,969	3,050	3,278	3,616
12 Payroll taxes—fixed	4,070	4,235	5,170	5,480	5,480
13 Repairs and maintenance	2,485	1,760	3,697	2,490	2,878
14 Utilities	6,285	6,505	6,765	7,010	7,300
15 Depreciation	1,900	13,285	832	2,650	478
16 Loss on equipment	—	4,700	—	—	—
Total historical expenses	105,760	128,687	121,625	128,993	135,236

1. Using the correlation function in Microsoft Excel, variable salaries and benefits appear to have a strong 95.9% relationship with patient revenue.

2. A problem was found within the fixed salaries and benefits account. This account shows what was paid to the office manager. It appears that the business seller refused to increase the office manager's pay in anticipation of retirement. Unless addressed, this could lead to employee turnover and other unforeseen problems.

3. A problem was also found within the advertising account. In anticipation of retirement, the business seller started spending less on advertising. This could negatively impact revenues in future time periods even if current revenue levels do not allude to the potential impact. In order to ensure that revenue levels will continue to grow as projected, the business seller must step up marketing efforts.

4. Dues and subscriptions increase with inflation and appear fixed.

5. Insurance grows with inflation, but the buyer should obtain a quote from an insurance company to determine how much malpractice insurance will cost personally.

6. Lease payments grow with inflation and appear fixed.

7. Legal and professional services grow with inflation until the final year where costs have increased to deal with issues related to the business sale.

8. Meals and entertainment appear spurious with no clear trend.

9. Amounts in the miscellaneous account appear spurious, but a large $3,500 nonrecurring item exists.

10. Office supplies show a strong uptrend beyond the rate of inflation.

11. Variable payroll taxes positively correlate with expenses in the variable salaries and benefits account.

12. Fixed payroll taxes also positively correlate with expenses in the fixed salaries and benefits account.

13. Repairs and maintenance appear spurious with no clear trend. The buyer has inspected the office for any potential major repairs and has found nothing specific to include into the cash flow projection.

14. Utilities grow according to the rate of inflation and appear fixed.

15. The organization makes use of IRS Code Section 179, which allows expensing of fixed assets in the year they are placed in service. Depreciation expense equals what was spent on fixed assets within each given year.

16. The loss on equipment was a nonrecurring item. Fixed assets that the buyer will use going forward appear in good working order.

5. Draft Assumptions Regarding Future Expenses

The following assumptions were drafted for each expense line noted above as a result of the review of historical activity.

A. Variable salaries and benefits have averaged 10.6% of patient revenues and should continue as such.

B. In order to keep the office manager from leaving, the buyer intends on increasing fixed payroll salaries and benefits by 10% immediately and 4% thereafter.

C. The business seller let advertising diminish. The buyer wants to boost advertising to $1,000 and then adjust it for inflation thereafter. If the business seller does not immediately increase marketing efforts, adjustments should be made to the projected revenue stream or the discount rate.

D. Dues and subscriptions are fairly immaterial and should grow with inflation.

E. Insurance has trended with inflation but the buyer will need to obtain a different malpractice policy. An adjustment is made to reflect the policy cost per a quote received from an insurance company and then as adjusted by inflation thereafter.

F. The lease payments should steadily grow according to the estimated rate of inflation.

G. Legal and professional services were artificially high in the prior year because of legal work related to the business sale. Since this amount should not reoccur in future periods, only four of the five historical years have been used to project related expenses. Amounts should grow according to the estimated rate of inflation.

H. Since meals and entertainment appear spurious, an average of the past five years was taken and used for all future periods.

I. A nonrecurring item of $3,500 was removed from the historical miscellaneous expense account. Since miscellaneous expenses appear spurious, an average of the past five years was taken without this nonrecurring item and used for all future periods.

J. Using the =LOGEST function in Microsoft Excel, it was discovered that office supplies grew at a 6% compound rate historically—about twice the rate of inflation. The buyer assumes that office supplies will continue to increase in price at this larger rate based on discussions with vendors.

K. Variable payroll taxes averaged 13% of *variable* salaries and benefits and should continue as such.

L. Fixed payroll taxes averaged 11% of *fixed* salaries and benefits and should continue as such.

M. Since repairs and maintenance appear spurious, an average of the past five years was taken and used for all future periods. No adjustment has been made for specific items.

N. The buyer sees no purpose in a digital cable package that costs $1,200 annually. The future projection reflects the removal of this item and all remaining utilities adjust each year per the estimated rate of inflation.

O. The depreciation account equals the total cost of equipment and appears to have various nonrecurring items. A $12,000 purchase was removed from the historical cash flow stream because a similar expenditure should not arise in future time periods. Since amounts reported for depreciation appear spurious, an average of the past five years was taken without this $12,000 nonrecurring item and applied to future time periods. The buyer expects to buy an x-ray machine in Year 3 that has a *future value* of $13,500. This unique item was placed directly in the projected cash flow stream.

P. Equipment sales are not expected.

6. Project Future Expenses

The cost projection shown in Table D was formulated using assumptions A through P as previously outlined.

TABLE D	Projected Expenses					
		2012	2013	2014	2015	2016	Terminal
A	Salaries and benefits—variable	26,487	27,285	28,108	28,956	29,829	30,728
B	Salaries and benefits—fixed	54,802	56,994	59,274	61,645	64,111	66,675
C	Advertising	1,000	1,033	1,066	1,101	1,136	1,173
D	Dues and subscriptions	316	326	337	348	359	371
E	Insurance	1,390	1,435	1,482	1,530	1,580	1,631
F	Lease payments	23,925	24,703	25,505	26,334	27,190	28,074
G	Legal and professional services	3,056	3,155	3,258	3,364	3,473	3,586
H	Meals and entertainment	1,783	1,783	1,783	1,783	1,783	1,783
I	Miscellaneous	443	443	443	443	443	443
J	Office supplies	4,367	4,629	4,907	5,201	5,513	5,844
K	Payroll taxes—variable	3,443	3,547	3,654	3,764	3,878	3,995
L	Payroll taxes—fixed	6,028	6,269	6,520	6,781	7,052	7,334
M	Repairs and maintenance	2,662	2,662	2,662	2,662	2,662	2,662
N	Utilities	6,298	6,503	6,714	6,932	7,158	7,390
O	Depreciation	1,429	1,429	14,929	1,429	1,429	1,429
P	Loss on equipment	—	—	—	—	—	—
	Total projected expenses	137,429	142,197	160,642	152,273	157,596	163,118

The buyer feels that fixed costs should be matched with supporting revenues based on the difference between unadjusted and adjusted patient revenue as calculated in Table E. The amounts reported for fixed expenses should be reduced by the percentage found through this comparison. Approaching the calculation in this manner is highly subjective and other allocation schema may be more appropriate under different circumstances.

TABLE E **Fixed Expense Allocation Rate**						
	2012	**2013**	**2014**	**2015**	**2016**	**Terminal**
Projected patient revenue	249,876	257,410	265,171	273,166	281,402	289,886
Adjusted patient revenue	203,649	194,345	184,294	146,144	84,421	32,612
Fixed expense allocation rate	81.5%	75.5%	69.5%	53.5%	30.0%	11.3%

Reducing the adjusted revenue stream by *all* expenses would grossly underestimate the value of the future business. Table F presents the total of adjusted expenses, which better reflects the amounts necessary to support the revenue provided by the business seller.

TABLE F **Adjusted Expenses**						
	2012	**2013**	**2014**	**2015**	**2016**	**Terminal**
* Salaries and benefits—variable	21,587	20,601	19,535	15,491	8,949	3,457
* Payroll taxes—variable	2,806	2,678	2,540	2,014	1,163	449
Salaries and benefits—fixed	44,664	43,031	41,195	32,980	19,233	7,501
Advertising	815	780	741	589	341	132
Dues and subscriptions	258	246	234	186	108	42
Insurance	1,133	1,084	1,030	819	474	183
Lease payments	19,499	18,651	17,726	14,089	8,1057	3,158
Legal and professional services	2,491	2,382	2,264	1,800	1,042	403
Meals and entertainment	1,453	1,346	1,239	954	535	201
Miscellaneous	361	334	308	237	133	50
Office supplies	3,559	3,495	3,410	2,783	1,654	657
Payroll taxes—fixed	4,913	4,733	4,531	3,628	2,116	825
Repairs and maintenance	2,170	2,010	1,850	1,424	799	299
Utilities	5,133	4,910	4,666	3,709	2,147	831
Depreciation	1,165	1,079	10,376	765	429	161
Total projected expenses	112,005	107,359	111,646	81,466	47,279	18,351

*Variable expenses correspond directly to adjusted patient revenue. All remaining expenses have been calculated by multiplying the allocation rate of adjusted to total projected patient revenue for each year by the corresponding expense item reported in the original expense projection.

7. Summarize Final Net Profit The projected net profit stream shown in Table G captures the estimated cash flows that will accrue to the buyer from the existing business. Product revenue is reintroduced into the cash flow projection at this point. The cash flows reported for product revenue represent the historical average observed over the past five years.

TABLE G	Net Profit Summary					
	2012	**2013**	**2014**	**2015**	**2016**	**Terminal**
Projected patient revenue	203,649	194,345	184,294	146,144	84,421	32,612
Projected product revenue	770	770	770	770	770	770
Projected expenses	(112,005)	(107,359)	(111,646)	(61,466)	(47,279)	(16,351)
Projected net profit	92,414	87,756	73,418	65,446	37,912	15,031

The buyer does not want to pay for net profit that can be personally generated meaning that only revenues and related expenses provided by the seller's community, assets, reputation, human resources, and existing patient base should form part of the valuation. The business valuation in this case study would amount to $520,000 [calculation not shown] if the buyer's contributed value were included in the calculation. Although this amount has not been reduced for risk and inflation, it would be absurd to pay anything close to this amount, let alone lend money at this level.

8. Free Cash Flow Adjustments

The final net profit figures must be further adjusted to remove any cash flows that will not accrue to debt or equity holders.

Free Cash Flows to the Firm (FCFF) Table H shows all the FCFF adjustments made to net profit. Interest expense has not been deducted to arrive at net profit, thus no adjustment is necessary. A tax professional reviewed both personal and business activity and felt that the projected business profit will trigger an income tax consequence averaging 22%. The buyer intends on invoking U.S. Tax Section 179 resulting in depreciation expense equaling the total for fixed asset purchases. This adjustment will net to zero as a result. The buyer expects accounts receivable to increase $10,000 in 2012 and $5,000 in 2013 since the newfound organization will have a slower collection rate than the former organization. The buyer feels that the newfound organization can gain traction and collect the outstanding accounts receivable resulting in the $5,000 and $10,000 being recuperated in 2015 and 2016, respectively. No other changes to working capital are expected to occur.

TABLE H	FCFF Adjustments					
	2012	**2013**	**2014**	**2015**	**2016**	**Terminal**
Projected net profit	92,414	87,756	73,418	65,448	37,912	15,031
Interest expense	n/a	n/a	n/a	n/a	n/a	n/a
Projected tax liability	(20,331)	(19,306)	(16,152)	(14,399)	(8,341)	(3,307)
Capital purchases and depreciation	n/a	n/a	n/a	n/a	n/a	n/a
Δ in working capital	(10,000)	(5,000)	—	5,000	10,000	—
Free cash flow to the firm	62,083	63,450	57,266	56,049	39,571	11,724

The buyer wants to use a risk premium of 14.75% based on conversations with other business owners in the marketplace. The discount rate would equal 18% after adding the estimated inflation rate of 3.25%. Terminal year activity is discounted using an estimated long-term economic growth rate of 2%. The discounted cash flows would produce a net present value of $211,271 as presented in Table I. This amount reflects the total free cash flow available to both debt and equity holders on a risk and inflation adjusted basis. A lending institution would want to review this amount before extending a practice loan to ensure enough value exists.

TABLE I	Discounted FCFF					
	2012	**2013**	**2014**	**2015**	**2016**	**Terminal**
	62,083	63,450	57,266	56,049	39,571	11,724
Step 1						(DR-g)
Step 2	$(1 + DR)^1$	$(1 + DR)^2$	$(1 + DR)^3$	$(1 + DR)^4$	$(1+ DR)^5$	$(1 + DR)^6$
Step 1						73,275
						11,724/(.16)
Step 2	52,613	45,569	34,854	28,909	17,297	32,029
	$62,083/(1.18)^1$	$63,450/(1.18)^2$	$57,266/(1.18)^3$	$56,049/(1.18)^4$	$39,571/(1.18)^5$	$73,275/(1.18)^6$
NPV = 211,271						

Free Cash Flow to Equity (FCFE) Imagine that the buyer establishes a line of credit charging 7% annual interest to cover the change in working capital and protect against negative cash balances. The interest would accrue for the entire year causing the organization to make interest payments of $700 or $1,050 in relation to the loan balances of $10,000 and $15,000, respectively. Unlike with the FCFF calculation, interest expense related to an operating loan should reduce net profit when calculating the FCFE stream. Table J shows the free cash flows that would accrue to the equity holders of this business. Notice how the change in working capital is offset by the amounts borrowed to fund the imbalance.

TABLE J	FCFE Adjustments					
	2012	**2013**	**2014**	**2015**	**2016**	**Terminal**
Projected net profit	92,414	87,756	73,418	65,448	37,912	15,031
Projected interest expense	(700)	(1,050)	(1,050)	(1,050)	(700)	
Projected tax liability	(20,331)	(19,306)	(16,152)	(14,399)	(8,341)	(3,307)
Capital purchases and depreciation	n/a	n/a	n/a	n/a	n/a	n/a
Δ in working capital	(10,000)	(5,000)	—	5,000	10,000	—
Δ in operating loan	10,000	5,000	—	(5,000)	(10,000)	—
Free cash flow to equity	71,383	67,400	56,216	49,999	28,871	11,724

The net present value of the FCFE stream would tentatively equal $214,176 as presented in Table K using a discount rate of 18% and a long-term economic growth rate of 2%. However, this value would need to be further reduced by the present value of a practice loan.

Imagine that the business seller wants $160,000 for this practice. How much in free cash flows would be available to the buyer if a lending institution requires a 25% down payment and charges 8% interest rate on a ten-year loan?

TABLE K	Discounted FCFE					
	2012	**2013**	**2014**	**2015**	**2016**	**Terminal**
	71,537	67,631	56,447	50,230	29,025	11 ,724
Step 1						(DR-g)
Step 2	$(1 + DR)^1$	$(1 + DR)^2$	$(1 + DR)^3$	$(1 + DR)^4$	$(1 + DR)^5$	$(1 + DR)^6$
Step1						73,275
						11,724/(.16)
Step 2	60,625	48,572	34,355	25,908	12,687	32,029
	$71,537/(1.18)^1$	$67,631/(1.18)^2$	$56,447/(1.18)^3$	$50,230/(1.18)^4$	$29,025/(1.18)^5$	$73,275/(1.18)^6$
NPV = 214,176						

9. Reduce FCFE Value for Any Practice Loan

Using the =PMT function in Excel, the monthly loan payments are found to equal $1,346.75 on an after-tax basis as shown in Figure C. Note how the interest rate of 8% has been adjusted for the estimated tax rate of 22% (1 – Tax Rate) and divided by 12 months. A total of 120 (10*12) monthly loan payments would be made over ten years. The sales price of $160,000 is reduced by the 25% down payment that the lending institution will not provide. A lending institution will only extend a loan in the amount of $120,000.

FIGURE C Payment Function in Excel

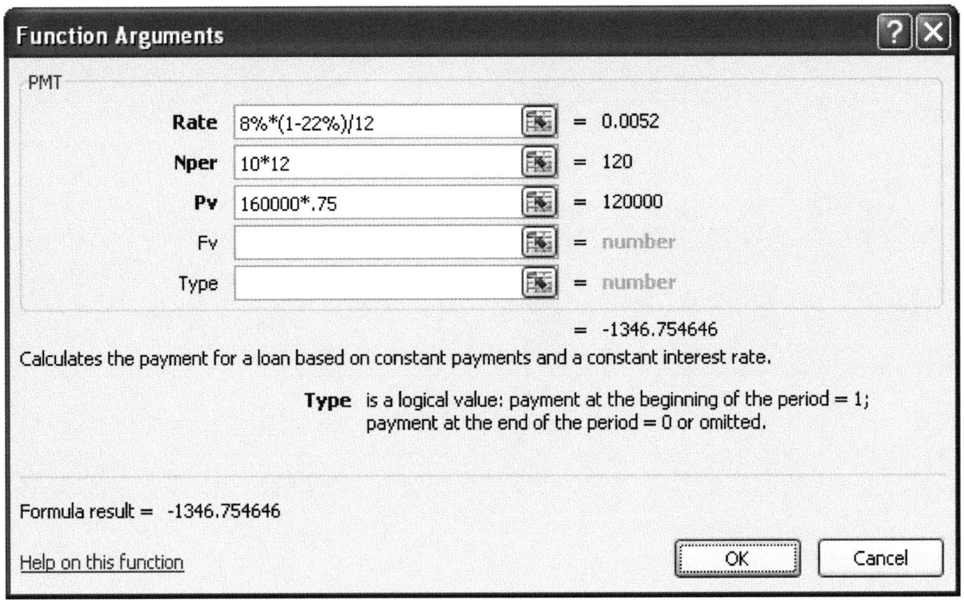

The buyer now needs to discount the $1,346.75 monthly cash flow stream into present value terms. All the projected cash flows of the organization need to be discounted, including cash outflows related to a practice loan. If a discount rate of 18% is applied, the 120 monthly payments will equal a present value of $74,743 using the =PV function in Excel as presented in Figure D.

Funding this transaction with 75% debt would decrease the net present value available to equity holders (FCFE) to $139,433 ($214,176 – $74,743) on a risk and inflation adjusted

FIGURE D Present Value Function in Excel

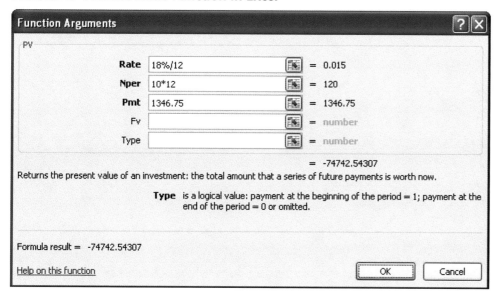

basis. The buyer has a significant chance of *losing* around $20,567 ($139,433−$160,000) on a risk and inflation adjusted basis if the business was purchased for $160,000 in total. The buyer should either bargain for a lower sales price or find a different opportunity based on this business valuation.

Funding Sources

AUTHOR'S NOTE

Family members, friends, or a significant other can help in a number of different ways, not just financially, but raising expectations of such people could sour relationships. A business owner will endure a high degree of stress when forming a new business or managing operations. Be careful not to unload those pressures onto others in a thoughtless manner. A common and straightforward way for a health care provider to obtain financing is through a line of credit or seller-financed loan. In terms of venture capital, many health care providers seem perplexed over the notion that unknown people can provide capital funding to a fledgling business. It's very common for businesses to seek investors and sell them on an investment idea. Make sure to secure proper loan terms no matter what the situation is. The Small Business Administration (SBA), or an affiliated group, can provide assistance throughout the lending process. Put forth the effort to speak with an attorney and access the resources that the SBA makes available.

A health care provider should conduct a cash flow projection to determine if a venture will provide sufficient value on a risk and inflation adjusted basis as discussed in previous chapters. If a venture is ultimately accepted, the next step involves finding a source of capital financing. An organization with current business activity can rely on future profit levels or existing cash savings. A health care provider starting business activity or an organization with limited resources may need to find external sources of capital in an effort to seize upon opportunity.

An organization should secure operating capital or maintain a cushion of savings to guard against an unexpected cash shortfall. An imbalance in *working capital* can arise if current obligations must be satisfied before current assets are received. A loan is generally required when needing to purchase a practice, building, or land. A lending institution will review various forms of documentation along with a borrower's personal integrity as part of conducting a risk assessment.

A seller-financed loan represents a common funding option when buying the assets or patient base of an existing business. The seller takes on the role of a lending institution and the borrower makes loan payments directly to the seller per a loan agreement. The two parties have tremendous flexibility in formulating this agreement according to the general nature of contract law. The buyer and seller remain connected over the life of the loan per the agreed-upon terms.

This chapter closes with an overview of contract law to highlight important legal matters that organization members should take into account when making decisions and establishing agreements with others. For example, an oral agreement can be legally binding despite the absence of a written contract. A business that offers goods and services to the public is held to higher legal standards as well.

14.1 Personal Sources

Building a savings base can be viewed as a challenge when considering the high costs of a health care education. Health care students have little ability to work during their academic programs and most accumulate sizable school loans. Saving a portion of school loans to use after graduation can pose a problem since the loan agreement requires that funds be used for education-related purposes only. Accruing a large savings base might not be possible until finishing school. As a student or health care professional, it becomes important to live frugally and stick to a budget.

Personal savings are an ideal source of funding because no interest charges will accrue, but amounts held in savings will generally cover a relatively minor part of any future capital need. Still, a health care provider should build personal savings to the extent possible in an effort to pursue opportunity when it arises. Amounts held in savings could cover equipment purchases, the down payment on a loan, moving costs, or a working-capital imbalance.

Since personal savings are generally appropriated for near-term activity, amounts should be held in a low-risk money market fund or government-insured savings account.

Live within your current means.

A retirement plan or insurance policy may contain a low-risk money market fund as part of its investment offerings. Although retirement or insurance products tend to lock up investor money for a long time, the account owner may be allowed to borrow against the current balance. Any interest charged on such loans would accrue to the account holder personally, thus eliminating any real impact from borrowing funds in this manner. Contributions into specific retirement accounts and insurance products enjoy certain tax advantages enabling the account holder to save more. However, withdrawing funds prematurely could trigger penalties and tax consequences that may erase the initial tax advantages. The rules governing retirement plans and life insurance policies are discussed in further detail in Chapter 15. Speak with a financial advisor to evaluate the use of investment and insurance products as a vehicle for savings.

> The Federal Deposit Insurance Corporation (FDIC) will insure up to $250,000 in savings deposited in a covered banking institution.

Personal Legal Rights

A health care provider in an associate position must negotiate for the right to retain patients attracted through personal efforts as well as to receive a percentage of revenue generated from such patients. These rights will facilitate the formation of a new organization later, especially when savings are deficient and other sources of capital are limited. An associate position that disallows the personal formation of a patient base will make it harder for a health care provider to transition into a stable practice. Upon forming a new organization, always be prepared to work additional jobs in case cash balances fall too low. Compile a list of other job opportunities within the health care field (or an unrelated field) in order to find work if the need arises.

> Patient revenue represents the best source of capital.

Summary

A health care provider should make every effort to save money personally. Thrift and proper budgeting can lessen the dependence on external sources of capital. Establishing a savings base allows a health care provider to remain prepared for any potential situation, such as needing to relocate for an associate position or start a practice. Savings should be placed in a low-risk money market fund or government-insured savings account. A health care provider in an associate position must negotiate for the right to retain control over personally attracted patients and patient revenue, thus decreasing or eliminating the need to rely on personal savings or external parties for capital.

14.2   Private Sources

Most private sources of capital involve a significant other or family member. Friends may also show willingness to help with financial matters. Using these individuals as a source of capital can place stress on the relationship. A health care provider must determine how much stress the relationship can bear before divisions will give way. Take time to understand how much importance the other person places on money, especially after the risks are communicated. Refrain from using someone who has a great need for the money or does not deal well with monetary losses.

A significant other, family member, or friend might be able to lend alternative forms of support, thus softening the need for capital. Such assistance might include remodeling an office space, passing out marketing materials, or fulfilling administrative roles. This assistance would allow a health care provider to move forward with building a patient base and generating capital personally through patient revenue. Private individuals could *cosign* for a loan, accepting responsibility to make loan payments in case of default. A **cosigner** can also increase the chances of a loan being approved and result in a lower interest rate. Still, a health care provider should not have expectations or place unfair demands on anyone.

> **Cosigner:** A person who agrees to bear responsibility for a loan in case the original borrower defaults.

In situations where borrowing money from a private source appears sensible, tax authorities like to see both parties forge a loan agreement. *Even a health care provider who lends money to the business itself should forge a loan agreement.* A loan agreement must contain specific repayment terms, including a set interest rate and payment schedule. Speak with a licensed professional about any minimum interest rate levels required by tax authorities. The objective of a loan agreement is to show clearly that the money is not a gift. An unreasonably low interest rate or lack of clear terms could cause the loan to be treated as a gift whereby the person lending the money would be charged a gift tax. At the same time, a private lender cannot forgive indebtedness without invoking tax consequences for the borrower. Debt forgiveness under any circumstances results in taxable income to the borrower per the amount of obligation discharged.

Venture Capital

Venture Capital: Amounts solicited from external private investors looking to fund a fledgling business in exchange for an equity share.

In a manner similar to finding new patients, marketing efforts will unearth people with a willingness to provide **venture capital**. This source of capital involves soliciting external investors where a close relationship does *not* exist. Investors often look for alternative investment options that include providing capital to a fledgling business. It becomes a matter of finding investors and presenting a convincing business plan.

Review the tax advantages of an *S* corporation in Chapter 9.

A health care provider will seldom access venture capital because most investors will want an equity share in the business. If operating under a corporate business form, equity owners will automatically receive net profit or dividends in accordance with their respective ownership percentage. A partnership agreement allows greater flexibility in how net profit is divided among equity owners. Business owners often form partnerships because of this *legal* advantage even though a corporation may offer better *tax* advantages.

Summary

Family members, friends, or a significant other can provide many types of support, including marketing assistance, administrative help, or capital financing. Placing demands on such individuals should be avoided and an effort should be made to review the relationship, communicate risks, and determine if the other person can bear the consequences of those risks. To avoid complications with tax authorities, a loan agreement should always be forged whenever money is borrowed from a private source, even amid a health care provider's own business.

14.3   Commercial Loans

A more traditional approach to borrowing involves forming a loan agreement with a commercial lending institution, such as a bank. Even though the lending institution will most likely present the terms of the agreement first, the borrower may be able to negotiate different terms thereafter, especially with assistance from the SBA. If a loan size falls under a certain dollar threshold, a lending institution may require less paperwork and leave the lending decision up to a local office. For instance, a loan officer at a bank branch might deal with loans under $50,000 and require no business plan. This can facilitate the process of borrowing money for furniture, equipment, or working capital. Building strong rapport with bank personnel and maintaining a good history of activity with a bank could prove highly beneficial.

The lending decision may be routed to a commercial lending division when dealing with loans above this threshold. The commercial lending division may require a business plan, personal financial statements, and a professional appraisal of assets. A personal credit score is generally always reviewed regardless of the size of the loan.

Credit Score

The Fair Isaac Corporation (FICO) devised a system to measure personal lending risk referred to as a FICO score. A FICO score looks mainly at a borrower's historical record of making timely payments on revolving debt accounts. Credit cards are viewed as the standard for revolving debt. A credit card can help build a FICO score as long as payments are made on time, debt levels remain historically low, and the card was issued many years earlier.

A person's FICO score depends largely on making timely payments on revolving debt but missing such payments—even by mistake—could cause this strategy to fail. *The best strategy for raising a FICO score appears to involve rarely using a credit card but keeping it active for as long as possible.* The Fair Isaac Corporation does not advise opening up a new credit card in an effort to improve a FICO score. A new credit card has no history and will trigger a recalibration of average account length, thus automatically lowering the FICO score.

A bankruptcy, foreclosure, repossession, or collections proceeding will significantly reduce a person's credit score for up to seven years. After seven years, the credit reporting agencies will remove these items from a person's credit report. Borrowers should request a free copy of their credit report from one of the three credit agencies to review for mistakes. A borrower might have to report a bankruptcy, foreclosure, repossession, or collections proceeding directly to a lending institution *even though it occurred more than seven years earlier.*

CREDIT AGENCIES	
Experian	experian.com
TransUnion	transunion.com
Equifax	equifax.com

Business Plan

A business plan should include a marketing section covering how the organization intends to generate revenue. The financial section of a business plan presents the forecasted values for revenue along with supporting expenses. Forecasted cash flows should be discounted for risk and inflation in order to confirm that an organization will generate positive net present value, thus generating enough profit to cover the costs of debt (interest charges) and equity. The net present value of a business must be equal to or greater than the requested loan value.

A business plan should also include a management section that sets benchmarks for an organization and demonstrates how hypothetical problems, such as the onset of new competitive pressures, will be resolved. The SBA has free educational programs that provide borrowers with assistance in writing a business plan. The SBA offers additional classes on general business topics and can help with negotiating loan terms. Contact a local SBA office, or an affiliated group, when attempting to acquire funding through a lending institution.

SCORE is affiliated with the SBA, score.org

Personal Financial Statements

A personal financial statement examines information related to a borrower's personal balance sheet and current sources of income. Unless self-employed, a lending institution could ask for wage details, including any wage encumbrance, such as a court-ordered garnishment. A lending institution may want an accounting of cash, investments, real estate, and life insurance on the asset side. For liabilities, a borrower may need to list loans made with other lending institutions, relatives, or other persons. Taking a loan from a life insurance policy or retirement account might also need to be reported. The same reporting requirement applies for cosigning or guaranteeing the loan of another person. A lending institution may require a borrower to secure a loan using personal assets. Such actions would override any personal protection afforded by an organization's business form.

Loan Covenants

A loan agreement usually comes with positive and negative **covenants** that protect the lending institution and borrower, respectively. *Positive* covenants prevent the lending institution from setting unreasonable terms. *Negative* covenants prevent the borrower from engaging in activities that could increase risks, such as taking out additional loans or using funds or collateral in an undesired way. Most loan agreements will contain debt and liquidity ratios that must be maintained by a borrower's business. Table 14.1 lists some of the main ratios

Covenants: Restrictions placed on either the borrower or lender as noted within a loan agreement.

TABLE 14.1   Key Loan Ratios

Times-Interest Earned:
(Net Profit + Interest Expense + Depreciation + Amortization) ÷ Interest Expense

Long-Term Debt to Total Assets:
(Long-Term Debt + Obligations under Capital Leases) ÷ Total Assets

Current Ratio:
Current Assets ÷ Current Liabilities

---

seen in loan agreements. Failure to maintain ratios above the threshold set by a lending institution could result in loan default.

Noncompete Agreement

A separate contract should set limitations on a business seller's ability to turn around and establish another practice. Without such limitations, the buyer might experience a high degree of patient turnover. A standard *covenant not to compete* specifies the time frame during which the seller cannot reestablish a new practice—usually one year. The agreement may define a geographic region in which the seller cannot relocate or engage in marketing activities. The buyer might want to identify specific community organizations or businesses toward which the seller cannot direct marketing resources. A court may alter a noncompete agreement if the terms appear unreasonable or impose an undue hardship on the seller.

Cash Flow Loan

Cash Flow Loan: A loan where the basis of repayment depends on expected future income streams.

A **cash flow loan** has *no underlying support* that a lending institution could access in case of borrower nonpayment. Similar to how a personal credit card functions, a practice or working-capital loan relies on a borrower's future income stream as a means for repayment. If a borrower goes into default because future cash flows prove inadequate, a lending institution could not recover the remaining loan balance by selling the borrower's personal or business assets. Cash flow loans face a high degree of risk as a result, usually forcing lending institutions to charge a high interest rate.

Could you recruit enough patients in the time it takes to accumulate relevant work experience?

Could a health care provider afford a practice loan at an interest-rate level similar to what a credit card company charges? The SBA administers the *7(a) loan program,* giving borrowers access to affordable cash flow loans. Section 7(a) of the Federal Small Business Act authorizes the SBA to work with lending institutions to (1) reduce the overall risks lenders face, (2) establish standard interest rates, (3) reduce down-payment requirements, and (4) extend the maturity length of loans. A lending institution must follow guidelines set forth by the SBA to remain eligible for assistance under the 7(a) loan program. One such guideline requires that a borrower have relevant work experience including at a management level. A lending institution can require several years of work experience, especially if a borrower appears to lack the skills needed to successfully run a particular health care organization.

SECTION 7(A) LENDERS	
CIT Small Business Lending	cit.com
GE Health Care Finance	gehealthcarefinance.com
Wells Fargo Practice Finance	practicefinance.wellsfargo.com
Professional Practice Capital	ppcloan.com
Coffman Capital	coffmancapital.com
Rx Financial Group	rxfinancialcorp.com

Reduced Risk The SBA does not directly protect the borrower. The borrower is able to receive a reasonable interest rate on a cash flow loan because of protections offered to the lending institution.

Standard Interest Rates The interest rate on a cash flow loan supported by the 7(a) loan program is calculated by adding a *risk premium* to the U.S. Federal Reserve prime rate, which is the rate large institutional borrowers receive. The risk premium differs based on the loan size and length of the loan. Per SBA requirements, lenders cannot charge interest rates above the levels shown in Table 14.2.

TABLE 14.2	7(a) Loan Interest Rates	
Loan Amount	**Maturity < 7 years**	**Maturity > 7 years**
>$50,000	Prime + 2.25%	Prime + 2.75%
$25,000 − $50,000	Prime + 3.25%	Prime + 3.75%
<$25,000	Prime + 4.25%	Prime + 4.75%

The fed prime rate can be found at primerate.net.
Source: sba.gov

Reduced Down Payment Suppose a health care provider negotiates to buy a practice for $100,000. A lending institution may provide only $72,000 of this total. The remaining $28,000 represents a down payment that would need to come from a separate capital source. The SBA can work with a lending institution to reduce the required down payment.

Extended Maturity Practice and working-capital loans will generally not exceed seven years. A lending institution can even set a maturity date as short as three years. A maturity of ten years may be approved if a lending institution believes the longer time horizon will allow a questionable loan to become fully repaid. The SBA can work with a lending institution to increase a loan's maturity length.

U.S. SMALL BUSINESS ADMINISTRATION

A health care provider should request assistance from a local SBA office in setting up a loan. A lending institution may agree to adjust the interest rate, down payment, or loan maturity based on the SBA's recommendation, especially in regard to a borrower in a disadvantaged class. More importantly, overall approval for a loan may be the result of having worked with the SBA. Apart from a business plan and personal financial statements, a lending institution *and* the SBA will assess the borrower's character as part of the loan package that is reviewed. Both parties will want to see significant work experience before initiating the loan process. When a loan is offered, an organization might run into difficulty meeting loan payments later whereby the lending institution could exercise the right to foreclose on the loan and require immediate repayment. A lending institution will usually want to renegotiate the terms first, in which case solid relationships with SBA officials and loan officers can prove beneficial.

Collateralized Loan

A **collateralized loan** involves assets (collateral) that a lending institution could recover in case of default. A lending institution only sustains losses if a loan balance plus administrative costs are greater than the proceeds from the sale of collateral. A collateralized loan provides a lending institution with greater security, and interest rate levels are lower as a result. Banks and community credit unions offer collateralized loans with competitive

Collateralized Loan: A loan secured by an underlying tangible asset that could be sold to cover the loan balance in case of default.

terms as part of their normal banking operations, offering a health care provider more access to a loan when purchasing assets, such as equipment, land, or a building. SBA loan programs exist for collateralized loans, but a borrower may find reasonable interest rates while working directly with a lending institution apart from such programs.

A lending institution can require that personal assets be used as collateral to secure a loan. Protections granted by a particular business form would not apply in situations where a loan agreement specifies personal collateral be made available. An SBA official can help remove such terms from a loan agreement and reestablish proper personal protections. A borrower must pay attention to loan terms that prevent taking on new debt. A loan agreement may contain negative covenants against borrowing additional funds later. A health care provider may need to finance a practice and fixed assets together through SBA loan programs in order to sidestep such covenants.

A standard down payment for a collateralized loan equals 25%, requiring a borrower to have additional sources of capital financing. Maturity lengths for collateralized loans vary between 10 and 25 years depending on the type of asset. The maturity length will almost never exceed the useful economic life of the underlying collateral. For instance, an x-ray machine might function properly for an estimated 20 years, but the lending institution might figure that this particular machine will be useful in a clinic setting for only 15 years. In this case, a lending institution may require the loan to be repaid over a 15-year timespan to ensure the collateral remains valuable. Loan terms may also limit the ability to dispose of the underlying collateral securing a loan.

Line of Credit

Line of Credit: A loan arrangement resembling a credit card that allows a borrower greater flexibility to withdraw amounts up to a preset limit as needed.

Note how a line of credit functions very similar to a credit card.

Instead of borrowing a predetermined amount of money, a **line of credit** represents a more flexible lending arrangement where the borrower can take out only what is necessary and repay amounts when possible. Consider a health care organization that arranges a line of credit with a local bank. Money would not have to be withdrawn at first and interest charges consequently would not accrue. Imagine that a working-capital imbalance several months later results in a cash shortfall. The organization could withdraw a specific amount of funds from the line of credit to cover the negative cash balance, repay amounts within a reasonable timeframe, and bear interest charges only while an outstanding balance exists.

A lending institution can structure a practice loan to include a line of credit. Additional funds can then be accessed if a need arises, unless the loan agreement prohibits certain transactions. A lending institution may require (personal) collateral to secure a line of credit or rely solely on future cash flows. A line of credit usually has an approved limit and preset interest rate, which are generally more reasonable than those a credit card offers, yet are still influenced by the level of risk faced by the lender. A lending institution will often penalize borrowers for repaying a regular loan faster than what its amortization schedule designates. No such penalties exist for a line of credit. In most cases, a line of credit will need to be reapproved once per year.

Home Equity Line of Credit (HELOC): A line of credit tied to the equity value of a person's home.

A person's home can serve as collateral for a **home equity line of credit (HELOC)**. Using a house as collateral reduces risk and keeps the designated interest rate low even when funds are withdrawn for a business purpose. A HELOC could present challenges for a homeowner trying to sell a house if an outstanding loan balance exists. Since the line of credit depends on a home's equity value, refinancing a home may be necessary to establish the equity value and increase the available limit. If a home's market value subsequently declines, the HELOC may not be reapproved or the available limit may diminish.

Mortgage Equity Withdrawal (MEW): A lump-sum withdrawal of equity from a person's home requiring establishment of a new loan that combines the old loan with the total withdrawal.

A homeowner may have the ability to pull equity out of a home through a **mortgage equity withdrawal (MEW)**. This process involves reestablishing a new home loan that combines the current loan balance with the amount of MEW. A homeowner must have a sufficient level of home equity to make this withdrawal. If a home's market value subsequently declines in value, the homeowner may face a negative equity value as a result of having made the MEW. Negative equity could make the process of selling a home more challenging. Refinancing a loan or reestablishing a new loan can lead to higher loan payments and additional fees. Before using a personal home (or a third party's home) as collateral for a HELOC or source of MEW, examine and assess the *costs* and *risks* of both refinancing and default for all parties involved.

Summary

A local bank branch might manage the entire lending process for a smaller loan. Past a certain threshold, a commercial lending division could review additional documentation and provide ultimate approval for a loan. A lending institution may require a business plan and personal financial statements in addition to a good credit score. FICO is generally regarded as the key source for credit scores.

Because a cash flow loan provides insufficient levels of security to a lender, the Small Business Administration administers the 7(a) loan program, which works directly with lenders to reduce their risks. The security afforded by collateral allows lending institutions to offer loans apart from any SBA program at low interest rates. Still, the SBA can work on behalf of a borrower to renegotiate better lending terms and offer assistance when putting together documentation. A borrower should pay attention to negative covenants that could prohibit certain activities.

Instead of taking out a lump sum of money all at once through a cash flow or collateralized loan, a line of credit allows for a more flexible lending arrangement resembling how a credit card functions. As with a credit card, the line of credit can provide small amounts of capital when needed and limit interest charges to periods when an outstanding loan balance exists.

14.4 Seller-Financed Loans

Using a lending institution as a source of capital has its drawbacks, especially when dealing with larger loans. A borrower will most likely face a large down payment, which could represent 25% or more of the total capital need. A loan agreement may contain negative covenants limiting further capital procurements. A lending institution may want to secure a loan using personal assets as collateral. A loan package might be denied by a lending institution or the SBA because of credit issues, such as a prior bankruptcy or low FICO score. Other issues may exist that make it practical for a borrower to avoid working with a commercial lending institution. For example, a borrower may want to take over a practice in stages or buy several fixed assets one at a time.

A seller-financed loan does not involve the use of a formal lending institution. The party selling an asset functions as a lender by exchanging the asset with the buyer and then accepting loan payments directly. The seller may receive nothing upfront unless a down payment is specified. The loan could be for equipment, land, a building, or a practice being sold. The buyer and seller must negotiate the loan terms from scratch since there is no formal lending process already established. For example, if the buyer defaults on the loan, an agreement could state that the seller will regain the asset. An **escrow agent** should be part of the arrangement in order to keep an outside record of payments and verify that the loan agreement is being upheld. The loan payments would pass through an *escrow account* before being received by the seller.

The party selling an asset may have the upper hand and use the opportunity to secure an interest rate above current market rates or sell the asset at a price that a lending institution or the SBA would not approve. Seller-financed loans can be dangerous for buyers who do not properly value the asset being sold, such as through a net present value calculation. The buyer and seller should involve the SBA and other professionals in the negotiation process to ensure that loan terms are reasonable for both parties. Lawyers should officially draft the loan agreement in compliance with contract law and confirm that the arrangement is both legal and fair. Apart from a loan agreement, both parties should sign a *noncompete agreement* to prevent the seller from establishing a new practice that competes with the one just purchased by the buyer.

The buyer or seller can fill out a **negotiation matrix** as a way to better understand how to approach the contract process. A negotiation matrix covers the advantages and disadvantages that either party faces as listed in Table 14.3 as a way to pinpoint bargaining

Escrow Agent: A third party hired to maintain a proper accounting of loan payments and ensure that all parties fulfill contractual obligations.

Negotiation Matrix: A structured method of looking at the advantages and disadvantages faced by the parties working to establish a legal agreement.

TABLE 14.3	Negotiation Matrix

This negotiation matrix contains the *general* advantages and disadvantages to a seller-financed loan. A negotiation matrix normally contains *specific* items related to a particular transaction.

	Borrower	**Seller**
Advantages	Smaller down payment Longer maturity Efficient transition Better default options No loan-initiation fees Flexible terms	Higher sales price Efficient transition Sell to a preferred buyer Flexible terms
Disadvantages	Overpaying for an asset No incentive to explore other financing options Less oversight on the loan process Expense of contract and escrow	Remain bound to situation Dependence on loan payments Reestablish practice if default occurs Expense of contract and escrow

strengths and weaknesses. Realize that bargaining power helps when trying to wrestle for favorable lending terms. Use of this matrix can benefit a health care provider when negotiating in other situations as well.

> The other party should not see the negotiation matrix you put together.

Loan Payments

The buyer and seller must establish payment terms when arranging a seller-financed loan. A loan agreement could stipulate a fixed rate or establish a variable rate that changes once per year (within a set range). The interest rate selected could reflect long-term averages as opposed to the current market rate of interest. Current rates may be abnormally high (or low) and the borrower or seller may not want to get stuck with an abnormal interest rate.

A seller-financed loan provides the ability to establish a longer maturity length, thus reducing the size of monthly loan payments. A balloon structure could allow for smaller loan payments during an initial trial period to ensure the buyer can maintain the practice being sold. Payments would then increase after the trial period ended. A loan agreement could call for a large lump-sum payment at some point. This lump-sum payment may be required upfront—such would be the case with a down payment—or occur after several years. Problems could arise if loan payments start to increase or a lump-sum payment is required and the buyer is not prepared financially.

A down payment is not normally required with a seller-financed loan unless it is part of the lending terms. A borrower could even use a seller-financed loan to cover a portion of the capital need that a lending institution will not provide; that is, the down payment on a commercial loan.

Collateralization

> The seller will most likely retain the right to collect on accounts receivable that existed before the business was sold.

The buyer could require that personal assets *not* be used as collateral, thus maintaining legal protections afforded by a business form. The seller may require that business equipment, land, or a building serve as collateral, even when selling a patient base, as long as such assets are not covering another loan. A seller-financed loan agreement often specifies that *future* accounts receivable will become the property of the seller in case of default. The seller will need to retain rights over applicable patient records for the duration of the loan in order to collect accounts receivable if default occurs.

Practice Transition

A seller-financed loan provides more flexibility in how the transition of assets can occur. Instead of making a clean break and handing assets over to the buyer all at once, the two parties could slowly transition assets and increase the loan balance in segments. For instance, a contract could require that the borrower pay $100,000 overall for a practice yet the obligation would accrue in annual segments of $25,000. The buyer would slowly assume more leverage risk and the seller could begin working less in anticipation of retirement. The seller could exit the practice entirely after four years or continue helping with marketing and administrative tasks to keep the practice stabilized.

A health care provider who anticipates buying a practice could work as an associate and receive a set salary or earn a percentage of patient revenue based on patients who were attracted through personal efforts. A prospective buyer could work as an independent contractor and retain control over all personally generated revenue. An independent-contractor position may require payment of a monthly fee to help cover an organization's administrative costs. If an associate eventually agrees to buy a practice, a portion of the monthly fees paid in the past could be applied against the seller-financed loan balance.

Breach of Contract

Any failure to fulfill the terms of a seller-financed loan will result in **breach of contract**. The buyer and seller must clearly specify the various terms in a contract, especially patient receivables, patient records, third-party lawsuits, collateral, management decision making, and proper forms of communication (mail, email, and fax). The two parties can determine the relevant penalties in advance depending on the type of breach that occurs. The damages will be set by legal proceedings unless clearly set forth in a contract.

Imagine that a borrower slowly takes on a seller-financed loan but struggles to maintain the patient base. After two years, both parties agree that taking on the entire practice loan appears excessively risky and the buyer should hand back the practice. The contract could stipulate that the buyer is required to pay a lump sum representing liquidating damages. The seller could reestablish the practice and sell it to a different health care provider thereafter.

Breach of Contract: Failing to fulfill obligations as set forth in a legal agreement.

Summary

A lending arrangement can be made directly with the party selling assets through a seller-financed loan. The buyer would take over assets and begin making payments through an escrow account to the seller. The loan agreement should make plain the exact terms of the lending arrangement and what will occur if the terms are breached. A contract can specify unique terms related to loan payments, collateral, the transition of assets, and breach of contract. Either party can put together a negotiation matrix in an attempt to obtain better contract terms personally.

14.5   Leasing Equipment

Vendors may provide the option to lease medical or office equipment instead of selling it outright. Acquiring equipment on lease can decrease the need for capital financing. A lease agreement rarely entails a down payment except in terms of a damage deposit. A business plan and personal financial statements should not be required either. A leasing company may review a FICO score to verify that the *lessee* will be able to make lease payments on time.

Obtaining equipment on lease allows an organization to modernize the patient experience and avoid getting stuck with outdated equipment. An organization may need to

Vendors may also provide long-term financing options enabling equipment to be purchased on loan directly.

make updates to equipment with a growth plan or because of changing patient demands. Leasing affords certain financial benefits by keeping leverage risk down and avoiding payment for surprise repair costs. An organization may even have the option to later purchase the equipment being leased at a reduced rate.

The overall costs associated with leasing equipment may be higher than if the equipment was purchased originally. An organization will generally not build equity in leased equipment, removing any potential gain upon its disposal. A net present value calculation can identify the overall value between leasing versus buying. The projected sales price (salvage value) of equipment should be viewed in contrast to its original purchase price, projected repair costs, or related loan payments. The present value found from this analysis should then be compared to the cost of lease payments.

An organization must pay attention to how a lease should be reported to external parties, such as a tax authority. If a lease has the economic appearance of a loan where ownership may likely trade hands, *capital lease* reporting requirements may be triggered. The leased asset would be placed on the balance sheet along with an artificial long-term loan. A licensed tax professional can help determine if a lease arrangement must be reported as a capital lease.

> Capital versus operating lease reporting requirements are covered in Chapter 7.

Summary

Leasing equipment instead of purchasing it outright may allow an organization to need less capital financing. An organization may acquire leased equipment without a down payment, business plan, or personal financial statements. Leasing equipment can provide a health care organization more flexibility in modernizing the type of equipment being held from one time period to another. A leasing company may want to review a FICO score or other credit rating to verify the likelihood that lease payments will be made. A lease arrangement that functions more like a loan must be reported as a capital lease.

14.6   Contract Law

> This book should not be relied upon for legal guidance. The legal code of each state can vary significantly and involve more complexity then discussed here. Seek the help of a licensed attorney to thoroughly review legal issues related to a given situation.

> The employee handbook is discussed in Chapter 18.

Extending services to the public or making business arrangements with other individuals directly or indirectly falls under the scope of contract law. A loan agreement, insurance policy, and commercial lease are examples of contracts that are normally in writing. Promising employees certain benefits or making concessions to patients can be considered a contract, even when communicated orally. Organization members who make oral promises to external parties could unknowingly lock the entire organization into a legally binding contract. Organization members should receive adequate training on how to communicate (or not communicate) on behalf of your organization. An employee handbook should explicitly restrict employees from forming unauthorized contracts or agreements.

Legal Formation

A contract is considered a legally binding agreement in most states if four criteria are met.

1. Capacity The parties involved in a contract must be mentally competent, over the age of 18, and properly authorized to form a particular contract. A staff member may not have legal capacity to establish contracts on behalf of an organization unless otherwise granted the authority by an appropriate person.

2. Legality A contract cannot set unreasonable terms or run contrary to federal, state, or local laws and regulations. A court may release an individual's obligation to fulfill a particular contract term if it cannot be realistically performed.

3. Consideration A fair exchange must occur among all parties to a contract. A court may release an individual's obligation to fulfill a particular contract term if an exchange is not fair. Imagine a case where a buyer pays $125,000 for a practice but forgot to ask for a covenant not to compete and the seller establishes a new practice that is located two blocks away after one week. How would a judge perceive the fairness of the **consideration** if much of the patient base remains with the seller?

4. Mutual Assent The contract process begins when one party makes an *offer*. The contract is then formed when the party receiving the offer communicates *acceptance*. The contract process may be interrupted by *revocation* of the original offer before acceptance is made; also, the party receiving the offer could *reject* the original offer or *counteroffer*. The two parties must agree to enter into the contract within a reasonable amount of time and by a suitable form of communication. The form of communication may need to adhere to agreed-upon terms. If the party receiving an offer begins to perform services related to an oral or written contract, formal acceptance may not be necessary for the contract to become legally binding.

Breach of Contract

If one party fails to perform terms of a contract in a reasonable or specified manner, that party can be in breach of contract. This may not release an injured party from fulfilling obligations under a contract unless the breach is considered *material*. Nonperformance of a contract term could result in damages owed to an injured party. Unless a contract specifies the exact damages, a court will generally attempt to restore conditions for an injured party comparable to what existed before forging the contract. The **remedy** offered to an injured party may cover reductions in asset value, legal or professional fees related to the breach, or a small lump-sum payment for miscellaneous items. A remedy will rarely involve punitive damages or amounts in excess of apparent losses unless actions are highly injurious. The parties to a contract may decide to renegotiate certain terms in an effort to ensure that contractual obligations can be fulfilled going forward.

Uniform Commercial Code

Almost all states have adopted the **Uniform Commercial Code (UCC)**, or substantial parts of the UCC, as a way to govern various forms of business activity, including the sale of tangible goods (excluding services). A merchant who runs a business selling tangible goods to the general public is held to a high standard. For example, a merchant must usually accept returns for up to 30 days. Many businesses will offer in-store credit after 30 days but there is no obligation to return a customer's money thereafter unless some other agreement has been forged—such an agreement can be made orally. Contracts made orally are usually legally binding if the legal formation was appropriate. **Statute of Frauds** provisions within the UCC specify which contracts must *always* be evidenced in writing to be legally binding. The Statute of Frauds provisions that relate to business activity include the following.

1. One-Year Performance A contract must be in writing to legally bind both parties if full performance of obligations will take more than one year *no matter the circumstances*. A loan agreement falls under this category whenever the terms define a maturity date past one year. However, if a borrower has the option to pay a loan in less than one year, a contract made orally might prove legally binding.

2. Land Contract Contracts that involve land ownership must always be evidenced in writing to legally bind both parties. If an agreement to purchase or sell land is made orally, there may not be any remedy for nonperformance of contractual obligations.

Do any contract terms conflict with a health care provider's scope of practice?

Consideration: The items of value constituting a fair exchange among parties to a contract.

Remedy: Amount of reparation offered to a party injured by a breach of contract.

Uniform Commercial Code (UCC): Set of standard rules governing (business) contracts as adopted by most states.

Statute of Frauds: Provisions of the UCC that specify the types of contracts that must be evidenced in writing.

3. Sale of Goods over $500 If the asking price for tangible property exceeds $500, an agreement must be evidenced in writing in order to legally bind both parties. There may not be any remedy for nonperformance of contractual obligations if an agreement is made orally.

Principal and Agent

Principal: An entity that has authorized others to act on its behalf.

Agent: An entity granted certain rights to act on behalf of a principal.

A principal-agent relationship is established when one person has the authority to act on behalf of another person. A **principal** grants the authorities while an **agent** acts in accordance with the authorities granted by the principal. An employee acts as an agent of an employer (principal) and has a legal duty to support the organization. An employee should never use the organization's resources to the detriment of the organization or engage in activities that conflict or compete with an employer. For example, quitting an associate position and leaving with patient contact information without proper authorization would breach this duty.

A legal contract should clearly define the authorities granted to an agent as well as terms for breach of the principal-agent relationship. Independent contractors should be told directly that they do not have the right to act as an agent of the organization. A principal can be held responsible for negligent or unauthorized acts performed by an agent or unauthorized person if external parties had reason to believe that such actions were proper. If a principal fears that an agent or unauthorized person might act erroneously or fraudulently, the principal should set specific limitations by a contract and communicate proactively with market participants about such limitations. For example, should the buyer of a practice have the right to open a bank account in the organization's name or set agreements with vendors before the practice is fully transitioned? A health care provider selling a practice should impose specific limitations on the buyer and mention such limitations to current and former patients along with vendors.

Summary

A contract is considered legally binding if four criteria are met: capacity, legality, consideration, and mutual assent. Agreements made orally can prove legal in most situations as long as an offer to a contract is properly accepted. The Uniform Commercial Code contains Statute of Frauds provisions that define which contracts must be evidenced in writing. An injured party may have difficulty recuperating damages for nonperformance of contractual obligations if written evidence is unavailable. Damages awarded for breach of contract normally attempt to restore conditions for an injured party to what existed before the contract was forged.

CHAPTER ASSIGNMENT

Working in a group of three to four students or fellow professionals, complete the following items.

1. How could a person access funds maintained in a retirement account or insurance policy to cover business expenditures?

2. What drawbacks exist when borrowing money from a significant other, family member, or friend? Why should a private borrower and lender forge a loan agreement?

3. How could a health care provider access funds from investors looking for alternative investment opportunities?

4. What key items will a lending institution (or the Small Business Administration) want to review when determining if a borrower is a good credit risk? How will those items differ if the loan size is large versus small?

5. How does a cash flow loan differ from a collateralized loan?

6. Why might a health care provider wanting to buy a building and practice need to acquire financing through SBA loan programs? What does the 7(a) loan program entail?

7. Describe how a line of credit functions and how it could provide a borrower with greater flexibility than a regular loan. Are there any drawbacks to using a home equity line of credit or taking a mortgage equity withdrawal?

8. How does a seller-financed loan function for both the buyer and seller of an asset? What loan terms should both parties consider and potentially include in a loan agreement?

9. What are the advantages and disadvantages to leasing equipment?

10. What types of contracts could be legally binding if only made orally?

11. How might a health care organization limit an employee or independent contractor from forging unwanted contracts with external parties?

Over-the-Counter (OTC)
Regulated Exchange
Initial Public Offering (IPO)
Market Capitalization
Coupon
Indenture Agreement
Callable Bond
Yield-to-Maturity (YTM)
Derivative Securities
Call Option
Put Option

Mutual Fund
Sales Load
Asset Allocation
Nondiscrimination Rules
Vest
Defined Benefit Plan
Defined Contribution Plan
Term Life Insurance
Permanent Life Insurance
Annuity
Business Continuity Insurance

Financial Planning

AUTHOR'S NOTE

Be wise with your money in both the short and long term. Do not regard the stock market as a way to get rich quickly. Investors often get into trouble by believing that high investment returns can be sustained over the long term. The best investment will be the one you make in your education and practice. It is more realistic to assume that your practice can sustain high levels of profit over the long term. It then becomes necessary to live comfortably, yet within your means, protect what you have through the right insurance products, and find the discipline to save for retirement using a portfolio of low-risk investment products.

A practice that generates a great deal of revenue can still experience financial problems if expenses are not properly managed. A working capital imbalance can come about if expenses must be paid before revenue is received. A cash shortfall could sour relationships with vendors or employees and result in penalties being imposed. A line of credit or business credit card can serve as protection against cash shortfalls, but persistent reliance on external financing will waste money through interest charges and expose an organization to higher leverage risk. A significant lack of money could lead to loan default and bankruptcy. Any of these events could disrupt an organization's culture and increase the stress level of a business owner.

A significant part of financial planning involves learning how to use resources effectively, including fixed assets, equity, human resources, and a marketing network. An organization should adhere to budgets and build a cushion of savings to deal with operating needs or a random emergency. Financial problems can easily surface if a roof starts to leak, equipment breaks, or a key employee leaves. What would happen if you became injured or sick? Insurance products may require a long waiting period before coverage begins. A health care organization always needs to save for future purposes, which could be urgent or unforeseen.

Various investment products provide a vehicle for savings when trying to attain short- and long-term goals. Investment products can be used to plan for asset purchases or provide for retirement. A retirement plan refers to an account that confers tax advantages to the investments held in it as long as specific rules are followed. A health care provider might have access to a retirement plan when working as an associate or upon buying a practice. Licensed professionals can help administer a retirement plan and select proper investment products.

This section on finance ends with taking components of accounting and finance learned thus far and assembling the financial section of a business plan. A financial plan should contain a cash flow projection based on relevant assumptions. Other financial calculations, such as a profitability analysis, should accompany a cash flow projection. Creating a financial plan will compel a health care provider to thoroughly examine the financial needs of a current or future organization and plan accordingly. Moreover, lending institutions and the U.S. Small Business Administration (SBA) may require a financial plan in order to ascertain the risks related to a loan and verify the overall monetary need. Even where a health care provider has no capital need currently, maintaining a financial plan can prove useful if an urgent or unforeseen event occurs.

15.1   Investments

Amounts set aside to meet short- and long-term financial goals can be placed into an investment account. The account holder can allocate amounts to various investment products to prevent savings from sitting idle. Investment products offer varying rates of return according to the underlying risks involved. Table 15.1 lists the main categories of investment products available to a general investor.

An investment *product* can also be referred to as an investment *security* or *vehicle*.

TABLE 15.1	**Investment Products**
Banking products	
Equity securities	
Debt securities	
Tangible property	
Derivatives	
Mutual funds	

An investment exchange can take place **over-the-counter (OTC)** where private parties set their own terms. Borrowing money from a friend to start a practice or asking unknown investors for *venture capital* illustrate types of OTC exchanges. **Regulated exchanges** open to the general public have greatly facilitated capital transfers between investors and companies by arranging transfers to take place in one central location with preset terms. The New York Stock Exchange (NYSE) and the National Association of Securities Dealers Automated Quotation (NASDAQ) system are two regulated exchanges through which investment products can be formally traded.

Over-the-Counter (OTC): A transaction involving investment products where private parties arrange the transfer and set their own terms.

Banking Products

Money held in a *savings account* earns a small rate of interest because a bank will use such funds as a source of new loans to other customers. Lending institutions also offer certificates of deposit (CDs) that typically offer more interest income than a savings account since funds are locked up for a period of time. A penalty will be assessed if funds are withdrawn from a CD early.

Regulated Exchange: A controlled environment open to the public where investment products can be transferred based on preset terms.

Equity Securities

An investor can obtain ownership in a company by purchasing shares of *common equity*. An equity security represents a legal contract detailing the ownership exchange. Participating in the ownership of a company grants an investor certain rights. These rights may involve voting on major decisions, receiving dividends, or receiving proceeds upon liquidation of the business. A company's balance sheet will generally not reflect the true value of common equity since asset accounts are presented at their *historical cost*. A *free cash flow to equity* calculation is required to determine the market value of common equity.

Preferred equity represents a rare hybrid investment product that resembles both debt and equity securities.

The exchange of equity securities can occur OTC. For example, a health care provider could sell a portion of stock OTC in an incorporated health care organization to an outside investor. A company that receives approval from the Federal Securities and Exchange Commission (SEC) and submits to an annual independent audit can sell stock certificates through a regulated U.S. exchange. Investors can purchase stock certificates more easily on a regulated exchange because of the predetermined structure. Regulated exchanges increase price efficiency since more buyers and sellers are calculating the net present value of the traded securities.

The term stock certificate is synonymous with equity security.

NASDAQ and the NYSE are the two most common regulated exchanges for equity securities in the United States. An **initial public offering (IPO)** refers to the first issue of

Initial Public Offering (IPO): The first issue of equity securities offered by a company on a regulated exchange.

Market Capitalization: The total amount of value that a company's equity securities are worth.

stock a company trades through a regulated exchange. **Market capitalization** represents the total value of all the stock a company has trading. A company is typically categorized as small, medium, or large based on the total market capitalization of its equity.

Debt Securities

Bond holders used to remit paper coupons to receive each interest payment. The term coupon has become synonymous with bond interest.

A company can issue debt securities as a vehicle to borrow funds from investors. A debt security issued by a company represents a legal contract and is generally referred to as a *bond*. Most bonds do not amortize the loan balance, as would a commercial loan. A bond normally pays interest (termed **coupon**) biannually and returns the original amount borrowed upon maturity. Bonds are sold OTC via bond dealers that match buyers and sellers using electronic systems. The investment terms are listed in an **indenture agreement** drafted by the company issuing the bonds. A **callable bond** contains terms that allow a company to end the bond indenture early before the stated maturity date.

Coupon: Term used to represent the interest given to holders of a bond security.

The coupon rate stated in a bond indenture may conflict with the current market rate of debt securities. The buyer will pay either a *premium* or receive a *discount* to adjust a bond's value and bring it in line with current market rates. Suppose a company issues 20-year bonds in the principal amount of $20,000 paying a 6% coupon rate biannually. If investors want to earn 8% on their money, these bonds would be discounted in price to $16,041 (calculation not shown) in order to create an artificial **yield to maturity (YTM)** of 8%. Investors will receive $1,200 (6% × $20,000) each year along with the $20,000 principal upon maturity but the bond will have been purchased for only $16,041 originally.

Indenture Agreement: The loan agreement set forth between a bond issuer and the investor lending funds.

Bond rating agencies evaluate bond issues and assign a rating according to the estimated risks. The rating can greatly influence the YTM that investors want to earn while holding a particular bond. Table 15.2 shows the classification schema for two of the major bond rating agencies: Moody's and Standard & Poor's (S&P).

Callable Bond: An indenture agreement with terms allowing the bond issuer to return the borrowed funds early ending the bond indenture before the normal maturity date.

Yield-to-Maturity: An artificial rate of return created by altering the price at which a bond sells.

TABLE 15.2		Agency Credit Ratings	
	Moody's	S&P	
Investment Grade	Aaa	AAA	Very strong ability to meet all obligations
	Aa	AA	Fairly strong ability to meet all obligations
	A	A	Fairly strong ability to meet all obligations, but could be impacted by poor economic conditions
	Baa	BBB	Should meet all obligations, but could be severely impacted by poor economic conditions
Speculative Grade	Ba	BB	Could have trouble fulfilling the long-term portion of the debt obligation
	B	B	Could have significant trouble fulfilling the long-term portion of the debt obligation
	Caa	CCC	Could have significant trouble fulfilling the entire obligation
	D	D	Coupon or principal payments have been missed

Source: Moody's, Standard and Poor's.

Government Bonds The U.S. government offers short-term *bills*, medium-term *notes*, and long-term *bonds*. Federal agencies and foreign countries also issue government bonds. Income from U.S. government and agency bonds may be exempt from taxes at the state level.

Municipal Bonds State and local governments can issue various types of municipal bonds, some with unique investment terms. The income from bonds issued by state and local governments may be exempt from federal taxes. States will normally tax income from bonds issued by other states, but will exempt the income from municipal bonds issued within the state.

Corporate Bonds A for-profit or not-for-profit organization can issue bonds to investors as a way of raising capital. Publicly-traded corporate bonds receive a rating from one of the bond rating agencies. A corporate bond indenture may specify collateral that can be used in case of default.

Structured Products Certain commercial loans can be packaged together by investment companies and sold as debt securities. Borrowers would make loan payments as usual, but amounts would flow past the original lending institutions and be received by outside investors who purchased these loans as structured bond products.

Tangible Property

Investors can exchange tangible property, such as commodities, real estate, and currency. Typical commodities include agricultural products, gold, silver, and oil. An investor can earn cash flows from rent or attempt to earn a rate of return on appreciation of real estate values. Changes in international exchange rates provide an additional form of investing.

Derivatives

Certain investments *derive* their value from other investment products. Many **derivative securities** exist in the marketplace and can be acquired OTC or through a regulated exchange. An investor should understand that derivatives allow profits to be made when market prices both increase and decrease. For example, a **call option** allows investors to make money when stock prices *rise* and a **put option** allows investors to make money when stock values *fall*. A call option would grant an investor the right to *buy* an equity security at a set price. At the same time, a put option would grant an investor the right to *sell* an equity security at a set price. If the right conditions are present, an option holds value because of the set price specified in the contract. Derivative products can either reduce the risks inherent in a portfolio of investments or exponentially increase those risks.

Mutual Funds

A **mutual fund** represents a collective investment account where the money from many different investors is pooled and allocated to various investment products based on an agreed-upon strategy. The mutual fund company must send each investor a *prospectus*, which specifies the contract terms and investment strategy. An example strategy may involve buying equities from only large capitalization (large cap) companies or investing in select commodities. A money market fund invests in low-risk securities set to mature in less than one year and functions as a savings account within an investment portfolio.

A **sales load** might be charged when an investor enters or exits a mutual fund. An annual fee is normally charged to all investors in a fund, but the annual fee is generally lower in cases where an investor also pays a sales load. An investor will generally benefit by paying a sales load and low annual fee in cases where a mutual fund is held long term. An investor might be able to jump from one fund into another within a distinct family of funds administered by the same mutual fund company without incurring an additional sales load.

Asset Allocation

An investor must establish an **asset allocation** method to divide savings among the different investment products available. Many inexperienced investors base allocation decisions upon emotion. Investors may look for the greatest potential return without taking into account overall risks. The risks involved with the various investment products should be compared against an investor's personal circumstances.

A well-structured portfolio of investments will mitigate risks as a whole through *diversification*. A portfolio should include a wide variety of investment products in the form of debt and equity securities. Diversification can be increased by including investment vehicles from

Derivative Securities: An investment product that derives its value from an underlying investment product, such as a bond, stock, or commodity.

Call Option: A derivative agreement that lets an investor buy an investment product at a set price thus allowing an investor to make money when the underlying security is traded above the set price.

Put Option: A derivative agreement that lets an investor sell an investment product at a set price, thus allowing an investor to make money when the underlying security is traded below the set price.

Mutual Fund: An investment account run by a mutual fund company where investor money is pooled and invested per a predefined strategy.

Sales Load: A percentage levied on either the contributions or withdrawals of investor money into or from a mutual fund.

Asset Allocation: Targeted framework of how amounts should be distributed among different categories of investment products to balance between risks and desired return levels.

international markets or by using mutual funds that automatically offer diversification. The goal of diversification involves finding investment products with *uncorrelated* risks.

One class of investment products may grow faster than others, leaving a portfolio bloated in one area. A portfolio can lack diversity over time whereby an investor should *rebalance* the portfolio back to a more varied allocation distribution. As retirement nears, the asset allocation of a portfolio should be restructured to decrease risks and provide an income stream for retirement. A licensed professional should be used to construct a portfolio and manage it over time in relation to various personal matters specific to an investor.

Time Horizon An investor with a longer time horizon can normally expose a portfolio to more risk than an investor nearing retirement. If amounts are held in savings for urgent or unforeseen contingencies, the time horizon should be viewed as very short.

Income Level An investor with strong employment income potential can recover more easily from portfolio losses as compared to an investor with heavy dependence on future investment income.

Portfolio Size Investment losses will appear more significant with a small portfolio in contrast to a large portfolio.

Risk Tolerance An investor's individual preference toward risk should be a consideration.

Summary

The main categories of investment products include equity securities, debt securities, tangible property, derivatives, and mutual funds. The process of transferring investment products can occur through a regulated exchange or over-the-counter. Equity securities tie their value to the free cash flows available to equity holders. Debt securities are issued in the form of bonds by governments, municipalities, and corporations, or by packaging loans into structured products. Mutual fund companies pool investor money and manage the purchase of investment products per an agreed-upon strategy. A diversified portfolio of investment products should be constructed according to an investor's time horizon, income level, portfolio size, and risk tolerance.

15.2   Retirement Plans

Since interest income and investment returns can *compound*, planning early for retirement years can greatly amplify the overall result. Consider an investment portfolio of corporate bonds that generates an average growth of 8% over a 30-year time horizon where the average inflation rate equals 3%. The portfolio as shown in Figure 15.1 would grow in total by a factor of ten; however, the portfolio would only provide *purchasing power* of $41,457 when viewed in present value terms. This example illustrates how compound growth greatly enhances investment value over time, but inflation is also a concern when planning for retirement.

Retirement accounts differ from regular investment accounts in that they convey certain tax advantages. Money inside a retirement account is used to purchase investment products, but some limitations may be imposed. For example, an account holder may not be able to withdraw funds until reaching retirement age without facing penalties. Certain retirement accounts allow penalty-free withdrawals if proceeds are used for exempt purposes, such as covering education or health care costs. Using money in a retirement account to buy property for personal use would also not comply with U.S. tax law. Other investment products that already convey tax advantages, such as municipal bonds, may not generate appropriate returns if placed in a retirement account.

Small businesses that enact a retirement plan must adhere to **nondiscrimination rules**. These rules may differ according to the type of retirement plan adopted, but the expectation

Nondiscrimination Rules: Retirement plan rules that limit high-paid employees from receiving a disproportionate amount of benefits compared to other qualified plan participants.

FIGURE 15.1 Discounted Investment Returns
An investment is shown to grow at 8% in the first row and then amounts are adjusted into present value terms by an estimated inflation rate of 3%. The $10,000 will achieve purchasing power of $41,457 after 30 years according to these assumptions.

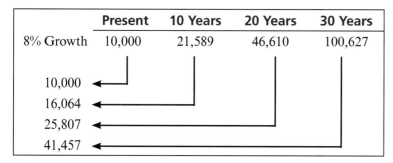

is that high-paid employees will not receive a disproportionately higher amount of benefits. Nondiscrimination rules prevent a health care provider from making contributions personally while disregarding the need to fund the retirement accounts of qualified staff members. If nondiscrimination rules are not followed, a retirement plan can lose its tax advantages.

Eligibility rules exist to define which staff members qualify to participate in a retirement plan. An organization may have the right to omit part-time or brand new employees. Contributions made by an employer on behalf of an employee may not automatically **vest**, requiring an employee to work a certain number of years before amounts officially transfer ownership. In the United States, retirement plan rules are set forth largely in the Employee Retirement Income Security Act (ERISA). Plans should be selected and administered with the help of a licensed professional in order to ensure applicable rules are followed. Table 15.3 presents the retirement plans available in the United States along with specific features of each.

> **Vest:** A requirement that an employee work a certain number of years before employer contributions officially transfer ownership.

Defined Benefit Plan

Very few small businesses enact **defined benefit plans** to fund retirement needs. Such plans define the exact amount that organization members will receive upon retirement based on years of service, salary level, age, or other acceptable criteria. Because an organization is responsible for making *guaranteed* retirement benefits, the tax code requires that the projected future amount of benefits be estimated and minimum amounts be invested each year. Licensed professionals can help project the future benefits, but the risk of not having enough to meet future obligations persuades most small organizations to adopt a more flexible type of retirement plan. Still, a health care provider may be able to save significantly more for retirement with a defined benefit plan than with other plan types.

> **Defined Benefit Plan:** A retirement plan that provides guaranteed benefits during retirement years according to a predetermined formula.

Defined Contribution Plan

Small businesses mainly enact **defined contribution plans** that allow organization members to save money in a tax advantaged retirement account without requiring payment of guaranteed benefits. Account holders may not possess enough for retirement if contributions prove inadequate or investment products do not perform as expected. Individuals over 50 may make additional contributions beyond what a plan ordinarily allows. U.S. tax law provides for several different defined contribution plans, some of which function together as a hybrid plan.

> **Defined Contribution Plan:** A retirement plan where the retirement benefits depend on the total amount contributed and the investment performance of the account portfolio.

TABLE 15.3	Types of Retirement Plans				
	Guaranteed Benefit	Borrowing Possibility	Nondiscrimination Rules	Maximum Contributions	Contribution Source
Defined Benefit Plan	Yes	No	Yes	Very high	Employer
Individual Retirement Arrangement (IRA)					
Traditional IRA	No	No	None	Low	Employee
Roth IRA	No	No	None	Low	Employee
401(k) Plan	No	Yes	Yes	Moderate	Employee*
Savings Incentive Match Plans for Employees (SIMPLE)					
SIMPLE IRA	No	No	Yes	Moderate	Employee*
SIMPLE 401(k)	No	Yes	Yes	Moderate	Employee*
Simplified Employee Pension (SEP-IRA)	No	No	Yes	High	Employer
Qualified Plan (Keogh/HR 10)	No	Yes	Yes	High	Employer
401(k) component	No	Yes	Yes	Moderate	Employee*

*With limited employer match.

Individual Retirement Arrangement (IRA) IRA accounts are personal retirement plans that allow an individual to set aside a small amount each year. A *traditional IRA* allows contributions to be made tax-free. Upon retirement, amounts withdrawn are subject to income taxes. Similar contributions to a *Roth IRA* are made on an after-tax basis and do not receive a tax advantage upfront. However, funds withdrawn at retirement are not subject to taxes. A Roth IRA is preferred if moderate investment returns can compound over a long time horizon, say 15 years or more. Both account types grow tax deferred. Investors cannot borrow against amounts held in an IRA.

401(k) Plan The name given to a 401(k) plan refers to U.S. tax code. A 401(k) plan enacted by a business allows employees to set aside part of their salaries into a retirement account. The maximum contribution allowed by an employee is fairly moderate. The nondiscrimination rules are more complex with a 401(k) plan, but an employer only needs to contribute to a 401(k) account if an employee also personally funds the account through salary reductions.

An organization can provide employees with the option of treating 401(k) deferrals as *Roth* contributions. If a *Roth* election is made, salary reductions are still subject to income taxes, but qualified withdrawals would be tax-free. Investors can take loans against amounts held in a 401(k) account, usually up to 50% of the account balance. Interest charged on a retirement plan loan accrues to the account holder, thus the borrower will personally benefit from the interest charges. A loan may be subject to repayment once an employee leaves an organization unless the 401(k) plan permits the employee to keep the account active.

Savings Incentive Match Plans for Employees (SIMPLE) A SIMPLE plan enacted by a business lets employees set aside money from their salaries into a retirement account that retains characteristics of either an IRA or 401(k) plan. A SIMPLE IRA confers an account to the individual employee whereas a SIMPLE 401(k) is structured as a business plan. In both instances, the employee cannot contribute more than the maximum limit allowed, which is usually a moderate amount. An employer must adhere to nondiscrimination rules with either type of SIMPLE plan. An employer can contribute 2% of gross salary for each qualified employee or match employee contributions up to 3% of gross salary. For example, an employee earning $30,000 per year who sets aside $800 in a SIMPLE plan would receive $600 ($30,000 × 2%) if the first nondiscrimination rule is followed or $800 if the employer adopts the other. Note how the employer would not have to contribute the full $900 ($30,000 × 3%) since the employee only set aside $800. Investors cannot borrow against amounts held in a SIMPLE IRA, but they can take loans against amounts held in a SIMPLE 401(k).

Simplified Employee Pension (SEP) Instead of employees personally funding their retirement accounts through salary reductions, a SEP plan is funded solely through employer contributions. Since the investment accounts are conferred to each individual employee, the plan is considered a SEP-IRA. A *Roth* election is not available. An employer will contribute to SEP-IRA accounts according to a written formula, usually a set percentage rate not to exceed 25% of gross salaries. For example, a health care provider with earned income of $100,000 could receive a maximum of $25,000 ($100,000 × 25%) whereas an employee making $30,000 would only receive $7,500 ($30,000 × 25%) in benefits. A written formula is subject to nondiscrimination rules, thus it cannot favor highly compensated organization members unfairly. Still, an employer can change the written formula each year. Contributions to a SEP-IRA are subject to annual dollar limitations ($50,000 in 2012), which are generally three times greater than what a regular 401(k) plan allows. Investors cannot borrow against amounts held in a SEP-IRA.

Qualified Plan Sometimes referred to as a Keogh or HR 10 plan, a qualified plan is funded solely through employer contributions according to net profit levels, gross salaries, or another written formula. The written formula can change each year. A qualified plan has the same annual flat dollar limitation as a SEP-IRA, but contributions can reach as high as 100% of gross salary. For example, a health care provider with earned income of $100,000 could contribute a maximum of $50,000 (annual limit for 2012) whereas an employee making $30,000 could receive a full $30,000 ($30,000 × 100%) in retirement benefits. A qualified plan can incorporate features of a 401(k) plan, which would allow employees to defer part of their salaries as well. Contributions to a qualified plan or 401(k) component of a qualified plan must adhere to nondiscrimination rules. Investors can take loans against amounts held in a qualified plan or its 401(k) component.

Summary

Investors can place money into a retirement account in order to achieve certain tax advantages. Penalties may apply if money is withdrawn from a retirement account prematurely. An account holder may be able to withdraw funds before retirement for select purposes or borrow a portion of the current account balance. Contributions to a business retirement plan cannot be made in a way that unfairly discriminates in favor of highly compensated organization members. A defined benefit plan requires an organization to provide guaranteed benefits to employees upon retirement. The outcome of a defined contribution plan is uncertain. The amount available upon retirement depends on the total amount contributed and investment performance of an employee's portfolio.

15.3 Insurance Products

What would happen to patients, employees, you, and your family if a catastrophic event occurred? A sizable amount of savings might *not* be enough to cover a major natural disaster, health emergency, or lawsuit. A health care organization should explore insurance products to protect against misfortune and provide alternative investment opportunities.

Life Insurance

In case of untimely death, life insurance products as listed in Table 15.4 can provide for family members as well as cover end-of-life expenses, such as burial costs. Life insurance can be used to pay down financial obligations of the business as well. For example, the person selling assets through a seller-financed loan should take out a life insurance policy on the buyer. If the buyer passes away, insurance proceeds could cover any remaining loan balance. Most life insurance products require that an *economic interest* be present when taking out a policy on another person. Payments made to fund an insurance policy can occur monthly over the life of the policy or upfront during an introductory period.

TABLE 15.4	**Types of Life Insurance**
Term life insurance	
Permanent life insurance • Fixed whole life • Variable whole life • Fixed universal life • Variable universal life	

Term Life Insurance: A life insurance policy that will provide death benefits for a set number of years only.

Permanent Life Insurance: A life insurance policy that will provide death benefits no matter when death occurs and may include a cash value portion that builds over time.

Term life insurance does not usually contain a cash value component.

Annuity: An investment account administered by an insurance company that provides tax-deferred growth and various distribution options.

Term life insurance is more common in business situations because it provides death benefits for only a set time period. **Permanent life insurance** provides a death benefit across an indefinite time period and the policy usually contains a cash value component that builds tax-free and acts like an investment account. In terms of permanent life insurance, a *fixed whole life policy* would pay a defined death benefit using in part the cash value that an investor builds with the insurance company. A *variable whole life policy* would pay a guaranteed minimum death benefit and may provide additional death benefits depending on the investment performance of the cash value that the policyholder directs. *Universal life insurance* products are similar to whole life insurance in that they provide fixed or variable benefits. Universal life insurance provides more flexibility in how premiums can be paid and may allow a policyholder to adjust guaranteed minimum death benefits.

A policyholder can borrow against the cash value component offered by a permanent life insurance policy. If the amount borrowed is not fully repaid, death benefits will be reduced in proportion to the outstanding loan plus interest expense charged by the insurance company. The cash value can also be returned to a policyholder if a permanent life insurance policy is cancelled.

Insurance Annuity

Insurance companies allow investors to save money in an **annuity** account. Amounts placed in an annuity grow tax deferred. Contributions can be made over time or in one lump sum. An annuity may contain a lock-up period where the investor cannot withdraw funds without incurring penalties. A *fixed annuity* is directed by the insurance company and guarantees a set value upon maturity. The value of a *variable annuity* depends on how the underlying investments directed by the annuity holder perform. Combination annuities contain elements of both fixed and variable policies.

An annuity can mature within months if a lump sum is made or after a set number of years. Upon maturity, an annuity holder can withdraw funds immediately in one lump sum, take withdrawals when desired, or *annuitize* the account value. If the maturity value is annuitized, the insurance company will base fixed monthly distributions on the annuity holder's *expected* life span. Annuitized distributions will continue until the annuity holder's death or beneficiary's death, even if the distributions exceed the total value of the annuity. An annuity can benefit an investor in cases where retirement plans are not available or if an investor wants an annuitized distribution plan upon retirement. Some annuities allow investors to borrow against the current balance.

Business Insurance

A *health* insurance policy is necessary to at least cover major medical emergencies. A health care provider has the option to obtain a personal health insurance policy or open coverage through a business policy. A policy held under a business confers different tax advantages and it affords the opportunity to cover qualified employees.

A health care provider should maintain a *disability* policy in case of long-term injury or permanent disability. A disability policy could provide income for the remainder of a health care provider's expected working years in an amount comparable to what could have been earned otherwise, but a disability policy usually ends upon retirement where an insurance company expects the policyholder to rely on retirement assets. Most disability policies have a waiting period of around three to six months before benefits start. A health care organization should always maintain a savings base to protect against urgent or unforeseen events, especially considering an insurance policy may require a deductible or contain a long waiting period before distributing benefits.

Business continuity insurance can cover a temporary interruption in business activity caused by a disaster or accident, such as a fire or earthquake. Such policies normally cover administrative expenses whenever operations cease or slow down due to some sort of catastrophic event. Business continuity insurance would protect against having to lay workers off or default on liability obligations.

A health care organization should obtain a *property and liability* insurance policy to cover any damage or theft of assets and protect against general legal disputes that may arise. A *malpractice* insurance policy is needed to cover legal disputes specific to the presumed mishandling of care. Review policies to ensure the actions of all organization members are properly covered. Imagine if an associate injures a patient and the malpractice policy had not been updated to include the associate.

Business Continuity Insurance: An insurance policy that covers business overhead in case of emergency or disaster.

Business continuity insurance is also referred to as business interruption or asset protection insurance.

Take pictures of equipment and the office for insurance purposes in case of theft or damage.

Summary

Insurance products offer protection against catastrophic events as well as provide investment opportunities. Term life insurance is common in a business situation when the policyholder wants coverage for only a set time period. Permanent life insurance will confer a death benefit no matter the date of death. Differences exist among policy types based on whether the permanent life insurance is fixed or variable, whole or universal. Permanent life insurance contains a cash value portion that a policyholder can borrow against or receive upon policy cancellation. The cash value grows tax deferred and can become part of the future death benefit.

Annuities allow investors to place money with an insurance company and experience tax-deferred growth. Amounts can be withdrawn in one lump sum, as the need arises, or through an annuitized structure. A health care provider should maintain various insurance policies, such as health, disability, business continuity, malpractice, and property and liability insurance.

15.4   Example Financial Plan

A business plan will contain a financial section to evaluate the projected financial value of an organization. A lending institution, the SBA, and other funding sources will not want to fund a venture that cannot generate a positive net present value after consideration of risk and inflation. A cash flow projection does not always need to be created for external parties. The process of compiling a cash flow projection offers a tremendous amount of insight into how an organization operates. The following *hypothetical* financial plan was put together by a beginning health care provider. This health care provider is working in an associate position but wants to form a new organization. All details in this plan are fictitious and the content of your actual financial plan may differ substantially.

Cash Flow Projection

The following assumptions were used to construct a cash flow projection covering my transition into an individual practice and the three-year period thereafter. These assumptions are based on experience with the current patient base in my associate health care provider position, results of historical marketing efforts, and thorough research into the material needs of the upcoming organization.

Macroeconomic Outlook

The economy appears to be recovering from a recession because the Federal Reserve Bank of New York has started increasing interest rates. The business climate should be ideal for starting a new practice and obtaining financing at inexpensive rates. A reputable economic survey reports that the expected rate of inflation will average 4% in each of the next three years.

Industry Outlook

Health care providers operating in the surrounding area have stated that they are extremely happy about net profit levels. My new practice will differentiate itself based on quality, but will not attempt to compete for a particular target market. After speaking with the statewide professional association, I learned that no material legal or regulatory changes are expected over the time period covered by this cash flow projection.

New Patients

Table A shows the total number of new patients over the past 12 months as well as a projection of new patients for the next three years. The number of new patients should decline right after transitioning the patient base because of the disruption caused by moving my location and getting reestablished. The number of new patients in the second quarter of the first year should increase by four. Thereafter, it is projected that one additional new patient will be recruited each quarter until Q2 of Year 3. The organization should reach capacity at that point where ongoing marketing efforts will attempt to stabilize the practice at 75 new patients per quarter. Experience with marketing techniques is steadily increasing and should ensure that this continual growth of new incoming patients will occur as forecasted.

TABLE A	New Patients															
Historical				**Projected**											
Q1	Q2	Q3	Q4	Q1	Q2	Q3	Q4	Q1	Q2	Q3	Q4	Q1	Q2	Q3	Q4
8	12	16	21	12	16	21	27	34	42	51	61	72	75	75	75

Returning Patients

Before starting as an associate with my current employer, we agreed that any patients attracted through personal efforts could be retained. The agreement called for a fee of $50 per each patient who transitions to my new organization. A charge of $50 will accrue once a request for patient records is made. Based on my employer's experience, about 40% of patients reinstitute care within two years from the point their care previously ended. Since I have attracted 57 patients through personal marketing efforts over the past year, an estimated 22 (57 × 40%) patients will restart care at a later point in time.

According to conversations with the patients of my employer, an estimated 10% are expected to use my services if a future need arises. As a result of treating 118 of my employer's patients over the past year and assuming 40% will return for care, an estimated 3 patients (118 × 40% × 10%) will join my new practice at some point.

The cash flow projection also includes nine returning patients in Year 3 who originally started care under the new practice for the first time in Year 1. These patients will not be subject to the $50 fee since they originally started care only at the new practice.

Continuing Patients

Of the 57 patients attracted through personal efforts over the past year, 16 are expected to continue receiving care at my new clinic unabated. Only five of the 118 patients seen by my employer are expected to continue their care using my new practice. An agreement made with my employer requires that $200 be paid for each patient who transitions over to my new practice who was *not* attracted through personal efforts as opposed to $50 for one of my own patients. Because I exercised extreme caution when approaching patients of my current employer, no conflicts of interest or disputes over money are expected.

Patient Margin

Patients seen in the past have conveyed strong positive feedback about my treatment approach. My employer has noted no increase in patient turnover related to the patient base I have treated. My employer calculated that the average patient seen by me provided $875 in revenue. This amount should be approximately 10% less ($788) because of different agreements with select insurance carriers.

Patients who are receiving care during the transition will be considered midway through their care and will only provide an average of $394 ($788 ÷ 2) to the new organization. Collection rates should be similar to my current employer since I will ask for payment upfront. Table B presents the revenue projection based on assumptions about new, returning, and continuing patients along with the corresponding patient margin. Table C summarizes the results of the revenue projection. Since insurance companies typically lag several months before covering their portion of a patient's bill, the actual collection of estimated revenue as shown in Table D has been shifted ahead one quarter to show when much of the cash flow will most likely take place. This projection follows the *cash* method of accounting, which differs from the *accrual* method, and could influence the amount of net present value reported.

TABLE B   Revenue Projection

	Projected											
	Q1	Q2	Q3	Q4	Q1	Q2	Q3	Q4	Q1	Q2	Q3	Q4
New patients	12	16	21	27	34	42	51	61	72	75	75	75
Returning patients[a]	–	–	–	–	–	3	5	6	8	5	6	8
Returning patients[b]	–	–	–	–	–	1	1	1	–	–	–	–
Total patients	12	16	21	27	34	46	57	68	80	80	81	83
Total patients × $788	9,456	12,608	16,548	21,276	26,792	36,248	44,916	53,584	63,040	63,040	63,828	65,404
Continuing patients[a]	16											
Continuing patients[b]	5											
×$394	8,274											

[a]Patients attracted through personal efforts.
[b]Patients that originated from my employer's efforts.

TABLE C   Summary of Revenues

	Projected											
	Q1	Q2	Q3	Q4	Q1	Q2	Q3	Q4	Q1	Q2	Q3	Q4
Revenues	17,730	12,608	16,548	21,276	26,792	36,248	44,916	53,584	63,040	63,040	63,828	65,404

TABLE D   Projected Collections

Amounts have been shifted ahead one quarter to reflect when collections will occur.

	Projected											
	Q1	Q2	Q3	Q4	Q1	Q2	Q3	Q4	Q1	Q2	Q3	Q4
Collections	–	17,730	12,608	16,548	21,276	26,792	36,248	44,916	53,584	63,040	63,040	63,828

Projected Expenses

The expense projection shown in Table E reflects the 14 categories of expenses the new organization is expected to face. The assumptions used to formulate the expense projection are shown below.

TABLE E   Projected Expenses

	Projected											
	Q1	Q2	Q3	Q4	Q1	Q2	Q3	Q4	Q1	Q2	Q3	Q4
1 Salaries and benefits	–	–	–	–	2,880	3,120	3,120	3,120	3,275	3,275	3,275	3,275
2 Advertising	1,150	250	250	250	365	260	260	260	380	270	270	270
3 Dues and subscriptions	270	–	–	–	280	–	–	–	290	–	–	–
4 Entertainment	650	650	650	650	675	675	675	675	700	700	700	700
5 Insurance	924	924	924	924	960	960	960	960	1,000	1,000	1,000	1,000
6 Lease payments	11,400	7,600	7,600	7,600	7,600	7,600	7,600	7,600	7,600	7,600	7,600	7,600
7 Legal and professional	3,360	360	360	360	894	375	375	375	930	390	390	390

TABLE E		Projected Expenses (continued . . .)											
8	Maintenance	100	100	100	100	105	105	105	105	110	110	110	110
9	Miscellaneous	250	250	250	250	260	260	260	260	270	270	270	270
10	Office supplies	355	252	331	426	536	725	898	1,072	1,261	1,261	1,277	1,308
11	Patient charges	1,800	–	–	–	–	350	450	400	200	–	–	–
12	Payroll taxes	–	–	–	–	374	406	406	406	426	426	426	426
13	Utilities	1,200	1,200	1,200	1,200	1,250	1,250	1,250	1,250	1,300	1,300	1,300	1,300
14	Depreciation	5,000	–	–	–	520	–	–	–	540	–	–	–
	Total expenses	26,459	11,586	11,665	11,760	16,699	16,086	16,359	16,483	18,282	16,602	16,618	16,649

1. A part-time receptionist will be hired for $12 per hour in Year 2 to help with seating patients and answering the phone. A $1 raise will be offered after 90 days and then a 5% raise will be given after one year of service.
2. New business cards, brochures, and signage will cost approximately $1,150 at the start. Additional orders of brochures costing $250 will be needed each quarter. Business cards costing $100 to reprint should last an entire year. Design work has already been completed. Amounts adjust for estimated inflation.
3. Six magazine subscriptions averaging $20 each per year will be needed for the waiting room, plus an annual fee of $150 for professional association dues. Amounts adjust per estimated inflation.
4. Each week, a $50 lunch will be brought to a new business in order to build a networking base. The total cost equals $650 per quarter and amounts adjust per estimated inflation.
5. Monthly payments of $20 will be made for universal life insurance, $80 for health insurance, and $208 for malpractice insurance. Amounts adjust per estimated inflation.
6. A leased office space is available for $1,900 per month. The landlord is requiring a set five-year lease with last month's rent and upfront deposit.
7. Legal and accounting fees used to establish an S corporation will amount to $3,000. A certified public accountant can supervise bookkeeping and complete all tax returns for a flat fee of $360 per quarter. An attorney will need to compile documents each year to maintain the corporate business form. Current fees equal $500 and amounts adjust per estimated inflation.
8. The landlord expects to pay for repair and maintenance costs, but $100 is projected to address potential upgrades to the interior each quarter. Amounts adjust per estimated inflation
9. Miscellaneous charges of around $250 per quarter are expected. Amounts adjust per estimated inflation.
10. Office supplies typically correspond to patient revenue at a rate of 2% according to what my current employer experiences.
11. The charge owed to my employer for transitioning each of my own patients equals $50, and then $200 for the patients of my employer.
12. Payroll taxes should equal 13% of salaries and benefits according to a licensed tax professional.
13. Utilities include water, electricity, telephone, and Internet. Charges are currently $300 per month and this amount adjusts per estimated inflation.
14. Most furniture and equipment needs have been fulfilled. An additional $5,000 of furniture and equipment is expected at first as well as $500 each year to cover upgrade costs. The projected amount of $500 is adjusted per estimated inflation. The full amount of depreciation should be allowed in the year assets are placed in service per Section 179 of the U.S. tax code.

Projected Net Cash Flows

The net cash flows remaining after deducting projected expenses from projected collections are show in Table F. A source of capital is required to cover the cash shortfall in Q1 of Year 1.

TABLE F	Net Cash Flows											
	Projected											
	Q1	Q2	Q3	Q4	Q1	Q2	Q3	Q4	Q1	Q2	Q3	Q4
Collections	–	17,730	12,608	16,548	21,276	26,792	36,248	44,916	53,584	63,040	63,040	63,828
Expenses	26,459	11,586	11,665	11,760	16,699	16,086	16,359	16,483	18,282	16,602	16,618	16,649
Cash flows	(26,459)	6,144	943	4,788	4,577	10,706	19,889	28,433	35,302	46,438	46,422	47,179

Terminal Activity

Activity after Year 3 has not been included in this analysis. By including such information into the cash flow projection, the net present value of the practice might increase. This projection isolates the first three years to better examine near-term cash flow needs.

Cash Flow Evaluation

A 21% risk premium is assumed in addition to the expected inflation rate of 4%.

NPV and IRR

Based on a combined discount rate of 25%, the projected cash flow stream will possess a net present value of $118,829. The internal rate of return equals 36%. Calculations were performed using financial functions in Microsoft Excel. The amount of net present value would be larger if the *accrual* method was used instead of the *cash* method and terminal activity was included after Year 3.

Payback Period

Ignoring personal expenses, the initial loss in Q1 of ($26,459) should be fully recovered by Q2 of Year 2 using *undiscounted* cash flows as presented in Table G. If personal expenses and student loan payments total $2,000 per month, a negative balance in total should persist until Q4 of Year 2. Personal expenses extend the payback period by approximately six months.

TABLE G	Payback Period (undiscounted)											
	Projected											
	Q1	Q2	Q3	Q4	Q1	Q2	Q3	Q4	Q1	Q2	Q3	Q4
Cash flows	(26,459)	6,144	943	4,788	4,577	10,706	19,889	28,433	35,302	46,438	46,422	47,179
Personal expenses	(6,000)	(6,000)	(6,000)	(6,000)	(6,240)	(6,240)	(6,240)	(6,240)	(6,490)	(6,490)	(6,490)	(6,490)
Personal income	(32,459)	144	(5,057)	(1,212)	(1,663)	4,466	13,649	22,193	28,812	39,948	39,932	40,689

Funding Sources

A personal home currently has $60,000 of equity value. A lending institution will offer a home equity line of credit (HELOC) for 75% of this amount. The entire available HELOC of $45,000 should not be needed. The projected negative cash flow deficit inclusive of personal expenses may total $40,246 at its worst. Since the HELOC is secured by a home, the interest rate will be approximately 5.75%. Interest charges will equal roughly $2,500 per year if the entire balance remains open on the line of credit. The HELOC should be fully repaid after Q4 of Year 2.

Two additional sources of capital exist in case the practice does not perform as expected. A personal 401(k) plan was funded over the last year with total employee and employer contributions of $6,000. The amount has been placed in a low-risk money market fund. Per the plan administrator, 50% of this balance could be borrowed. If the need arises, the total sum of $6,000 could be liquidated but will be subject to taxes and a 10% penalty payable in the next calendar year. The tax liability generated from the liquidation of this account should be low due to offsetting business losses. A universal life insurance policy has been in effect for six years and has a cash value of $3,000. The insurance company would permit 75% of this amount to be borrowed. The full $3,000 would be available if the insurance policy is canceled. Certain business and personal expenses can also be reduced if the practice does not perform as expected. For example, a part-time employee will not be hired if the practice does not earn sufficient revenue in the first year.

Profitability Analysis

The projected cash flows may not materialize as expected. The following analyses show the current strength of operations and the extent that actual cash flows could vary before the new organization starts to face financial problems.

Ratio Analysis

The ratios listed in Table H were compiled to better understand operating performance over the next three years. The operating ratio drops significantly showing that fewer expenses will be needed to generate revenue in later periods. The marketing ratio also declines to 2% by Year 3. Such a low percentage shows that positive word of mouth will play a strong role in attracting new patients instead of marketing expenditures. The net profit margin will also grow precipitously over the first three years.

TABLE H	Financial Ratios		
	Year 1	Year 2	Year 3
Operating ratio	131%	51%	28%
Marketing ratio	10%	3%	2%
Net profit margin	−31%	49%	72%

Sensitivity Analysis

The analysis reflected in Table I shows what would happen if collections dropped by 20% because of decreased revenue levels. This analysis examines the impact that unforeseen events could have on current estimations. Although this analysis only reflects a 20% decline, the degree of impact helps to illustrate the organization's overall sensitivity to events. This analysis assumes that office supplies are the only expense that will vary according to revenue levels. Also, a part-time employee would not be hired in Year 2 under this scenario.

TABLE I	Sensitivity Analysis											
	Projected											
	Q1	Q2	Q3	Q4	Q1	Q2	Q3	Q4	Q1	Q2	Q3	Q4
Collections	−	14,184	10,086	13,238	17,021	21,434	28,998	35,933	42,867	50,432	50,432	51,062
Expenses	26,388	11,536	11,599	11,674	13,338	12,415	12,654	12,742	14,329	12,649	12,661	12,686
Cash flows	(26,388)	2,648	(1,512)	1,564	3,683	9,019	16,345	23,190	28,539	37,783	37,771	38,376

The IRR would fall to 29% under this scenario but would still remain slightly higher than the discount rate of 25%. The net present value of the organization would equal $86,509. This 20% drop in collections would cause the organization's value to drop by 27%. Ignoring any discounting of cash flows, the payback period would occur sometime in Q3 of Year 2. If personal expenses were included in this analysis, the payback period would not occur until Q1 of Year 3 as demonstrated in Table J.

TABLE J	Payback Period (Sensitivity Analysis)											
	Projected											
	Q1	Q2	Q3	Q4	Q1	Q2	Q3	Q4	Q1	Q2	Q3	Q4
Cash flows	(26,388)	2,648	(1,512)	1,564	3,683	9,019	16,345	23,190	28,539	37,783	37,771	38,376
Personal expenses		(6,000)	(6,000)	(6,000)	(6,000)	(6,240)	(6,240)	(6,240)	(6,240)	(6,490)	(6,490)	(6,490)	(6,490)
Personal income	(32,388)	(3,352)	(7,512)	(4,436)	(2,557)	2,779	10,105	16,950	22,049	31,293	31,281	31,886

The organization would have a maximum projected financing need of $50,245 under this scenario. The HELOC would cover $45,000 of this need. Loans made against a personal 401(k) plan and life insurance policy could cover an additional $5,250 ($3,000 + $2,250) of the estimated cash flow need. The organization appears able to sustain a 20% drop in projected collections by a narrow margin of $5 ($45,000 + $5,250 − $50,245). If collections fall more than this, the new organization would need to consider other financing options, including liquidating the 401(k) plan and life insurance policy.

Business Form

The organization will operate as an S corporation, which should reduce the cost of payroll taxes owed personally. S corporation status with the IRS will allow all business information to flow to the individual level. No taxes will be due at the corporate level. The net loss occurring in the first year will not give rise to an income tax liability and it should carry forward reducing the income tax liability in subsequent years. Personal deductions for home mortgage interest, education loan interest, and real estate taxes should further reduce taxable income.

Status as an S corporation should provide personal protection in case of bankruptcy. However, the HELOC used to fund the practice is secured by a personal home. If default occurs, the home could be put into foreclosure. The HELOC does not require repayment at set intervals but the bank must approve the HELOC annually.

CHAPTER ASSIGNMENT

Working in a group of three to four students or fellow professionals, complete the following items.

1. What is the difference between selling an investment product over-the-counter versus through a regulated exchange?

2. How does acquiring common stock in a company translate into equity ownership? What rights does equity ownership bestow? Provide a definition for IPO and market capitalization.

3. Why would an investor care if a bond held in an investment account falls from a BBB rating to a BB rating?

4. Explain the four categories of bonds and give an example of each.

5. What type of investment product would base its value on another investment product, such as oil or common stock?

6. Go online and find examples of mutual fund strategies. Why might paying a one-time sales load benefit an investor as compared to paying high annual fees?

7. How do the tax advantages and compound growth in a retirement account shape how the account balance will grow over time?

8. Which retirement plans expect employees to make contributions? Which retirement plans allow account holders to borrow against their current balance?

9. What personal criteria should an account holder examine when determining how to allocate funds among different investment products?

10. Explain the difference between term and permanent life insurance. What categories of permanent life insurance exist?

11. What are the five categories of business insurance policies? What types of policies could protect a health care provider who is seriously injured in an automobile accident?

12. Review the revenue and expense assumptions used in this chapter's example financial plan. How do these differ from the ones listed in Appendix III?

Entrepreneurship

AUTHOR'S NOTE

This textbook took nine years to develop and two years to write—well, the third attempt took two years to write. Don't expect to create a thriving organization overnight. Work each day toward building the knowledge and know-how you will need to succeed. If you have read thus far, you have shown a clear dedication toward acquiring business skills. It may still take several more years before you gain strength with business concepts and can fully apply them to business situations. Set goals and action steps in relation to the core strengths you possess and work to overcome any personal or business weaknesses.

As Aristotle maintained, "You are what you repeatedly do. Excellence is not an event—it is a habit." Solidifying good habits will expand your capacity to deal with challenges related to starting and operating a business. Getting an early start on developing marketing skills will support the future generation of revenue streams. Knowledge of accounting and finance will enable you to capture and analyze business information. This final section on management is meant to turn a business into a cohesive organization where all parts work together symbiotically.

Almost anyone can start and run a business. Becoming a true entrepreneur means standing upon a foundation of knowledge and know-how in order to create something dynamic and solid. An entrepreneur works hard to reach the highest rungs of success possible for a venture. Success requires a willingness to learn, openness to change, and resilience to make forward progress each and every day. The accumulation of business skills will slowly turn feelings of fear and anxiety into the upshot of foresight and achievement. The freedom that comes from running an organization cannot be fully enjoyed unless risks and emotions are properly managed. A well-managed organization allows more time and energy to be dedicated to health care matters instead of business concerns. Strong management also facilitates a successful livelihood in terms of compensation and personal satisfaction.

Setting out to start an organization should involve a thorough analysis of what seems feasible in a given marketplace. An entrepreneur will want to explore different options to find the right opportunity. Putting together a business plan will add to the knowledge and experience needed to make a specific venture successful. As a way of avoiding disorder, an entrepreneur can slowly develop a health care organization over time and judge progress toward goals using predetermined metrics.

Ask for help but avoid placing demands and relying on others.

A support network of family members, friends, and other professionals can provide assistance in numerous ways. An entrepreneur should never feel timid asking others for help. Starting and operating an organization will present major challenges and working with others to overcome them should be considered part of the adventure.

16.1   The Entrepreneur

In order to take an idea and transform it into something tangible in the marketplace, a person must decide to undertake a new venture and become a business owner. The typical emotions of fear, uncertainty, and doubt (FUD) will inevitably surface, but knowledge and experience will help to mitigate those emotions. To illustrate this point, consider a car mechanic attempting to fix a car without any tools. The car mechanic might encounter a high degree of FUD because the task seems impossible without proper equipment. In much the same way, an entrepreneur must accumulate a toolbox of skills to apply toward

CONQUER YOUR FEARS

Public speaking often provokes fear in people, yet a health care provider needs to feel comfortable talking to others. What are some ways to overcome such adverse feelings and develop strong public speaking skills? A health care provider could become a member of Toastmasters International, a community organization that provides a structured forum for members to work on their public speaking skills. Communication courses are normally available at local (community) colleges during the evening. Organize your own speaking group using family, friends, classmates, or other professionals to work on building public speaking skills as well as other business skills.

situations that might arise. As the capacity to take on future challenges increases, the emotions of FUD should eventually decline. Often, the required skill set rests outside the scope of health care. Overlooking or resisting the need to adopt a diverse set of business skills will make starting and operating a successful health care organization more difficult.

Vision

Entrepreneurship begins with an idea. The idea could involve a broad vision for the future or relate to some minor thought. If an entrepreneur struggles with the creative process, structure can be set in place to facilitate the expansion of ideas.

1. Meet regularly with other professionals to brainstorm ideas.
2. Uncover ideas by reading appropriate books, journals, or websites.
3. Document ideas in writing and slowly map out context around them.
4. Schedule time to concentrate alone and consider ideas holistically.

Goal Setting

Bringing an idea to life will prove challenging without setting specific goals. Goals keep the mind focused, assist with motivation, and foster a sense of purpose. Display goals prominently either at home or work using a dry eraser board or other bulletin board mounted on a wall as illustrated by Figure 16.1. Linking goals together (where applicable) can identify how to focus resources best. Central goals within this framework can reinforce what matters the most while secondary goals can highlight additional plans for the future.

The process undertaken to reach a particular goal should be clearly outlined through detailed *action steps*. These action steps should present a realistic path that takes shape incrementally over time. Action steps should be reviewed and adjusted as circumstances change.

FIGURE 16.1
Goal Board

Central Goal:

Hire a receptionist after revenues hit $75,000

Secondary Goal:

Streamline processes to decrease administrative duties

Action Steps:

■ Review interview techniques

■ Prepare to hold staff meetings

■ Find a payroll service

Implementation

Confronting a major decision or working intently on making ideas come alive can take tremendous resolve and sacrifice. There must be a good reason to take on risks, alter standards of living, or put forth tremendous effort toward launching an idea. Market research and discussions with successful business owners can provide useful insight into what ideas will work. Drafting a business plan, forming a support network, and considering details in advance will reduce the anxiety felt about implementing new ideas. Associated risks can be managed through knowledge and experience, but an entrepreneur might still feel uneasy about launching a major venture or encounter skepticism from community members.

An entrepreneur must come to terms with any perceived risks and possess a high degree of desire to undertake the action steps needed to reach a goal. Ideas, goals, and action steps that engender happiness or passion are generally easier to pursue.

Leadership

The path toward success does not always follow a clear course or satisfy all parties involved. Leadership means letting go of secure situations and venturing into unknown territory with only a foundation of knowledge and experience. Keeping an organization progressing forward may require taking charge of situations and walking ahead of the crowd. An entrepreneur must embody the vision of an organization at all times even when no one else may understand or care about that vision.

An entrepreneur may need to implement action steps without assistance from others. It becomes important to overcome personal weaknesses and further develop strengths. The natural reaction when faced with stress or uncertainty is to push responsibility onto others. Actions may negatively impact organization members, family members, friends, or a significant other. For example, it would not be uncommon for an entrepreneur to see friendships fade as success grows. An entrepreneur must approach matters holistically and remain mature about handling challenges.

Maturity

Starting a practice will let loose a cascade of future events with both good and bad consequences. An entrepreneur needs to fully consider potential outcomes and develop ways to deal with the corresponding emotions. Imagine a situation where a patient becomes angry over a billing error. Taking a course on conflict resolution might improve your ability to understand the anger, calm emotions, and provide a meaningful solution. An assertiveness training course might instill the confidence needed to maintain composure during an emotionally charged exchange. What other courses could help prepare an entrepreneur for emotional challenges?

An entrepreneur must have the maturity to accept responsibility for past decisions, clear away negative feelings, and find the resolve to move forward. If left unchecked, emotions can compile and create an unhealthy distraction. Impetuous reactions will not realistically move an organization forward. It becomes necessary to discover innovative solutions and resolve matters expeditiously instead of dwelling on past events or taking thoughtless actions.

Motivation

Working for oneself can be challenging without self-imposed structure. An entrepreneur must get into the habit of initiating activities and following through until completion using nothing more than personal resolve. Setting action plans into small, easy-to-manage stages makes the process of reaching goals seem less overwhelming. To initiate efforts and remain motivated throughout the day, especially in light of any unpleasant tasks, artificial structure should be imposed.

1. Plan relaxation at set time periods so that down time can be anticipated instead of taken spontaneously.
2. Create a sense of urgency and overcome procrastination by setting deadlines.
3. Impose consequences if work does not get done, such as the loss of a personal monetary allowance.
4. Ensure the work environment is free from unnecessary distractions, such as computer games.
5. Decorate the workspace with energizing colors and furniture.
6. Get to work on time, log in hours, and stick to a set schedule.
7. Place work in plain sight, especially items considered unpleasant.
8. Consume healthy foods and beverages that support high energy levels.

Orderliness

An entrepreneur must learn how to multitask a diverse workload. All workspaces should be neatly organized and free of messes. Systems should be put in place to make sure the workload is completed. Internal controls can ensure that processes are performed as specified. A practice management software program may contain an appointment calendar that could double as a workload calendar. Microsoft Outlook has a computerized calendar system that can send automatic alerts so tasks are not missed. A cell phone or personal digital assistant (PDA) may have a calendar system as part of its functionality that automatically syncs with Microsoft Outlook or a specific calendar program. Consider carrying around a daily planner to keep track of events and write down information. Consider offering patients a daily planner to keep them organized as well.

Regulation

Rules ensure that processes remain structured and that the workload is performed diligently. Rules could apply to keeping the office clean and tidy. The front area of an office must be maintained throughout the day or it can negatively impact the patient experience. Imagine putting forth tremendous effort to provide quality health care services only to find that patients complain about a dirty restroom. Enact rules for handling patient records. For example, an organization can have a rule that states no one can leave for the day until all chart notes have been fully compiled. Enact deadlines for when work should be completed. For instance, if a patient leaves a phone message, the phone call must be returned within 24 hours. A good set of rules will give organization members guidelines to follow and introduce discipline into the work environment.

Excellence

An entrepreneur needs to uphold high standards and take every opportunity to surpass expectations. Patient care must reach a level of quality that will guarantee positive word of mouth. Remembering information on patients, offering free secondary services, and paying attention to sacrifices will greatly enhance the patient experience. Open multidirectional channels of communication with patients, network participants, and referral sources to uncover problems, find solutions, and enact positive change.

DIALOGUE

WRONG
Provider: Call me if you ever have concerns.

RIGHT
Provider: I would like you to call me immediately with any concerns that arise. I welcome patient phone calls. I am here to help you all hours of the day.

Discussion Most patients will hesitate to contact an organization and voice concerns, especially outside of regular business hours. Take the time to understand the patient's point of view and communicate a *narrative* that is both calming and motivating.

Seek out complaints proactively and find meaningful solutions to keep your organization progressing forward. Work to prevent underlying events that give rise to the original complaints. For instance, if patients start complaining about traffic congestion, hold conversations to figure out what type of scheduling environment will favor patients. Give patients the power to control a situation and make suggestions.

An entrepreneur must be willing to learn early and learn often. Complete education and training beyond the minimum requirements and involve staff members. Take ownership of weaknesses and ask for constructive criticism to find a path toward growth and transformation. Discover more about yourself in a mature fashion and implement goals and action steps that will allow you to evolve personally and professionally.

Community Leader

A health care provider must become a respected figure within a vast community of people. It becomes important to feel a high degree of empathy for others and listen to concerns with interest. By taking time to understand what others experience (theory of mind), a health care provider will make people feel important and build a strong reputation throughout the community as a true provider of care. Professional sales techniques offer ideas on how to foster long-lasting relationships better.

Being an entrepreneur in the health care field requires a high level of professionalism at work and during off hours. A health care provider may encounter patients or come across opportunities to market at random. Maintain a clean appearance out in public even when running a quick errand. Any controversial topics that will raise eyebrows or blood pressure should be avoided. Running a health care practice will require making a firm commitment to patients, staff members, and the surrounding community.

> Theory of mind is a concept in psychology referring to a person's ability to consider how other people may be experiencing life.

1. Volunteer with community organizations and donate to local causes.
2. Support local businesses by referring patients and obtaining products and services from them.
3. Cultivate relationships in a meaningful way by remembering information and remaining in contact.

Summary

Emotions that arise when faced with the challenge of starting and operating a health care organization can be calmed with experience and knowledge. Becoming a successful entrepreneur involves accumulating good habits and a diverse set of skills. An idea should be carried through to fruition using goals and action steps. Implementing action steps occurs more easily when the work involved provides personal satisfaction. An entrepreneur will need to keep motivated over time, especially if work includes any unpleasant tasks. Artificial structure can increase the ability to become motivated and complete tasks on time. Organization members need to remain organized and adhere to rules when performing work in order to prevent a disordered work environment. Every attempt should be made to conduct oneself as a professional and provide patients with the best experience possible.

16.2   Feasibility Analysis

An entrepreneur should explore a collection of options to find the best conditions in which to launch a venture. A **feasibility analysis** is used to list all the preliminary opportunities being considered and isolate the key features of each. An entrepreneur needs to have a refined sense of what market participants want (and do not want) and what is involved with a particular venture. A feasibility analysis may include the option to work as an associate, form a new organization, or purchase an established practice. Table 16.1 lists ways to transition into a personally owned health care practice.

> Feasibility Analysis: A review of business opportunities to isolate the one option that will offer the most financial value and personal satisfaction.

The feasibility questionnaire shown in Table 16.2 is used to make initial inquiries into a potential opportunity. The best three to four opportunities should be selected

TABLE 16.1	Transition Options

A health care provider can transition into a personal practice in the following ways:

1. Work as an associate and be paid a salary; retain the right to hold onto patients who were personally attracted.
2. Pay for space as well as the use of office resources, but maintain full control over your patient base as well as patient revenue.
3. Form a new organization alone or with others.
4. Buy a large practice all at once or over several years.
5. Buy a small practice to add patients to an existing practice.
6. Work for a franchising company and buyout the franchise later.
7. Work outside of health care or in a related field and build a practice on the side.

TABLE 16.2	**Feasibility Questionnaire**

Marketing Potential

Has an in-depth territory worksheet been compiled on the marketplace?
What persons could serve as network participants or referral sources?
How much time, energy, and money will need to go toward marketing?
Should marketing efforts be focused on the general community or a target market?

Service Potential

Is there any potential legislation that could have an impact on services?
What core services will be offered and at what price?
What secondary lines of service will be offered and at what price?
If buying a practice, what types of services are currently performed and at what price?

Location Potential

What type of commute must patients endure at different times of the day?
Does the area inside and outside of the proposed building appear professional?
Can the inside be renovated to meet the needs of patients and staff members?
Will patients have easy access to the building and surrounding amenities?

Growth Potential

How might the surrounding area change over the next five years?
How might competition evolve in the future?
Should the proposed organization grow in stages?
What additional skills are needed to grow the proposed organization?

Management Potential

What kind of staff members will the proposed organization need?
How will the internal systems be structured, such as billing and scheduling?
How much experience is needed to properly handle this type of organization?
If buying a practice, does the current organization contain any major deficiencies?

Risk Potential

What is the greatest potential risk to success with this option?
Do any foreseeable economic or marketplace risks exist?
How will the proposed organization react if profit levels prove insufficient?
What do successful business owners say about this option?

Return Potential

How much revenue could the proposed organization generate?
What amount of fixed and variable expenses will be needed to support revenues?
How will the proposed organization be taxed at various governmental levels?
What is the net present value of all future free cash flows?

Satisfaction Potential

Does the marketplace offer enough profit for health care providers to remain satisfied?
Will organization members work well together?
Could this option negatively impact a significant other, family member, or friend?
Will this option evoke passion and happiness personally?

The different parts of a business plan are shown at the end of the marketing, finance, and management sections of this book, respectively.

and reviewed in greater depth according to each category noted. This process of asking questions and seeking answers should reveal the one opportunity that presumably offers the greatest overall benefit with all things considered. A full business plan should be put together on this one opportunity to confirm that the anticipated venture will offer enough value. Preparing a business plan might show that a selected venture has major drawbacks that were not previously considered. When a business plan shows that a venture will provide a high degree of financial value and personal satisfaction, an entrepreneur should consider moving forward with starting the actual organization.

Summary

A feasibility analysis begins with a list of business opportunities that may exist for a health care provider and involves narrowing down that list through a feasibility questionnaire. The results of the feasibility questionnaire support the effort to explore opportunities in greater depth and pinpoint the one single opportunity that would provide the most value. Putting together a business plan on a selected venture helps confirm that sufficient value will be available.

16.3   Enterprise Development

An organization needs to provide an overall positive experience from day one. The process of assembling an organization that conveys an atmosphere of warmth and healing can take a considerable amount of time, but steps toward this goal can be initiated while a person is still in school or employed as an associate. Creating a marketing plan, building a network, and conducting marketing campaigns should begin as soon as possible. Items that might be needed for a future organization can be *identified* in advance. Such items can be budgeted for and then purchased later once the needs of a specific organization become apparent. Compile a comprehensive list of items according to the following categories.

A tax deduction occurs once an item is placed into service. Items purchased in advance can be deducted later once an organization begins operations.

1. Decorations, furniture, magazine subscriptions, and books.
2. Computers, software programs, and network devices.
3. Diplomas, licenses, and accolades placed within nice frames.
4. General office supplies as well as billing (invoice), collection, and insurance forms.
5. Medical supplies and equipment, including a filing cabinet for patient records.

A health care provider should begin communicating in a specific manner with network participants and referral sources once a particular venture has been selected. Dialogue *applications* and *narratives* should be modified to fit a specific venture. A grand opening should be announced once it becomes certain that an organization will start accepting patients. An organization should increase marketing efforts and launch new marketing campaigns to foster growth of the patient base.

Staged Growth

An organization should consider growing in stages and making expenditures strategically. Financial problems can emerge if resources are expended too quickly even when product or service demand appears strong. A large timing difference between cash inflows and outflows can lead to a cash shortfall, higher debt levels, and even bankruptcy. Maintaining a savings base will help in case of an urgent or unforeseen event. Money held in savings should reside in a low-risk money market fund or government-insured savings account.

An organization should start with the minimum set of items needed to ensure a high-quality patient experience and grow in planned stages thereafter. It may not be necessary to have staff members when first opening doors to the public. A growth plan could establish a staff position as part-time at first and then outline how to expand the position to full-time. Specific fixed asset and remodeling needs can wait until patient volume increases.

An organization can set metrics that specify when to move to the next stage of a growth plan. For example, an associate could be hired once revenue levels increase to $15,000 per month. The following list of actions should be considered when forming a growth plan.

1. Replace or add furniture, decorations, and equipment.
2. Open or close service lines and change prices.
3. Hire new staff members or change job duties.
4. Provide more employee benefits.
5. Transition to a new location or remodel the current office.
6. Initiate major marketing campaigns.

Contingency Plan

If an organization later falls below a growth metric it had surpassed earlier, certain actions may need to be reversed. A different base set of metrics could trigger new actions if business activity declines too much. To maintain sufficient profit levels, an organization might reduce an employee's hours or terminate a position. A *contingency plan* should outline how each expense account could be reduced or eliminated if necessary. A contingency plan must consider the importance of a particular expense in terms of revenue production. Removing expenses may bring down revenue levels, actually resulting in a reduction of net profit.

A contingency plan should include a section on how to prepare an organization for bankruptcy if profit levels fall excessively low. This section should outline robust measures meant to reestablish profitability according to the reason for bankruptcy, that is, poor financial management, catastrophic event, or inability to recruit and retain patients. A new marketing plan might need to be drafted centering on grassroots marketing campaigns and other low-cost marketing efforts. Consider focusing resources around core services that offer the highest profit margins. An organization should contact all parties to whom it owes money in order to investigate the option of modifying repayment terms. A borrower may be able to work with the Small Business Administration to renegotiate loan terms with any lending institution. Put together a *turnaround plan* detailing how an organization could best make payments to vendors and lending institutions and satisfy obligations over time.

A *succession plan* should also be formulated to know how to handle a business owner's untimely death or anticipated departure. A succession plan must detail how to wind down operations, sell a business, or purchase back a partner's equity share, especially if a partner's significant other or dependent relies on income from the business. A list of related professionals could be included to know which persons to contact for assistance. A budget should outline how much to pay employees and other professionals helping with related administrative duties.

Skills Accumulation

To attain a high level of success, it is necessary to learn as much as possible about business by taking classes, reading books, and exploring existing organizations. Attend business classes, workshops, or events through a regional Small Business Administration (SBA) office or a local community college. Obtain the motivation to learn new software programs and marketing techniques. A health care provider should have a proven marketing ability in regard to recruiting and retaining patients before attempting to operate a business. The accumulation of skills can offset any negative emotions that might arise.

Organization members should receive ongoing training through continuing education classes, seminars, publications, and so forth—and cross-train with each other. For example, an office manager could attend a weekend seminar alone and summarize key information at the next staff meeting using handouts. Every organization member would learn about what took place during the seminar and the handouts could be referenced in future time periods. As skills accumulate, organization members become more valuable and their ability to face challenges improves.

Many recent graduates fail to explore how the office they are currently working within operates. Seize upon this opportunity!

Summary

Many of the essential items that a future organization will need can be identified in advance. Once an organization is ready to start operations, expenditures can occur in stages. A growth plan can protect an organization from becoming overextended financially. Metrics can be used to specify when to move to the next stage of a growth plan. An organization should draft various contingency plans to understand how to approach major events that might occur. Organization members should take every opportunity to gather additional skills and cross-train with each other as a way of developing an enterprise further.

16.4   Balanced Scorecard

Balanced Scorecard: A management device used to outline goals and identify when goals are being met.

Setting goals will greatly enhance an entrepreneur's ability to lead an organization toward a desired vision. Drs. Robert Kaplan and David Norton devised a **balanced scorecard** system in the 1990s to organize goals and combine them with distinct metrics. The four categories they outlined in their system included financial, customer (patient), internal processes, and learning perspectives:

1. Financial Perspective Entails cash flow management and financial health.
2. Patient Perspective Encompasses ways to improve the patient experience.
3. Internal Processes Perspective Considers the job duties of organization members.
4. Learning Perspective Focuses on the improvement of skill sets and job satisfaction.

Metrics attempt to clarify when goals are being reached and to what extent an organization needs to make improvements. Actual results should be compared to the metrics listed on the balanced scorecard with some frequency and discussed during meetings with staff members or participants of a support network. A balance scorecard should be prominently displayed in the back-office area and at home. Action steps outlining how to reach goals can be listed on the scorecard itself or on a separate document. Figure 16.2 represents an example balance scorecard and follows with related action steps.

FIGURE 16.2 Balanced Scorecard

Balanced Scorecard			
Financial Perspective		**Patient Perspective**	
Goal	Metric	Goal	Metric
Increase revenues	Year 1: 8% increase each quarter Year 2: 5% increase each quarter	Improve the overall patient experience	The results of our patient survey should be greater than 85%
Improve savings	Minimum of $15,000	Focus more on a target market	Talk to a member of our target market each week
Decrease leverage	Assets to liabilities ratio greater than 1.25	Reduce patient wait times	No more than 15 minutes
Internal Processes Perspective		**Learning Perspective**	
Goal	Metric	Goal	Metric
Digitize note taking	Training will be done by December and implementation by January	Finish the business plan	Marketing section will be done by May and the financial section by June
Improve staff communication	Schedule a monthly staff meeting and review patient activity daily	Learn how to recruit high-quality staff members	Review five books on interviewing and practice techniques with someone in my support network
Reduce insurance billing errors	Keep under 3% of forms filed	Increase personal motivation	Complete a daily "To Do List"

FINANCIAL ACTION STEPS

Increase revenues: Positive word of mouth will help attain the desired growth rates in patient revenue. An estimated 20 hours will need to be spent each quarter practicing professional sales techniques with other individuals to improve personal marketing skills. Three other health care providers have shown interest in meeting once per month.

Improve savings: Place approximately 5% of net profit each month in a savings account until the $15,000 minimum is reached.

Decrease leverage: After setting aside 5% of net profit into a savings account and distributing amounts to cover personal expenses, the remainder needs to be used to reduce debt levels.

PATIENT ACTION STEPS

Improve the overall patient experience: Put together a survey addressing the main concerns that patients face. The survey should be no more than four questions and contain a rating system on a scale of 1 to 5, where a 5 response is best. Distribute the survey to a random selection of 50 patients.

Focus more on a target market: In order to improve job satisfaction and increase revenue levels, more patients should come from a specific target market. Narratives need to be compiled along with a relevant territory worksheet. An organization member needs to research the best sources of food to bring to sales luncheons.

Reduce patient wait times: Patients need to be transitioned from the waiting room within 15 minutes into either a treatment room or a room with free preliminary or secondary services. An organization member needs to talk with patients and apologize if wait times exceed 30 minutes in total.

INTERNAL PROCESSES ACTION STEPS

Digitize note taking: A net present value calculation showed that a new electronic note-taking system would save the organization money, especially when considering the equivalent hourly rate of the health care provider's time. Training should end by December to verify that organization members can run the system as intended.

Improve staff communication: A bulletin board in the back-office area needs to be updated daily with the number of total patient visits, number of missed visits, and corresponding lost revenue. This information must be discussed during regular staff meetings.

Reduce insurance billing errors: Insurance companies will not pay claims until the form is correct. In order to attain revenue metrics and reduce inefficiency, insurance forms need to be done properly the first time.

LEARNING ACTION STEPS

Finish the business plan: Although operations have started, a business plan still needs to be completed in order to acquire financing for a later stage of a growth plan [not shown]. The management section is done, but the marketing and finance sections are still unfinished. The marketing section should include more detail on our target market.

Learn how to recruit high-quality staff members: More experience is needed with interviewing techniques in order to find high-quality employees. Three other health care providers have shown interest in meeting once per month to practice interviewing.

Increase personal motivation: In an effort to reach goals, a written *To Do List* must be completed each day before watching TV at home or surfing the Internet.

Summary

A balanced scorecard outlines goals according to financial, patient, internal processes, and learning perspectives. Metrics are then aligned with each goal in order to identify when a goal is being met. Action steps should accompany the balanced scorecard in order to provide detail on how best to attain goals. A balanced scorecard should be placed somewhere visible in the back-office area for all organization members to review. Actual results should be frequently compared to the established metrics and discussed during staff meetings.

16.5   Support Network

Do not reinvent the wheel!

Part of managing a business involves accessing the expertise and support of other entrepreneurs and business professionals. Ask for advice on how to approach a situation instead of figuring out everything from scratch. Patients, family members, or a significant other should not be used as a source of support unless the situation seems appropriate. Heavy or improper reliance on such persons could strain relationships.

1. Maintain contact with SBA officials and lending institution personnel in case a capital need suddenly arises.
2. Establish a *brainstorming group* with other entrepreneurs and professionals to discuss business issues or practice using job skills.
3. Keep lines of communication open with established small business owners and successful health care providers.

Holding discussions with a well-established health care provider or business professional should involve taking the person to lunch and following up with a thank-you card. Make sure to have questions outlined beforehand to ensure the meeting takes place efficiently. An associate position can provide a continual opportunity to learn from a well-established health care provider and gain knowledge on how to operate a successful business. In order to deal with the emotional challenges of operating a business and dealing with people's health, a support network can include a psychologist, career counselor, or business coach.

Some cities have *Tips Clubs* to organize brainstorming meetings in a more structured manner. The Internet gives brainstorming groups an innovative way to stay connected. For example, health care students can remain in contact after graduating by using a social networking website, such as Facebook or LinkedIn. Meetings can be organized online and conversations can expand over time as participants post responses to a topic.

Summary

An entrepreneur should proactively structure a support network and consider it part of the adventure of starting a business. A support network can include other business owners, professionals, and health care providers. To deal with the strong emotions involved with operating a business, a support network can include a psychologist, career counselor, or business coach. Using a close friend, family member, or significant other as a source of support might strain relationships.

CHAPTER ASSIGNMENT

Working in a group of three to four students or fellow professionals, complete the following items.

1. How could an entrepreneur who struggles with creativity develop an idea further? *p305*

2. What kind of artificial structure could ensure that an entrepreneur remains motivated? *p306*

3. List some of the main qualities that an entrepreneur should possess. Do you struggle with displaying any of these qualities? How might you further develop entrepreneurial traits? *p308 summary*

4. What are the main categories of a feasibility questionnaire? List a relevant question for each category. *p309*

5. List examples of items that can be identified in advance before launching a new venture. Why should an organization grow in planned stages? *p310*

6. What are the four perspectives of a balanced scorecard? For each perspective, create an example goal, metric, and action step. *p312*

7. Who should an entrepreneur place (or not place) in a support network and how could participants in a support network stay connected? *p314*

Health Insurance Portability and
  Accountability Act (HIPAA)
Stark Laws

Patient Conversion
Explanation of Benefits (EOB)
Travel Slip

CHAPTER

17

Care Management

AUTHOR'S NOTE

The health care process is by far the most important part of the patient experience. It becomes essential to figure out what a new or returning patient wants and then continually make sure that such wants have not changed. A health care provider needs to confirm an understanding of the patient's expectations before recommending any type of care. Communication and feedback are essential in making certain that a patient is comfortable with the recommended health care process. Throughout the entire process, a health care provider needs to provide the best level of service possible.

What kind of experience do you encounter when shopping at your favorite store? How often do you spread positive word of mouth about this store? Would you frequent the store as often if it sold products or services that you did *not* want? At every step of the way, a health care provider needs to strive for excellence in the face of challenging situations. The pursuit of excellence requires good management and a strong desire to enhance the overall patient experience. The most important aspect of the patient experience involves the health care process—this is ultimately why a patient has expended resources and scheduled an appointment.

The health care profession exists to provide high-quality services to community members in need of care. Providing high-quality services involves more than walking into a treatment room, taking notes, recommending care, and then leaving. A health care provider should constantly look for ways to improve the patient experience. The health care process can be enhanced by empathizing with a patient, articulating an understanding of a patient's concerns, and asking for feedback about treatment recommendations. Continuing to develop professional skills and upgrading equipment and supplies (in planned stages) can also improve the quality of care delivered.

A patient needs to understand the reasons for the health care process during an initial visit. In subsequent visits, it becomes important to refine the health care process and ensure that the patient experience remains positive. To this aim, a health care provider needs to use all available tools to improve a patient's health. Referring patients to another provider who can assist in the health care process should always be considered. Managing a patient's care might require tackling the underlying habits causing a health issue. Since health care tends to encroach upon a patient's personal space, a health care provider needs to maintain a professional approach at all times. Hard marketing tactics or unnecessary care can generate more revenue in the short term, but any discomfort such actions create may cause a patient to shy away from accessing services later or passing along positive word of mouth.

Successful practices are built over time by offering patients a high-quality experience. A slight nuisance in the beginning can transform into a major issue later, leading to potentially negative word of mouth or patient turnover. Patient complaints should be anticipated and addressed preemptively instead of being allowed to linger and interfere with the health care process. An organization needs to take steps to resolve matters expeditiously as patient complaints surface. Any problems should be fully noted in order to ensure that a resolution is properly achieved. The health care process itself should always be documented in chart notes. Such notes should also include patient concerns or important personal details that might bear upon the health care process. For example, if a patient recently experienced

Try not to put personal information unrelated to the health care process in a patient's chart note. Store unrelated personal information using a separate document or marketing software program.

a job loss, a treatment plan may need to be modified in order to address any new financial limitations. Constructing an overall positive experience for every patient grants an organization more opportunity to focus on patient care instead of marketing or administrative duties.

17.1   Professional Approach

Why does a patient decide to schedule an appointment? Patients will consume resources, including time, money, and energy, to address a specific health concern. A professional approach to care management involves respecting such resource expenditures and focusing on what the patient ultimately wants. Patients should have an opportunity to describe their health concerns on a small card while sitting in the waiting room or verbally within the first few minutes of an appointment. An intake form can provide a list of common health conditions, such as depression, that patients may be hesitant or forget to mention. When a health care provider finally meets with a patient during an office visit, the first few minutes should be spent building rapport, reviewing the intake form, and confirming what the patient ultimately wants. A health care provider should make a clear written note of main objectives and stay focused throughout the appointment. The communication with a patient should include practical information set in terminology that allows full comprehension.

> Save time and increase efficiency by having patients list subjective health information before the visit begins (to the extent possible).

Rapport Building

Rapport building is an essential part of forming long-lasting relationships. A health care provider should come across as personable and approachable and tailor rapport building to the individual patient. Keeping notes on prior conversations can simplify rapport-building efforts during future encounters. Never dominate a conversation or take the focus off what a patient holds important; instead, take a moment to understand the patient by asking relevant questions and stay on topics that interest the patient. Patients will feel better working with a health care provider who shows an interest in getting to know them. The health care process might entail treatments that intrude on personal space, but patients might not feel any displeasure if strong rapport with a health care provider exists. The effort to build rapport should remain on a professional level and should exclude controversial or negative topics as well as excessive or inappropriate touching. For example, complaining about being busy can cause patients to feel hesitant about requesting services or setting future appointments.

> Three Communication No-No's:
> 1. *Do not dominate the conversation.*
> 2. *Do not bring up irrelevant topics.*
> 3. *Do not recommend care without asking for feedback.*

Expect that patients are encountering a mental or physical health concern and they might become disengaged from conversation because of pathology. Don't take offense to abrasive personalities or react in an unprofessional manner. Matching a patient's energy

---

DIALOGUE

Provider: I want to confirm that you have listed all your current health concerns on the intake form. Please let me know if you feel uncomfortable talking to me about anything and we can try to find a proper solution.

Patient: Well, I have a regular health care provider and so I'd rather not cover everything today. I'm just here to talk about a new problem I've been having.

Provider: Okay, I will make a note of that. Let me know if you would like a second opinion. If not, we can focus on this new problem you came in for.

level can calm a patient, but always ensure the energy remains positive. Behaviors that seem disrespectful or inappropriate can easily form part of a patient's disease profile and a health care provider should have the competence to examine such behavior objectively without judgment.

Qualified Health Care Need

Some health care providers attempt to increase revenue by using hard marketing tactics that rope patients into structured treatment programs. Patients might benefit from maintenance care or secondary services, but most individuals will not come in for such reasons. Patients may submit to such services at first, but any later discomfort could cause early termination of the health care process, which could put their health at risk, or lead to negative word of mouth. Even where no consequences manifest themselves, an organization's needs are taking precedence over a patient's needs and that creates an ethical concern that a health care provider should try to avoid.

It is important to explain how treatments will address a *qualified health care need* and how a patient could benefit in other aspects of life personally. A qualification occurs when a health care provider determines how a patient's health care issue can be properly addressed with products and services the organization has available. A health care provider must always make a qualification to ensure a patient receives the proper form of care. The type of care and number of visits should appear reasonable to outside observers, especially if an external party has set authoritative treatment guidelines. Providing an excessive amount of care, beyond the level that appears normal for your particular health care profession, can give rise to litigation or board complaints. A referral must be offered if a health care provider cannot adequately address a health concern.

A health care provider may have good intentions and recommend a vast array of care after making a diagnosis, but does that fit within what the patient really wants? Patients will generally agree to a treatment recommendation during an appointment as a way of avoiding confrontation or because the recommendation has not yet been fully digested. Patients should recapitulate an understanding of recommended care and confirm acceptance. If patients ultimately view a recommendation as unnecessary or unwanted, feelings of displeasure can arise at some later point.

Since a patient will often need to make lifestyle changes to reach a higher level of health, time needs to be spent reviewing what a patient is willing to change or why old habits have been embraced. To maintain professionalism, a health care provider should not try to provoke change by drawing on negative emotions. A health care provider should work with patients over time to replace unhealthy habits with healthier ones and encourage implementation of treatment recommendations. Adequate rapport allows the health care process to be tailored in a manner relevant to each patient.

If a patient has an expectation of care that appears *unnecessary*, a health care provider must clearly communicate the reasons for that assessment. Explain that matters were given full consideration and a specific expectation will be reviewed again to confirm if the related care is still unnecessary. Tell the patient that a chart note will be made in order to hold a follow-up conversation later. An organization member should also take note of any other special requests made by a patient. The health care experience will run a lot smoother if patients feel their concerns are being addressed and remembered.

Care Management

The overall quality of service needs to be excellent at all times. A daily task list, calendar, and general administrative procedures can help ensure errands related to patient care are performed. A health care provider must keep organized in terms of reviewing labs, submitting prescriptions to pharmacies, ordering inventory, and returning phone calls (and emails). Failing to follow up with patients on matters related to their care could sour the patient experience or result in negative health consequences.

Sidebar notes:

Do not display favoritism with your patients. Respect and enjoy all of them equally.

Review the qualification phase of the selling process in Chapter 3.

What does a patient consider important overall in life?

Patients need to understand what you are doing and the importance of why you are doing it. You need to understand what the patient is perceiving.

You may want to avoid sending confidential (health) information when responding to emails.

In order to maintain high standards, written procedures should be followed when possible. Each procedure should outline what items to consider in a given situation and give rise to an alert if a procedure is not appropriately followed. For example, an assistant can review a list of procedures during a visit to confirm each item was addressed. Procedures should encompass any legal matters that may impact the delivery of health care. The **Health Insurance Portability and Accountability Act (HIPAA)** in the United States lists privacy rules meant to safeguard patient information. **Stark Laws** place restrictions over a health care provider's ability to receive remuneration, either directly or indirectly, for referring Medicare and Medicaid patients. Other laws may affect the health care process and should be included in any relevant procedures.

Root Cause Analysis

A health care provider should always ask, "What is the root cause of this patient's health problem?" Health care providers often address overt symptoms but overlook the need to remove any causal source. Every health problem is caused by either an external or genetic factor. Certain external factors may be causative only to the extent they exacerbate genetic factors. Human beings are now exposed to a tremendous amount of harmful substances in food, air, water, and topical agents. Sorting through each of these potential sources to confirm if they might be a factor may require an extensive amount of laboratory work or office visits. A patient should be advised of the expected costs and receive enough information to make an informed decision about how best to proceed with the health care process. A patient can reduce costs by compiling a list of potential toxins or engaging in other activities while at home.

Health Insurance Portability and Accountability Act (HIPAA): Federal legislation that regulates the transition of patient health care coverage from one insurance provider to another and includes additional regulations on patient privacy.

Stark Laws: Federal legislation directed at preventing health care providers from receiving a direct or indirect financial benefit from referring Medicare or Medicaid patients.

CASE STUDY

Tolle Causum

After discovering a patient has low levels of thyroid hormones, the next step involves looking for antibodies. A thyroid peroxidase test can be used to confirm a diagnosis of (Hashimoto's) thyroiditis as the cause of the patient's hypothyroidism. But what has caused the antibodies to surface? A health care provider will often stop with the thyroid peroxidase test and overlook the need to explore further. Have the antibodies come about because of other issues occurring with the immune system? The patient could be facing other autoimmune problems that have not yet become symptomatic. What is the true root cause of the thyroid antibodies and how many resources is the patient willing to spend to find this out? Ask!

Only follow a written procedure when applicable. The health care process may need to be modified for a particular patient.

Summary

To maintain a positive health care experience, the first few minutes of an appointment should be spent building rapport, reviewing an intake form, and confirming what a patient ultimately wants. A health care provider must ensure that the nature of services fits within a patient's expectation of care. Patients normally do not want to expend resources unless it is to properly address a health concern. A health care provider should confirm that a patient understands what a treatment or diagnosis entails before delivering services. Providing unwanted care can lead patients to terminate the health care process prematurely and spread negative word of mouth. Maintaining written procedures and seeking out the root cause of a health problem can improve a patient's health outcome.

17.2   Initial Visit

The health care process for new patients needs to appear seamless right from the start. The first impression that patients derive of an organization can be the strongest. The patient experience must remain 100% positive, requiring that every subtle detail reflect an organization's commitment to high-quality standards.

First Impressions

A. A new patient will contact an organization usually by telephone to set up an initial appointment. Every phone call needs to be answered without fail during regular business hours. Outside of regular business hours, an answering machine should let patients know when the phone call will be returned and to call 911 if the call relates to an emergency.

B. An organization member should make an attempt to ascertain if a prospective patient has a qualified need that the organization could address appropriately. If not, the prospective patient should be offered a referral to another health care provider. The approximate cost of the appointment should be quoted to the patient to prevent surprises. Gather information on any third-party payor and research what the coverage involves.

C. An organization needs to remain flexible when scheduling an initial visit and accommodate a prospective patient's schedule even if that means working during a lunch hour or on a weekend. Whoever schedules a new patient's appointment should outline what will take place during the initial visit and suggest coming early to complete any outstanding documents.

A health care organization should also maintain an implied consent form and a handout detailing what the patient can expect during the initial visit.

D. Insurance and intake forms can be sent ahead of time either via email or regular mail as a way of saving time. Such documents can be kept on an organization's website for the convenience of patients. Bear in mind that average literacy rates are low and prospective patients should always be asked if they would prefer to complete forms with an organization member present rather than receiving such forms in advance.

E. Make sure to hire a *professional* language expert or interpreter when language barriers exist. Medical malpractice can arise if an unqualified language expert was used or no language expert was present. An intake form should ask about special needs related to cultural and religious norms, physical limitations, emotional boundaries, language, and personal preferences.

Tell patients to bring medications or supplements to ensure the dosages are correctly recorded.

F. A prospective patient should receive a reminder phone call the day before an initial visit to prevent a missed appointment and ensure relevant documents, such as an insurance card, are brought. If an organization decides to email appointment reminders, intake forms should be attached as a convenience. Clarify what any third-party payor will cover and what the patient's obligation will be based on research conducted in *Part B* above.

G. A new patient should never feel disoriented when walking into an office. As soon as a new patient arrives, an organization member should immediately provide a brief orientation. The orientation should involve making an introduction, presenting a tray of beverages and snacks, describing the bathroom location, and pointing to any magazines, toys, or entertainment options. An organization member can quickly review what will take place during the initial visit, clarify the approximate charges, and confirm that all documents have been completed (or not completed).

H.   Wait times should be kept to a bare minimum (less than ten minutes) before a health care provider either starts the initial visit or stops by to apologize for the delay. If a health care provider needs to leave the room for any reason after the actual visit has started, the patient should be told how long it should take.

A patient's insurance card and driver's license can be scanned electronically using a special dual-sided scanner.

Introduction

The introduction when a health care provider finally meets with a new patient should keep in mind cultural norms, personalities, and potential health problems that could influence how a person likes to be approached. For example, a patient with mental health problems may require more personal space and may not like to shake hands.

Ask the patient, "How would you like to be addressed?"

Rapport Building

A health care provider needs to remain focused on a new patient and spend a few moments building rapport. The conversation can begin by ascertaining if any problems existed in getting to the office. A health care provider can discuss the commute to make sure the full experience remains positive. Covering the commute can bring forth more information about a patient's general routine as well.

A stressful commute could cause an abnormally high blood-pressure reading.

DIALOGUE

Provider: Thank you for coming in this morning. Was this a good time for your appointment? Did you have any problems getting here?

New Patient: The afternoons work better for me, but this is the only time the receptionist said you had available.

Provider: I apologize if this time was inconvenient. I'll make a note right now to my receptionist to schedule your next visit in the afternoon. Are you commuting from somewhere far or through traffic?

New Patient: No, I just like walking in the morning, but the commute is fine.

Provider: Okay, good. It sounds like you are dedicated to walking then. I like to hear that. How far do you usually walk in the morning?

Rapport building can take place during the entire visit and does not need to dominate the early part of an appointment. This differs from professional sales where the selling process cannot move forward until rapport is sufficient. Rapport building can often be combined with the health care process by reviewing a patient's quality of life. This type of conversation can involve having a patient rate any pain, discomfort, or limitation before following up with a qualitative review of what that concern means in terms of the patient's daily routine.

Personal information is highly relevant to the health care process. How might asking about travel help diagnose an infectious disease?

Health Care Process

A health care provider's main task involves managing the health care process. A health care provider needs to review medical forms and compile a patient's health history (intake) until it becomes clear that a proper level of understanding has been reached about a patient's

Obtain a complete intake to diagnose a patient's health problem and configure the best form of treatment.

Consider having patients sign a waiver if they refuse a recommendation for care.

Foster long-lasting and mutually beneficial relationships.

Simply ask! "Are you satisfied with the care you received today?"

Don't delay! Getting to a new patient quickly makes a strong first impression.

Don't be pedantic! Don't overload a new patient with information or use complex terms just to sound smart.

Don't assume! Check with a new patient to ensure everything is acceptable and document the response.

health concerns. This understanding should be communicated back to the patient to confirm its accuracy. The communication style during an initial visit should involve simple terms that attempt to educate a new patient. Where other health care providers have been seen in the past, efforts should be made to discover what took place and what treatment recommendations were offered. Gathering historical information can shorten the learning curve and move the health care process forward in a more precise manner.

Describe to a new patient what the health care process will entail and ask about feelings of discomfort before moving forward with any in-depth examination. Since a new patient might not immediately voice complaints, try to anticipate how a particular patient will perceive the patient experience. Providing unwanted or unnecessary care can lead to negative word of mouth and high patient turnover. Ask permission before touching a patient and frame questions in a way that permits a smooth and open dialogue. In instances where uncomfortable subjects are discussed, thoroughly listen at first and then attempt to reduce a patient's emotional burden.

Avoid passing any form of judgment and give a patient space to feel a certain way. For example, a health care provider should ascertain if a patient has any aversion to needles before drawing blood and then ask if concerns exist after explaining the procedure. Ask a new patient in a polite manner what the expectation of care is if the health care process encounters obstacles. Make the patient ultimately responsible for decisions. Avoid provoking negative emotions to force patients into engaging in unwanted activities. Coming to terms with an uncomfortable subject or examination can take time and most patients can be rescheduled to continue the health care process later.

Make the best use of a new patient's time and work through the health care process at an appropriate speed. Some health care providers refrain from certain activities during an initial visit as a marketing strategy, thus forcing every new patient to wait until a second visit to have health issues addressed. This approach can increase revenue over the short term, but patients can grow frustrated about spending money needlessly. An organization that fosters long-lasting and mutually beneficial relationships with patients will profit from repeat business, positive word of mouth, and direct referrals. The amount of revenue possible from long-term relationships is far greater than what a short-term sales ploy could provide.

Toward the end of a visit, a health care provider should summarize the main points of a diagnosis, treatment, or examination to affirm that services were rendered as desired. Always *ask the patient* for feedback to confirm that the health care process falls in line with what the patient really wants. Although a patient may go along with an examination or treatment recommendation at the moment, this same patient may grow frustrated when given time to digest its implications. Ask questions to ensure that the health care process is perceived as reasonable and that the patient did not have a different expectation of care. Nothing will damage the patient experience more than providing unnecessary or unwanted services.

A clear explanation should be given if there were any difficulties with the health care process or if certain care was withheld. A new patient should feel encouraged to ask questions and contact the health care provider outside of regular office hours. A health care provider may want to follow up with a phone call after an initial visit to confirm the patient's satisfaction—a patient might not appreciate a phone call made for marketing purposes. A small packet of information to take home should be reviewed with a new patient as well as any personalized list of activities to perform or key information to remember. Patients may struggle with changing habits and writing goals and action steps along a timeline can help reduce the energy involved in setting change in motion.

Posttreatment

In ending an appointment, a new patient should be rescheduled if the need exists and handed a reminder card. An organization member should explain what might take place during a subsequent visit (if applicable). In an effort to avoid surprises, any unique situations expected to occur should be explained. The amount of information delivered overall during an initial visit should not prove overwhelming. A new patient should be asked about making payment at the very end but should already know in advance what the approximate charges will be.

Summary

A prospective patient should view the process of setting an initial appointment as seamless. An organization member should provide a new patient with a brief orientation on how the office functions and what the initial visit will involve. A health care provider should make contact within the first ten minutes or apologize for any delay. The initial part of the health care process should involve building rapport, taking a complete health history, and confirming the nature of a patient's health issues. As long as a patient is comfortable with the health care process, an appointment should be spent addressing health issues in an expedient manner. Confirm that a patient did not view any actions as unnecessary or unwanted—communicate about the qualified reasons for care. At the end of an initial visit, a new patient should receive a modest amount of information to take home and receive instructions on any subsequent visits.

Wash your hands in between meeting with patients!

17.3 Subsequent Visits

After an initial visit, a patient might need to schedule subsequent visits to continue addressing a health concern. A former patient might also contact a health care organization to renew care. A former patient restarting care may need to fill out medical forms again and receive a thorough examination similar to one that would be provided during an initial visit.

Phone calls and emails should always be answered during regular office hours and organization members should respond quickly to phone messages or emails left outside of regular hours. The schedule should provide patients with a good range of open availability. An organization member should call the day before an appointment as a reminder and suggest bringing any questions or concerns that might have arisen since the last appointment. A patient who comes in frequently does not always need to receive a reminder phone call before every appointment.

A patient can spend time in the waiting room filling out a small card outlining the expectations for the visit. Secondary service offerings can improve the waiting experience and help spread positive word of mouth. Organization members working near the waiting room can use this time to engage in rapport-building efforts. Wait times should be kept under ten minutes, but brand new patients should receive a higher priority if an organization gets behind. After ten minutes, an organization member should check in and apologize for the long wait. Chronically long wait times should be analyzed in terms of how patients are scheduled and the amount of time needed with a particular type of patient.

Occasionally ask patients if there have been any changes to insurance coverage. Confirm what the new coverage involves.

Rapport Building

A health care provider should continue conversations with patients where they last ended. Notes kept in a patient's file or marketing program can point to what was discussed before. Compare this approach to quickly popping into a treatment room, looking intensely at a patient's chart, and immediately wanting to get started. No one wants to feel like a number and patients will appreciate a brief conversation that closely tracks what was talked about before—even if it only lasts 30 seconds. A professional approach should be maintained even though the relationship might become more familiar. Inappropriate conversations can damage rapport as well as the overall patient experience.

Health Care Process

A health care provider must review a patient's health history, consider taking more history, and ask relevant clinical questions until reaching a *new* understanding of a patient's health care needs. *A dangerous assumption involves thinking that the health care process can pick up where it last ended.* Discuss your *report of findings* from any prior visit, including lab results and diagnostic imaging. Ensure that a patient is comfortable with the entire health care process before an examination begins. Ask permission or frame questions in a way that permits a smooth and open dialogue. New expectations may have formed in a patient's

If you are unable to figure out what's causing a patient's health problem, consider taking more health history or provide a referral.

mind about how the health care process should take place. Attempt to discover what a patient wants to focus on during each specific visit and then summarize this understanding back to the patient. A health care provider should expand a patient's knowledge of technical matters as time progresses.

DIALOGUE

Provider: We did some lab work last time and I mentioned that we will be going over your results today. Does this sound like a good plan and is there anything else that you want to discuss?

Patient: Well, I started having pain on the side of my face.

Provider: You mentioned that on the form you filled out in the waiting room. You rated it as a 5 out of 10. You didn't note what the cause was on the form. Have you been doing anything different since we last met?

Patient: My life has been fairly routine. I've been sleeping about the same. My appetite has not changed. Work has been stressful but not more than usual.

Provider: Would you like to investigate this new facial pain further today?

Patient: I'd rather go over what my labs said. Plus, I need to pick up my kids at day care. Maybe if we have time we can talk about it, but I'm not too worried right now.

Provider: Okay, I'm just going to make a quick note on your chart so I remember to ask you about this pain next time.

Discussion Notice how the prior visit is tied into the current visit and an effort is made to clarify if anything has changed. Instead of launching into a comprehensive health intake regarding the facial pain, the health care provider asks for the patient's feedback about how to proceed with the health care process. Even though the patient decides against addressing the facial pain currently, the health care provider makes a chart note to document the patient's decision and create a reminder to review the facial pain during a future appointment.

An appointment should move along seamlessly and in an expedient manner. A fine line exists between too much time spent with a patient and too little. A patient could potentially have other commitments and other patients could be waiting. At a minimum, focus on the main aspects of what a patient wants and communicate about any expectation of care that appears *unnecessary*. A patient can be given additional information to take home (if applicable). Let the patient know how many more visits are anticipated until reexamination and the approximate cost. Any unique situations should be explained in order to avoid surprises. At the end of a visit, an organization member should reschedule a patient (if applicable), provide a reminder card, handle any payment requirements, and confirm that the patient has no unanswered questions.

Recommending Care

A health care provider needs to review prior recommendations to determine if a patient has performed activities as outlined. Do not expect every patient to follow a treatment recommendation as specified, especially at first. Do not pass judgment on patients who have not followed a recommendation or look down upon their efforts. It takes time for people to form new habits depending on how their lifestyles are arranged. A health care provider should determine how much time, energy, and money must be put toward implementing a recommendation and then review how to restructure goals and action steps to be more realistic for a particular patient's situation. A patient who fails to follow a specific recommendation may view some aspect of it as unwanted or unnecessary.

Simply Ask! "How could this treatment plan be structured to better fit your lifestyle?"

> **DIALOGUE**
>
> *Incorrect*: I'm going to have you take an additional supplement.
>
> *Correct*: I recommend that you take an additional supplement, but I want to make sure that you are in agreement first. Are there any concerns that you might be experiencing?

If a patient feels treatments are not working or have created other health problems, consider revising a patient's treatment plan, obtain more medical history, and explain what will change during future visits. Performing a reexamination is usually appropriate when treating a patient on a frequent basis in order to track progress and substantiate the need for care to external parties. Thank the patient for raising concerns and make an appropriate notation in the patient's file. A patient should be advised to obtain a second opinion in order to protect both the patient and health care provider against the negative consequences of a misdiagnosis.

Treat the entire system and not the symptoms: cause versus effect.

Treatment Plans

A structured treatment plan can give a patient a clear vision of how to tackle a chronic health concern. Such plans are best discussed after *two to four visits* because a patient may need to grow comfortable with the health care process before accepting a long-term care program. A treatment plan should have an approximate end date or involve a specific number of visits and it should not be used as a ploy to simply make money. If a treatment plan needs to be modified, a health care provider will need to communicate why the change is important and review comfort levels. A patient should be encouraged to set unplanned appointments apart from a treatment plan if unexpected pain, discomfort, or limitation develops.

Summary

A health care provider can make the transition from one visit to another appear seamless by keeping good notes about general conversations held in the past. A subsequent visit should start with rapport-building efforts and proceed with the establishment of a *new* understanding of a patient's concerns. The level of terminology used to explain the health care process can expand during each subsequent visit but a professional approach should always be maintained. After several visits, a health care provider might want to formulate a treatment plan that addresses a chronic health concern. A health care provider needs to review the effectiveness of a treatment plan as well as other recommended activities that a patient is meant to perform.

17.4   Patient Conversions

A **patient conversion** occurs any time another health care provider administers a patient's ongoing care either on a temporary or permanent basis. The patient experience should remain consistent when a conversion occurs.

Patient Conversion: The process of creating a seamless transition for a patient from one health care provider to another.

Temporary Conversion

An organization must proactively communicate with patients if an *alternate* health care provider might at some point take charge of the health care process temporarily.

Integrated Clinic An associate might work underneath an established health care provider or multiple health care providers might form an integrated clinic as a way of delivering care. Any *alternate* health care provider who might temporarily take over a patient's care must confirm that the patient has not previously requested to be seen only by the *regular* health care provider. A patient may have reservations about seeing an alternate health care provider, especially one with less overall experience. The patient load can be reviewed during a morning meeting to identify the patients who should *not* be seen by an alternate health care provider. Review chart notes to become familiar with the health care process in relation to patients available to be seen. Attempt to learn as much as possible about each patient on a personal level so that the same conversations are not repeated time and again.

At the start of an appointment, an alternate health care provider should reconfirm that a particular patient is okay with being seen. Efforts at building rapport should correspond to the patient's level of acceptance toward receiving care from an alternate health care provider. If available, the patient's regular health care provider should briefly check in and review matters at the end of a visit.

DIALOGUE

Provider: Hello, I'm Jim, an associate with the office. I will be handling your care today. I met with your regular provider this morning and we discussed what should be done today. I also hear that you're a college football fan.

Patient: Yep, I used to play college ball.

Provider: Was that at Florida State?

Patient: That's right. I played on the defensive line.

Provider: Very cool! Well, I want to make sure you're comfortable working with me. I will understand if you want to see your regular health care provider. Would you prefer to wait?

Patient: Oh, no, that's fine.

Provider: Please let me know if you change your mind. I want to quickly review why you're here today and if there is anything special you would like to discuss. At the end, I will try to have your regular health care provider check in with you.

Temporary Absence There might be instances when a *substitute* health care provider fills in temporarily due to a vacation or illness. Patients should be warned in advance (if possible) about the regular health care provider's absence. For example, suppose a health care provider becomes ill and needs a substitute for only one day. The organization should contact patients as soon as possible to see if they want to reschedule. A substitute health care provider should try to hold a meeting with organization members to discuss how the patient load should be handled and also confirm the best form of contact with the regular health care provider in case a problem arises. A substitute health care provider must review patient files and ask about anything that might be missing, such as new lab results. Calling and discussing the patient load each day with the regular health care provider is ideal, but this may not be possible. A follow-up meeting should be arranged with organization members once the regular health care provider returns to discuss how everything went and to highlight any special issues.

If a patient comes in for an appointment and is surprised to learn the regular health care provider is unavailable, an organization member needs to give an approximate return date and offer the patient top priority when making a new appointment (if applicable). The regular health care provider should call the patient to apologize for the inconvenience and consider offering a price discount or gift certificate, especially if a patient was not properly alerted to the absence.

Permanent Conversion

A *permanent* conversion occurs when a health care provider buys an existing practice and patients will no longer be seeing their regular health care provider. Tremendous effort on the part of both the incoming and outgoing health care providers is required to ensure a smooth transition. The transition can occur in stages over time, allowing both health care providers to slowly change their roles within the organization. Both health care providers need to thoughtfully communicate with patients well in advance to prepare for the permanent conversion. The outgoing provider needs to discuss the upcoming transition with patients individually, address any concerns they might have, and provide assurances that the level and type of care will remain excellent.

Marketing tools can be used to disseminate announcements to current and former patients. Around the time of the transition, the incoming provider needs to stage open-house functions, remain highly accessible, communicate often with patients, and offer more appointment availability. Organization members should make a special effort to orient former patients who return for care under the newfound organization. The incoming provider should study historical and current records in order to become familiar with the entire patient base. Analysis must be performed to remove patients who will not continue on with the newfound organization from a business valuation. If patients will ultimately leave and never return, the incoming provider should not spend money on this absent value.

To ensure that patients remain with the newfound organization, the incoming health care provider should make every effort to maintain the same level and type of services. Procedures, techniques, philosophies, and so forth should remain comparable to those of the former organization, especially at first. This may require special training sessions with the outgoing health care provider to learn exactly how to keep patient care similar. The best approach toward understanding a patient base involves working directly as an associate or independent contractor for an organization long before a permanent conversion takes place.

An incoming health care provider might envision a different direction for an organization, but changes should be made in small steps to prevent any major disruptions to the patient experience. A *growth plan* could outline when to make changes according to predetermined metrics. A former organization may have been poorly managed, located, or equipped whereby immediate changes may be warranted. A newfound organization must ensure that the patient experience will improve in a way that the existing patient base will find favorable.

> A seller-financed loan offers a health care provider the flexibility to hand over a practice in stages.

Summary

When taking over patient care from another health care provider, steps should be followed to ensure a smooth transition for patients. Review patient files in advance so that the same conversations are not repeated and the health care process continues to progress. The option to only be seen by a patient's regular health care provider should be extended (if possible). When buying a practice, both the incoming and outgoing health care providers must communicate with patients well in advance. The incoming provider must put forth additional effort to update notes and learn about the patient base, especially when trying to piece together a business valuation.

17.5   Patient Complaints

A health care organization must deal with patient complaints in a professional manner or risk provoking negative word of mouth. Communication plays a key role when examining the patient experience and finding a solution if the experience contains negative elements. Problems caused by forces outside the control of an organization can often be eliminated through communication efforts. For example, a health care organization can apologize to patients if a neighboring tenant is producing excess noise. Health care providers who become frustrated over patient complaints fail to understand the value of knowing about problems.

> Do not wait for a patient to complain. Be proactive about uncovering problems that may be occurring.

Most patients will not readily voice complaints about a negative experience. These same patients may terminate the health care process prematurely, which could put their health at risk, or spread negative word of mouth to others. Discovering problems must occur in a proactive manner and be done in a way that enables a smooth and open dialogue. Table 17.1 lists common reasons that patients complain about a particular health care provider. Show appreciation to patients and organization members who bring forth concerns. An organization member with the right authority should immediately address a problem that is found. Allow patients to contribute ideas on how to resolve matters. An organization should take precautions to ensure that the same problems do not resurface in the future.

Patients may feel more comfortable expressing complaints to an organization member other than yourself.

If a conflict occurs, *narratives* committed to memory can help guide the conversation. Attending classes on conflict resolution can provide insight into what drives emotions and how to reduce tension. Organization members should place related notes in a patient's file to confirm later that complaints are fully resolved.

Don't assume anything. Ask questions!

TABLE 17.1	Common Patient Complaints
1. Feeling of being overcharged	
2. Inadequate care	
3. Visits too short	
4. No end goal with treatments	
5. Lack of information	
6. Discomfort from marketing tactics	

Scheduling Complaints

Offer a specific referral if a patient cannot find a time that works in the schedule.

Patients might make an appointment but later have a negative experience because an appointment time was not the most convenient. An organization needs to offer sufficient availability and maintain open lines of communication about what times are most ideal. Calling to remind new or returning patients of their next appointment will help reduce missed visits. As patients arrive at appointments, wait times should be kept to a minimum even if patients come early or walk in unexpectedly. Preliminary service offerings can preoccupy patients as they wait. A health care provider should remain open to being contacted outside of regular office hours in order to deal with emergencies or meet with patients by appointment. Regular office hours should extend into lunch breaks, the evening, or the weekend if necessary.

Billing Complaints

Prices should be quoted to new and returning patients when setting an appointment to avoid surprises. If an organization member quotes a price either orally or in writing, the organization might be legally responsible to uphold that price, especially if services have already been rendered. To avoid misunderstandings, the full price for services should always be quoted with clarification when a discount would apply. For example, a patient might be told that the full price for a particular service is $85, but insurance coverage can reduce the price to $65. The $20 discount would only apply if a patient had the appropriate insurance coverage at time of service.

Explanation of Benefits (EOB): A general document sent by insurance providers that describes the nature and cost of benefits.

Organization members need to alert patients to additional billing information and invoices they might receive, such as an **explanation of benefits (EOB)** listing what charges an insurance company will cover. When patients do not customarily pay for services directly, a summary of amounts accrued on their account should still be presented each visit. If a patient account contains an unpaid balance, try to collect the full amount at first. If payment is still not submitted, ask what the patient believes is reasonable given the circumstances and then base a decision on that information. The solution should ensure that negative word of mouth is kept under control, organization needs are met, and both parties feel it's a fair compromise.

Diagnosis Complaints

A health care provider needs to review the specific health issues that a patient wants to cover and form a proper understanding of the issues each visit. A diagnosis should be clearly explained to a patient using plain terminology. If a patient remains skeptical about a diagnosis or one cannot be ascertained, a health care provider can take more history, list additional tests or examinations to perform, or advise the patient to obtain a second opinion. The name of a specific referral should be written down for a patient along with any current diagnosis.

> Make sure to thank a health care provider who refers a patient to you.

A health care organization should be ready to discount prices or offer free care if a misdiagnosis occurs. A health care provider could mention how a patient was advised to obtain a second opinion. The health care process should be properly documented in chart notes in case a legal dispute does arise.

REFERRING PATIENTS

It's perfectly fine to refer patients to other health care providers. You may not have the expertise to properly handle all aspects of care when working with a specific type of patient or when faced with a complex situation. Providing a referral allows a patient to receive an appropriate level of service elsewhere. It may also prevent a patient's care from being mismanaged as a result of error on your part. If you fail to build rapport with a particular patient, it might benefit your organization to make a referral before the patient spreads negative word of mouth. Always make sure to document situations where the doctor-patient relationship is being dissolved.

Treatment Complaints

Services provided to patients should be wanted or necessary. Insisting on unwanted or unnecessary treatments might cause patients to consent at the moment but feel frustrated later. A health care provider should use plain terminology to clearly explain what a treatment will entail or what might occur afterward. Anticipate how patients might react to a particular treatment and communicate proactively about potential concerns. For example, some patients might feel worse after a particular treatment as the body repairs itself. Ask permission before initiating services and make certain that patients are comfortable with the health care process. After providing treatment to a patient, ask if the process occurred as expected. In order to avoid any letdown over the health care process, communicate why certain actions were not taken (or taken) and make a note to review expectations during a subsequent visit.

> Always list on paper the side effects of drugs, herbs, or supplements being recommended to patients.

A health care provider must understand that treatment recommendations might run contrary to a person's lifestyle. A recommendation must be modified or reexplained if a patient fails to follow it. If a patient does not get better or dislikes some aspect of the experience, attempt to provide a meaningful solution, including a referral. When referring a patient to a specific health care provider, contact that health care provider later to find out what the patient said about your organization—did the patient complain about your services?

> Suggest healthier alternatives to replace a patient's unhealthy habits.

PARQ CONFERENCE

Structure should be set in place to minimize diagnostic or treatment problems. According to the Oregon Revised Statute, for example, a health care provider must complete a PARQ conference in order to obtain implied consent. The acronym stands for procedures, alternatives, risks, and questions. The PARQ conference ensures that all aspects of care have been properly communicated and the patient is given an opportunity to question what is taking place. A health care provider should also communicate a diagnosis and referral, thus forming the extended acronym DR PAR-Q.

D – Diagnosis.

R – Referral

P – Procedures

A – Alternatives

R – Risks

Q – Questions

Summary

Patient concerns will inevitably arise and a health care organization should be prepared to deal with matters in a professional way. Communication plays a key role in discovering problems and finding solutions. An organization needs to look at the patient experience holistically and prevent complaints from happening. Always thank patients and organization members for raising concerns if they do exist. Proper communication can assist with quieting tensions, finding solutions, and improving the patient experience. In order to minimize conflict if a mistake is made in diagnosis or treatment, make certain that the health care process is properly documented and encourage patients to obtain a second opinion. Be prepared to discount prices or offer free care if an issue arises.

17.6   Record Keeping

Note taking should occur during a patient visit or directly afterward. By waiting too long, information can be forgotten and remaining motivated to complete notes can become more challenging. A new or returning patient should be informed about the note-taking process and how it might cause a slight distraction during the actual visit. An organization member might assist a health care provider by taking comprehensive notes during normal appointments or in cases where patients have unique issues. Forming good habits around note taking is essential, especially when third parties will heavily review the notes. For example, an insurance company will most likely scrutinize the records of a health care provider attempting to gain membership on the company's panel. Good chart notes also serve as a mechanism to verify patient charges and to make sure billing records are never erased fraudulently or erroneously.

At the start of each day, patient files should be gathered according to the appointments listed on the daily schedule. Patient files should be stored somewhere safe for the remainder of the day until used. Organization members should meet in the morning, quickly discuss the patient load, and review prior notes. Organization members can become reacquainted with prior conversations (that were documented) in order to create a seamless experience for patients from one visit to the next.

An organization should examine whether using electronic or handwritten notes would provide more value since both methods have pros and cons. A net present value calculation can be prepared to examine the benefit versus cost of using a particular note-taking system. For instance, reading through pages of an electronic chart might be harder than flipping through pages of a written chart.

Travel Slip: A condensed form that lists common procedures and allows for an abbreviated version of note taking.

If a health care provider's time is limited, a **travel slip** can be used to abbreviate the note-taking process. An administrative person can write formal chart notes later using items noted (circled) on the travel slip if applicable. An organization can create an assortment of travel slips to deal with different situations and place written procedures, common labs, and examinations on their backside. A health care provider must ensure that notes become properly transcribed in a patient's chart before disposing of a travel slip.

The standard note-taking format contains a subjective, objective, assessment, and plan (SOAP) component. A health care provider should adhere to this format in an effort to manage patient care appropriately and document the health care process for external parties. A patient's file could contain special requests made by the patient or highlights of past rapport-building efforts. Such information should not be comingled with medical chart notes unless appropriate.

A travel slip itself might be extensive enough to function as the chart note eliminating the need to transcribe it.

Internal Control Measures   The overall patient file, including notes, is subject to privacy rules covered under the HIPAA Act in the United States. Such rules require that an organization appoint a *privacy officer* to ensure compliance. Organization members must sign a document saying that they understand and will comply with privacy rules.

Organization members should receive training and sign a confidentiality agreement annually.

Even where HIPAA rules do not apply, internal control measures must be in place to ensure that unauthorized people never review patient files. Steps should be taken to ensure patient files are kept safe from fire and theft. Electronic notes must always be secured with a password and backed up daily. Written or electronic files should be kept away from the waiting room, check-in counter, or common walkway. An organization should have select areas where files can be placed that are clear of other documents. As soon as files are no longer needed, they should be immediately placed in a filing cabinet in the back office. A special filing cabinet can house files that are more frequently accessed. If patient files no longer need to be kept, they must be disposed of properly. Hard drives containing electronic files should be destroyed. Paper documents should be shredded in-house or collected by a shredding company. Putting shredded documents in a garbage bin for pickup may not sufficiently protect patient records.

Your state may have specific laws governing how to handle patient files.

Summary

A health care provider should maintain high standards when taking notes and consider using the SOAP format. Organization members should meet in the morning to review patient files regarding scheduled appointments for the particular day. Use of a travel slip can expedite the note-taking process, especially during busy times. An electronic system may prove more beneficial than writing notes by hand depending on the circumstances. A net present value calculation can help determine the best approach toward note taking. An organization must maintain compliance with laws, such as HIPAA, that govern patient files and privacy. Patient files should only be kept in certain places to avoid theft, misplacement, or unauthorized viewing.

CHAPTER ASSIGNMENT

Working in a group of three to four students or fellow professionals, complete the following items.

1. Why is it important to refrain from bringing up negative or controversial topics with patients? Under what circumstances do you find yourself talking negatively? *p 320*

2. Consider the last time you saw a health care provider. What sacrifices did you make as a result of the appointment and did the health care provider recognize those sacrifices? Did the health care provider advocate for any unwanted care and, if so, how did that make you feel?

3. How might talking about a patient's commuting experience help you understand the patient's daily routine? In what way could personal information about patients influence the health care process? *p 323*

4. What type of issues should a health care provider discuss before, during, and at the end of a new patient visit? *p 325*

p326   5. Are there any situations where a recommendation for care might be perceived as unwanted or unnecessary?

p327   6. Under what circumstances would a long-term treatment plan prove helpful to a patient?

p328-329   7. How should an organization communicate with patients about a temporary or permanent conversion of their care?

p330-331   8. How could an organization prevent problems related to scheduling, billing, diagnosing, and treating patients? In each of these four categories, what types of solutions could be implemented if a problem does arise?

p322-323   9. What are some pros and cons regarding the use of an electronic note-taking system as opposed to a paper system? What steps should an organization take to ensure chart notes are recorded properly and kept safe from unauthorized viewing? Are there any laws that must be upheld relating to patient files?

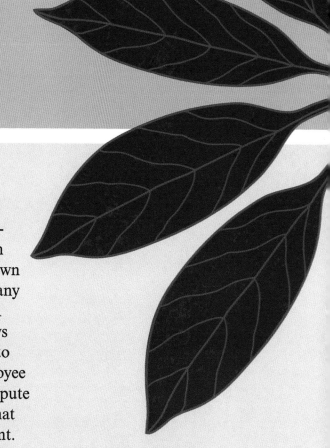

Human Resources

AUTHOR'S NOTE

Make sure to do the appropriate groundwork before hiring an employee. Put together an employee handbook in which you outline job duties for each position. Write down appropriate interview questions to ask. A payroll company can handle compliance issues for a relatively low cost. A licensed attorney should create a list of employment laws that your organization is required to follow. Make sure to keep proper documentation on the hiring process, employee performance, and termination process in case a legal dispute arises. The most important concept to bear in mind is that poor performance may be the result of poor management. Employees need supervision and structure without which they can become unmotivated and perform work at minimum standards.

Find more information about managing employees online through the Society of Human Resource Management, shrm.org

Employee costs typically represent the greatest expense for a health care organization. A health care provider forming a new practice might be able to handle the administrative workload at first, especially if a significant other, family member, or friend offers assistance. As an organization grows, it could quickly become necessary to hire an employee. Employment activity must be anticipated well in advance in order to formulate the correct budgets and assess the ability to meet payroll expenses. An organization needs to maintain procedures manuals and an employee handbook that clearly define the employment relationship. An organization will also need to adhere to a set of laws that aim to protect employees.

The process of hiring employees should be handled with utmost care because many questions and actions could be considered unprofessional or illegal. A work environment needs to allow employees to fulfill job duties without harm to their physical or emotional selves. An organization should not tolerate unprofessional actions, behaviors, or comments from anyone in the office, including patients. Employees are an expensive resource and should be provided with a supportive environment. Employees might have foregone other job opportunities to work for a particular organization and that sacrifice should be respected through proper management.

As a way of managing an organization holistically, regular meetings should take place to relay problems, discuss solutions, and keep organization members updated on changes and events. Staff members should have individual goals that can be assessed during performance reviews. Such reviews, along with an organization's financial performance, should influence compensation changes and promotions. If an organization or an individual staff member underperforms, the root cause may involve poor management. Organization members tend to adapt to the environment that has been formed around them. An organization must determine whether poor performance is the result of poor management or if a certain staff member needs more skills and training. If an employee cannot perform as required even with management participation and proper training, the employment relationship may need to be terminated. The hiring process may need to be reworked thereafter in order to ensure new hires are a better fit for the organization.

18.1   Human Resource Planning

Some health care providers may not need a staff person during the initial stages of growth. The need for staff may quickly emerge as marketing efforts gain traction and an organization naturally evolves. Two issues make human resources planning essential: Employee costs tend to be high overall and government agencies do not tolerate unpaid wages or payroll taxes. An organization must confirm through a *cash budget* that it can realistically afford a new staff member before starting the hiring process. An organization that becomes unable to cover payroll costs will face repercussions from both staff members and government agencies, namely the state labor department. A *growth plan* can outline metrics to pinpoint exactly when a staff member should be hired (or laid off). This plan should anticipate employee turnover and include steps on how to make changes to the workflow if an employee departs. For instance, an organization can prepare to hire a temporary worker or require overtime if a particular staff member suddenly leaves. A health care organization should preregister with an employment agency in case a temporary worker is suddenly needed.

Organization members in charge of hiring should practice interviewing (and terminating) employees before actually staffing the organization. Many legal disputes can arise if interview questions are deemed inappropriate. It would *not* be uncommon for an employer to have a legal confrontation with an employee or interview candidate at some point. Because payroll forms can be highly complicated, a payroll company can minimize the challenge involved with reporting employment activity. Payroll companies represent a simple and fairly inexpensive way to manage payroll compliance.

Government Compliance

An organization must register ahead of time with government agencies to provide sufficient notification of employment activity. A health care provider operating as a C, S, or personal service corporation will need to register as an employee personally. At the federal level, an organization must apply for an Employer Identification Number (EIN) using IRS Form SS-4 before engaging in employment activity. A paper version of Form SS-4 can be downloaded or the full submission can be done electronically online though the IRS website.

An organization engaging in employment activity will need to register with the state labor department although this can often be done indirectly. Documents used to register a business form with the Secretary of State's office may also contain a section on employment activity, allowing an employer to indirectly notify the state labor department about the intent to hire workers. If not, an employer will need to file additional documents directly with the state labor department. The state labor department requires an employer to maintain *unemployment* and *worker's compensation* insurance, which covers employees in case of job loss or injury while on the job, respectively. For example, an employee injured in an auto accident while running job-related errands would be covered under worker's compensation insurance and not through personal auto insurance. Some states maintain a government fund for worker's compensation while other states require that the employer find private coverage. The Small Business Administration, or an affiliated group, can provide guidance on government forms and offer classes on human resources.

Owners of a sole proprietorship, partnership, or LLC are never paid wages.

Form SS-4, irs.gov

Payroll taxes, such as unemployment and worker's compensation insurance, were discussed in Chapter 9.

Staffing Decisions

An organization can either find the right skill set to fit current needs or rework current job functions to fit the right candidate. Reworking job functions may disrupt other staff members already employed. Communication with staff members is important, especially when finding a desired skill set among job candidates appears difficult. An organization should gauge the flexibility to alter the staffing framework when adding (or subtracting) employees.

The job duties to be performed by each organization member should be outlined in a procedures manual. A health care provider in charge of an organization should also formulate a procedures manual to create more personal structure. A procedures manual should encompass an employee's work schedule, job duties, and general office duties.

Work Schedule
A procedures manual should contain a work schedule for an employee. Because benefits do not accrue to most part-time workers, a procedures manual should clarify the worker's status and the policy for working hours in addition to those outlined.

An organization should prevent a part-time worker ordinarily ineligible for certain benefits from working a full-time schedule and indirectly becoming eligible for such benefits.

Job Duties The main section of a procedures manual should list the various job duties involved with a position and provide examples or metrics that clearly define good performance.

General Duties Staff members should understand their responsibility to the organization in general. Such duties might include keeping the office clean, answering the phone promptly, attending regular meetings, filling in for other staff members, and so forth.

Employee Handbook

Employee Handbook: A complete set of policies set forth by an employer meant to clearly define the employment relationship.

An organization must give each employee a handbook that covers major policies governing the employment relationship. Software products are available online that can provide a starting framework. A licensed attorney should review a draft of the **employee handbook** for legal conformity. A job candidate slated for hire should read through the handbook before officially starting work and sign a document confirming that the employment terms are understood and agreeable. The signed document should be kept in the employee's file in a locked cabinet. The employee handbook should mention that written policies contained therein supercede any oral agreements. An employee handbook should contain at least the following sections.

Introduction

An employee handbook should start with a general overview of the organization including types of services, prices, general number of patients, hours of operation, and contact information.

Core Values

An organization's philosophy or mission statement should be stated and will most likely refer to expectations of service quality and the importance of supporting the organization internally.

Duty to Employer

Stark Laws prevent health care providers from receiving a direct or indirect financial benefit from referring Medicare or Medicaid patients.

This section should make reference to any procedures manuals and how described job duties can change. This section should stipulate that the employee must report any potential conflicts of interest to management, such as potential violations of *Stark Laws*. This section should cover the unauthorized use of resources, competition with the organization, or holding another job elsewhere. An employee generally has a duty not to deny an organization of any skills, knowledge, or abilities.

Performance Reviews

Most organizations will conduct performance reviews annually, after 90 days from the date of hire, or upon request. The policy on conducting performance reviews should mention the need to properly fulfill job duties. This section should specify any initial evaluation period for new hires.

Timekeeping

Employees need to receive instructions on timekeeping policies, including a list of job codes to use on timecards. Employees must take breaks at designated times and they cannot forego breaks or lunches by law. If intending to hire employees under 18, the rules governing safety limitations and additional breaks should also be covered.

You are responsible by law for ensuring employees take breaks on time!

Compensation

Changes in compensation should be based on the combined performance of the organization and the individual staff members. This section can clarify what denotes an exempt or nonexempt employee from overtime pay as set forth by law. Salaried employees eligible for overtime must receive an amount based on a corresponding hourly rate, which is usually calculated as the worker's salary divided by 2,080 (52 weeks $\times$ 40 hours). The timing of payroll disbursements should be noted, such as weekly, biweekly, bimonthly, or monthly. This section should mention that the organization must garnish wages when required by law.

Benefits

This section needs to define eligibility rules for benefits. Most full-time employees working more than 20 hours per week will qualify for existing benefits. The types of benefits available to employees can be fixed or form part of a **cafeteria plan**, which offers preferred tax status to a *menu* of benefit options. An organization can either pay for benefits directly or use a method of salary reduction that allows employees to pay for benefits by reducing their taxable income personally. Such benefits may include life, health, disability, and dental insurance as well as a retirement plan, public transportation pass, parking reimbursement, and educational assistance.

Cafeteria Plan: A benefit plan organized under Section 125 of the U.S. tax code allowing an employee to select from a "menu" of benefit options, and which reduces an employee's taxable income.

Time Off

This section outlines how vacation and sick time (if offered) will accrue and describes the employee's responsibility to reimburse any overdrawn paid vacation or sick time. Paid or unpaid time off might apply for jury duty, military obligations, or bereavement. An organization should define eligibility rules for paid time off, and these rules can apply to part-time employees. The employee handbook should list recognized holidays when the organization will be closed along with any eligibility for holiday pay.

Leave of Absence

An organization might have a responsibility to provide a leave of absence for qualified reasons if required by law. Such reasons could include childbirth, adoption, military service, personal illness, or to assist an ill family member. Even when not required by law, an organization can list the circumstances when it will grant a leave of absence.

Expense Reimbursement

By law, an organization must reimburse employees for reasonable expenses incurred while performing job duties. A policy might state that expenses will not be reimbursed unless prior approval is granted. Such items may include the purchase of office supplies, auto mileage, travel, or a *per diem* for food and lodging.

Per Diem: A standardized amount provided to an employee meant to cover the cost of food or lodging when away on work-related travel.

Professional Conduct

The sensitive and confidential nature of providing health care services should be mentioned in this section. A general discussion about appearances should touch on cleanliness and appropriateness, but an organization might not have the legal right to enforce dress policies unless a standard uniform is used. A proclamation should be included that states any alcohol use, illegal acts, theft, gross misconduct, or inappropriate conduct toward patients and other organization members will not be tolerated and will result in immediate termination.

Unauthorized Actions

This section should cite any specific actions that an organization will not allow, which may include dating patients, improper use of resources, personal communications, forming contracts, or unauthorized handling of patient records. This section should encourage employees to bring forth concerns related to other organization members engaged in unauthorized actions.

Privacy Rules

An employee should review and resign a confidentiality agreement each year.

Privacy rules (HIPAA) should be referenced and a clear description of how to handle patient records should be outlined. This section needs to define what constitutes an improper release of patient information—while employed or after the employment relationship has ended. An organization needs to have employees sign a *confidentiality agreement* apart from the employee handbook in order to reinforce privacy expectations.

Harassment

An organization should provide anti-harassment, antidiscrimination, and safety training to new hires and enact a policy to retrain employees on an ongoing basis.

A clear definition of harassment should be given along with the consequences of engaging in harassing behavior. The definition should touch on specific activities, such as sexual advances, jokes, comments, looks, and other behaviors that would make a reasonable person feel uncomfortable. This section should encourage employees to bring forth concerns related to other organization members or patients engaged in harassing behaviors.

Discrimination

A clear definition of discrimination should be given along with the consequences of engaging in discriminatory behavior. The definition should cover factors related to gender, race, creed, national origin, religious affiliation, and sexual orientation. This section should encourage employees to bring forth concerns related to other organization members or patients engaged in discriminatory behaviors.

Safety Issues

Dangerous activities should be listed in the employee handbook in an effort to comply with various labor laws. Such activities may include taking diagnostic images, handling biohazardous materials, cleaning up chemical spills, and dealing with disasters. This section should clearly explain what to do in case of an emergency and how to direct patients.

Termination

This section should outline grounds for termination and specify if the employment relationship is *at will* or *for cause*. Some government authorities allow an employer to terminate the relationship at any time (at will) whereas other jurisdictions require an employer to have a justified reason for termination (for cause). The employee handbook should list policies related to severance, compensation, benefits, and the accrued vacation or sick time of departing employees.

Summary

Hiring a new employee is an expensive undertaking and an organization needs to adequately plan for the event. A cash budget can help determine if an organization has enough money to cover payroll expenses. An employee, along with the state labor department, will react strongly against any nonpayment of compensation, benefits, or payroll taxes. Because reporting employment and payroll activity can be highly complicated, a payroll company can serve as a simple and fairly inexpensive way to manage payroll compliance.

New positions can be filled according to a desired skill set or in relation to a desired candidate. Procedures manuals are used to outline the specific and general job duties of each position. An organization must put together an employee handbook and confirm that staff members understand the major policies governing the employment relationship contained therein.

18.2   Employment Law

Various employment laws may apply only to organizations with more than a minimum average number of staff members. For example, the Americans with Disability Act only forces compliance at the federal level if an employer has 15 or more regular staff members. State or local governments may have versions of these same laws that come into effect at lower levels. An organization needs to verify the specific employment laws that must be upheld. As a way of fostering a positive work environment and avoiding any unknown legal conflicts, an organization could decide to fully comply with employment laws even where no legal requirement is apparent.

> Seek the advice of a licensed attorney to confirm what employment laws apply.

Employee Protection Laws

The employee protection laws mentioned in this book apply to all organizations regardless of the number of employees. These laws govern work conditions, employee compensation, and the employment relationship.

Occupational Safety and Health Act (OSHA) OSHA requires that employers review the workplace for safety issues and maintain a log of even minor incidents using OSHA Form 300. A health care organization should outline safety standards for dealing with x-ray equipment or biohazardous materials. Additional safety efforts should include training employees on how to deal with a disaster or fire. Employers must display appropriate *safety* posters prepared by the U.S. Department of Labor prominently in a visible part of the clinic, such as a breakroom.

> OSHA, osha.gov

Fair Labor Standards Act (FLSA) An organization will not have to withhold payroll taxes, file payroll-related forms, provide benefits, or worry about various employment laws when using the services of an independent contractor. Employers have a clear incentive to take advantage of the independent contractor status as a result. In order to prevent the treatment of valid employees as independent contractors, the FSLA provides a framework meant to help organizations determine a worker's proper status.

> Department of Labor, dol.gov

1. Behavioral Control How much control can the organization exert over how work is performed? Does the worker perform such services for others in the community using a customary skill set?

2. Financial Control Does the organization provide the worker with supplies, equipment, and workspace? Does the worker receive pay in regular intervals or after accomplishing a project?

3. Nature of Relationship Will the worker perform work on an ongoing basis and are job duties considered normal for the organization?

> More information about how to determine a worker's status can be found in Chapter 9.

An independent contractor will generally perform work for other organizations in the community and maintain control over how work is performed. Consult a licensed professional if the status of an independent contractor seems questionable. More information related to payroll matters can be found in IRS Publications 15 and 15A. An organization can also file Form SS-8, Determination of Worker Status, with the IRS. When in doubt, an organization should treat a worker as a *bona fide* employee in order to prevent legal disputes or an assessment of unpaid payroll taxes.

The FLSA further establishes two categories of employees—exempt and nonexempt—to determine eligibility for overtime pay. An *exempt* worker is not entitled to overtime pay when working more than 40 hours in a week. An employee is considered exempt if one of the six standards is met as listed in Table 18.1.

> An associate or office manager may qualify as an exempt employee. Check with a licensed professional if unsure about an employee's status.

TABLE 18.1	**Overtime Exemptions**
Executive officer	
Administrative manager	
Professional worker	
Computer employee	
Outside sales agent	
Highly compensated employee	

A *nonexempt* employee must earn at least the minimum wage and receive overtime pay when the hours worked surpass 40 in relation to an organization's standard workweek (seven consecutive days that can begin on any day). Paying a nonexempt staff member a salary does not sidestep the requirement to pay overtime. The hourly rate used for overtime purposes is calculated by dividing the annual salary by 2,080 hours (52 weeks × 40 hours). A different set of minimum wage laws apply to salaried employees to prevent employers from offering an unreasonably low salary.

> The state labor department or regional SBA office should be able to furnish FLSA or OSHA posters that must be posted somewhere visible in the clinic.

The FLSA also defines what constitutes a payable instance of work and addresses work conditions for minors. There are no federal limits as to how many hours an employer can require an employee to work within a week although state laws may impose stricter standards. Employers must display appropriate *worker protection* posters prepared by the U.S. Department of Labor prominently in a visible part of the clinic, such as a breakroom.

Equal Opportunity Laws

Federal equal opportunity laws may not apply to a small business depending on the average number of employees retained throughout the year. State and local laws may parallel these federal laws and stipulate lower thresholds for applicability. Equal opportunity laws attempt to prevent unfair practices during the hiring process and period of employment.

> Equal Employment Opportunity Commission, eeoc.gov

Title VII of the Civil Rights Act Title VII prevents discrimination based on race, color, religion, sex, and national origin. One of the most common behaviors considered discriminatory is an inappropriate sexual advance or conversation. Sexual harassment laws are based on Title VII and subsequent civil rights acts. An organization should define inappropriate actions and educate staff members about the consequences of harassment and discrimination. Organization members should sign a code of conduct at the time of hire, usually as part of an employee handbook, and annually thereafter upon retraining efforts. The code of conduct should be reviewed with *patients* who display inappropriate behaviors as well. Penalties and lawsuits can be severe if actions are not immediately taken to prevent further incidents. Such actions might include increasing preventative training, terminating an offending staff member, or advising an offending patient to seek care elsewhere.

Equal Pay Act The Equal Pay Act prohibits unequal pay among male and female staff members performing roughly the same job duties unless such pay differential is based on seniority or merit.

Age Discrimination in Employment Act (ADEA) The ADEA prohibits discrimination against persons over the age of 40 during the hiring process and during any period of employment. The ADEA prevents the use of age in determining compensation, benefits, opportunity, and job functions.

Americans with Disability Act (ADA) An employer must give equal consideration to a disabled candidate as long as the person requires only *reasonable* accommodations to perform job duties. An employer is *not* required to provide accommodations that would impose an undue hardship on the organization.

Pregnancy Discrimination Act An employer must give equal consideration to a pregnant candidate. Upon being hired, the candidate shall be afforded the same rights and benefits as other employees, such as the right to acquire health insurance or take a leave of absence for childbirth.

Benefit Protection Laws

Federal benefit protection laws may not apply to a small business depending on the average number of employees retained throughout the year. State and local laws may parallel these federal laws and stipulate lower thresholds for applicability. Benefit protection laws permit an *employee* to maintain certain benefits during a time period where employment activity has been halted.

Department of Labor, dol.gov

Consolidated Omnibus Budget Reconciliation Act (COBRA) COBRA affords an eligible staff member the right to extend health insurance benefits that were previously provided through an employer's group health plan. An employer must notify the plan's administrator within 30 days of the event that led to an employee no longer being covered by the group health plan. The group plan might have been terminated, an employee might have left the organization, or an employee could have had a change in worker status. The employee is financially responsible for the cost of health insurance coverage under most circumstances.

Family and Medical Leave Act (FMLA) If FMLA rules apply, an employer must grant an eligible employee an unpaid leave of absence for up to 12 workweeks over any 12-month period for childbirth, adoption, military service, serious personal illness, or family member's serious illness. Employees become eligible after having worked 12 months in a full-time capacity. An employer must extend health benefits during a leave of absence and reconstitute an employee's same employment status immediately after the leave has ended.

Summary

Various federal employment laws may not apply depending on the average number of regular employees retained by an organization. State and local laws may parallel these same federal laws, but impose a smaller number in terms of this minimum threshold. A licensed attorney should be consulted to verify which laws apply to a particular organization. The Occupational Safety and Health Act along with the Fair Labor Standards Act will apply to every health care organization regardless of the number of employees. OSHA sets safety standards whereas the FLSA governs the status of workers and corresponding pay requirements. An organization should give due consideration to following equal opportunity and benefit protection laws regardless of the number of employees. Preventing harassment and discrimination during the hiring process and in the workplace is essential to creating a positive experience for patients and organization members.

18.3   Hiring Process

An organization can start the recruitment process to attract and hire a new staff member after carefully reviewing staffing needs, compiling an employee handbook, and checking to ensure compliance with laws and regulations. An organization should keep a record of recruiting and hiring efforts in case a legal dispute arises. Notes should *not* be written on materials submitted by candidates, such as an application or résumé.

A common way to attract job candidates entails the use of a job posting. A comprehensive job posting can describe the organization, relevant job duties, expected qualifications, and best method for candidates to submit information. Every candidate should submit a résumé or job application listing prior work experience, education, and skills. Asking candidates to write a brief cover letter detailing their ability to perform related job duties can assist an organization with finding a proper match, especially when considering that not all candidates will submit well-developed résumé. Candidates should be asked for references and salary requirements, but it may not be necessary to request these items upfront.

Post a job online, craigslist.org

A help wanted sign might not appear professional.

A job posting can be placed with newspapers, recruiting agencies, or online websites. An organization should use caution when recruiting network participants, referral sources, or patients—or a friend or relative of such persons. What types of concerns could surface if a person is not hired or the employment relationship sours? An organization may also want to keep its business name undisclosed in a public job announcement to avoid disrupting relationships. Not hiring a candidate or terminating the employment relationship could lead to problems within a health care provider's community. Assess the strength of relationships and clearly communicate expectations in advance in order to minimize negative backlash.

An organization may want to work with an employment agency to receive interviewing assistance and obtain guidance on the hiring process. An employment agency can help find the right candidate or place a worker temporarily if more flexibility is needed. A temporary or temp-to-hire arrangement might work best when an organization faces financial constraints or expects major changes to take place. The employment agency fee might be worth the cost in relation to the time saved by not having to sort through a pile of résumés and interview candidates directly. A job posting could easily draw over 50 responses and finding the right fit could take weeks. An organization might want to ask general interview questions to verify that a temporary placement is appropriate since incorrect judgment by an employment agency could waste resources or negatively impact the patient experience.

Interview Guide

An organization will want to select a few candidates to interview based on responses to a job announcement or referrals from an employment agency. An interview should be used to explore a candidate's skill level in more depth and consider how the person would fit socially. An ideal staff member in the health care field will be personable, likable, trainable, and sustainable. Most candidates will not possess all the required skills immediately, but will a candidate's background, work ethic, and aptitude suggest that the job duties could be learned within a short time? Current organization members and patients must be able to establish rapport with a new employee. An abrasive or dissimilar personality could cause tension among organization members or lead to a negative experience for patients. Table 18.2 outlines a common process to follow when interviewing candidates.

An office manager or employment agency can conduct both interviews, but an organization member (owner) with the power to hire an employee should participate in at least the second interview. A general overview during the first interview allows a candidate to assess the situation and give proper consideration to working for a health care organization. Interview questions should be general at first and then cover technical matters later.

TABLE 18.2 Interview Process	
First Interview	**Second Interview**
1. Give an overview of the organization	1. Meet organization members
2. Give an overview of the position	2. Ask remaining interview questions
3. Ask interview questions	3. Perform a skills assessment
4. Allow for candidate questions	4. Allow for candidate questions
5. Discuss general logistical expectations	5. Discuss compensation
6. Outline the next step	6. Outline the next step

Table 18.3 illustrates standard interview questions that a health care organization could ask. A candidate should have an opportunity to ask questions toward the end of an interview. A lack of questions could mean that a candidate is not interested in the position or has not come to the interview prepared. Key logistical matters should be mentioned if a candidate appears viable, such as work hours, potential compensation, and potential

TABLE 18.3   Standard Interview Questions

General Questions

1. What prompted you to respond to our job posting?
2. Why would you like to work for a health care organization?
3. How would you describe your ideal job position?
4. Why do you think you will be successful here?
5. What are your long-term career goals?
6. Why did you leave your last employer?
7. How would your last employer describe your work?
8. Do you anticipate leaving this position in the near term?
9. Are you willing to work overtime or on a weekend?
10. What is the pay range you would like to stay within?

Technical Questions

11. How much experience do you have using our software programs (list)?
12. How many words per minute can you type over an extended period?
13. Tell me about an experience you've had speaking in front of a small audience?
14. What would you do if a patient complained about poor service?
15. What would you do if a staff member complained about our organization?
16. What type of management style do you prefer—structured or hands off?
17. In what way do you feel your skills relate to this position?
18. What job skill would you like to learn next?

Behavioral Questions

19. Tell me about a time when you were unsuccessful at work and how you responded?
20. Have you ever taken on work unexpectedly without being asked?
21. Give me an example of a conflict you had at work and how it was resolved.
22. Discuss any career goals you have set for yourself and what steps you are taking to reach those goals.
23. What has motivated you in the past to do a good job at work?
24. Provide an example of when you took the lead on a work project and was it done properly?
25. Has there been a situation when you needed to build rapport with customers and what actions did you take to form long-term relationships?

benefits. Steps 1 through 3 of the second interview should also be outlined in cases where a candidate might be selected for a second interview.

If called back for a second interview, a candidate needs to have a tour of the facilities and meet other organization members so all parties can fully assess the relationship. The interview portion might include more technical questions. The use of behavioral interview questions is meant to assess a candidate's skill level in handling situations. For example, a candidate could be asked the best way to handle a phone call from a patient angry about a billing mistake. Behavioral interview questions explore past instances of problem solving, conflict resolution, rapport building, motivation, and so forth assuming that future actions will be handled in a similar manner.

A candidate should receive a skills assessment covering the specific job duties of a position. A skills assessment must directly pertain to the job duties under consideration to avoid any discriminatory appearance. Avoid asking a candidate to solve general math problems or demonstrate general reading comprehension. An appropriate assessment involves tasks that will be performed later as part of the position, such as typing, filing, reconciling accounts, or writing chart notes.

If a candidate seems viable, the organization member in charge of hiring should discuss compensation near the end of the second interview. By planning ahead, an organization should already know an approximate salary range to work within. Any final steps of the interview process should be outlined if it appears that a candidate might be hired, namely the candidate will receive a phone call and offer letter if selected. Candidates who are not selected after the first or second interview should receive a general thank-you letter or phone call showing appreciation for their time and effort. The organization should wish them well in their career pursuits and encourage them to apply again if another position becomes available. Valid reasons why candidates were not selected should be documented in notes.

Discriminatory Questions

Practice asking interview questions to make certain they are phrased correctly. Questions should relate to work and comply with equal opportunity laws.

Interview questions must not give the appearance of discrimination. It must be clear how each question *directly* relates to the specific job position being offered and any personal information mentioned by a candidate should not be discussed further. An interview question must not broach subjects deemed inappropriate under equal opportunity laws. The conversation needs to be immediately changed if a candidate brings forth inappropriate subject matter. Use the following mnemonic as presented in Table 18.4 to remember what question topics walk a fine line: **B**adly **P**hrased questions will have **CRASHED** the interview.

Offering Employment

Avoid asking inappropriate questions when calling to verify a candidate's references.

After the completion of the interview process, an organization must decide if a particular candidate would be appropriate to hire or if recruitment efforts should continue. A new staff member must be personable, likable, trainable, and sustainable. An improper fit can lead to unforeseen problems, including poor job performance and higher patient turnover. Keep in mind that candidates are often nervous during an interview and they may not present an accurate image of how they normally behave. The organization member in charge of hiring should confer with other organization members, an employment agency, or a support network before making a final decision.

The starting salary and benefits can be discussed during the second interview, but both parties might still negotiate the exact terms thereafter. An organization should look at other job postings to understand the current market rate for similar positions. An employment agency can help determine the proper wage and benefit structure as well. An organization can establish an initial evaluation period (90 days) when compensation is automatically lower than normal. A new hire may receive a salary increase and certain benefits after successful completion of the initial evaluation period. An organization should specify if bonuses will fully or partially apply to a new hire depending on the start date. For example, will a new employee who starts near the end of the year be eligible for an annual bonus?

TABLE 18.4	Inappropriate Interview Questions

Note the acronym BP CRASHED in the left-hand column. If a job candidate brings forth personal information during an interview, the conversation should be changed immediately.

	Subject	Inappropriate	Appropriate
B	Background	Would you submit to a polygraph test?	Would you take a drug test? Can we run a background check?
P	Pregnancy	Do you anticipate having kids? Do you have children?	Will you need any specific time off?
C	Criminal acts	Have you ever been arrested?	Have you ever been convicted?
R	Religion	What religion do you practice? Will you need time off to observe religious holidays?	Will you need any specific time off?
A	Age	When is your birthday? How old are you?	Are you over 18?
S	Sexual orientation	Do you live with anyone? Are you married?	Are you comfortable working with a diverse group of people?
H	Health	How much do you weigh? Do you smoke or drink? What is the nature of your disabilities?	Can you perform job duties without limitation? Will anything conflict with the proper performance of job duties? What kind of reasonable accommodation will you need?
E	Ethnicity	What is your nationality? What is your first language?	Are you eligible to work in the United States?
D	Documents	Can you submit a photo, driver's license, or ID card?	Can you submit a résumé, cover letter, letter of recommendation, references, or salary requirement?

Once the salary and benefit terms have been agreed upon, the selected candidate should be called to ask if any questions remain and to be notified that an offer letter will be sent. An offer letter should outline the start date, starting salary, and initial benefits being offered as well as request the employee handbook be read. An organization might want to send a copy of the employee handbook and procedures manual along with the offer letter. A candidate should be instructed on how to reply to the offer letter in order to accept the position.

On an employee's first day, the organization member in charge of hiring should provide a general orientation of the organization, cover the employee handbook, and take care of payroll forms, such as Homeland Security Form I-9 and IRS Form W-4. A new employee will need to sign a form confirming that the employee handbook was read and agreed to. All relevant documents should be placed in a personnel file and kept locked in a filing cabinet. An effort should be made to arrange a paid lunch among organization members and perform other team building activities within the first week of employment.

FEDERAL EMPLOYMENT FORMS		
Form I-9	uscis.gov	Employment Verification Worksheet
Form W-4	irs.gov	Employee's Withholding Allowance Certificate

Summary

A job posting describes the position being offered and instructs a candidate how to apply. An employment agency can place a temporary or temp-to-hire worker with an organization as part of a growth plan or as a way of simplifying the hiring process. After finding candidates of interest, at least two interviews should be conducted to assess the relationship. Interview questions can be general, technical, or behavioral in nature. Questions that relate directly or indirectly to subjects covered by equal opportunity laws should be handled with utmost care. A **B**adly **P**hrased question will have **CRASHED** the interview and could result in a legal dispute. Once a candidate is selected, an organization should negotiate salary and benefit terms and then send a letter extending an offer of employment. Once hired, a candidate must complete relevant payroll documents and confirm an understanding of the employee handbook.

18.4   Employee Management

Employees are an expensive resource that must be properly managed.

Although a health care organization may be started without employees, staffing needs can grow over time. Employee-related costs represent the greatest expense on the income statement for most established practices. Besides wages, benefits, and payroll taxes, an organization might encounter other expenses related to equipment, training, professional fees, and so forth. The time and energy involved with managing employees should also be considered as a cost.

Poor job performance can negatively impact net profit levels due to either work inefficiencies or higher patient turnover. It would not be uncommon for an organization to experience theft or legal disputes, especially if job duties are not properly supervised. In order to prevent employees from wasting time and engaging in unwanted activities, proper management involves checking in with them frequently throughout the day to review what they are accomplishing. An organization needs to be proactive about removing games from computers, restricting website use, and establishing a policy against personal phone and email activity. The use of timesheets and job codes allows an organization to keep tabs on employee productivity indirectly. An organization can analyze how time is spent and modify job duties or work hours if productivity appears low.

Management Styles:
A. Linear chain of command with top to bottom hierarchy.
B. Flat (no hierarchy), team based, and project oriented.

Office Culture

Mission Statement: To provide excellent health care to community members and provide them with an unparalleled health care experience.

If left unmanaged, an office culture often takes on a life of its own. A cultural dynamic could emerge that is in direct opposition to professionalism. For example, staff members might start complaining about a particular patient and later begin acting disrespectful toward the patient. An office culture needs to be proactively managed in order to prevent destructive behaviors and attitudes from forming. The employee handbook should make the first attempt at connecting employees with a general *mission statement* and an overall philosophy. An employee's job performance, behavior, and attitude can be tied to the mission statement during performance reviews. The employee handbook should outline acceptable and unacceptable actions, especially in terms of harassment, discrimination, and patient privacy. Such topics should be further discussed during individual or group staff meetings and during training events. If an employee engages in unwanted activities or expresses inappropriate behaviors or attitudes, an individual meeting should be held to prevent further occurrences. The meeting should be documented and the employment relationship should be discussed.

An organization should cultivate an inclusive environment among staff members. Stressing teamwork and meeting together as a group can eliminate cliques from forming. Organization members will appreciate celebrating birthdays together or engaging in team-building activities. When hiring a new employee, all organization members should eat lunch together as a way of getting to know each other.

Staff Meetings

An organization should hold *morning* meetings to discuss the upcoming patient load. Morning meetings can be fairly brief and might occur daily, weekly, or before busy days. This type of meeting gives organization members a chance to review patient files, hear an inspirational thought, and mention any special issues. It also forces organization members to arrive at work on time.

A *monthly* staff meeting should cover progress toward reaching organizational goals (balanced scorecard) and examine general issues impacting the organization. A monthly staff meeting should be held at the office or a restaurant with free lunch provided and last around one hour. Management will have more opportunity during a monthly staff meeting to inspire employees, redirect the office culture, and strengthen relationships.

Management may find that an *individual* meeting is required to address unwanted activities or disruptive behaviors and attitudes. For example, if an employee is sending personal text messages during work hours, management should hold a closed meeting with the employee to discuss how such actions are against policy and could be grounds for termination.

Meetings can be used to encourage employees to voice any problems they might have encountered. Employees might feel hesitant about bringing forth concerns because (1) they might not be motivated to solve a problem or (2) it might show that they caused the problem initially. An organization might suggest setting an individual meeting if a problem is personal or involves other staff members.

Apart from work-related meetings, an organization should arrange events where staff members can bring family members, hang out, and be rewarded for a job well done. An annual event could center on the anniversary of the organization's opening. Other events could relate to seasonal activities, such as a summer picnic or winter ski trip.

> The cost of meals is normally only 50% tax deductible. In contrast, amounts spent on lunch for a staff event may be 100% deductible. Consult a tax professional for more information.

Training and Development

Positive feedback for a job well done can empower an employee and it can reiterate what sort of job performance is desired. Management should congratulate organization members during meetings for major accomplishments and give praise throughout the day for superior work.

Receiving only negative feedback during a training session can cause an employee to feel belittled and complain about the training experience. To circumvent this sensitivity, *prearranged* training sessions covering multiple job duties should be conducted thus allowing employees to observe mistakes directly or indirectly. A more complete overview of job duties allows an employee to receive both praise and guidance concurrently. An employee can also have an easier time remembering or understanding all aspects of training if such activity is placed into a greater context. Prearranged training sessions should occur almost daily for new hires and then less frequently as performance improves. The employee handbook should reference this training pattern so that employees expect it. When an employee needs immediate correction due to the circumstances, a training session should still cover more than one job duty.

> A full training session can correct mistakes indirectly without having to make an employee feel bad.

An organization should put together training sessions to enhance current skill sets. Continuing education, seminars, publications, and in-house presentations can make employees more valuable from a productivity standpoint. Training can cover how to handle patient concerns, market more effectively, or perform internal processes better. Organization members should learn how to handle patients with mobility limitations, language barriers, reduced literacy, and so forth. Employees must sign a confidentiality agreement and receive training in order to ensure patient privacy is not violated.

Antiharassment, antidiscrimination, and safety training must be conducted upon hire and at least annually. Organization members can also cross-train with one another to diversify skill sets, break apart monotonous routines, and soften any impact from employee turnover. Ensure that employees always maintain notes to minimize retraining efforts.

Training efforts can occur during regular business hours, at lunch, after closing, or on the weekend. Consider the patient experience along with how an employee might feel. Would an employee learn more being trained in front of patients? Or, would conducting a training session during regular business hours negatively impact the patient experience? An organization may need to establish a blend of training times to benefit all parties.

Performance Reviews

Performance reviews typically occur 90 days after the date of hire, on an annual basis, or upon request. The evaluation process should involve three perspectives.

1. The employee's evaluation of management
2. An individual self-assessment
3. Management's evaluation of the employee

Each person is different and should be managed differently.

Management Evaluation Employees should receive a survey to rate management and overall job satisfaction. The survey should provide management with insight into the root cause of poor job performance. Has an employee performed poorly because of management's unwillingness or inability to address specific issues? Employees will often see a lack of oversight or directive as a reason for doing the bare minimum. Employees will come to understand boundaries and put forth just enough effort to avoid a reaction from management. Most employees need structure and failing to provide that structure places part of the blame for poor job performance on management's shoulders. It becomes important to ask employees if they would like to be managed differently.

Self-Evaluation A self-assessment encourages each employee to set goals and devise action steps needed to meet those goals. An employee can be asked an open-ended question to derive feedback, such as "How would you improve your position?" An employee should rate personal job performance and list ways to make improvements. Management can compare responses among organization members and review performance with a more complete picture. Thereafter, management needs to work with employees to refine goals, move action steps along, and provide the resources each employee needs to perform job duties well.

Employee Evaluation Finally, management should evaluate employees based on their specific job performance and how much they have assisted the organization in general. A procedures manual serves as a platform to inform employees about performance expectations. Compensation changes, bonuses, and promotions should reflect the extent to which an employee has exceeded, met, or failed to meet expectations. Management should address any performance concerns in conjunction with what the employee is doing correctly. Offering only negative feedback without concurrently showing appreciation for an employee's work effort can cause an employee to feel belittled and to complain about the review experience.

Compensation and Benefits

An organization must use caution when agreeing orally to compensation, bonuses, and promotions because such actions might prove legally binding. Adjustments to compensation and job status should reflect individual job performance as well as an organization's overall financial health. A *cash budget* can demonstrate that an organization can fully cover employee costs. This type of analysis is crucial since cash flows can fluctuate wildly and an organization will face strong repercussions from both staff members and the state labor department if payroll expenses are not paid on time.

A bonus or raise can be given to employees with greater responsibilities, seniority, or performance ratings (merit pay). A compensation or bonus system based on net profit can provide employees with a strong incentive to support revenue growth and prevent waste. This system also ensures an organization has enough money to cover payroll costs.

An organization may want to offer steady increases to base salaries and treat compensation related to exceptional job or financial performance as a bonus. An organization that underperforms will find it easier to deny a bonus than decrease base salaries since employees tend to be highly sensitive about their incomes. At a minimum, an organization may want to provide a cost of living adjustment (COLA), giving employees a raise based only on the change in inflation and thus keeping the purchasing power of their incomes the same.

Paying employees a low wage might *not* result in an overall increase to net profit. An underpaid worker might not strive to cultivate an ideal patient experience resulting in higher *patient* turnover. Low wages can also result in higher *employee* turnover, productivity issues, and diminished job satisfaction. Wage levels should correspond to the degree of job skills and performance quality desired.

Organization members might decide to forego a salary increase in favor of more benefits. An organization will receive a tax advantage for only **qualified benefits**, such as certain insurance policies, retirement plans, a cafeteria plan, or transportation costs. An **unqualified benefit** may not receive a tax advantage and a tax authority may consider it indirect compensation, subjecting the employee to more taxable income. Except for small ***de minimis*** items, providing employees with cars for personal use, allowing them to live rent-free in a building, or giving them expensive gifts typically represent an unqualified benefit subject to recharacterization as taxable income. An amount spent on qualified benefits in excess of any legal benefit limitation could be recharacterized as taxable income as well.

Staff Promotions

Employees should have a chance at upward mobility, which might be difficult within a small organization. In order to offer employees promotions and keep job satisfaction high, certain advantages can be bestowed upon employees who perform well. A staff member could earn a closer parking spot or get to move into a nicer workspace. More decision-making authority or responsibility can be conferred upon employees. An organization can create a new position or present a new job title. As employees rise in seniority, they could be allowed more control over the job duties they would like to perform. Job duties can be rotated among employees automatically in an effort to provide variation and cross-training. An organization should pay attention to how monotonous tasks appear and try to make such tasks livelier where possible.

Summary

Management should prevent staff members from forming an unhealthy office culture. A general mission statement can act as a guide when trying to mold a positive office environment. Regular staff meetings as a group or individually are key to opening lines of communication and discussing important matters. Training and development activities make staff members more valuable and help correct any problems that might be occurring with job performance. Since employees tend to be sensitive to negative feedback, establishing prearranged training sessions that cover multiple job duties allows for a review of what employees are doing correctly and incorrectly. If job performance is adequate and net profit levels are sufficient, employees could receive more compensation, benefits, or a bonus based on

Make sure that employees do not aggressively sell products and services in an effort to increase their potential bonus.

Qualified Benefits: Indirect payments of money to employees that tax authorities allow as a tax deduction for the business and which are not treated as compensation to employees.

Unqualified Benefits: Indirect payments of money to employees that tax authorities disallow as a tax deduction for the business and which may be treated as taxable compensation to employees.

De Minimis: Indirect payments of money considered immaterial by tax authorities allowing treatment as a qualified benefit automatically.

responsibility levels, seniority, or merit. Although promoting staff members may be difficult in a small organization, various advantages can be conferred on well-performing staff members apart from monetary rewards.

18.5   Termination Process

The right of an employer to terminate employees differs depending on the location of the business. An organization should always maintain proper records of job performance and termination in case a legal dispute arises. In the United States, an *at will* state allows an employer to terminate the employment relationship at any time and without reason. A *for cause* state requires an employer to provide the employee with an opportunity to correct poor performance. The employment relationship can only terminate where fair warnings have not led to sufficient improvements in job performance. Regardless of the location, an employer has the right to terminate the employment relationship where illegal or hostile actions have been committed or might occur. For example, if a receptionist is caught stealing money, the organization should send the employee home, contact the state labor department or a licensed attorney, and take action to terminate the employee.

In cases where a termination is caused by gross misconduct, the employee will most likely be denied unemployment benefits. If terminated or laid off exclusive of any misconduct, an employee may be eligible to receive unemployment compensation. This might affect an organization's *contribution rate*, thus increasing the amount charged each year for mandatory unemployment insurance coverage.

Termination Guide

A. Immediately terminate all relationships when the employee poses a threat to others. The employee should be told verbally that coming back on premises will be considered trespassing. The organization should contact the state labor department or a licensed attorney to confirm that legal steps have been appropriately followed.

B. If an employee is suspected of illegal activity or appears under the influence of substances, the employee should be sent home until matters can be investigated further. Theft and alcohol abuse are common reasons for immediately terminating an employee. Depending on the circumstances, an organization should contact the state labor department or a licensed attorney to confirm that legal steps have been appropriately followed. In some cases, an employee might need to rest at home for understandable reasons, such as experiencing side effects from prescribed medication.

C. An organization should always document job performance by a standard evaluation process. Job performance considered *poor* should be adequately documented in order to maintain a record and help the employee make adjustments. Hiring and training a new staff member requires resources and an organization should not hastily terminate the employment relationship. Often, an employee will correct poor performance after a warning has been issued. Management's lack of employee oversight, training, opportunities, and incentives may contribute to performance issues as well. An employee should have an opportunity to critique management as a result.

D. In *for cause* jurisdictions, an organization must give employees the opportunity to correct poor performance by law. An organization in an *at will* jurisdiction should afford this same opportunity to ensure that employees are not hastily terminated. A *progressive discipline structure* should normally be followed to protect against legal disputes and formally address performance issues. The topic of poor performance should initially be discussed in reference to one item (if possible) and a written letter should be signed by the employee and placed in the employee's file. If sufficient corrections are not made in a timely manner, a second warning needs to be given. Management should write a letter clearly explaining how performance was not adequately corrected, two fair warnings have been given to date, and a third fair warning will result in termination of the employment relationship. The second written letter should be signed by the employee and placed in the employee's file.

E. Poor performance that is not eventually corrected should result in termination of employment. The reasons should be clearly stated in a document placed in the employee's file. Ignoring poor performance can create a legal appearance that job performance was in fact satisfactory. The communication should occur on a *Monday morning* to lessen the employee's emotional distress. An organization should say as little as possible about the reasons for termination, simply apologize for the circumstances, and tell the employee what will happen next.

F. An organization can give an employee a two-week notice or decide to end the relationship immediately. In some cases, an organization must legally compensate an employee for those two weeks even if termination becomes effective immediately. Employees who leave or are terminated are usually legally eligible to receive in-kind payment for unused accrued vacation time. An employee might be eligible for *severance* if an employment contract exists or as set forth in the employment handbook. A key, uniform, or other organization property will need to be returned by the employee, but an organization may not be able to withhold compensation in the interim. The state labor department or a licensed attorney should be contacted to verify compliance with applicable laws and employment terms.

G. After an employee's final day, an organization should arrange a staff meeting to address any concerns among remaining staff members and delegate workloads until a replacement is found. Staff members should feel welcome to meet with management individually. Management should specify how to talk to patients about the termination. Narratives should be used in order to avoid unprofessional statements and provide assurances that the employee departed on good terms.

1. _____ decided to explore another opportunity.

2. I'm not sure why _____ left, but we will miss having him/her here.

3. _____ is no longer with the organization, but we wish him/her the best.

H. An organization should consider reworking the hiring process to ensure that a more precise selection is made going forward.

The state labor department may require an organization to reinstate an employee who was improperly terminated.

Employees are at an increased risk for suicide if terminated on a Friday.

Employees are usually not eligible to receive in-kind payment for unused accrued sick time.

Summary

A health care organization needs to determine if relevant laws allow for *at will* termination or require *for cause* justifications. In either case, documentation of poor performance is an essential management tool because (1) employees are an investment that should be properly managed and (2) good records can protect an organization if a legal dispute arises. When termination has been deemed appropriate, the employment relationship may need to be immediately terminated or the employee may receive a two-week notice and work the remaining time. The employee handbook and relevant laws will spell out how to compensate employees who leave or are terminated. Speak with the state labor department or a licensed attorney to ensure compliance with applicable laws.

CHAPTER ASSIGNMENT

Working in a group of three to four students or fellow professionals, complete the following items.

1. What financial tools help an organization determine if it can afford to hire staff members? *p 337*

2. Review the different categories of an employee handbook. Discuss the type of information that each category should contain. *p 338 - 340*

3. Under what circumstances could specific employment laws *not* apply? Within the United States, what role does the Fair Labor Standards Act play in defining the employment relationship and overtime eligibility? *p 341*

4. What are the main steps of an interview? What should occur if a candidate is selected for hire? *p 345*

5. What does the mnemonic **BP CRASHED** refer to and why should an organization avoid trying to uncover personal information about a candidate? *p 346*

6. How might an unmanaged office culture disrupt the patient experience or result in a legal dispute? *p 348*

7. What types of meetings should an organization hold and what specific topics should be discussed during each one? *p 349*

8. Why might scheduling a training session in advance make a staff member feel more comfortable than being told directly that a job duty was not performed correctly? *p. 349*

9. Could an employee's poor job performance emanate from poor management? How should strong job performance be rewarded? *p 350 - 351*

10. What is the difference between a qualified and unqualified benefit for tax purposes? *p 351*

11. What is the difference between an *at will* and *for cause* jurisdiction? What could happen if an organization does not document poor job performance? Why might an organization always want to follow a progressive discipline structure? *p 352 - 353*

12. When should an organization cease the employment relationship and what persons should be contacted? *p 352*

Chief Executive
Fixed Asset Turnover

Form CMS-1500
Conditional Formatting

Practice Management

AUTHOR'S NOTE

Administrative functions must be performed efficiently and have adequate structure in terms of management supervision and internal control measures. Learn how to set up internal processes by exploring other health care practices, especially while working as an associate. Any inefficiency, mistake, or fraud that occurs could waste resources or negatively impact the patient experience. A health care provider can run into financial difficulties or be forced to charge patients higher prices when resources are wasted. Most importantly, it shows how you want to spend your day—either marketing to prospects, managing crises, feeling frustrated, or actually caring for patients. It becomes hard to focus on patient care when your mind is distracted by disorganization. The word *organization* is used throughout this textbook to reinforce how a business should truly operate.

Chief Executive: The organization member possessing the highest level of authority and responsibility.

A health care office is in fact an organization with many working parts that feed into one another. A health care provider normally stands as the **chief executive** of the organization and must formulate and manage all of the working pieces. Billing, scheduling, and accounting are some of the main administrative functions. Poor management of internal processes can lead to high expense and debt levels. Moreover, a patient might encounter a negative experience from part of an organization that has nothing to do with the actual health care process, leading a patient to terminate care prematurely, which could put the patient's health at risk, or spread negative word of mouth. In order to maximize success, all aspects of an organization must be properly managed.

Problems big and small will always exist when running a business. It becomes necessary to proactively discover problems, create meaningful solutions, and implement changes. An organization can become inflexible and inefficient without proactive management. The lack of good management can lead to significant disruptions when an organization is placed under stress. Imagine a case where a key employee leaves, placing a tremendous workload on the remaining organization members who have not received sufficient cross-training and feel overloaded with work already. These organization members may resent the lack of good management and perform job duties poorly leading to even worse problems.

A chief executive must set goals and implement action steps toward establishing a well-functioning organization. As part of offering patients a 100% positive experience, the chief executive needs to consider problems in advance and stand ready to tackle any problems as they surface. A chief executive should use resources efficiently and protect the organization from any random eventuality. Internal-control measures help ensure that systems are indeed working as designed and the potential for fraud and errors is minimized. Organization members must check and recheck work in order to guarantee that administrative tasks and patient records are properly handled.

The final part of this chapter explores the management portion of a business plan. The management plan details goals and action steps as well as examines ways that a business owner can guarantee a venture will have a successful outcome. When combined with the marketing, accounting, and financial concepts discussed in previous chapters, an entrepreneur has all the pieces needed to weave together a full business plan.

19.1   The Chief Executive

This word *organization* has been mentioned often throughout this textbook because of its importance in conveying what running a successful business means. A chief executive must look beyond forming a business and construct a living, breathing system that will not function well or even survive unless all parts are working together in an organized fashion.

Many of the traits that an entrepreneur needs apply to the chief executive position. Having vision and a course for implementation backed by solid motivation are meant to keep a health care organization progressing forward in a productive manner. Leadership traits ensure that decisions are thoughtfully crafted and the chief executive serves as an example for all organization members to follow. Ethical leadership should come without saying when running a professional health care organization. Knowing that disorganized administrative functions can compromise an employee's ability to work effectively or a patient's ability to receive quality health care, a chief executive has an ethical duty to manage operations properly.

A chief executive should take every opportunity to understand how to personally operate internal processes. Too often, health care providers working at a clinic will not seize upon the opportunity to gain knowledge from their surroundings. Management skills take time to develop and a chief executive should make a long-term investment toward optimizing abilities.

A chief executive must remain calm, review a situation, and approach each challenge methodically. Management inexperience can lead to hesitation when confronted with a challenging situation. Acting on impulse rather than relying on research, analysis, and communication can take an organization in the wrong direction unexpectedly. Although staff members and external parties may provide assistance with moving an organization forward, a chief executive should not rely on anyone else to take on the responsibility of properly managing an organization.

Summary

Many of the same traits that define a successful entrepreneur apply to the chief executive position. Ethical and assertive leadership is needed to ensure an organization heads in the right direction. A chief executive should take every opportunity to develop the knowledge and skills needed to manage a health care organization properly. Indecisive or unskilled management can easily lead to unwanted consequences for all organization members as well as patients. In order to put together a successful business, a chief executive must construct an organization where all parts function together in a holistically sound manner.

19.2   Executive Decision Making

A *management information system* is meant to gather information useful in executive decision making. Regular staff meetings, management reports, feedback forms, and constant communication represent the bulk of this system. A chief executive needs this system to proactively look for problems, synthesize meaningful solutions, review a solution's effectiveness, and then implement action steps to resolve matters going forward. Preemptive measures, such as internal controls, can keep problems from ever occurring. Since a business functions as a diverse organization, a chief executive must think through the potential effects of all decisions. Situations should be examined holistically in order to uncover the full scope of an issue.

Suppose a new patient has a sudden health care concern and calls to make an appointment. The schedule appears full in the near term and the only way to accommodate the new patient is to extend regular office hours. If an organization remains flexible and allows a special appointment for this new patient, could this decision lead to other positive outcomes? To what extent would the decision-making process differ if a new patient works for a large company and can easily refer coworkers? Holistically, the decision-making process must take into account all the material benefits and drawbacks to a situation. Extending office hours one time to accommodate a new patient could generate a tremendous benefit later. A chief executive with good management skills will benefit an organization over the long term by seizing upon good opportunities, avoiding hollow initiatives, and making the most of every situation.

Information Collection

A chief executive must know an organization in depth and get a feel for how smoothly it is running by actively collecting information. Remaining alert throughout the day represents the best approach to staying informed. Staff meetings are essential for keeping tabs on employees and gathering information from their perspective. Employees should follow a *chain of command* (where applicable) in order to keep relevant supervisors informed. Other ways for a chief executive to stay informed include reviewing reports, directly communicating with people, or handing out feedback forms. A chief executive will want to consistently communicate with employees, patients, network participants, referral sources, and other professionals.

Reports containing both quantitative and qualitative information can be used to assess situations and gather opinions. General management reports include employee performance reviews, a balanced scorecard, and the results of surveys. Financial reports include the income statement, balance sheet, cash budget, or daily *net profit summary.* A profitability analysis can shed more light on an organization's financial strength. When new or unique issues need examining, an *ad hoc* report can be created from scratch.

CASE STUDY

Executive Decision Making

Imagine that an associate health care provider working for a clinic experiences a visit turnover of 5.6 and a patient margin of $960. The associate decides to leave the position and form a new practice based on these strong performance figures. After one year, the financial position of the new organization looks surprisingly weak. The health care provider believes that low patient retention could be the cause and creates a financial report to evaluate patient ratios. Information gathered reveals a visit turnover of 1.9 (460 ÷ 240) and a patient margin of $133 ($31,900 ÷ 240). A total of 240 patients seems sizeable for the first year of operation, but seeing each patient only 1.9 times appears problematic. Experiencing revenues of $133 per each patient as compared to $960 in the previous year warrants an examination as well.

Why are patients spending so much less on average and coming in fewer times— and could these two phenomena correspond? These declines may reflect problems with the patient experience that the health care provider would have an ethical duty to correct. Since the health care provider is offering a different range of services than before, a survey is sent out to a sample group of patients to gather more information. The sample group involves patients who did not reschedule a follow-up appointment after an initial visit.

Dear Patient,

My goal is to provide excellent health care services to community members. I would greatly appreciate your feedback to help make my organization stronger. Please take a moment to complete this survey at your convenience. A self-addressed, stamped envelope has been included so you can return the survey when completed.

Warm Regards,
Health Care Provider

(1) Circle the types of services that you need a health care facility to offer?
Service 1   Service 2   Service 3   Service 4

(2) Were you dissatisfied with any part of your health care experience? If so, please explain.

(3) Please feel free to comment on any additional topics that you find relevant.

Ten patients responded to the survey within two weeks. Responses showed that patients wanted service lines that the organization did not offer currently. A few respondents mentioned that they did not like driving across town to get x-rays taken. Other respondents commented that they disliked how rapidly visits took place. Based on information gathered from the survey, the health care provider decides to implement a series of reforms. Research was conducted to discover all the x-ray centers nearby. The health care provider evaluated the quality of each one to ensure that the patient experience did not suffer indirectly. The top five x-ray centers were placed on a list displayed next to the front desk. Two new service lines were initiated based on the survey results in an effort to give patients more options. In order to address concerns over improper care management, the health care provider set lunch meetings with more experienced health care providers to review procedures and internal controls. A balanced scorecard in combination with action steps was drafted to ensure that changes are made within a reasonable amount of time.

Managing Transitions

The human brain does not adapt to change effortlessly. Patients and staff members might feel resistant to transitions that need to occur. Communication should begin long before a transition takes place in order to prepare individuals mentally and give them time to voice concerns. Instead of waiting for problems to emerge, expect that people will feel uneasy about a transition. It is important to address matters explicitly and build support for change by highlighting how the organization or patient experience will improve. People involved in a transition could receive a special gift or perk in an attempt to offset any potential impact. When one person brings up a concern, an organization should assume that others are experiencing a similar set of thoughts and emotions. Potential concerns should be addressed in a preemptive manner with all parties who could be impacted.

Imagine a transition that involves a weeklong remodeling of the front-desk area. Any patients with scheduled appointments during this time period should be alerted to the construction and have an opportunity to reschedule. The organization might want to open more appointment times in the weeks surrounding the remodeling. During the week of construction, patients could be offered free secondary services and staff members could receive a *de minimis* gift just to show a little appreciation for having to deal with any potential disorder.

Patient Conversions   Selling a practice can cause significant problems for existing patients and staff members. Communication efforts should alert patients and staff members to a major transition well in advance. The level and type of communication should ensure that there will be no surprises and everyone will have a good understanding of the positive aspects of the transition. As the transition takes place, feedback must be continuously gathered from patients and staff members to ensure undetected problems do not surface. The incoming health care provider needs to keep the experience for staff members and patients as consistent as possible.

Partnering with other health care providers may benefit patients overall. An integrated clinic allows for shared resources and can provide a more diverse range of service offerings. Always make sure to present patients with a simple way of specifying who they would like to be seen by at an integrated clinic. A partnership arrangement should not be taken lightly because management confrontations are common. Legal contracts should clearly define the partnership relationship, ensure fairness, and allow a smooth exit to occur if the arrangement does not function as expected.

Employee Turnover   As part of human-resources planning, management should outline steps to follow in case an employee leaves either by choice or through termination. If an employee leaves the organization, management should hold staff meetings and look for problems that the transition might cause. Would organization members be able to take on the job duties of a departed coworker? Current organization members should receive

An organization can preregister with a temporary employment agency in case a future need arises.

cross-training on a continual basis to ensure any new job duties could be performed properly. A part-time or temporary worker could be hired to alleviate the excess workload until a replacement is found. Professional *narratives* should be conveyed to patients who held strong rapport with a departed worker.

Information Technology (IT) Conversions IT conversions that replace computer hardware or software can result in a loss of data if managed improperly. Sufficient resources should go toward converting a software program or a computer system. This entails training staff ahead of time, having access to the software or hardware vendor, and checking the system to make sure data are converted properly. Before making an IT conversion, management needs to review what will occur if the transition is unsuccessful or if access to data is needed during the process. Data should be thoroughly checked to ensure integrity after the conversion.

Back up data daily!

Summary

A chief executive must proactively look for problems, synthesize meaningful solutions, review a solution's effectiveness, and then implement action steps to resolve matters going forward. The collection of information should occur proactively through direct contact with various groups and indirectly using feedback forms and reports. Instead of waiting for problems to emerge, management must anticipate what might occur given the circumstances of a situation and address matters proactively. Often, individuals will feel uneasy about transitions that must take place and thoughtful communication in advance can prevent problems from arising. Sufficient resources and planning should go into making any major transition to ensure change occurs smoothly and an organization stabilizes afterward.

19.3 Resource Management

An organization must face the reality of having access to only a finite amount of resources. A chief executive must maximize the amount earned in relation to the time, money, and energy consumed through the process of starting and operating an organization. Part of resource management involves protecting an organization against major threats that could materially impact operations, such as a lawsuit or natural disaster.

Insurance Products

Insurance products are explained in greater depth in Chapter 15.

Typical insurance products, such as liability, malpractice, disability, and health, can protect an organization in case a mishap occurs. Business continuity insurance can cover business expenses for a period of time after a catastrophe, such as a fire or earthquake. Manufacturer warranties and property insurance can cover fixed assets in case of damage or theft. Insurance policies should be reviewed to ensure all relevant parties are included in coverage. For example, will a malpractice insurance policy cover a new associate an organization has recently hired?

Human Resources

Employee-related costs usually represent the largest expense for an established health care practice. Human-resources principles, discussed in Chapter 18, explore how to manage employees effectively in order to minimize costs and maximize productivity. Poorly managed employees tend to cost more on average and yield lower productivity concurrently. Without proper structure and oversight, employees are more likely to underperform, make errors, or attempt to defraud their employers.

Inventory Levels

An inventory system needs to strike a balance between too many and too few products on hand. Housing a large inventory takes up space, increasing the cost of rent or taking away from other revenue-producing activities. However, failing to keep adequate levels of inventory on hand can frustrate or disappoint patients who expect the inventory to be available. An inventory system should provide feedback about demand factors for each item of inventory along with a signal warning when inventory levels are low. Understanding demand factors will enable an organization to reorder an appropriate quantity of products at the correct time. An organization should review if demand factors change depending on the season, time of month, or general level of economic activity. Management should take note of the net profit derived from each product line and review if products *complement* or *cannibalize* demand for other products and services. An organization with a small amount of inventory may find that tracking inventory manually apart from a computerized system works more efficiently.

> Consider using Quickbooks or a practice management software program to track inventory. Store inventory on a bookcase or at home to save space.

CONFLICT OF INTEREST

Recommending the same health care products that your organization sells at retail price can create a conflict of interest. Patients might grow frustrated if they feel that such products were recommended for the main purpose of generating profit. Consider selling health care products at wholesale prices or providing patients with information on where to obtain these same products elsewhere.

Fixed Asset Turnover

Fixed assets, such as equipment, furniture, or a building, tend to require large cash outlays at the time of purchase. The **fixed asset turnover** ratio looks at how well the investment in such assets has helped to produce revenue. Compare an organization (1) that earns $150,000 per year and has $30,000 in health care equipment versus a similar organization (2) that earns $80,000 per year and has $40,000 in equipment. The fixed asset turnover ratio would equal 5 and 2, respectively. These figures indicate that the first organization uses equipment 2.5 (5 ÷ 2) times more effectively that the second organization. Management should attempt to derive the maximum amount of revenue from the least number of fixed assets, especially when such assets have been purchased using debt.

> **Fixed Asset Turnover:** A profitability ratio that compares net revenue over total fixed assets.

Net Profit Margin

Each expense account (and subaccount) should be reviewed at least annually to determine if a particular expense could be reduced or eliminated. For example, could an organization switch telephone carriers or change to a different cell-phone plan? Does a particular employee really need a cell phone? An organization should remove all expenses that do not support the production of revenue. Increasing expenses will not make financial sense if revenue levels cannot increase to an even greater extent. A business owner might also want to account for the time and energy spent trying to generate profit.

> Profitability ratios look at how efficiently management uses resources, such as assets and equity.

CASE STUDY

Expense Management

A health care provider has operated a practice for two years and wants to review each expense account in order to improve the organization's net profit level. The following questions were posed in relation to each account in order to determine if expenses could be reduced or eliminated—or if an increase to a particular expense account would help boost the production of revenue.

Advertising   How do advertising expenses support word of mouth and could other resources in terms of time, money, and energy promote the organization better?

Computer Expense	Would new computers help increase worker productivity? Should any software be purchased to block personal Internet use?
Continuing Education	Are there any continuing education events that would provide training on professional sales?
Dues and Subscriptions	Should different magazines or newspapers be placed in the waiting room? How else could the waiting room experience be improved?
Insurance	Does insurance coverage provide adequate protection against all potential contingencies? Are there any additional forms of insurance that the organization should consider?
Interest Expense	Can the organization afford to pay down debt levels in an effort to reduce leverage risk?
Landscaping	Would landscaping upgrades help boost the patient experience enough to offset the cost?
Lease Payments	Should the organization consider buying a building instead of leasing office space?
Legal and Professional Fees	Is there a licensed accountant with more health care industry experience who could advise the organization on financial matters better?
Meals and Entertainment	Would any professionals or business owners want to meet over lunch to discuss referring customers?
Office Supplies	Could the organization save time and money by using electronic documents, especially patient charts?
Payroll Taxes	Could the organization receive worker's compensation coverage at a cheaper price through another insurance company?
Repairs and Maintenance	Are there any upcoming repair and maintenance expenses that should be displayed in the cash budget?
Salaries and Benefits	Could more training, staff meetings, or direct supervision increase worker productivity? Would an increase to salaries and benefits achieve a similar objective?
Utilities	Would energy-efficiency modifications reduce utilities? Could the organization switch to another utilities provider?

Summary

Resources must be used efficiently and an organization must be protected against accidents and disasters. Various insurance products can provide protection against unforeseen events. Good resource management involves giving employees structure and providing them with oversight. An organization needs to ensure that financial outlays will properly contribute to the production of revenue. For example, an organization should review the *fixed asset turnover* ratio to determine how fixed assets are used. Expense accounts should be examined at least annually to determine if changes could lead to higher net profit levels. An inventory system should ensure that an organization houses the right number of products for resale—not too many or too few.

19.4 Internal Processes

Administrative functions must be properly designed to reduce costs, prevent errors, and increase job satisfaction even when a health care provider works alone. Internal processes that are poorly designed can cause employees to grow frustrated with the work environment, underperform job duties, and seek opportunity elsewhere. A system of internal processes must contain *internal control measures* to protect the validity of information. What happens if a patient's name is misspelled on a contact form? How might that impact the patient experience, especially if mail is sent to the patient's home and other family members see the misspelled name?

Take note of how internal process can occur manually, electronically, or both.

With today's state of technology, computer programs have streamlined many of the internal processes that used to occur manually. For example, a software program can populate a Health Insurance Claim Form, also known as **Form CMS-1500,** with billing information and then submit the form electronically to insurance companies or other third parties. Generating information for analysis purposes and putting together management reports can be a mouse click away. When using a computer program to manage internal processes, the following internal control measures work to uphold the integrity of data.

Form CMS-1500: The Centers for Medicare and Medicaid Services (CMS) requires a standard format for health care forms used to bill insurance companies and certain other third parties.

A. Well-developed software programs will have internal control measures automatically built into the computer code. For example, software programs should possess **conditional formatting** in data screens. Such formatting might involve an error box that appears if information is not entered properly into a specific field.

Conditional Formatting: An input screen with functional limitations set forth in the software program's underlying computer code.

B. Software programs should limit what a specific user can do or see (segregation of duties). Password protections should block access to information or prevent users from executing certain functions. For instance, a staff member who handles cash might need to review patient records, but having access to modify patient records as well could enable an undetected theft of cash.

C. Information should be backed up every day and audited periodically to ensure its integrity. Suppose 30 patient files were reviewed and 2 errors were found. Should all files then be reviewed for similar errors and what steps could prevent errors in the future?

D. Software programs should maintain a log of user activity, especially in relation to sensitive information, such as SOAP notes or billing records.

Since even minor issues can negatively impact the patient experience, managing every detail of each internal process becomes an essential part of creating a successful organization. A well-structured system of internal processes will prevent minor (and major) problems from happening. The following overview outlines how to perform administrative functions to increase efficiency and allow for internal controls.

Sign-in Sheet

The day's appointment schedule should be reviewed in the morning as a way of preparing to meet with patients. As patients arrive, they should write their names on a sign-in sheet. A sign-in sheet can be used to confirm that walk-in appointments are recorded in the system and regular appointments are not erroneously or fraudulently deleted. An accurate sign-in sheet gives an organization the chance to (1) check on missed appointments and (2) verify that chart notes have been taken on every patient seen throughout the day.

Put the sign-in sheet on a nice clipboard. Set out pens carrying your organization's logo.

Placement System

Organization members must communicate about where to place patients and the order in which to see them. A placement system often involves putting patients in treatment rooms according to a standard room order. A health care provider may direct where to place patients using hand gestures or verbal instructions. A patient's chart may specify what room to place the patient in if special equipment is needed. A new patient should be placed into a treatment room quickly and given priority by the health care provider.

Consider displaying information in other languages, such as Spanish or Russian, depending on your patient base.

Access to patient files must be limited as discussed in Chapter 17.

Posting Charges

A patient's chart is the ultimate guide in figuring out how much to bill. After a health care provider has finished an appointment, charges need to be established in the billing system based on the chart notes or *travel slip*. A separate document with billing codes can also be used, but the charges should still be verified against what the chart notes or a travel slip have listed. The appointment schedule and sign-in sheet can confirm that chart notes were compiled for every patient seen throughout the day.

Some type of journal entry or management report should be produced to confirm that charges were posted correctly. Billing errors can occur if charges are posted to an incorrect account or in the wrong amount. Staff members should not have the ability to erase charges once established in the system. Only the chief executive or a person with proper segregated job duties should have access to modify billing records. Make sure to periodically audit a sample group of patient charges in the system against chart notes to confirm no errors exist. If an error is found, more investigation may need to take place.

Billing Charges

After posting charges to patient accounts, any unpaid balance needs to be invoiced. Many software programs can populate and then transfer CMS-1500 forms directly to third parties electronically. Sending patient invoices and CMS-1500 forms once per week gives an organization time to conduct a comprehensive review of patient accounts and verify the accuracy of amounts being billed. The patient experience can definitely sour if an organization bills twice for services or misstates the amount due. An organization will also lose money if it underreports charges or fails to include certain charges on billing documents.

Have a sign saying, "Let us know about any changes to your health care coverage or mailing address."

Recording Payments

An organization must ensure that patient accounts are updated correctly when payment is received at the time of service or according to billing documents sent to patients or third-party payors. The patient experience will definitely sour in instances where an organization resubmits a bill after a patient has already made payment. One organization member should gather the mail and list all payments received before depositing amounts in a bank. A deposit slip, journal entry, or *cash log* could serve as this list. A cash log reports how much was received from a particular patient. A cash log should include detail on check and charge card payments.

Job duties can be segregated using an external bookkeeper.

A different organization member should update patient accounts according to the list prepared earlier in the day. The receipt of cash or cash equivalents represents a significant area for potential fraud. Separate organization members should oversee the job functions of (1) handling money and (2) posting charges to patient accounts. Checks should be photocopied and stored along with any charge card receipts. Some type of journal entry or management report must be examined to confirm that information was posted correctly in the system according to these supporting documents. The organization member in charge of posting payments should not have the ability to destroy or alter checks, charge card receipts, or a cash log.

Collection Efforts

A patient with a long-standing unpaid balance should be handed an invoice during a subsequent appointment (if possible). If payment cannot be made at that time, the organization should hand the patient a self-addressed, stamped envelope along with a nice letter explaining any collection policies. An organization must attempt to collect unpaid balances in a professional manner and draft a compromise that benefits all parties if collection efforts prove difficult. Billing documents should be sent several times over the course of many months, taking note that excessive billing efforts can sour the patient experience and drain organizational resources. An organization should call a patient with a long-standing unpaid balance to understand the situation better. Unless a fair compromise can be reached, an organization may need to write off an unpaid balance or turn a patient's account over to a collection agency.

Summary

The various administrative functions must be designed properly to reduce costs, prevent errors, and increase job satisfaction. Computer programs should include internal controls to prevent errors and protect data against fraud. Manual reviews can confirm the integrity of data along the entire range of data collection. The lack of internal controls over administrative processes can lead to problems with the patient experience and subject an organization to damage caused by error or fraud. A sign-in sheet helps to verify that chart notes are completed on every patient seen. Chart notes specify how much to bill patients. A review of patient accounts can confirm that billable charges and payments were posted correctly.

19.5   Example Management Plan

The following *hypothetical* management plan involves a health care provider who has been working as an associate for two years and intends to form a new organization. All of the details in this plan are fictitious and the content of your actual management plan may differ substantially.

Character and Experience

I graduated *cum laude* two years ago. The last two years have been spent working as an associate health care provider at a midsized clinic. I was able to gain a great deal of experience acquiring new patients using marketing and sales techniques. I have been attending the following community organizations to expand my marketing network and referral system:

Member, Toastmasters International
Member, Rotary International
Volunteer, Habitat for Humanity
Volunteer, Biking Association

While working as an associate, I met with administrative staff members regularly in an effort to learn how to operate a health care organization internally. Each quarter, I focused on a different area of the business and spent roughly 15 hours per month reviewing systems. Taking four classes through the regional Small Business Administration office supported this business training. Work references and a résumé are available upon request to confirm this experience.

Key Success Factors

The following list summarizes key factors that will contribute to my success.

1. I have taken the opportunity to learn fully about the internal processes of a health care organization.
2. I have a proven track record of building a network, recruiting new patients, and retaining them. I have steadily increased the size of my network through effective marketing and sales techniques.
3. I know how to create a positive patient experience in terms of delivering quality health care services and managing the office environment.
4. I have financial support from personal savings and a family member has structured a loan agreement to function as a line of credit.
5. Research shows that competitive pressures are low within a specific target market and current health care providers tell me that net profit levels are high.

Financial Ratio Targets

The new organization will seek to achieve the following financial ratios.

1. Times Interest Earned: Greater than 6
2. Long-Term Debt to Total Assets: Less than 50%
3. Current Ratio: Greater than 1
4. Net Profit Margin: Greater than 20%
5. Return on Assets: Greater than 30%
6. Worker Productivity Ratio: Less than 30%
7. Visit Turnover: Greater than 5
8. Patient Margin: Greater than $500

Balanced Scorecard

The new organization will seek to achieve the following goals using an array of action steps [not listed]. The metrics shown next to each goal specify the point where a goal is being attained.

Goal Board			
Financial Perspective		**Patients Perspective**	
Goal	**Metric**	**Goal**	**Metric**
Increase fiscal responsibility	No more than $1,000 in credit card charges per month	Improve the waiting room experience	Review verbal feedback about magazines, toys, and furniture
Increase financial stability	Maintain a rolling six-month cash budget	Review prices	Achieve 85% positive feedback about price levels
Decrease expenses	Review expense items and find one way to save money each month	Increase service levels	Consider two new services that could increase the quality of patient care
Internal Processes Perspective		**Learning Perspective**	
Goal	**Metric**	**Goal**	**Metric**
Convert to a better inventory-tracking program	Training done by June Implementation by July	Improve cross-training	Schedule 30 minutes of cross-training each week
Improve internal-control measures	Confirm that data input is reviewed once per week	Memorize narratives	Memorize one new narrative per week for marketing purposes
Personal motivation	Complete a weekly *To-Do List*	Morning meetings	Memorize patient names on the daily schedule

Strategic Planning

The new organization could implement the following strategies if the current operating environment changes.

New Competition

If other health care providers start competing within the organization's target market or profit levels contract within the marketplace, I can begin offering more services. A comprehensive territory worksheet has been compiled detailing various marketing efforts that could be initiated. The organization may experience low profitability at first until current marketing efforts take hold. My proven track record with recruiting and retaining patients should ensure that profit levels remain sufficient.

Economic Downturn

The economy appears to be stabilizing after a deep recession. The demand for health care services appears highly *inelastic* since demand levels did not decline during the last recession. If the economic recovery falters and revenue levels decline within the health care industry, the new organization can focus more attention on a target market or offer additional services. The organization has identified ten ways to reduce expenses if revenues decline, resulting in a potential savings of $22,000. Certain expenses would not be needed in cases where revenue levels dropped below set thresholds. A separate *contingency plan* has been drafted that addresses these thresholds. The use of a line of credit should keep debt leverage at a minimum as well.

Industry Changes

A strong professional association has been instrumental in improving the legal environment over the past decade. A lobbyist with the association has confirmed that there are no current pieces of legislation being considered that could impact the profession. The professional association has a fair amount of resources available to combat any negative publicity. If consumer trends change, the organization has a strong ability to change service lines, modify prices, and launch new marketing campaigns.

Transition Planning

A legal contract was drafted with my current employer to properly define the employment relationship before starting work. In order to make a smooth transition into my own practice, it was agreed that any patients attracted exclusively through personal efforts could be retained without charge. The legal contract defines what qualifies as personal efforts. Any conflicts of interest have been minimized by not actively marketing to my employer's patients. If a patient of my employer decides to convert to my new organization, it would result in charges of $250.

My employer authorized narratives that I could use when talking to patients about the transition. A noncompete agreement will enforce these policies for two years after the transition has occurred. Patient records are stored digitally and can easily be converted to my new system. Records will be acquired only in cases where they relate to personally attracted patients or after paying $250 for a patient of my employer. Files will be examined before and after conversion in order to verify the integrity of data.

Since I am currently employed and in a principal-agent relationship, planning efforts have been conducted only during my personal free time. As a result of thoughtful management of the transition process, I do not anticipate any legal complications with my current employer or disruptions in care for patients.

Resource Management

The practice management software program used by the new organization will have a wide range of internal controls to protect against errors and fraud. Internal processes have been structured to prevent erroneous data from getting into the system.

I will also follow procedures designed to protect against mistakes in patient care. An expert in Occupational Health and Safety Act (OSHA) laws will review the organization for safety concerns. In order to protect against lawsuits or catastrophic events, the organization has budgeted for adequate malpractice, liability, business continuity, health, and disability insurance.

Staff members hired by the new organization will receive training on how to operate internal processes efficiently. A comprehensive employee handbook will clearly define the employment relationship. Finally, I have obtained video training modules on the topics of harassment and discrimination to ensure that organization members understand what constitutes proper behavior.

CHAPTER ASSIGNMENT

Working in a group of three to four students or fellow professionals, complete the following items.

p 357   1. How long might it take to gather the skills needed to succeed as the chief executive of an organization and under what circumstances can a person develop such skills?

p357   2. To what extent should the chief executive of an organization solve problems in a pre-emptive and holistic manner?

p358   3. In what ways could organization members, especially the chief executive, gather information needed to make executive decisions?

p. 359-360   4. Cite examples of transitions that an organization might undergo. What actions could make these transitions proceed smoothly?

p. 360-361   5. How can an organization ensure that resources are used efficiently and remain protected? What are the main resources that an organization should closely manage?

p. 363   6. Review the four types of internal control measures that a computer program should contain. What could occur if such quality control measures are absent from part of a program?

7. How should internal processes be structured to ensure that
   a. detailed chart notes are compiled for every patient?
   b. charges are correctly posted to patient accounts?
   c. patients are billed the correct amounts?
   d. payments are correctly posted to patient accounts?

Computer Systems

AUTHOR'S NOTE

Welcome to the last chapter of this book. I congratulate your efforts to learn so much about business and entrepreneurship. A lot of smaller health care organizations still rely heavily on manual systems to perform administrative and clinic functions. Manual processes can be faster and less expensive when the patient load is easily manageable. As an organization becomes more difficult to manage or the range of services expands, the use of electronic equipment and management software becomes more practical. Finding suitable equipment and software has its own unique set of challenges. Make sure to budget enough time to explore the medical supply industry and experiment with different software to find a strong fit. The market for software is saturated with vendors, each providing a slightly different product across a wide price range.

A health care organization will typically use electronic devices, such as diagnostic equipment, to assist with patient care. Possessing a range of medical equipment in a clinic can limit the need to refer patients for imaging and testing services. An organization has better control over the patient experience in this case and a patient may face fewer inconveniences. However, the increase in types and cost of medical equipment has made housing all necessary devices impossible. Patients may benefit more by being referred to a trusted diagnostic center that has all the latest equipment.

An organization may possess medical equipment that only serves to enhance the patient experience. For example, a health care provider can use an electronic device to present various images of the body. Such equipment can allow a patient to *visualize* a health problem better and appreciate the qualified reasons for care. Spend time browsing medical supply stores (online) and conduct a cost-benefit analysis to identify suitable equipment.

> Patients like to "see" their health problem.

General administrative functions are normally performed using peripheral devices, such as a telephone, fax machine, copier, and printer. Almost all health care organizations make use of a computer (or computer system) that ties into these peripheral devices and may interact with medical equipment. As an organization grows in size, it may decide to link multiple computers together using a central computer (called a server) that runs **network** software.

> **Network:** A system of two or more servers, computers, or peripheral devices interconnected as a way of communicating or functioning together.

A health care organization should not only consider the costs of equipment and software before making a purchase decision, but also training, personnel time, and management requirements. A computer system must provide for internal controls to protect the integrity of information. Health care organizations must safeguard patient records in compliance with HIPAA regulations and other applicable laws. Safeguards must restrict both internal and external access to the entire computer system or specific areas thereof and prevent authorized viewing.

A basic practice management software program can be used to perform administrative tasks related to scheduling, billing, and maintaining patient contact information. A more comprehensive system may integrate marketing and bookkeeping functions as well. Advancements in technology have led to the increased use of electronic health records (EHR) software that often works in conjunction with a vendor's practice management program. An EHR system will generally comprise charting, prescription drug ordering, and treatment or diagnostic procedures. Since the market for practice management and EHR software is highly saturated with different vendors, a health care organization will need to conduct research to determine which program will work best. Despite all the electronic devices and software made available, certain processes are still performed more efficiently using manual systems.

EHR can also be referred to as EMR (electronic medical records).

20.1   Information Technology

Electronic devices can allow an organization to perform activities in a highly efficient manner. A computer system has quickly become the central hub for internal processes. Devices all around the *periphery* of the computer system support the performance of administrative functions. A health care provider should explore the use of medical equipment to perform diagnostic tests, enhance the patient experience, and expand service lines. A health care organization must explore what equipment, software, and peripheral devices will add value by performing a cost-benefit analysis.

Table 20.1 lists various administrative devices and categories of software programs along with additional costs to consider. Computer hardware and software can be expensive to install, upgrade, and repair. An organization will also need to consider training costs and IT support in any cost-benefit analysis compiled.

Peripheral Devices

Normal peripheral devices include a telephone, fax machine, copier, printer, scanner, and calculator. Although telephone systems are generally not connected to a computer system directly, new technology referred to as **Voice over Internet Protocol (VoIP)** demonstrates how telephone communication may become increasingly linked to a computer system in the future. To manage the sale of products, an organization can use point-of-sale (POS) technology involving a barcode printer and scanner, a specialized computer, and POS software. An organization should consider the purchase price along with ongoing maintenance and upkeep of peripheral equipment, such as the cost of ink cartridges, batteries, paper, and electricity usage. Training costs or paying for IT support may be a concern

Voice over Internet Protocol (VOIP): An emerging system of technologies that allows video and audio transmissions across the Internet in a manner similar to landline telephones.

TABLE 20.1	Electronic Devices and Related Costs		
Peripheral Devices	**Computer System**	**Software Programs**	**POS System**
Telephone	Desktop system	Office suite	Barcode scanner
Fax machine	Monitor	Practice management	Barcode printer
Copier	Keyboard	Electronic health records	Charge card reader
Printer	Mouse	Calendar	Special computer
Scanner	Pads	Charting	Software
Calculator	Laptop	Virus protection	
Ink cartridges	Backup system	Firewall	
Batteries	Network server	Internet filter	
Paper	Training and support	Network	
Electricity	Electricity	Point-of-sale	

when managing more complex machinery or processes. If an organization decides to go *paperless* and use a scanner to convert any physical documents into electronic files, the ongoing cost of paying organization members to scan documents should be considered.

Computer Hardware

The essential working parts of a computer system rest inside a desktop tower or underneath a laptop's keyboard. A hard drive houses all the software applications and data files whereas a **random access memory (RAM)** chip pulls those applications and files from the hard drive and holds them in short-term memory while in use. A processor chip does the actual thinking by performing functions based on information held in RAM. The quality of both the processor chip and RAM play a vital role in creating a fast and reliable system. A computer system along with peripheral devices should be protected against bursts of electricity by plugging devices into a *surge protector*.

Random Access Memory (RAM): Working memory of a computer system or peripheral device that holds information temporarily while software and data are in use.

Hard Drive = Storage Memory

RAM = Working Memory

Ergonomics   A workstation should be arranged in a way that supports organization members ergonomically. Approaching devices from an awkward position over time can cause physical pain and stifle productivity. An ergonomic workstation will take into account the chair, desk, and monitor position along with the arrangement of a keyboard and mouse. Special computer pads can dampen stress placed on wrists while typing or using a mouse. Stands should be used to hold any paper documents that organization members interact with while using a computer. Apart from the workstation setup, walking around equipment in the office should be considered in addition to lighting. Substitute generic fluorescent lights with full-spectrum light bulbs to reduce eyestrain.

Local Area Network (LAN)   A computer can exist as a stand-alone device separate from any other equipment. As an organization grows in size, the need for multiple computers to access the same information can increase. Several computers can be linked together using a central computer (server). A **local area network (LAN)** refers to the use of a server to house all the key software applications and data files whereas workstation computers connect to the server via a (wifi) router and access the software and files when needed. Instead of each computer containing all the same hardware and software individually, a LAN places the key hardware and software on one central server only. An organization may still need to purchase separate software licenses for each workstation computer accessing the software housed on a server. Placing the main hardware, software, and data files onto one central computer (server) allows the workstation computers to be easily replaced or modified. A server arrangement also ensures that data remain consistent within software applications.

Local Area Network (LAN): A computer system involving workstation computers that access software and data files housed on a central computer (server).

Computer Software

An operating system allows software applications to interact with a computer's hardware. The main operating systems sold by Microsoft and Apple include network software making it unnecessary to buy a separate program to establish a computer network. Administrative functions are usually performed in part using an office suite, such as Microsoft Office. An organization may also use practice management or EHR software as well as a POS system.

System Security

A computer network needs to assign at least one user administrative rights over the entire system. A system administrator controls how individual users interact with the software and data files stored on a server. A system *administrator* must assign each user an account and then partition the system to keep user accounts separate. Each user should have an individual data folder on the server to store work materials that no other user can access except for the administrator. Administrator permissions should limit user functions in an effort to maintain internal controls and prevent unauthorized activities. For example, a staff member who handles cash should be restricted from modifying the cash balance reported in an accounting program. A system administrator needs to back up files daily and remove old or unwanted files from the server, especially when an employee leaves the organization.

A computer system or individual software programs should maintain a record of each user's activity to deter unauthorized actions or ascertain which user made unauthorized changes to data. A computer's operating system needs to be locked when a user steps away from a workstation computer in order to prevent an unauthorized person from performing tasks through another user's account. As part of proper employee management, all unnecessary software should be removed from a computer system, including games, media players, and instant messaging programs. Employees will undoubtedly waste a tremendous amount of time if software programs meant for entertainment are left on the system.

The Windows operating system can be locked by holding down the Windows Logo Key + L on the keyboard. The Windows Logo Key is normally left of the space bar.

Internet Security

A computer system must be protected by a **firewall** to prevent unauthorized external access *directly* from the Internet. A firewall may consist of software or hardware placed on a central server or an individual computer. An Internet Service Provider (ISP) normally incorporates a firewall into the hardware and software that were provided when the Internet connection was established originally.

Firewall: A software program that regulates external access to a computer system from the Internet.

Data must be sent over an encrypted line when transmitted electronically to an external source or whenever an authorized user accesses a computer system remotely to work from an external computer. A *remote computer* allows a user to operate programs directly by accessing a workstation computer tied to the computer system. A remote computer does not house any of the software applications or data files itself. An organization must grant permissions directly to a remote user in order to bypass the firewall. Posting information to a third-party's website, such as Google Docs, can allow an organization member to work remotely without needing to access a computer system. Organization members must take caution when posting information to a third-party's website because of the risk of unauthorized access.

Unauthorized external access to a computer system can also occur *indirectly* if malicious software becomes unknowingly downloaded from the Internet. Viruses, malware, spyware, and so forth can communicate to an external party if software becomes installed unintentionally. An organization should install protective software that can detect and isolate malicious software in case it becomes loaded somewhere on the computer system.

Malicious software may grant an unauthorized external party administrator rights over a computer system.

Software that blocks Internet sites can prevent malicious software from being downloaded and it can keep employees from wasting time surfing websites unrelated to work. An organization should block a maximum number of websites possible, including all the major social networking and gaming websites, and specifically grant access to work-related websites only as the need arises.

Summary

A health care organization requires a mix of computer hardware, software, and peripheral devices. These devices along with other elements of the office should be arranged in a way that supports organization members ergonomically. Devices can be connected using a central computer (server). An administrator needs to oversee how computer users interact with information on the server. The computer system must be protected overall using a firewall, virus protection software, and website filter.

20.2   HIPAA Compliance

The Health Insurance Portability and Accountability Act (HIPAA) of 1996 set forth strict rules regarding how a computer system should be kept secure. HIPAA rules regulate patient privacy in terms of **protected health information (PHI).** An organization must understand what constitutes PHI and then maintain and document the safeguards used to secure it. The safeguards must be adequate and an organization must take steps to ensure the safeguards are properly followed. A regulatory review or lawsuit can arise if PHI is improperly handled.

Protected Health Information (PHI): Specific types of health and personal information about patients that health care organizations must take steps to protect from unauthorized viewing.

Find more information on HIPAA regulations through the Department of Health and Human Services, hhs.gov.

Computer monitors, fax machines, and other electronic devices should be located or positioned so unauthorized persons cannot accidentally view PHI. Any physical chart notes or documents containing PHI must be stored in a secure location at all times. A computer system or software program should maintain a record of activity over what a specific user has altered or attempted to alter. A computer network must be set up with proper administrator permissions restricting what each individual user can access or modify.

Security Measures

Even when an organization member sends information through an encrypted line, that information may not remain in an encrypted format. Consider the example of a patient who wants a health care organization to send PHI to a personal email account. The organization sends PHI in a secure manner, but a virus on the patient's computer results in the PHI becoming compromised. Patients should be informed of safeguard limitations whenever PHI is sent to them or other external parties, even at their own request.

To ensure that PHI does not become compromised, an organization may want to avoid sending PHI electronically to any recipient who is *not* required to maintain compliance with HIPAA regulations. An organization should consider using the telephone or regular mail to send information even if a patient sends an email or fax originally. A patient should be asked what form of communication works best and have the right to opt out of receiving emails or faxes. If a patient requests that information be sent electronically, an organization should maintain a signed waiver noting that the patient understands and accepts any potential safeguard limitations.

Even after deleting PHI, a computer's hard drive houses an imprint of the data that can be recovered with forensic equipment. Sometimes peripheral devices, such as copiers, printers, and fax machines, contain internal hard drives as well. Hard drives should be destroyed properly when selling or disposing of electronic equipment.

External Contracts

Any outside vendor or independent contractor that interacts with PHI must sign a contract stating that PHI will be protected. For example, an outside interpreter service hired to translate for a patient should sign a contract stating that the patient's PHI will be kept secure. An organization needs to verify that external parties have proper safeguards in place and are actively following them. The need to enter into a contract would not apply if an external party is *not* expected to interact with PHI, such as a painter or cleaning service. Make certain that an external party does not view PHI accidently.

Disaster Recovery

HIPAA regulations require that PHI be secure in case of disaster and data can be recovered immediately after an event. In order to meet these regulations, off-site storage of PHI with a secure vendor has become increasingly common. An organization would need to sign an appropriate contract in this case and ensure that the vendor has adequate safeguards in place. The process of backing up data with the vendor should occur on a daily basis. Even when off-site storage is used, an organization should still back up the system internally and store any backup copy in a disaster-proof container that is password protected. Internal control measures should be enacted to prevent the backup copy from becoming lost or stolen, such as from a car or office desk.

EHR software may offer secure backup as part of its features.

Summary

Safeguards must be in place to ensure unauthorized viewing of protected health information (PHI) does not occur. Access to patient files should be limited and PHI should not be sent over the Internet unless recipients are in compliance with HIPAA regulations. External contractors expected to interact with PHI must sign documentation stating that they have adequate safeguards in place. Off-site storage of PHI with a secure company has become commonplace because of the need to protect data in case of a disaster.

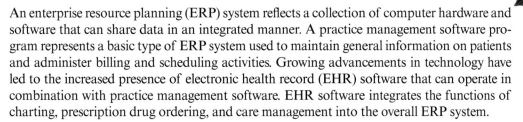

20.3   Enterprise Resource Planning

An enterprise resource planning (ERP) system reflects a collection of computer hardware and software that can share data in an integrated manner. A practice management software program represents a basic type of ERP system used to maintain general information on patients and administer billing and scheduling activities. Growing advancements in technology have led to the increased presence of electronic health record (EHR) software that can operate in combination with practice management software. EHR software integrates the functions of charting, prescription drug ordering, and care management into the overall ERP system.

Basic System

A small health care organization or one running a cash-only practice may not experience an overall benefit by implementing an ERP system. Such organizations often maintain the daily schedule of patients using a general calendar program, such as Google Calendar or Microsoft Outlook. A cell phone or personal digital assistant (PDA) may have the functionality to synchronize with such calendar programs. Patient charges may be tracked using Quickbooks or Excel unless a manual process proves easier. Small or cash-only organizations normally use Quickbooks to maintain general bookkeeping records even if patient charges are tracked elsewhere. All remaining administrative and clinic functions, such as charting and marketing, are normally performed using manual processes.

ERP System

A larger sized health care organization or one that bills insurance companies on behalf of patients may generate value by using an ERP system. The industry for medical software has evolved to where most practice management software vendors offer a separate EHR program or an all-inclusive practice management and EHR program. A complex program may integrate marketing, bookkeeping, and other administrative functions. Most health care organizations still use Quickbooks to manage general bookkeeping functions even when a practice management program contains accounting features.

Make sure programs are compatible with each other and will run at an optimal speed without crashing.

ERP Vendors

The market for practice management and EHR programs has become heavily saturated with vendors and determining what program will work best, especially when considering the various types of costs, may prove daunting. General lists of practice management and EHR vendors can be found on websites, but rapid changes within the industry have resulted in these lists becoming outdated quickly. A health care organization must conduct

ERP VENDORS (SELECT FEW)		
Practice Fusion*	www.practicefusion.com	Practice Fusion
Office Ally	www.officeally.com	Office Ally
Lytec	www.lytec.com	McKesson Corporation
Vitera Integrity	www.viterahealthcare.com	Vitera Healthcare Solutions
MacPractice	www.macpractice.com	MacPractice
Eclipse	www.galactek.com	Galactek Corp.

*Practice Fusion offers free software that displays third-party advertisements at the bottom of the screen.

Set up a separate email account to communicate with software vendors because their sales teams will bombard you with follow-up emails.

research and contact other health care organizations to learn more about the available software and compare the various pricing options. From there, determining what system would work best may involve browsing vendor websites, viewing online demonstrations, or installing a trial version. Most vendors offer a free trial version that lasts several weeks and is accessible online as a download or via the mail on a compact disc. Work with programs before making a final purchase decision to confirm they function as needed.

Cost-Benefit Analysis

A cost-benefit analysis can be conducted to determine the overall advantage of implementing a particular program. Table 20.2 lists common costs associated with an ERP system. Ask the vendor about other costs that may apply and talk to other health care organizations that use the same program to determine what costs they have incurred. Ensure the vendor has exceptional technical support since software can be complex to implement and understand. A vendor should be willing to pretest the program and test it again after implementation to confirm compatibility with the overall computer system. A suitable ERP system should boost the patient experience, increase user satisfaction, and minimize administrative and management time beyond what the underlying costs total.

If a vendor does not return emails or phone calls, that should be a red flag in terms of your ability to receive technical support when you need it.

TABLE 20.2	ERP System Costs	
Software program	Updates	
Related software	Technical support	
Hardware requirements	Administration time	
Installation	Repairs and maintenance	
Training		

Practice Fusion is a free online ERP system that can be used to manage patient charts. CMS-1500 forms can be uploaded into Office Ally's website and submitted to insurance providers for free as well.

Using a *medical billing service* to manage the billing process can prove valuable. A professional medical biller might be able to maximize reimbursement rates by using appropriate codes and avoid rejections from improper codes. Certain billing codes are considered "red flags" that could subject the organization to an audit, resulting in the potential repayment of money to an insurance company or government entity. The time, energy, and employee costs involved with handling the billing process internally, along with following up with any rejected claims, could outweigh the cost of using a medical billing service. A health care provider should calculate how much additional revenue could be produced from seeing patients as a result of not having to manage the billing process internally.

Preferred ERP System Features

Consider the following items when assessing the functionality and value of a particular practice management or EHR program.

Scheduling
Time slots on the schedule should be formatted according to desired intervals and length. The formatting should help with managing patient flow among rooms. The schedule should take note of patients who have been checked in and are waiting to be seen along with patients who missed an appointment.

Let patients know about services that will not be covered by their insurance provider before the appointment.

Billing Charges
Patient contact information and billable charges should be automatically printed on billing forms to minimize mistakes and reduce the need for extra data entry. The program should prevent the unauthorized deletion of billable charges from the system. Certain programs can submit electronic claims (including superbills) directly to third-party payors, such as insurance companies or Medicare. The third-party payors usually establish criteria to automatically reject incomplete forms. A health care organization must confirm that ERP software and any third-party payor can submit and receive data

across encrypted lines. The program should also check the eligibility of insurance coverage, copayment requirements, and deductibles.

Collection Efforts The program should display amounts owed from patients or third-party payors and print contact information and billable charges on invoices or collection letters automatically. Programs generally offer reports that list outstanding *accounts receivable* for each patient who has an outstanding balance.

Care Management The program might contain procedures related to general or specific health concerns. Key health information should be clearly visible, such as drug allergies or significant health issues. Any concerns that a patient has expressed in the past should be available through notes. The program should allow labs and diagnostic images to be uploaded into a patient's file.

Patient Charts The program may allow a health care provider to document the health care process in electronic chart notes. The program may offer functionality similar to a travel slip wherein a health care provider can enter abbreviated terms that are automatically extended by the program. Templates might exist related to general or specific health concerns that can be edited during a visit. The program should block any unauthorized viewing of patient files and prevent the deletion or alteration of chart notes after they have been saved originally.

Bookkeeping A few practice management programs include comprehensive bookkeeping functions. An organization may find that using Quickbooks is more practical because of the complex nature of maintaining accounting information.

Marketing A few practice management programs include comprehensive marketing functions that allow an organization to keep track of marketing efforts, organize marketing campaigns, and maintain notes on network participants, referral sources, and patients. A separate marketing program may be used if an organization requires increased functionality.

Security Measures The program should be in full compliance with HIPAA regulations and other applicable laws, and contain safeguards to ensure data are kept secure. Users must have their own accounts, restrictions must be placed over user accounts, and data must only be transmitted over encrypted lines. The program should contain other internal control measures to ensure unauthorized persons cannot modify or view data.

Medicare Claims In accordance with the Health Information Technology for Economic and Clinical Health (HITECH) Act, a health care organization that does not meet an exception must transmit Medicare claims using a software program certified by the Certification Commission on Health Information Technology (CCHIT). Smaller health care organizations with fewer than ten full-time employees may meet an exception. An organization should contact the Centers for Medicare and Medicaid Services (CMS) or review the CMS website to confirm if an exception is met. Free Medicare billing programs exist in case an organization is not currently using a certified program.

Centers for Medicare and Medicaid Services, cms.gov

Summary

A small health care organization will often use a range of software programs and manual processes to manage the flow of information. As an organization grows in size, it may find that using a more complex software system holds more value in terms of time and capabilities. Many software vendors now offer a practice management system that controls billing and scheduling functions in combination with an electronic health record system used for charting, prescription drug ordering, and maintaining patient charts.

CHAPTER ASSIGNMENT

Working in a group of three to four students or fellow professionals, complete the following items.

1. What is the role of a workstation computer versus a network server? Why is it usually unnecessary to individually purchase network software? *p372*

2. How might an organization form an ergonomic workstation to reduce the risk of an employee filing a worker's compensation claim for on-the-job injuries? *p372*

3. How can a network administrator protect a computer system against unauthorized activities? *p372*

4. What is the importance of removing games from a computer system and blocking websites? *p373*

5. What is the purpose of a firewall and how can an *authorized* remote user bypass the firewall? *p373*

6. What constitutes protected health information (PHI)? Under what circumstances should an organization refrain from sending PHI electronically? *p373·374*

7. When does it become important to sign a contract with an external party to safeguard PHI? *p374*

8. Why have health care organizations started to store backup files off-site with third-party vendors? *p374*

p 376 9. What kind of analysis can be conducted to determine the value of computer hardware or software? List four to five costs related to a practice management or EHR program.

10. If an organization does not use a practice management or EHR program, how might administrative processes be conducted?

1. Thank anyone in writing who has provided assistance during this learning process, including your study group members.

2. Please recommend this textbook to any health care provider who could benefit from this information.

3. Email **info@remedybooks.com** and list ways in which the author could improve the content of this textbook.

BIBLIOGRAPHY

CHAPTER 1

James D. Gwartney, Richard L. Stroup, and Russell S. Sobel. "Economic Fluctuations, Unemployment, and Inflation." Chap. 8 in *Economics: Private and Public Choice*. 9th ed. Fort Worth, TX: Dryden Press, 2000.

Charles T. Horngren, George Foster, and Srikant M. Datar. "Cost-Volume-Profit Analysis." In *Cost Accounting: A Managerial Emphasis*, pp. 441–42. 10th ed. Upper Saddle River, NJ: Prentice Hall, 2000.

CHAPTER 3

N. Thomas Ingram et al. "Planning Sales Dialogues and Presentation." Module 6 in *Professional Selling: A Trust-Based Approach*. 4th ed. Cinncinnati, OH: Thomson Learning, 2008.

Nusaybah Bey in discussion with the author via telephone, March 2011.

CHAPTER 5

Charles T. Horngren, George Foster, and Srikant M. Datar. "Cost-Volume-Profit Analysis." In *Cost Accounting: A Managerial Emphasis*, pp. 441–42. 10th ed. Upper Saddle River, NJ: Prentice Hall, 2000.

CHAPTER 6

Don Warnecke in discussion with the author in person, July 2010.

Donald E. Kieso, Jerry J. Weygandt, and Terry D. Warfield. *Intermediate Accounting*. 10th ed. New York: John Wiley & Sons, Inc., 2001. See esp. Chaps. 8 and 11, "Valuation of Inventories: A Cost Basis" and "Depreciation, Impairments, and Depletion."

CHAPTER 7

Don Warnecke in discussion with the author in person, July 2010.

Donald E. Kieso, Jerry J. Weygandt, and Terry D. Warfield. *Intermediate Accounting*. 10th ed. New York: John Wiley & Sons, Inc., 2001. See esp. Chaps. 8 and 11, "Valuation of Inventories: A Cost Basis" and "Depreciation, Impairments, and Depletion."

CHAPTER 8

Charles T. Horngren, George Foster, and Srikant M. Datar. "An Introduction to Cost Terms and Purposes" and "Cost-Volume-Profit Analysis." Chaps. 2 and 3 in *Cost Accounting a Managerial Emphasis*. 10th ed. Upper Saddle River, NJ: Prentice Hall, 2000.

CHAPTER 11

Gitman, J. Lawrence. "Capital Budgeting Techniques." Chap. 9 in *Principles of Managerial Finance*. 12th ed. Boston: Prentice Hall, 2009.

CHAPTER 13

Aswath Damodaran. *Investment Valuation*. 1st ed. New York: John Wiley & Sons, Inc., 2002. See esp. Chaps. 14 and 15, "Free Cash Flow to Equity Discount Models" and "Firm Valuation: Cost of Capital and Adjusted Present Value Approaches."

CHAPTER 14

Richard A. Mann and Barry S. Roberts. "Contracts." Part III in *Essentials of Business Law and the Legal Environment*. 7th ed. Cinncinnati, OH: Thomson Learning, 2001.

myFico. "Credit Q&A." Last modified June 14, 2012. www.myfico.com/crediteducation/questions

United States Small Business Administration. "7(a) Loan Program." Last modified June 14, 2012. www.sba.gov/category/navigation-structure/loans-grants/small-business-loans/sba-loan-programs

CHAPTER 17

Dr. Stephen Liston in discussion with the author in person, February 2012.

CHAPTER 18

Marne Garcia in discussion with the author via telephone, January 2009.

United States Department of Labor. "Wage and Hour Division (WHD)." Last modified March 20, 2012. www.dol.gov/WHD/flsa/index.htm

Society for Human Resource Management. Accessed June 14, 2012. www.shrm.org

CHAPTER 19

Nancy Hagen in discussion with the author via telephone, January 2009.

CHAPTER 20

Jacob Redding in discussion with the author via email, September 2010.

John Ross and Kelly L. Murdock. "Using Windows Remote Desktop." Chap. 41 in *PC User's Bible*. Indianapolis: Wiley Publishing, 2007.

United States Department of Health and Human Services. "Health Information Privacy." Last modified June 14, 2012. www.hhs.gov/ocr/privacy

GLOSSARY

Accrual Method System of accounting that requires that a transaction be recorded when a business exchange occurs or when cash is exchanged.

Ad Hoc Report An unconventional report meant to explore the circumstances of an atypical situation.

Adjusting Journal Entry (AJE) A secondary journal entry used to modify amounts already recorded in the accounting system according to an original journal entry.

Advertisement Information about an organization displayed by a third-party vendor.

After-Tax Interest Rate The net cost of debt that reflects the benefit derived from deducting interest charges on a tax return.

Agent An entity granted certain rights to act on behalf of a principal.

Amortization Schedule A detailed listing of how each loan payment is applied to interest charges and the principal balance.

Annuity An investment account administered by an insurance company that provides tax-deferred growth and various distribution options.

Applied Network Network participants with a trained ability to market on your behalf.

Array A specific list of numeric values categorized together within a data set.

Asset Allocation Targeted framework of how amounts should be distributed among different categories of investment products to balance between risks and desired return levels.

Assets Items that have value extending into future time periods.

Authorized Stock The amount of stock a corporation could potentially transfer to owners.

Bad Debt The amount of a valid billable charge that is never collected.

Bank Reconciliation The process of matching the cash balance reported on a bank statement against the corresponding cash balance reported on the balance sheet.

Balanced Scorecard A management device used to outline goals and identify when goals are being met.

Board of Directors An elected body that oversees a company's management team on behalf of owners.

Branding Inspiring a particular feel or reputation through a common name, icon, message, or marketing campaign.

Breach of Contract Failing to fulfill obligations as set forth in a legal agreement.

Breakeven Analysis An examination of the approximate revenue level needed to cover all fixed and variable expenses.

Business Continuity Insurance An insurance policy that covers business overhead in case of emergency or disaster.

Cafeteria Plan A benefit plan organized under Section 125 of the U.S. tax code allowing an employee to select from a "menu" of benefit options, and which reduces an employee's taxable income.

Call Option A derivative agreement that lets an investor buy an investment product at a set price thus allowing an investor to make money when the underlying security is traded above the set price.

Callable Bond An indenture agreement with terms allowing the bond issuer to return the borrowed funds early ending the bond indenture before the normal maturity date.

Cannibalization The loss of demand for one type of service because of the addition of a more desirable one within an organization's service mix.

Capital Lease A lease agreement that acts as a loan or transfers substantial rights of ownership leading to treatment of the leased item as a fixed asset.

Capitalization The act of taking a material expense applicable to multiple time periods and holding it on the balance sheet.

Cash Equivalent Any financial instrument that can function like cash, such as a check or charge card.

Cash Flow Loan A loan where the basis of repayment depends on expected future income streams.

Cash Method System of accounting that calls for a transaction to be recorded only when cash is exchanged.

Cash Practice A health care organization that does not accept third-party coverage directly but provides treatment codes (superbill) to patients so they can seek reimbursement personally.

Central Bank The entity in charge of an economy's banking system. A central bank normally controls the amount of loans that lending institutions can extend.

Chapter 7 A bankruptcy filing that results in liquidation of a business (or personal assets) in satisfaction of debts resulting in conclusion of business activity.

Chapter 11 An initial bankruptcy filing that attempts to keep a business solvent by reorganizing debts and setting forth a plan to meet future obligations.

Chart of Accounts A complete listing of active and inactive accounts used by an organization.

Chief Executive   The organization member possessing the highest level of authority and responsibility.

Coefficient of Determination   A formula that more specifically isolates how one array influences (or does not influence) another.

Collateral   Print or electronic documents that display information about an organization.

Collateralized Loan   A loan secured by an underlying tangible asset that could be sold to cover the loan balance in case of default.

Collusion   Two or more organization members working together to commit fraud despite the existence of internal controls.

Common Stock   The general class of stock offered by most corporations providing for ownership rights and access to owner distributions.

Complementary Service   A type of service that fits within the scope of other services leading customers to demand items together.

Conditional Formatting   An input screen with functional limitations set forth in the software program's underlying computer code.

Consideration   The items of value constituting a fair exchange among parties to a contract.

Consultative Selling   The express use of questioning tactics to build rapport and configure how a customer's needs best match with an organization's services.

Continuance   Moving forward with a long-term relationship through mutually agreeable actions.

Contra Account   An account that offsets the balance in another account, such as bad debts, accumulated depreciation, or product returns.

Contribution Margin   The amount of profit existing after deducting variable expenses from revenue.

Correlation   A formula used to determine the approximate relationship between two arrays.

Cosigner   A person who agrees to bear responsibility for a loan in case the original borrower defaults.

Cost of Goods Sold (COGS)   The total amount of inventory that is expensed in relation to the quantity of items sold or purchased.

Cost Leadership   Offering products or services similar to competitors but at lower prices.

Coupon   Term used to represent the interest given to holders of a bond security.

Covenants   Restrictions placed on either the borrower or lender as noted within a loan agreement.

Data Set   The complete list of numeric values under consideration.

De Minimis   Indirect payments of money considered immaterial by tax authorities allowing treatment as a qualified benefit automatically.

Defined Benefit Plan   A retirement plan that provides guaranteed benefits during retirement years according to a predetermined formula.

Defined Contribution Plan   A retirement plan where the retirement benefits depend on the total amount contributed and the investment performance of the account portfolio.

Deflation   A decrease to general price levels within an economy due to the lack of money in relation to what is needed to purchase all the products and services available in an economy.

Depreciation Expense   The amount of a capitalized expense that is applied to a specific time period.

Derivative Securities   An investment product that derives its value from an underlying investment product, such as a bond, stock, or commodity.

Description Account   An account that serves no other purpose than to describe what has occurred with cash or sometimes noncash items.

Differentiation   Offering products or services with unique, high-quality features at similar or higher prices than competitors.

Disengagement   A noticeable desire to discontinue with a certain line of conversation.

Disinflation   The overall rate of inflation decreases from one time period to the next.

Dividend   A distribution of stock or money made to an owner of a corporation.

Double Taxation   An approach to taxation where earnings are taxed at the corporate level and again at the individual level when distributed to owners.

Double-Entry Accounting System   A recording system for accounting information that uses debits and opposing credits as a quality-control measure.

Effective Interest Rate   The theoretical amount of interest a financial product will cost or earn based on the ability to retain cash flows in a separate financial product before year's end.

Effective Tax Rate   The average percentage of tax imposed upon taxable income after application of marginal rates.

Elasticity of Demand   The degree to which price changes inversely impact demand levels for a product or service.

Elevator Pitch   A brief sales narrative that could be expressed within the time it would theoretically take to ride an elevator.

Employee Handbook A complete set of policies set forth by an employer meant to clearly define the employment relationship.

Equity The residual amount of value held by a business owner after subtracting liabilities from assets.

Escrow Agent A third party hired to maintain a proper accounting of loan payments and ensure that all parties fulfill contractual obligations.

Estimated Tax Payments Payments made to a tax authority incrementally, usually quarterly, in an effort to satisfy a projected year-end tax liability.

Expenses Outflow of value or cash necessary to support the production of revenue.

Explanation of Benefits (EOB) A general document sent by insurance providers that describes the nature and cost of benefits.

Feasibility Analysis A review of business opportunities to isolate the one option that will offer the most financial value and personal satisfaction.

Firewall A software program that regulates external access to a computer system from the Internet.

First-in-first-out (FIFO) An inventory counting method whereby the first item placed into stock is expensed first.

Fixed Asset Turnover A profitability ratio that compares net revenue over total fixed assets.

Fixed Expenses Outflows of cash or value that bear little or no relationship to revenue activity and which tend to remain constant over time.

Form CMS-1500 The Centers for Medicare and Medicaid Services (CMS) requires a standard format for health care forms used to bill insurance companies and certain other third parties.

Free Cash Flow to Equity (FCFE) Amount of net cash flow available to equity owners of a business.

Free Cash Flow to the Firm (FCFF) Amount of net cash flow available to both debt and equity holders of a business.

Frequency The amount of exposure over a given time period to an organization's marketing efforts.

Gains Inflow of value or cash as part of a nonstandard transaction (usually related to fixed assets).

General Ledger Summary of all journalized transactions posted to each individual account.

Gross Domestic Product (GDP) Amount of products and services produced in a country.

Health Insurance Portability and Accountability Act (HIPAA) Federal legislation that regulates the transition of patient health care coverage from one insurance provider to another and includes additional regulations on patient privacy.

Home Equity Line of Credit (HELOC) A line of credit tied to the equity value of a person's home.

Impairment Adjusting an asset's historical cost downward to reflect a material reduction in the asset's market value.

Indenture Agreement The loan agreement set forth between a bond issuer and the investor lending funds.

Inflation An increase in general price levels within an economy due to the presence of excess money beyond what is needed to purchase all the products and services available in an economy.

Information System A framework that enhances the collection, transmission, and dissemination of information.

Integration Forming an organization with other types of health care providers giving patients access to a broader range of services.

Intensity Impact on the consumer from one or more instances of exposure to an organization's marketing efforts.

Interconnection The act of knowing people, places, events, or objects in common with another person.

Internal Rate of Return The overall rate of profit that a cash flow stream provides on an annualized basis.

Initial Public Offering (IPO) The first issue of equity securities offered by a company on a regulated exchange.

Introduction The process related to coming into contact with a person whether for the first time or after some delay.

Invoice A document used to request payment from an external party that includes relevant payment terms.

Issued Stock The amount of stock in total that has been transferred to owners.

Journal Entry A listing of debits and credits related to a transaction along with an explanation of the transaction.

Last-in-first-out (LIFO) An inventory counting method whereby the last item placed into stock is expensed first.

Liabilities Obligations to pay that extend into future time periods.

Line of Credit A loan arrangement resembling a credit card that allows a borrower greater flexibility to withdraw amounts up to a preset limit as needed.

Liquidity Reflects the rate at which an asset can be converted into cash.

Local Area Network (LAN) A computer system involving workstation computers that access software and data files housed on a central computer (server).

Losses Outflow of value or cash as part of a nonstandard transaction (usually related to fixed assets).

Macroeconomics Field of economics focused on the study of nationwide economic activity.

Marginal Tax Rate The tax rate imposed upon a specific layer of taxable income.

Market Capitalization The total amount of value that a company's equity securities are worth.

Market Value The price at which two willing parties agree to exchange goods or services.

Marketing Pendulum A symbolic representation of the relationship between seeing patients and engaging in marketing efforts.

Marketing Resources Time, energy, and money spent in relation to marketing efforts.

Materiality A quantitative benchmark constituting a significant amount set in reference to the particular circumstances of an organization or transaction.

Media Spots Audio or video clips placed on a website or transmitted by TV or radio stations.

Microeconomics Field of economics focused on the connection between demand and supply forces.

Microsale A condensed sales approach that lacks either a sufficient introduction, buildup of rapport, or qualification.

Modified Accelerated Cost Recovery System (MACRS) The system of depreciation prescribed by U.S. tax code.

Mortgage Equity Withdrawal (MEW) A lump-sum withdrawal of equity from a person's home requiring establishment of a new loan that combines the old loan with the total withdrawal.

Multiple Regression Line A linear pattern established between more than one independent array and only one dependent array that can be used to predict an unknown value in one of the arrays.

Multiplier A standard ratio multiplied against a numeric figure meant to derive the expected value of another numeric figure.

Mutual Fund An investment account run by a mutual fund company where investor money is pooled and invested per a predefined strategy.

Mystery Shopper A "fake" patient hired by a health care organization to work through an appointment as a way of secretly assessing the patient experience.

Narratives Memorized dialogues structured to effectively communicate important matters.

Negotiation Matrix A structured method of looking at the advantages and disadvantages faced by the parties working to establish a legal agreement.

Net profit Amount remaining after deducting all necessary business expenses from revenue.

Network (marketing) Collection of people with awareness of you or some aspect of your organization.

Network (computer) A system of two or more servers, computers, or peripheral devices interconnected as a way of communicating or functioning together.

Nondiscrimination Rules Retirement plan rules that limit high-paid employees from receiving a disproportionate amount of benefits compared to other qualified plan participants.

Normative Views Standard perceptions of an idea, event, or situation.

Operating Lease A lease agreement that results in a normal lease exchange in which case amounts are directly expensed on the income statement.

Opportunity Cost A theoretical loss incurred from engaging in a specific activity as opposed to a more profitable one.

Outstanding Stock The amount of stock that owners still currently hold.

Over-the-Counter (OTC) A transaction involving investment products where private parties arrange the transfer and set their own terms.

Patient Conversion The process of creating a seamless transition for a patient from one health care provider to another.

Par Value The minimum value stated on a stock certificate for which it can be issued.

Payback Period The time until any capital investment in a venture is recovered through the generation of future net cash flows.

Payment Voucher An internal petition used to request payment be made to an external party.

Per Diem A standardized amount provided to an employee meant to cover the cost of food or lodging when away on work-related travel.

Permanent Life Insurance A life insurance policy that will provide death benefits no matter when death occurs and may include a cash value portion that builds over time.

Pierce the Corporate Veil A situation where creditors gain access to personal assets as a result of owners improperly administering the corporate structure.

Point-of-Sale (POS) System Electronic devices used to manage data and process payments related to the sale of products or services.

Present Value The approximate amount of current-day money that a future cash flow would equal upon consideration of differences in risk and inflation.

Price Discrimination Charging distinct groups of customers different rates based on source or type of payment.

Price Incentive   A product or service provided at a steep discount or free of charge as a way to entice customers into patronizing an organization and further buying products and services.

Price Inelasticity   Reflects the extent to which demand levels for a product or service are not significantly influenced by price changes.

Principal (legal)   An entity that has authorized others to act on its behalf.

Principal (loan)   The total amount of borrowed funds or remaining balance thereof that is expected to be repaid to the lender (excluding interest charges).

Professional Perseverance   The frequency and intensity of contact with a person viewed in terms of professional appropriateness.

Prospects   People who have the potential to become network participants, referral sources, or patients.

Protected Health Information (PHI)   Specific types of health and personal information about patients that health care organizations must take steps to protect from unauthorized viewing.

Purchase Order   A form used to make a request for services or products.

Put Option   A derivative agreement that lets an investor sell an investment product at a set price, thus allowing an investor to make money when the underlying security is traded below the set price.

Quadratic Regression Line   A quadratic pattern established between one or more independent array(s) and a dependent array that can be used to predict an unknown value in one of the arrays.

Qualification   Affirming that a long-term and mutually beneficial relationship between a health care organization and prospect can form.

Qualified Benefits   Indirect payments of money to employees that tax authorities allow as a tax deduction for the business and which are not treated as compensation to employees.

Qualified Health Care Need   Identifying how a prospective patient will benefit by receiving specific health care services.

Quality-Control Measures   Structured processes that ensure steps are not overlooked or improper actions are not taken without some form of alert or barrier.

Random Access Memory (RAM)   Working memory of a computer system or peripheral device that holds information temporarily while software and data are in use.

Real Property   Land or larger structures placed on land with a definite long-term use.

Referral System   Collection of network participants trained to provide others with direct recommendations regarding seeking care from you.

Regression Line   A linear pattern established between an independent array and a dependent one that can be used to predict an unknown value in one of the arrays.

Regulated Exchange   A controlled environment open to the public where investment products can be transferred based on preset terms.

Relative Valuation   Use of industry metrics in relation to adjusted historical cash flow streams of a business to establish a sales price.

Remedy   Amount of reparation offered to a party injured by a breach of contract.

Resistance   Objections or barriers to fostering an effective long-term relationship.

Revenue   The total inflow of cash or value derived by exchanging services or products with consumers.

Sales Load   A percentage levied on either the contributions or withdrawals of investor money into or from a mutual fund.

Secretary of State   The statewide government department in charge of authorizing businesses.

Segmentation   The process of delineating information contained in an account or multiple accounts into distinct categories.

Sensitivity Analysis   An examination of how economic variables impact each other.

SPIN Selling   A selling process that incorporates four categories of questions: situation, problem, implication, and need-payoff (SPIN).

Spurious   Amounts that appear random across time periods and lack any clear pattern.

Stated Interest Rate   The amount of interest a financial product will cost or earn.

Strategic Planning   The main approach an organization takes when attempting to form and maintain a relationship with consumers.

Statute of Frauds   Provisions of the Uniform Commercial Code that specify the types of contracts that must be evidenced in writing.

Subsidiary Ledger   Detailed listing of information within a particular general ledger account categorized by relevant criteria.

Substitutes   Completely different products or services, usually of lower quality and price, but able to still satisfy a customer's same demand.

SWOT Analysis   Strengths, weaknesses, opportunities, and threats of an organization in relation to competitive pressures.

Target Market   A defined group of market participants that receive a unique allocation of marketing resources.

Tax Method System of accounting that incorporates tax code rules.

Term Life Insurance A life insurance policy that will provide death benefits for a set number of years only.

Terminal Value The last time period used in a cash flow projection meant to fully capture any persisting value from all future time periods thereafter.

Territory A defined area where the expenditure of marketing resources is planned.

Territory Worksheet A listing of important people, places, events, and objects in a marketplace along with detail on related marketing efforts.

Theory of Mind A personal observation that considers how another person could be observing situations.

Third-Party Payor A corporate or government institution that makes health care payments on behalf of a covered recipient.

Top-Down Analysis A review of macroeconomic, micro-economic, and marketplace forces that could impact a cash flow analysis.

Travel Slip A condensed form that lists common procedures and allows for an abbreviated version of note taking.

Treasury Stock Shares that have been issued and were once outstanding but have since been repurchased.

Trend An observable pattern seen across multiple time periods.

Trend Analysis Reviewing the balances shown for a particular account across multiple time periods to spot patterns or unusual activity.

Triple Net Lease A form of lease agreement where the lessor (property owner) has main responsibility for the outside area and the lessee (person leasing) has main control over the inside area.

Trust-Based Selling Showing clear effort to build a supportive relationship with a customer, overlooking any short-term advantage.

Uniform Commercial Code (UCC) Set of standard rules governing (business) contracts as adopted by most states.

Unproductive Assets Business ventures that do not generate a positive return on investment because of management inefficiencies or weak demand levels.

Unqualified Benefits Indirect payments of money to employees that tax authorities disallow as a tax deduction for the business and which may be treated as taxable compensation to employees.

Variable Expenses Outflows of cash or value that vary in direct relation to revenue levels.

Variance Difference between amounts budgeted at the beginning of a time period and the actual account activity over the entire time period.

Venture Capital Amounts solicited from external private investors looking to fund a fledgling business in exchange for an equity share.

Vest A requirement that an employee work a certain number of years before employer retirement contributions officially transfer ownership.

Voice over Internet Protocol (VOIP) An emerging system of technologies that allows video and audio transmissions across the Internet in a manner similar to land-line telephones.

Working Capital The net amount after subtracting current liability accounts from current asset accounts.

Yield-to-Maturity An artificial rate of return on a bond created by altering its purchase price.

INDEX

Made in the USA
Charleston, SC
04 October 2013